George Borrow
Eccentric

MICHAEL COLLIE

CAMBRIDGE UNIVERSITY PRESS

Cambridge
London   New York   New Rochelle
Melbourne   Sydney

Published by the Press Syndicate of the University of Cambridge
The Pitt Building, Trumpington Street, Cambridge CB2 IRP
32 East 57th Street, New York, NY 10022, USA
296 Beaconsfield Parade, Middle Park, Melbourne 3206, Australia

© Cambridge University Press 1982

First published 1982

. Printed in Great Britain by
New Western Printing Limited, Bristol

Library of Congress catalogue card number: 82–4397

British Library cataloguing in publication data
Collie, Michael
George Borrow: Eccentric
1. Borrow, George, 1803–1881 – Biography
I. Title
823′.8 PR4156
ISBN 0 521 24615 6

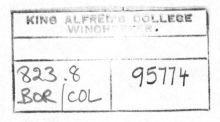

For Joanne Collie

I love all waste
And solitary places, where we taste
The pleasure of believing what we see
Is boundless, as we wish our souls to be.

Contents

Acknowledgements

A grant from the Canada Council allowed me to complete the research for this book a few years ago and it is a pleasure to have this opportunity to thank the Council once again for its generous assistance.

I thank, also, for help given at different times and for different purposes, Kathleen Cann, Martha de Narváez, Betty Parker, Cynthia Patterson and Diana Vipond. Angus Fraser and Mrs Ann Ridler both read the book at the typescript stage and made a large number of valuable suggestions, generously making available to me their extensive knowledge of many aspects of Borrow's life and work. The staff of the Inter-library loan office at York University has as usual been untiring in its support. Much appreciated, too, has been the advice and unfailing assistance of the staffs of those libraries in the United States and in Britain, which have significant Borrow holdings. It would have been quite impossible for me to finish the book without all this help and I am most grateful for it.

Finally, I owe a special word of thanks to John Murray for permission to quote from the daybooks and accounts. The frontispiece reproduces the portrait of Borrow by H. W. Phillips in the National Portrait Gallery.

The son of a recruiting sergeant

This book is a new account of the life of George Borrow, a remarkable Victorian eccentric whose mid-century best-seller, *The Bible in Spain*, brought his exploits to the public's attention and made him famous. In an age of intrepid travellers and explorers, he was one of those nineteenth-century Europeans who, becoming curious about some or other part of the world, simply set out, by whatever means of transport was available, to see what it was like. He lived in St Petersburg for two years, at a time when few Englishmen knew much about Russia. He lived in Spain for five years, travelling extensively throughout the west of the country during a savagely-fought civil war. Sometimes he wrote about his travels, sometimes he did not. His unpublished papers provide the evidence of more extensive travel than he revealed during his life-time, although sometimes only in hints, as when he says of an island that is as beautiful as 'the isles of Greece',[1] or when he describes seeing a 'raging rabble of fierce and animal propensities, men and women and children some of them of nearly negro blackness, most of them half naked, some especially the childen entirely so some on lean ragged ponies others on light creaking carts drawn by buffaloes'.[2] Borrow's early biographers did not know that he had been to the Greek islands, or that he had been in a country where carts were drawn by buffalo. There are countless other examples.

When he wrote about his travels, his experiences, his adventures, Borrow necessarily also wrote about himself, and it was Borrow's distinction to have done so with genius. Borrow depicted the often startling, sensational events of his own life in such a dramatic, sharply visual and compelling manner that, suspending disbelief, the reader is just carried along by the sheer virtuosity of his style. This is true both of his published books, which contain many brilliant passages, and of his unpublished papers, which contain many surprises. But Borrow's work is never documentary: everything he wrote is a function of his remarkable character. He is always singularly urbane but his is a brand of urbanity that alerts the reader to an unsettling ambivalence of tone, something that hints, suggests, or even makes blatantly obvious, that not everything is being said that might be said. The intrepid Victorian traveller so frequently writes like an extrovert that his reader can be quite chagrined to realise he is not. It is this paradox of character that is here analysed. That Borrow, in telling us so much, refuses to tell us all makes us inquisitive about his private life, especially (because he was a writer) about his private imaginative life. That he sometimes seems frank makes us wonder why he was not always frank, even allowing for the Victorian dislike of the explicit. To retell the story of his writing life involves, therefore, a marked shift of interest. The feats of endurance and the long journeys are still remarkable, are worth retelling. But we desire also an intimate knowledge of all the intimacies that inform them; we are interested in what Borrow did not tell us as well as in what he did; and we look for answers to questions that either did not perplex his early biographers or did not seem appropriate in an account of the life of a Great Writer.

Well off the beaten track of the Grand Tour, Borrow liked visiting places few of his contemporaries knew – Novgorod, for example: Bucharest. He tended to avoid the watering-places of the cosmopolitan middle class, because his interests were not social at all, but literary. And his literary interests were of a special kind. Though an educated man, he was less concerned about the movement of literary texts, or the knowledge of them, from the Eastern Mediterranean to Italy, France and England, than the earlier movement of languages themselves, from India, he thought, to the most westerly coastlines of Europe, a movement that coincided with the movement of peoples, including, to a degree, the gypsies. To test his sense of the relationships of languages and dialects he would go to a place to hear how people spoke. He did this often, by himself, without offering an explanation of what he was doing, because there was hardly anyone in his life who required an explanation, unless that person was his mother, and, as will be seen, she had early learnt the need to keep her secrets to herself. Borrow's travels were private and self-justifying, though his later talk about them, if and when it occurred, was rarely discreet.

On a number of occasions, he went to some trouble to conceal his whereabouts even from people with whom it would have been easy to be frank; at other times he revealed his whereabouts when to conceal them would have been more prudent. Possibly everyone is to some extent a manipulator of the truth about himself, not least those who inflict on others their supposed search for self-knowledge. Borrow, as will be seen, was an extreme case, an archetypal, eminently successful Victorian manipulator of the truth about self, which means that to think about him again one must submit the supposed facts of his life to the severest scrutiny, particularly when these 'facts' derive from Borrow himself, and at the same time analyse those marvellous published works that are so obviously, so delightfully ambivalent.

When Borrow returned from Spain in 1840, married the woman with whom he had been living in Seville and retired to Oulton Broad near Lowestoft, where his wife owned an estate, he took over for the sake of his writing a small octagonal, wooden summer-house between Oulton Cottage and the water's edge, a study retreat that for the remainder of his life functioned as a writer's den, like Dicken's chalet at Gad's Hill and Meredith's cabin at Box Hill later in the century. A friend remembered, after Borrow's death, that behind the door of this 'studio' there hung the military uniform and sword of the author's father – 'the household gods on which he would often gaze while composing'.[3] Possibly: it will be seen that Borrow's relations with his father are difficult to interpret. More to the point, perhaps, is that, although Oulton Cottage had five bedrooms, Borrow had a bedroom built onto the back of his summer-house, thus making it something more than a study. At all events, the man who filled notebook after notebook while on the road used this lakeside retreat as his base camp. Here, there accumulated over the years a large collection of rare books, many of them in little-known languages, together with a mass of papers, including the autograph manuscripts of both his published and unpublished works, discarded proof-sheets, letters and notes. When he died in 1881, these papers, together with his publications, constituted his remains. Borrow himself had done nothing to establish the significance, or otherwise, of these documents. He was not a theoretician, seldom talked with people about his work except to tell them how good it was and only rarely wrote about his method of composition. His life as a writer, his working and imaginative life, has to be reconstructed. It is in the reconstruction that a new biography can exist. What happened, one wants to know, in this primitive, rather quaint summer-house, within the imagination of Borrow, the writer, when he looked again at the words he had written, or wrote new words that by their originality would surprise those who knew him just as squire, linguist, missionary, traveller, literary lion or social humbug? Do the papers left there in such complete disarray help or not? And can our retrospective reconstructions in any way match his own?

When Borrow died at Oulton, at the age of seventy-eight, some forty years after the publication of *The Bible in Spain*, the book that made his reputation, his stepdaughter, Mrs Henrietta MacOubrey, became the owner of his papers. What happened to these papers greatly affected the image of Borrow after his death. Though she admired Borrow's work as she revered him, she had no idea what to do with his literary remains. Many personal papers she kept to herself but the papers in Borrow's summer-house she neglected and finally abandoned. As a consequence, the opportunity existed for them to be raided, purchased and dispersed, which is exactly what occurred. The curator of the Castle Museum in Norwich was authorised to purchase Borrow's literary remains for the City of Norwich and for that purpose travelled out to Oulton, but baulking at the price (£1,000) he missed his chance: the whole collection was bought instead by two booksellers, William Webber of Ipswich and Edward Allen of Henrietta Street, Covent Garden. Each of them then disposed of his share as best he could, either by publishing previously unpublished works or by resale. The dismemberment had begun. Interestingly, when Webber's Ipswich business was bought out by Jarrold's of Norwich many years later, Webber told Farrell that when 'he happened to look into the summerhouse', he saw a heap of waste paper 'awaiting the next visit of the ragman' and that on that very day he read letters 'revealing [Borrow's] character to a degree much modified by his tender-hearted biographer'.[4] This tender-hearted biographer, the one who most thoroughly whitewashed Borrow's character, was his first, an American clergyman and Professor of Spanish called W. I. Knapp, who in 1899 published the two-volume *Life, Writings and Correspondence of George Borrow*, a terribly confused and confusing book, which cannot safely be ignored, however, in as far as it provides clues to those papers he had in front of him which have not survived. Knapp prided himself on having collected every scrap of paper, down to laundry lists and hotel bills, which could possibly have a bearing upon Borrow's life. He once said to a friend: 'I have left no stone unturned ... Every hotel bill is amongst his papers which I bought. Every shred I have saved and registered.'[5] And in 1899 he said of his own biography, that it 'furnishes a sufficient and unalterable exhibition of the facts concerning the man and his work'. Augustus Jessopp, a Norwich clergyman and schoolmaster, who at one stage wanted to take this material over, reported that Knapp was 'paralysed' by the mere accumulation of detail. Knapp himself was far from sure what he should do with the material he had accumulated. In a letter to Wentworth Webster, Knapp said:

I am at a loss what to do – whether to tell the truth or *echar afeites*. If I tell the truth will Borrow ever be read again? If I embellish him, make him a hero, I must burn his papers and letters afterwards – that no quizzing fool 50 years later may make his fortune by bringing out a new life – and prove it by the tell-tale archives.[6]

Knapp seems to have forgotten what Borrow said about the heroic in the Appendix to *The Romany Rye*. He resolved his problem by first giving his 'every shred' of material to the Library of the Hispanic Society in New York and then taking much of it away again,[7] so that his portrait of Borrow as a sincere Christian, a sincere husband and a sincere writer could stand. No doubt acting in complete good faith, Knapp had little reason to ask himself after a lifetime's work whether, in 1981, people would prefer to have in hand his life of Borrow or Borrow's own papers. Meanwhile, correspondence in John Murray's archives shows that Henrietta MacOubrey did not for many years co-operate with attempts to gather materials for a life of her step-father. As has been the case with other writers, well-intentioned people deliberately suppressed evidence relevant to his biography so that the popular memory of George Borrow the great writer would be that of George Borrow the good man. In such circumstances, it seems reasonable to make a new attempt to write Borrow's life, both in justice to him and in centenary celebration of his fascinating books.

Fortunately there is little disagreement about Borrow's physical appearance. He was large and strong. When Borrow went to Cornwall to meet surviving members of his father's family, Anne Taylor described him as: 'A fine tall man of about six foot three; well-proportioned and not stout; able to walk five miles an hour successively; rather a florid face without any hirsute appendages; hair white and soft; eyes and eyebrows dark; good nose and very nice mouth; well-shaped hands; – altogether a person you would notice in a crowd.'[8] That was in 1853, when Borrow was fifty. After his death, his friend, Gordon Thomas Hake, remembered Borrow in similar terms.

His figure was tall and his bearing very noble; he had a finely moulded head, and thick white hair – white from his youth; his brown eyes were soft, yet piercing; his nose somewhat of the 'semitic' type, which gave his face the cast of the young Memnon. His mouth had a generous curve; and his features, for beauty and true power, were such as can have no parallel in our portrait gallery.[9]

Theodore Watts-Dunton's recollection of 1899, a recollection essentially the same as the two descriptions given above, involved a revealing comment on the effect of Borrow's remarkable physique.

The silvery whiteness of the thick crop of hair seemed to add in a remarkable way to the beauty of the hairless face, but also it gave a strangeness to it, and this strangeness was intensified by a certain incongruity between the features (perfect Roman-Greek in type), and the Scandinavian complexion, luminous and sometimes rosy as an English girl's. An increased intensity was lent by the fair skin to the dark lustre of the eyes. What struck the observer, therefore, was not the beauty but the strangeness of the man's appearance.[10]

In the chatter about Borrow after his death it amused gossips to describe him as effeminate. Thus his 'florid face without any hirsute appendages' and his complexion 'rosy as an English girls'. This of a man who, years before the gossips had known him, had travelled on foot halfway round the world, swam strongly, rode well, wandered about Scotland in the depth of winter with his shirt open at the neck and for years took his exercise by felling timber with a great axe given to him by Sir Shafto Adaire.[11] Borrow's face, and most of all his eyes, revealed something of the underlying complexity of character; the hair that turned white some time after his brother had painted it as dark certainly contrasted strangely with his impressive physique, particularly when he was young; his whole appearance with its supposed masculine and supposed feminine features constitutes, it is true, a biographical puzzle, not least when he draws attention to it himself; people scrutinised his bland exterior for a sign of the sexuality he signally concealed; but as to his strength, his imposing manner, his all-round athletic ability, there can be no doubt. He was a giant of a man, utterly fearless, and capable of great feats of endurance.

Borrow's physical appearance, his evident strength, his direct, rather aggressive way of looking at people, were to play a large part in his life, because wherever he went he impressed, either as a supremely confident person on whom you could depend or as a person to be feared. 'At seventy years of age', reported Watts-Dunton,

after breakfasting at eight o'clock in Hereford Square, he would walk to Putney, meet one or more of us at Roehampton, roam about Wimbledon and Richmond Park with us, bathe in the Fen Ponds with a northeast wind cutting across the icy water like a razor, run about the grass afterwards like a boy to shake off some of the water drops, stride about the park for hours, and then, after fasting for twelve hours, eat a dinner at Roehampton that would have done Sir Walter Scott's eyes good to see. Finally, he would walk back to Hereford Square, getting home late at night.[12]

Many of his exploits and many of his feats of physical strength and endurance will be mentioned in this book. What for Borrow was the psychological advantage of being large and strong will be constantly evident. He assumed there was nothing beyond his powers, which is why his fight with the Flaming Tinman in *Lavengro* is such an important part of his story. He had that disarming, sometimes objectionable confidence of a gentle person who knows his own strength. If someone barred his path Borrow was inclined to punch him in the face, but not without cause, for he was much more likely to use his huge presence for the sake of peace, as F. H. Groome said he did at Ascot.

The first time I ever saw him was at Ascot, the Wednesday evening of the Cup Week in, I think, the year 1872. I was stopping at a wayside inn, half a mile on the Windsor road, just opposite which inn there was a great encampment of gypsies. One of their lads had on Tuesday night affronted a soldier; so two or three hundred redcoats came over from Windsor intending to wreck the camp. There was a babel of cursing and screaming, much brandishing of belts and tent rods, when suddenly an arbiter appeared, a white haired, brown-eyed, calm colossus, speaking Romany fluently, and drinking deep draughts of ale – in a quarter of an hour Tommy Atkins and Anselo Stanley were sworn friends over a loving quart.[13]

Throughout his life this colossus had fits, a condition never properly diagnosed or treated. In childhood, he said, he was thought of as gloomy and withdrawn, sulky and perhaps stupid, at least by comparison with his talented brother. 'I was as a child in the habit of fleeing from society.'[14] In adolescence his fits and seizures were not frequent (the first definite record is of a fit at the age of sixteen) but they were devastating when they occurred. His mother taught him to call them 'the horrors', keeping the matter secret from the rest of the world as best she could. Later in life this sometimes proved difficult, as when he was unable to conceal a bad attack from fellow passengers while on his way to Russia. He himself gave a graphic account of the 'horrors' in the third volume of *Lavengro*, an account that shows well enough why Borrow throughout his waking days would live in fear of the next fit, why he felt different from other people, and why there was always an element of detachment and reserve in his dealings with them.

Suddenly I started up, and could scarcely repress the shriek which was rising to my lips. Was it possible? Yes, all too certain; the evil one was upon me; the inscrutable horror which I had felt in my boyhood had once more taken possession of me. I had thought that it had forsaken me – that it would never visit me again; that I had outgrown it; that I might almost bid defiance to it; and I had even begun to think of it without horror, as we are in the habit of doing of horrors of which we conceive we run no danger; and lo! when least thought of, it had seized me again. Every moment I felt it gathering force, and making me more wholly its own. What should I do? – resist, of course; and I did resist. I gasped, I tore, and strove to fling it from me; but of what avail were my efforts? I could only have got rid of it by getting rid of myself: It was a part of myself, or rather it was all myself. I rushed amongst the trees, and struck at them with my bare fists, and dashed my head against them, but I felt no pain. How could I feel pain with that horror upon me! And then I flung myself on the ground, gnawed the earth, and swallowed it; and then I looked round; it was almost total darkness in the dingle, and the darkness added to my horror.

Borrow attempted to compose himself by praying;

but it was of no use – praying seemed to have no effect over the horror; the unutterable fear appeared rather to increase than diminish, and I again uttered wild cries, so loud that I was apprehensive they would be heard by some chance passenger on the neighbouring road; I therefore went deeper into the dingle. I sat down with my back against a thorn bush; the thorns entered my flesh, and when I felt them, I pressed harder against the bush; I thought the pain of the flesh might in some degree counteract the mental agony; presently I felt them no longer – the power of the mental horror was so great that it was impossible, with that upon me, to feel any pain from the thorns.[15]

That Borrow is here describing an epileptic fit seems a safe conjecture, though it is impossible to know with certainty.[16] Perhaps because the phrase 'the horrors' became a euphemism that allowed biographers to gloss over the actuality of these fits even at the moment they were being referred to, not much of a connection has up to now been seen between what, by any standard, must be an extremely disturbing physical condition and Borrow's subsequent behaviour. As to behaviour, he was thought of by many early critics as wilful, perverse, wrong-headed, negligent in distinguishing between truth and falsehood and in-tolerant of the social practices others considered important, though admittedly a writer of great books. This is surely not good enough. A connection there must be between his fits, however rare their occurrence, and some of those aspects of his life that have puzzled biographers: his habit of secrecy, his limited sexual experience, his apparent ignorance of women and, more generally, his unremitting egoism, even though, again, these traits do not necessarily constitute a liability for Borrow as writer just because they might be regarded as a liability for Borrow as a human being. If this is to anticipate too much, it can at least be said that Borrow during his youth knew himself to be physically different from other people, radically different. This affected his relationship with them. He kept to himself. He buried himself in his books. He relaxed in the company only of people older than himself.

The family within which George Borrow grew up can be recollected only dimly, since neither his father nor his mother kept in touch with their own families or with their numerous brothers and sisters. Some families exert a good or even a bad influence on their members: others exert no influence whatsoever. In Borrow's case, there is next to no evidence of contact with grandparents, uncles and aunts, remoter rela-tives. Very few family letters have survived except those of Borrow to his mother, his brother, his wife, and his stepdaughter. He rarely re-ferred to family, except occasionally in indirect ways. An exception was when he went to Cornwall, late in life, to see members of his father's family, but it was the exception that proved the rule. If in some funda-mental biological sense there must have been exerted upon Borrow the influence of a 'family background' or a 'pedigree', the simple events of family life have certainly obscured it.

His father, Thomas Borrow (1758–1824), was the youngest of the eight children of a Cornish farmer, John Borrow, who farmed a 50-acre holding in the obscure hamlet of Trethinick near the village of St Cleer a few miles from Liskeard. He was of good height for that period – 5 feet 8 inches – and his sturdy physique was strengthened by the routine of farm-work up to 1778, when at the age of twenty he was apprenticed for five years to a maltster in Liskeard named Hambly or Hambley, a local worthy and Headborough or Constable of the Hundred of Liskeard. Why the apprenticeship did not begin until he was twenty cannot be ascertained, though it seems likely that without the parents (the father had died in 1758, the year of Thomas' birth, and the mother in 1773), the family just struggled on until it became obvious that the farm would not support them all. All that is known about the period of apprenticeship is the difficult-to-verify story that at the Menheniot Fair on 28 July 1783, the day his apprenticeship ended, Thomas became involved in a fight with rowdy factions from neighbouring towns and villages, resisted arrest by the Liskeard constables and, when his employer, acting in his legal capacity, remonstrated, happily if drunkenly knocked him to the ground – twice. Thomas left Liskeard quickly to avoid arrest and, as far as is known, never returned.

With nowhere to go that was safe from the constables, and no means to support himself, he seems just to have drifted about until Christmas of that year. Immediately after Christmas, on 29 December 1783, he was enlisted in the Coldstream Guards at Bodmin. He may indeed have realised that the army was the only career open to him, despite the arguments against such a course of action that legend has it that the commanding officer presented to him.[17] It is just as likely that he was pressed into service by the Coldstream Guards recruiting team as it visited the inns and taverns of Bodmin immediately after Christmas. The press-gang was to be a constant feature of George Borrow's early life. That he wrote about it once or twice with apparent nonchalance, as for example in the final pages of *The Romany Rye*, does not mean that he was not deeply affected both by the brutality of the activity itself and by the fact that he at least once, and probably countless times, saw his father forcing helpless recruits into the King's service. We will see later that George Borrow often steered away from events we might consider to have been formative, so to gloss over the involuntary nature of his father's initial enlistment would have been characteristic of him. At all events, Thomas Borrow spent nine years in the Coldstream Guards, being promoted to corporal on 17 September 1784 and to sergeant on 18 December 1789, at the age of thirty-one.[18]

Slightly more than two years later, on 25 February 1792, 'to instruct the young levies in military manoeuvres and disciplines', Thomas Borrow was transferred to the West Norfolk Militia, which at that time had its headquarters in King's Lynn.[19] Promoted almost immediately to sergeant-major, he began, as it were, a second military career, in as far as he could now expect to advance more rapidly than had been possible in the Coldstream Guards. George, Marquis of Townsend signed his promotion to ensign in June 1795 and to lieutenant-quartermaster in 1796, the original documents being preserved still in Norfolk Record Office. Army records show that he was then promoted to lieutenant-adjutant in 1798 and that some time later he acquired the rank, but apparently not the pay, of captain. So throughout George Borrow's life his father was always known as Captain Borrow. During the early years with the West Norfolk Militia, that is, between 1792 and 1802, the regiment was stationed mostly in King's Lynn and Colchester, though it was sometimes sent down into Kent, as happened, for example, in 1797. Thomas Borrow, however, spent some, perhaps much, of his time recruiting in Norfolk, both when he first joined the regiment and after becoming an officer. It was a job that frequently separated him from his wife.

In those short compassionate paragraphs about his father at the beginning of *Lavengro* Borrow said:

It may be as well to observe here, that I am by no means well acquainted with his early history, of which, indeed as I am not writing his life, it is not necessary to say much. Shortly after his mother's death, which occurred when he was eighteen, he adopted the profession of arms, which he followed during the remainder of his life, and in which, had circumstances permitted, he would probably have shone among the best. By nature he was cool and collected, slow to anger though perfectly fearless, patient of control, of great strength; and to crown all, a proper man with his hands.[20]

From the countless anecdotes about his father's army life which he must have heard, Borrow chose in *Lavengro* to recount the story of his father's hour-long fight in Hyde Park in 1790 with the famous pugilist, Big Ben, or to give him his proper name, Benjamin Brain, champion of all England from 1791 until his death in 1794. By this means the actuality of his relationship with his father was transformed into a loving and romantic memory, for 'smile not, gentle reader, many a battle has been fought in Hyde Park, in which as much skill, science and bravery have been displayed as ever achieved a victory in Flanders or by the Indus'.[21]

Borrow throughout his life admired as 'manly' anyone at all who was 'a proper man with his hands' and rather than attempt a documentary accuracy, preferred to give romantic colour to remembered episodes, except, that is, when he was writing about Roman Catholics, middle-class snobs and literary critics. Thus his way of saying that his father's military career was at best utterly undistinguished was the remark: 'had circumstances permitted, he would probably have shone among the best'.

On 11 February 1793, Thomas Borrow had married Ann Perfrement (1772–1858), the third of the eight children of Samuel Perfrement, a tenant farmer at Dumpling Green just outside East Dereham.[22] A man from an extremely isolated hamlet in a remote part of the Cornish countryside had by chance met a woman in an extremely isolated hamlet in a remote part of Norfolk. He was thirty-four and she was twenty-one.

Tradition has it that the Perfrements, who for at least a hundred years and maybe longer were concentrated in Norfolk and London, but apparently nowhere else in England, were originally Huguenot immigrants and that Samuel was a grandson or great-grandson of a family that had settled in East Anglia shortly after the Edict of Nantes. That Samuel's closest relations lived in North Norfolk, in East Dereham, Scarning and King's Lynn, has been convincingly demonstrated.[23] He himself rented a smallholding from a person called Starling or Sterling situated about a mile-and-a-half east of Dereham, in all probability remaining there from the time of his marriage to his death in 1804.[24] This smallholding with its house, buildings and stables, and surrounded at that time by unenclosed heath and common, was not the house identified by Knapp as George Borrow's birthplace, which is now marked by an appropriate, or rather inappropriate, plaque. Land-tax returns and enclosure-award maps show that Knapp had walked past the actual house on his expedition to Dumpling Green, misled apparently by a misreading of the relevant paragraphs in *Lavengro*. It was in any case only supposition that George Borrow was born in the house of his mother's parents. To the firm evidence about Samuel Perfrement's rental of this property from Starling for a period of about twenty years can be added the fact that all the other known children of Samuel and Mary Perfrement were baptised in East Dereham.[25] This makes it likely that the father of Ann and her seven brothers and sisters was indeed the same Samuel Perfrement as was named in the land-tax returns used to identify the smallholding. There is no evidence to support either Knapp's account of family and house at Dumpling Green, an account accepted more or less by most early biographers, or stories about the vagrant or gypsy background of Ann.[26] Knapp said that 'while occupied in recruiting and drilling', Captain Thomas Borrow 'occasionally allowed himself the diversion of the playhouse', that actors from the Theatre Royal, Norwich, sometimes put on plays in Dereham, that when they did so they often used local people for minor parts and that, in one such performance, Ann Perfrement was one of the 'graceful specimens of local talent'.[27] This story is unsupported. Although it is not known where Thomas Borrow was quartered when he visited East Dereham from King's Lynn in that particular year, there were countless ways in which they could have met. If there is a certain glamour in the idea that Ann was an actress, an element of romance in the picture of a world-hardened recruiting officer falling in love in the barn that was used for theatricals, next to the King's Head, a hint of respectability in a country wooing that led to marriage from the parental home, it nonetheless has to be noted that Ann's marriage was by licence, was witnessed by her sister, Elizabeth, not her father or mother, and may or may not have been a family affair. Because the headquarters of the West Norfolk Militia was in King's Lynn, it is likely that Thomas and Ann went there when the period of recruitment was over. Contacts between the Borrows and the Perfrements were minimal from that time on, so George was to grow up with two parents but not with the two families of his two parents, though in partial reconstructions of his early family life in *Lavengro*, he said that he remembered East Dereham and implied that some childhood experiences he also remembered had occurred there.

When or where the first son of Ann Borrow was born no one so far has been able to discover. Professor Knapp thought that this son, John, must have been born in 1800, because Borrow says in *Lavengro* that his brother was three years older than he was, and he thought the place must have been either Chelmsford or Colchester, because he believed the West Norfolk Militia was stationed there. Shorter, however, said that the date of birth was given as 15 April 1801 in one of the notebooks of Ann Borrow which he purchased from Henrietta MacOubrey's executors.[28] This latter date would have made him fourteen years old when promoted to the rank of lieutenant in the West Norfolk Militia in Ireland in 1815, which is possible but hardly likely, even though Borrow refers to him as 'the boy soldier'. These possibilities more compound the mystery than help to solve it. Ann Borrow's notebook is not available to be checked, while Knapp was mistaken in his account of the movements of the West Norfolk Militia.[29] It is not possible to demonstrate that Ann Borrow accompanied the regiment on all of its wartime expeditions. Nor is it possible to demonstrate that Thomas Borrow was the father of her first child, though there are a few hints to the contrary. Knapp, who certainly suppressed vital evidence when he thought the truth would damage Borrow's image, and who, after boasting about having every scrap of paper in his possession, said that he did not have the time or the money to do the necessary checking, called John a 'child of the regiment', thereby implying that he knew Ann

Borrow had been promiscuous. This phrase of Knapp's is consistent with Borrow's own description of his brother in *Lavengro*, where, in those teasing paragraphs on 'mirrors' and 'emblems', he emphasises how dissimiliar he and his brother were in childhood. The pattern of John Borrow's later career, his leaving home, his military career, his progress as an art student, with the implication of sponsorship from some source, make it reasonable to suppose that he might have been older than his brother, George, supposed and that he may not have been legitimate. What little evidence there is makes a birthday in 1797 or 1798 more probable than the dates suggested by Knapp and Shorter, even if that means abandoning the idea that Thomas and Ann Borrow were living in the same place as each other when the child was conceived.

In 1797 Ann Borrow was living in or near the new barracks at Sandgate, for it was there, and apparently there only, that she met John Murray II when he was visiting his mother, who two years earlier, after the death of John Murray I, had married Lieutenant Henry Paget of the West Norfolk Militia. This connection between the Borrows, Pagets, and the Murrays gave rise to a remarkable coincidence in George Borrow's own life, more than fifty years later, a coincidence at the heart of the story told in chapter 8 of the present book. Presumably it was during the 1790s that Ann Borrow led the uninhibited life that resulted in her son's characteristically ambivalent, though loving, recollection in *Lavengro*.

Thine is the peace of the righteous, my mother, of those to whom no sin can be imputed, the score of whose misdeeds has been long since washed away by the blood of atonement, which imputeth righteousness to those who trust in it. It was not always thus, my mother; a time was, when the cares, pomps, and vanities of this world agitated thee too much; but that time is gone by, another and a better has succeeded; there is peace now on thy countenance, the true peace; peace around thee, too, in thy solitary dwelling, sounds of peace, the cheerful hum of the kettle and the purring of the immense angora, which stares up at thee with its almost human eyes.[30]

Presumably John was born during this same period when his mother was agitated by the 'cares, pomps, and vanities of this world'. 'Misdeed' is a strong word to use about one's mother, but what else Borrow might have been referring to is not clear. Deleted, incidentally, from the manuscript page from which the above passage was printed was the interesting partial sentence: 'for thine was no common mind, one of those which are too obtuse to feel acutely the emotions either of joy or happiness; it matters not, dear mother'.

George, the second son of Thomas and Ann Borrow, was born on 5 July 1803, either in the home of his mother's family, if indeed the family was still there, or just as probably in the Borrows' own temporary quarters in a house on the site of the Co-operative Stores in what is now Norwich Street but was then Pound Street.[31] Thomas Borrow was a resident of East Dereham between April 1802 and August 1803 while on a recruiting drive for the regiment,[32] though when the war was renewed he presumably accompanied the regiment to Kent and Sussex when it was redeployed for coastal duties. Thus George was conceived and born in a brief period of matrimonial stability, a stability that was to be rare during the first ten years of his life.

Here, in what was then an extremely remote part of Norfolk, began the wayfaring career of the uprooted or rootless writer who at one stage was to sign himself George Olaus Borrow, not George Henry as his parents had determined, and who at later times was simply Shorsha in Ireland, Giorgio in Italy, Don Jorge in Spain and, in Russia, Yegor Phomitch Borrou. To the name 'Henry' he developed a distinct aversion. Probably important to his writing was the extremely disrupted life of his parents during the first thirteen years of his life, which corresponded, of course, with the Napoleonic Wars. Sometimes the boys were sent to school for a few months; sometimes they simply ran wild outside the walls of the barracks or the confines of the camp. Notable amongst these comings and goings were the family's stay in Norman Cross, near Peterborough, in 1810, when the regiment had a tour of duty guarding the French prisoners in the prisoner-of-war camp specially constructed for them there; the long, slow march north in 1812, with stops of various lengths at Harwich, Leicester, Tamworth, Macclesfield, Stockport, Ashton near Manchester, and Huddersfield; the winter of 1813–14 as part of the garrison of Edinburgh Castle; the demobilisation and return to Norfolk in 1814 at the supposed end of the war; and the remobilisation in 1815, when the regiment, not needed after all in the war against Napoleon, was sent to Ireland and stationed at Clonmel in Tipperary. The family returned to Norfolk in 1816 and in 1819 Captain Thomas Borrow retired on full pay,[33] after thirty-eight years' service.

With the exception of a small number of important incidents that can be independently verified, much of what we know about the first sixteen years of George Borrow's life derives from *Lavengro*, the book that he only began to write at the age of forty when, between himself and his own youth as he recollected it, lay the extensive travels and the extraordinary books that together made him famous. *Lavengro* is so splendidly written that few readers of it will readily forget those lively accounts of Borrow's youthful experiences that became anthology pieces, notably the passage about the vipers, which while extraordinarily vivid is also psychologically and politically enigmatic because of its symbolism, and the description of the fight between the Old and the New Town in Edinburgh, which was accepted as a model of good writing in so many school primers up to 1939 at least. These must be read and enjoyed for their own sake, for no discussion can improve upon them. The immediacy of so many of the well-known passages in *Lavengro* stems not from the recapitulation of verifiable fact but from his ability to write the type of prose that is always vigorous, unaffected, spontaneous and convincing. Consequently, to understand Borrow, and to think about the connection between his youth and his mature years, one must certainly start with *Lavengro*, but not, of course, stop there, despite his saying once that 'years pass by but we never undergo any radical change'. Borrow glossed over the facts of his family life, so it must be assumed from the outset that he glossed over other things as well.

When Borrow made the book called *Lavengro*, and filled it with many lively and convincing passages, he did not attempt to give a faithful record of the events of his life, least of all in volume 1, which was devoted to his earliest years. Boring days in married quarters, days of mere domestic activity, days of angry confrontation with one of his parents, or days of lazy and cheerful insignificance by the family hearth – these he chose to pass over. What he put into *Lavengro* were some of the highlights, some of the memorable events that retrospectively seem typical of his response to experience but, taken by themselves, have a charm all the greater for their not being seen as formative or in some way crucial. So he remembers, compassionately, the trials and tribulations of the French prisoners at Norman Cross, their meagre rations, their attempts to escape, their attempts to make a little money by wickerwork and work with straw, and by contrast the brutality of the English guards.[34] Characteristically, he leaves his reader with a visual impression, the picture of the French faces peering out through the tiny windows at the top of the huge casernes over the bleak Huntingdonshire landscape. In the same way, he remembers the stentorian voice of the parish clerk at East Dereham – 'thou wouldst be sadly out of place in these days of cold philosophic latitudinarian doctrine, universal tolerism, and half-concealed rebellion';[35] the magnificent Irish cob on which he first learnt to ride and the sight of the horse called 'Marshland Shales' to whom he said he doffed his cap at a Norwich horse-fair; and the striking characters of his childhood, too: Davie Haggart, the drummer boy whom his father had 'recruited' at Leith Races, who saved him in a fight in Edinburgh, and who was later hanged as a murderer; Joseph Gurney, the Quaker leader on whose property at Earlham Hall Borrow went fishing; and John Thurtell, the son of a Mayor of Norwich and a famous pugilist, whom the young Borrow says he first met by chance in the house of a magistrate. To this list of interesting people whom he got to know as he was growing up may be added a few famous figures from former eras, such as William Cowper, the poet who was buried in East Dereham. Borrow is remembering the strong impression made upon him by individuals who were essentially lonely and locked within themselves, despite their remarkable personalities. So of Cowper he says – 'who knows but within that unhappy frame lurked vicious seeds which the sunbeams of joy and prosperity might have called into life and vigour',[36] while in the case of Haggart, it is not the fact of his being a thief and a murderer that by itself interested Borrow, but the identification of a lonely and frustrated consciousness, as expressed in their talk on the crags of Edinburgh Castle and in the memoir Haggart wrote in thieves' cant in his death cell. Early on in life, Borrow is telling us, he had acquired that love of independence which goes with the loneliness and essential isolation of the individual and, also, that he preferred what he insisted on calling 'manly' activities, climbing, fighting, and horse-riding.

Exactly this was the reason for his delight in Defoe's *Robinson Crusoe*, a delight that grew into a lifelong imaginative association with an author whose other works must have been known to him at an early age. In *Lavengro* he gives a graphic description of his first looking at *Robinson Crusoe*; how a friend of his mother's, supposedly his brother's godmother, had brought it to the house as a gift; how, still unable to read, he looked at the pictures; how he 'remained motionless, gazing upon the pictures, scarcely daring to draw breath, lest the new and wondrous world should vanish of which I had now obtained a glimpse';[37] and how he did not rest until he had taught himself to read the book.

For hours together I would sit poring over a page till I had become acquainted with the import of every line. My progress, slow enough at first, became by degrees more rapid, till at last, under a 'shoulder of mutton sail,' I found myself cantering before a steady breeze over an ocean of enchantment, so well pleased with my voyage, that I cared not how long it might be ere it reached its termination. And it was in this manner [Borrow recollects] that I first took to the paths of knowledge.[38]

Defoe's direct, vigorous, colloquial and unaffected prose style had a profound influence upon the way in which Borrow later wrote, though it will be seen that there were also other influences, which Borrow himself identified. Equally attractive to Borrow was Defoe's habit, as a writer of fiction, of investing his principal characters with a forthright, down-to-earth, practical attitude to life, the attitude of someone who early in life learns that if he is to survive and manage at all it must be by dint of his own efforts, his own resourcefulness, his own determination. Thus there is a strong affinity between *Robinson Crusoe* and the fictional narration of *The Bible in Spain* and *Lavengro*, Borrow later showing himself as interested as Defoe had been in the imaginative blending of invention and knowledge into new fictions, a process that will be explored thoroughly in later chapters.

Borrow's love of Defoe was not a passing childhood phase but was sustained throughout his life. From *Lavengro* we know of his enthusiasm for *Moll Flanders*. He had the habit of reading the novel at the stall of his old friend, the applewoman, a recollection he repeats in *The Romany Rye*, perhaps because, as he asserted later, his understanding of the plight of Moll Flanders constituted the completion of his education. Defoe was a touchstone in later life. When he went to an exhibition, he commented on a remarkable scene by Poole, the idea of which was taken from Defoe's *Journal of the Plague Year*. When he started *Lavengro*, he said it was to be a life in the style of *Robinson Crusoe*. There are many stray hints of a continued interest throughout his papers, as for example his note (fossilised in a manuscript of *Lavengro*) on Defoe's *Account of Some Remarkable Papers* from a sale catalogue. In the British Library is a copy of *Zeldzame Levens-Beschriyving van Kolonel Jack*, that is, of a 1790 translation of *Colonel Jack* into Dutch with marginal autograph notes he made when teaching himself the language. In the library of Rutgers University and in the Lilly Library at Indiana are autographed manuscripts apparently forming part of a proposed essay on *Captain Singleton*. Consistent with these scattered morsels of evidence is the parallel between the careers of Defoe and Borrow as writers, made manifest, as will be seen, in Borrow's journalistic period in London, his later attempts to write about other parts of Britain as Defoe had done in *A Tour Through the Whole Island of Great Britain*, and in his neutral, worldly or amoral attitude to human behaviour, which allows him to lay stress upon the individual's efforts to survive in difficult circumstances without passing judgement one way or another on actions others would regard as immoral or undesirable. Borrow was not to become one of the great English moralists, unless a frank acceptance of human fallibility made him one.

Incidentally, the manuscript fragment at Indiana is interesting because Borrow is writing about how Defoe knew enough about central Africa in 1720 to give a realistic account of Captain Singleton's travels across the Continent. Borrow's response to this problem is characteristic of him. How does it happen, he asks, that in Defoe's *Captain Singleton* 'many of the modern discoveries of Africa are fore-shadowed, and the *great freshwater inland sea* is mentioned, and graphically described'? Because Defoe did not have 'second sight', there has to be a practical explanation.

In the early part of the eighteenth century Madagascar was a great nest for English pirates, amongst whom were individuals capable of conceiving and accomplishing enterprises the most extraordinary and romantic. A gang of these fellows may have crossed over to Mozambique, which is just opposite Madagascar, and from thence have traversed Africa, as Captain Singleton and certain of his companions are reported to have done, and Defoe may have met one of them in a certain dingy mughouse on Tower Hill much frequented by pirates come home, and other marine characters, and which he himself occasionally visited for the purpose of picking up materials for stories of adventure.[39]

Here is a clue, maybe, to what Borrow thought about knowledge. Borrow can contemplate with equanimity the likelihood that 'astounding secrets' can be obtained from 'tawny desperadoes' in a pub in which Defoe occasionally smoked a pipe. Books were a reliable source of knowledge, and so were people. Hard information did not necessarily come from books.

Very early in George Borrow's life began a process that was to shape his whole existence. Despite the comings and goings of his father's regiment, despite the war, despite his parents' lack of education, he discovered that it was easy for him to learn a foreign language, that he remembered all that he learnt and, most important, that he keenly enjoyed the experience of coming to terms with another language, whether by means of an undecipherable book or the strange sounds of someone met entirely by chance.[40] Why the son of an obscure recruiting sergeant should be blessed with the gift of tongues is, of course, impossible to determine. That he had a prodigious memory no one throughout his long life denied. It was always remarked upon and nearly always accepted as a fact. That he perhaps benefitted from the lack of formal schooling in his earliest years seems also to have been an important factor, for he soon showed himself to be a person with a very lively sense of the practical benefits to be derived from understanding what other people said. Though he later called himself a philologist, a 'Lavengro', an expert with words, his interest was always in a foreign language as used and hardly at all in a foreign language transposed into a school-room discipline. Though often criticised for his inaccuracy, though often presented as something of a fraud, he nonetheless made himself into one of the foremost linguists of the day, as later chapters will amply demonstrate.

While at the prison camp at Norman Cross, Borrow was taught by a local clergyman who was an old friend of his father's. In this somewhat improbable way, he began the study of Latin. This teacher was represented as thinking that the key to a sound education was the out-of-date Latin grammar, William Lily's *A Short Introduction of Grammar*.

If you are anxious for the success of your son in life, for the correctness of his conduct and the soundness of his principles, keep him to Lilly's grammar... I never knew a boy that was induced, by fair means or foul, to learn Lilly's Latin grammar by heart, who did not turn out a man, provided he lived long enough.[41]

This was in 1810, when Borrow was seven years old. The next three years were spent mostly on the road, with brief periods of stability in Colchester, East Dereham and Huddersfield, where Borrow had one of the longest periods at school to date, that is, the last four months of 1812. He recollected, quaintly, that by 1813 he had Lily's Latin grammar by heart, so that 'you only had to repeat the first two or three words of any sentence in any part of the book, and forthwith I would open cry, commencing without blundering and hesitation, and continue till you were glad to beg me to leave off'.[42] So far Borrow hardly understood a word of what he had learnt, but this was rectified during the year he spent at Edinburgh High School, the academic winter of 1813–14 being the first time he had experienced a complete school year. Given the extraordinary way in which Borrow's career was to develop, he was extremely lucky to have acquired this no doubt rudimentary yet soundly based knowledge of Latin at such a fine school. He began to learn Greek during a later, three-month stay at the Protestant Academy at Clonmel.

Borrow was admitted to Norwich Grammar School in 1814, at the age of eleven, but almost immediately had to accompany his father to Clonmel in Tipperary. Here he went wild, wandered about the Irish countryside and learnt to ride – at the insistence, according to *Lavengro*, of an army groom at Templemore who gave him the use of that great Irish cob which had proved too spirited for anyone else.

Oh, that ride! that first ride – most truly it was an epoch in my existence; and I still look back to it with feelings of longing and regret. People may talk of first love – it is a very agreeable event, I dare say – but give me the flush, and triumph, and glorious sweat of the first ride, like mine on that mighty cob.[43]

This horse was Borrow's passport to freedom, as he himself says in chapter 13 of *Lavengro*. It also gave rise, in the same chapter, to a line of thought that will be significant to anyone who takes the main drift of *Lavengro* seriously and is not too bothered by the frequent inaccuracies of detail. 'It was thus', said Borrow,

that the passion for the equine race was first awakened within me – a passion which, up to the present time, has been rather on the increase than diminishing. It is no blind passion; the horse being a noble and generous creature, intended by the All-Wise to be the helper and friend of man, to whom he stands next in the order of creation. On many occasions of my life I have been much indebted to the horse, and have found him a friend and coadjutor, when human help and sympathy were not to be obtained...I much question whether philology, or the passion for languages, requires so little of an apology as the love for horses. It has been said, I believe, that the more languages a man speaks, the more a man is he; which is very true, provided he acquires languages as a medium for becoming acquainted with the thoughts and feelings of the various sections into which the human race is divided; but in that case, he should rather be termed a philosopher than a philologist – between which two the difference is wide indeed! An individual may speak and read a dozen languages, and yet be an exceedingly poor creature, scarcely half a man; and the pursuit of tongues for their own sake, and the mere satisfaction of acquiring them, surely argues an intellect of a very low order; a mind disposed to be satisfied with mean and grovelling things; taking more pleasure in the trumpery casket than in the precious treasure which it contains; in the pursuit of words than the acquisition of ideas.[44]

At least for Borrow himself, it was important that 'the passion for languages' was 'always modified by the love of horses'. So he believed, that is, when he wrote *Lavengro*, for the high excitement of these first bare-back rides and the long expeditions about the Irish countryside, even as far as Cahir itself, had coincided with his learning Greek in Clonmel and Irish in his spare time from his friend Murtagh, with whom he exchanged a pack of playing cards for regular instruction so that for both of them the boredom of the long days and particularly the long nights would be alleviated. The full significance of Borrow being able to 'speak a considerable quantity of broken Irish' by the time he left Ireland would only become apparent a few years later, though he said that its initial appeal was that Irish was not 'a drawing-room language, drawled out occasionally, by the ladies of generals and other great dignitaries, to the ineffable dismay of poor officers' wives' but 'a speech spoken in out-of-the-way desolate places, and in cut throat kens, where thirty ruffians, at the sight of the king's minions, would spring up with brandished sticks and an "ubbubboo" like the blowing up of a powder magazine'.[45]

Borrow continued to learn Latin and Greek when the West Norfolk Militia returned to England and he returned to Norwich Grammar School, his father, on the point of retirement, having rented a small house in Willow Lane in the Parish of St Giles in Norwich. At the same time – that is, during his three years at Norwich Grammar School from 1816 to 1819 – he learnt French and Italian with an emigré priest called Thomas D'Eterville, who is described in quaint but loving terms in *Lavengro*,[46] acquired 'some knowledge of Spanish', and began to dabble in other languages, initially with the help of a 'tessara-glot' grammar, like the one that was then as now in the Norwich City Library called *The Guide into the Tongues. With their agreement and consent one with another, that is, the Reasons and Derivations of all or the most part of words in these nine languages.* Borrow said that the languages treated in *his* 'tessara-glot' grammar were French, Italian, Low Dutch and English; the nine languages in the Norwich City grammar were English, Low Dutch, High Dutch, French, Italian, Spanish, Latin, Greek and Hebrew. It will be seen that this question of where Borrow obtained his books is not unimportant. He somehow obtained or at least became acquainted with books that other people simply did not know about at all, enjoying the sensation of novelty and preferring the unorthodox to the orthodox method, even to the extent of being deliberately mysterious about it. As for the orthodox type of education that was briefly open to him, little is known about it because the headmaster of his day, the Rev. Edward Valpy, chose to destroy the school's records. The record of Borrow's three years at Norwich Grammar School would probably not have revealed very much, how-ever, for the books that proved influential were not in the school library, while the Rev. Valpy abruptly reduced the teenager's already limited enthusiasm for the schoolroom by giving him such a severe public thrashing for truancy that it was two weeks before Borrow was able to get out of bed. It was claimed, though there is no evidence to support this, that he was scarred for life. One of the stories that grew around this episode was that Borrow had persuaded three of his school-friends to leave school and rough it on Caistor Beach in Robinson Crusoe fashion, so that when they were spotted 11 miles from school they were not just giving themselves the day off, but were, dread thought, 'running away', and Borrow was in fact treated as the ringleader, being flogged severely on the back of James Martineau, who was required to 'horse' him and whom incidentally he never forgave, while the others, John Dalrymple and Theodosius and Francis Purland, got off more lightly.[47] The psychological, indeed the possible physical effects of this humilia-tion in front of the whole school are difficult to estimate, though the efforts some of his contemporaries made to minimise the episode give rise to the suspicion that, even by the standards of a notoriously cruel Christian schoolmaster, the beating was remembered as brutal and vindictive. James Martineau is supposed to have said that 'not for another life' would he again endure the misery he had experienced at school.[48] Borrow obviously shared this sentiment. Neither at home nor at school could this eccentric adolescent have any hope of being understood and, if he could not effect an escape physically, if he could not yet leave Norwich, then he would escape from local moral standards and proprieties into foreign languages and foreign books. So he read Dante with D'Eterville, at the same time casting around restlessly for new interests.

In 1819, when he was nearly sixteen, Borrow was articled for five years to a well-known and successful Norwich solicitor, William Simpson, who was senior partner in the firm of Simpson and Rackham with an office in Tuck's Court (no longer standing) and Treasurer of the County of Norfolk as well as Chamberlain and Town Clerk of Norwich.[49] Borrow at this time left the small attic bedroom that he had shared with his brother in their parents' house in Willow Lane to live for five years with Mr and Mrs Simpson in a house in Upper Close, near Tombland and with a garden next to what was then an open space used as a playground by the boys of Norwich Grammar School. A contemporary who recalled Borrow's chatting with school-friends over the fence that divided this playground from the Simpson's garden, remembered him then 'as a tall, spare, dark-complexioned man, usually dressed in black'.[50] A friend called Roger Kerrison[51] had told Borrow that he could usefully submit to the training of a law office, without intending to make a career of the law, which is what he did. He was at best an extremely nonchalant employee, for both in and out of the office he was bent on adding other languages to his repertoire, including Welsh, German, Romany, Hebrew, Arabic and Danish. Borrow himself said that he never achieved any proficiency in the law 'because he ever loved to be as explicit as possible'.[52]

Yes! Very pleasant times were those, when within the womb of a lofty deal desk, behind which I sat for some eight hours every day, transcribing (when I imagined eyes were upon me) documents of every description in every possible hand, Blackstone kept company with Ab Gwilym — the polished English lawyer of the last century, who wrote long and prosy chapters on the rights of things — with a certain wild Welshman, who some four hundred years before that time indited immortal cowydds and odes to the wives of Cumbrian chieftains — more particularly to one Morfydd, the wife of a certain hunchbacked dignitary called by the poet facetiously Bwa Bach — generally terminating with the modest request of a little private parlance beneath the green wood bough, with no other witness than the *eos*, or nightingale, a request which, if the poet himself may be believed, rather a doubtful point, was seldom, very seldom, denied. And by what strange chance had Ab Gwilym and Blackstone, two personages so exceedingly different, been thus brought together? From what the reader already knows of me, he may be quite prepared to find me reading the former; but what could have induced me to take up Blackstone, or rather the law?[53]

Here was the beginning of a lifelong interest, which was to be marked, some thirty years later, by three walking-tours through Wales and the publication, in 1860, of *Wild Wales*. In 1822 and 1823, however, Borrow was restricted to translating the poetry of Ab Gwilym and learning how to pronounce the language from a Welsh groom whom he happened to meet near the office. Borrow was often accused of being maladroit in the drawing-room, the language of gentility being the one he never cared to master, but in post-war Norwich, the scene of labour riots and disturbances, this inveterate, compulsive democrat never had difficulty getting on with a groom, which is a lot more than can be said for those superior social beings who were later so free with their criticisms.

Borrow was taught German by William Taylor, whom Borrow is said to have met through a mutual friend, a Jew – 'Mousha' in *Lavengro* – from whom Borrow had learnt Hebrew, or a smattering of the language at least. William Taylor had travelled widely, defended the French Revolution, having attended National Assembly debates in 1790, translated from the German and contributed to a number of well-known periodicals. Taylor gathered round him the hot-heads, the intellectuals, the 'interesting' people in Norwich, whom Borrow met when he began to go with some regularity to Taylor's house at 21 King Street. From the security of her drawing-room, Harriet Martineau much later condemned Taylor as being beyond the social pale, because of his atheism, his anti-establishment politics and his love of liquor. 'Matters grew much worse in his old-age, when his habits of intemperance kept him out of the sight of ladies, and he got round him a set of ignorant and conceited young men, who thought they could set the world right by their destructive propensities. One of his chief favourites was George Borrow.'[54] When Harriet Martineau wrote this in the 1870s, Borrow's own reputation was at a low ebb, so she was merely indulging her own destructive propensities by cattily linking together these two famous Norwich social rebels, who had stood aside from the political developments that allowed their contemporaries to believe in, for example, colonial wars and colonial exploitation. Borrow himself remembered William Taylor in different terms.

Methought I was in a small, comfortable room wainscotted with oak; I was seated on one side of a fireplace, close by a table on which were wine and fruit; on the other side of the fire sat a man in a plain suit of brown, with the hair combed back from the somewhat high forehead; he had a pipe in his mouth, which for some time he smoked gravely and placidly, without saying a word; at length, after drawing at the pipe for some time rather vigorously, he removed it from his mouth, and emitting an accumulated cloud of smoke, he exclaimed in a slow and measured tone: 'As I was telling you just now, my good chap, I have always been an enemy of humbug!'[55]

Over the gap of years, a person not encumbered with Harriet Martineau's superior judicial abilities can perhaps see that, intemperate or not, the fifty-five-year-old William Taylor simply brought Borrow along, talked with him when he needed talk, encouraged him in his literary interests when there were few people in his life who shared his enthusiasms and, with the experience and cosmopolitan *savoir-faire* that gave validity, or seemed to give validity, to his conversations about foreign countries and foreign languages, rescued Borrow in some measure from the provinciality of Norwich. He recognised Borrow's exceptional talents and became his friend and mentor. 'What I tell Borrow *once* he *ever* remembers', he reported;[56] and, on another occasion:

A Norwich young man is construing with me Schiller's *Wilhelm Tell*, with a view of translating it for the press. His name is George Henry Borrow, and he has learnt German with extraordinary rapidity; indeed he has the gift of tongues, and, though not yet eighteen, understands twelve languages – English, Welsh, Erse, Latin, Greek, Hebrew, German, Danish, French, Italian, Spanish and Portuguese.[57]

When Borrow left Norwich, his German was immediately subjected to an extremely severe test, but with William Taylor he simply enjoyed as ever the experience of grappling with something new. And he had the confidence to advertise himself as a teacher, for it was presumably at about this time that he posted the following notice found amongst his papers after his death: 'Mr. George Borrow, Willow Lane, St. Giles, Norwich. Gives instructions in German and in any other European language. Hebrew taught, if required.'[58]

Although Borrow was sometimes condemned as a dilettante, an amateur linguist, someone whose shallow understanding of grammar and structure was immediately exposed whenever he had to translate from English into the other language, there seems no doubt that he had an exceptional ear, an exceptional memory, an exceptional interest. Had he been alive in 1981 he might have failed to satisfy A-level examiners in any *one* of the languages listed above. On the other hand, he later in life used all of them, so what occurred while Borrow was articled to William Simpson in Norwich was not a mere display of youthful talent, but the restless yet rapid acquisition of the very basis of the whole of his later life. He should have stuck to the law, had a career, people might say – people did say. But Borrow in Rome, Paris, Lisbon and Madrid spoke the language of the people he was with. He liked this. It was important to him.

It was not as important, though, as the other 'events' of this period of his life: his learning Danish and the first inkling of what was to become a lifelong interest in the language of gypsies.

In *Lavengro*, Borrow gives a graphic account of how an old couple, who had done business with William Simpson and in the process been helped in small ways by the young lad who worked in the outer office and answered the door, felt grateful and arrived one day to give him a couple of presents, from the old lady a kiss on the cheek, and from the old man a book – a book that he had been given by three Danes whom the old couple had looked after for three days after their shipwreck. Danes! Borrow says – and is there at this point any reason to disbelieve him? – that 'the strange and uncouth-looking volume' was printed in gothic type on vellum and bound in wood 'compressed with strong iron clasps'.[59] There flashed through Borrow's mind all he had ever heard about the Danes, particularly in Ireland: their strength, their size, their magical powers and their ability to 'make strong beer from the heather that grows upon the bogs' – a useful attribute in the mind of a man like Borrow, who had a strong interest in survival techniques. He remembered, too, that earlier, as a child, he had seen the Daneman's skull in a Kent church, was then and there pervaded by 'an indefinable curiosity for all that is connected with the Danish race', and, as to the skull, supposed it 'must have belonged to a giant, one of those redhaired warriors of whose strength and stature such wondrous tales are told in the ancient chronicles of the north'.[60] He knew, too, that far inland from the East Anglian coast there were still people whose first language was Danish. Yet the language stumped him. He had never seen anything like it. He pored over it daily and nightly, he said, and became distraught. 'With all my poring I could not understand it; and then I became angry, and I bit my lips until the blood came out; and I occasionally tore a handful from my hair, but that did not mend the matter for I still did not understand the book.'[61] Eventually he conquered the problem, began to make sense of the words in front of him, by adopting a method he was to employ again and again. He locked the Danish book away, bought a Danish Bible from an Antinomian preacher who had once been a disciple of Ludowick Muggleton, and compared the Danish with an English Bible, until after working at the comparison for a month, he took the book from the closet where it had been locked away, and proceeded to master its contents.

Because Borrow developed a fanatical, obsessive interest in Danish literature, it is worth noting how this book, as yet only partly understood, so powerfully struck his imagination. By degrees, he said, he overcame the fact that the book consisted of poems written in an ancient dialect, for the book was a book of ballads, about the deeds of knights and champions, and men of huge stature; ballads which from time immemorial had been sung in the North, and which some two centuries before the time of which I am speaking had been collected by one Anders Vedel, who lived with a certain Tycho Brahe, and assisted him in making observations upon the heavenly bodies, at a place called Uranien Castle, on the little island of Hveen, in the Cattegat.[62]

In a small room in the house of the lawyer William Simpson, Borrow spent many hours trying to translate these poems; he later took them to London with him; he published some of them by subscription when he returned to Norwich; he showed them, later still, to his Danish friend, Hasfeld, in St Petersburg; he reworked the others and made repeated attempts to have them published. If this is to anticipate, the anticipation is important, because Borrow's struggles with the book given him by the old couple should not be dismissed as a trivial episode, a mere stage in his development, or a craze briefly exciting but soon forgotten. It was an experience Borrow never forgot, for indeed his imagination had been entirely captivated. He found there were books in Norwich that further whetted his appetite, particularly one with a somewhat off-putting title: *Runer: seu Danica Literatura antiquissima vulgo Gothica dicta luci reddita* by Olaus Wormius. Knapp said that the pencilled marginal notes in this copy, which are still there for anyone to inspect, are in Borrow's handwriting. It is difficult to tell, but certainly a measure of the importance of this book to Borrow is the fact that for a few years he signed himself George Olaus Borrow.

Borrow's interest in the old books, some of which were then in the Corporation Library and are now in glass-fronted bookcases in the basement of the Norwich Public Library, was not merely antiquarian. His interests were linguistic and, if he derived a profound, personal, aesthetic pleasure from inscription, unfamiliar calligraphy or exotic type in much the same way as someone else might enjoy a Bach score or a set of equations, he was never content to be a mere linguist but always thought of the acquisition of a language as a real extension of self, an acquisition certainly, but an acquisition with vast implications for his own future. These Danish poems that Borrow had come across, medieval Danish poems that the sixteenth-century poet, Anders Sorensen Vedel, had collected, and which Nyerup and Rahbek had edited in 1812 as *Udvalgte Danske Viser fra Middelalderen,* in an edition that Borrow knew, confirmed in him a sense – actually a type of knowledge – of European history which transcended what was taught in the school-room. England was part of Europe and the Danes had been amongst its earliest inhabitants: therefore an interest in Danish literature, or indeed any other early literature, was a valid alternative to the recently acquired moral prerogatives that dominated a city like Norwich in the 1820s. This may seem far-fetched, but Borrow did reject the 'gentility' and 'jobbery' of his own period and did consciously prefer the ethical and political standards of other periods. Borrow read the Danish *Kæmpe Viser* in 1822 or 1823; Meredith towards the end of the century began to write a book called *Celt and Saxon*. That between the two dates the Celtic was seen as an alternative to the Saxon, perhaps an alternative to be preferred, was a measure of the resistance (which Borrow represented) to establishment ideas acceptable to a district commissioner or a Church of England clergyman, though if some latter-day sociologist had labelled Borrow's interest in Scandinavian literature a 'counter-culture', Borrow would have been legitimately indignant because he knew, as a matter of fact, how deeply rooted in English life was the Scandinavian element. Furthermore, even as early as the 1820s, Borrow's interest in languages, especially Danish, involved his seeing a pattern to existence which transcended national boundaries. He became interested in the Vikings. It will become obvious, later, that a man who travels to St Petersburg and Novgorod, Portugal, Spain and Tangiers, Constantinople and parts of northern Greece, Wales, Ireland, the Isle of Man, Scotland and the Orkney Islands is not primarily interested, for example, in Roman history or British Colonial trade routes; he is interested in Vikings. In Norwich, in the early 1820s, a beginning was made when he taught himself Danish and began to read Danish poetry. Later in life, he pursued this interest to the fullest extent possible.

The gypsies, though, were as great an interest. Borrow recalled in *Lavengro* how he stumbled upon a gypsy encampment as a boy, how the gypsies were intrigued by him because he was carrying a viper inside his shirt and so called him *sapengro*, someone who knows the mysteries of snakes, and how he later met the same family at a horse-fair in Norwich and was taken by them to their new, but of course temporary, encampment on Mousehold Heath. Much of his time was spent tramping over the heathland and open countryside around Norwich, for he was already becoming a prodigious walker. His father's time in the army had accustomed George to a rugged, carefree existence, made him impervious to the weather, allowed him to enjoy day after long day out of doors without constraint of any kind and perhaps developed within him a tendency to regard other people, wherever he met them, as people met by chance on a walk whom one met again, or not, only as fate decreed. The ancient lineage of the migrant meant more to him than the recently acquired gentility of the English middle class. But as for the gypsies he came to know near Norwich, he felt a kinship with them long before he had a theory to explain it.

As his father had done before him, Borrow fulfilled the obligations of his apprenticeship and then turned his back on the profession he had learnt. His brother, meanwhile, had had a very different upbringing about which a word must be said, before we turn our attention to the main subject of this book, which is not family affairs, but George Borrow's writing life. In 1814 John was accepted as a student by Crome, the painter who had founded what became known as the Norwich School. Because John managed to eke out a living as an art student for most of the next ten years, it would be interesting to know what financial arrangement, if any, he had with Crome. Did he work strictly as an apprentice? Did his parents try to persuade him to find a job that would add to the family income? Or was he helped by someone who was not a member of the family? He seemed to enjoy a privileged position, for whatever reason.

The arrangement with Crome, whatever it was, lasted in the first instance for less than a year because when, as a result of Napoleon's escape, England once again seemed threatened and the West Norfolk Militia was called back to arms, John Borrow enlisted as an ensign and travelled to Ireland with the regiment, as did the rest of the family. In *Lavengro*, Borrow called him the 'boy-soldier'. The West Norfolk Militia's services were not required for very long, for the war ended with the Battle of Waterloo, but John Borrow was promoted to lieutenant on 23 December 1815,[63] which guaranteed him his 'disembodied allowance' when the regiment was disbanded shortly afterwards. Back in Norwich, John Borrow continued to study with Crome, exhibiting his work at the annual exhibitions of the Norwich Society of Artists. The five works he had in the 1821 exhibition included portraits of his father and his brother. When Crome died that year, John went to London to work with Benjamin Haydon, an arrangement that resulted in Haydon's doing that portrait of the Mayor of Norwich which Borrow described in such amusing terms in *Lavengro*. In 1823, John Borrow went to Paris, still an art student and still sending work back to the Norwich exhibitions. Then, unexpectedly, he himself was forced to return to Norwich when his father died on 28 February 1824, at the age of sixty-six.

While both George and John were living at home they may well have taken each other for granted as sometimes brothers do. When George began his own apprenticeship in 1819, and more certainly when John went to London in 1821, their paths began to diverge, because George became more and more engrossed in the study of languages, when he was not at the Simpsons spending much of his time with William Taylor, while, unbeknown to George, John had a private life of his own, a life which, kept secret from his friends in Norwich, had later to be disentangled by George, as will be seen in the next chapter. It will be seen, too, in later chapters of this book, that George by no means disregarded his brother's study of art, that he in fact shared it with him to some extent, and that his later references to Claude and Rembrandt, for example, are far from casual. Still, their paths had certainly diverged and for both of them all semblance of family life terminated when their father died.

When George Borrow's five-year period with Simpson and Rackham terminated only a few weeks after his father's death, he packed his trunk and set out for London, an already huge bundle of manuscripts carried in hand in a green box. He was determined to be independent, determined to make a name for himself, determined to lead the life of literature.

The metamorphosis of the recruiting sergeant's son into a writer of originality is the subject of the chapters that follow. It is often said that a biographer should present the facts of a person's life, to the extent that they can be ascertained, present them in chronological order and leave questions of interpretation to the reader, who may or may not feel that interpretation is useful or necessary. It is also often said that psychological interpretation is the imposition of the biographer's own proclivities, which the reader can well do without. These two points of view will no doubt be argued till doomsday, each new biography providing a fresh example of the biographer's attempt to establish a balance between a factual narrative, the details of which can be verified, and the explanation or interpretation of that narrative, which must ultimately depend upon the biographer's sense of his subject's whole life, viewed in its entirety. The present biography of George Borrow incorporates much information not available to most earlier biographers and thus constitutes a more complete version of his life, even on the level of factual detail. But its main purpose is to arrive at an understanding of Borrow the writer, to penetrate to the extent possible the eccentricity of his character, and to celebrate the marvellous transformations achieved by his pen in that remote summer-house in East Anglia where, despite the ups and downs of everyday life, his imagination ruled.

Borrow in New Grub Street

Borrow decided to leave Norwich because he had no intention of earning his living as a solicitor, because he already thought of himself as a writer, wished to do something of literary note in the world and therefore had to be in London, and in all probability because of the conflict he observed between the gentility of families where the children went to Norwich Grammar School or were privately educated and the political anger of the poor and the unemployed. Norwich was a cathedral city with a long tradition of culture and refinement: it was also a city that witnessed riots, protest meetings and unrest in the period immediately after the Napoleonic War, though during the period of Empire the extent of these disturbances was played down. Borrow rejected the refinement, sympathised with the protester. Though he was once sworn in as a special constable, together with (according to the *Norwich Mercury*) 1,800 other Norwich citizens – a figure that by itself shows how serious the unrest was – he throughout his life identified with the underdog, the dispossessed, the gypsy.

As his life proceeded, Borrow developed an almost pathological hatred of what he called 'gentility', that is, a mannered style of life governed by etiquette and disconnected from the problems, as well as from the real pleasures, of existence. He had a rooted objection to the acquisition of those social habits and forms which middle-class families found convenient and desirable. He disliked genteel dinner parties and the small talk of dinner parties. When, having become famous, he went out more frequently to dinner, he would sometimes leave the table and go off to another part of the house to talk to the servants, or the children. He disliked having to chatter to other people on subjects of no importance to himself, reacting badly towards people who condescended to disregard his bad manners so that they could go on talking, or try to get him to talk. From one point of view, he was truculent, maladjusted and socially gauche; from another point of view he was genuinely the democrat who saw gentility as the unacceptable face of bourgeois power politics, despite the fact that while decrying humbug in others he became a humbug himself. Early nineteenth-century Norwich cannot be blamed for the whole of this. Nonetheless, the virulent attack on 'gentility nonsense' in *The Romany Rye* must have had a deep cause, one that we may plausibly trace back to hot-headed radical talk in William Taylor's study. To judge by his subsequent actions he must have thought, when he left Norwich in 1824, that personal and political independence could be achieved with the pen, rather than by social action or involvement, for though he did not have a well-thought-out political position, or at least not as far as one knows, he at first associated himself with writers, radicals and socially alienated individuals, as well as with tramps, misfits, bohemians and eccentrics. Only later in life did he gloss this over with a Tory attitude.

His decision to leave Norwich preceded the death of his father and was not caused by it, for in January he wrote the following letter to his friend, Roger Kerrison, who, it will be remembered, had also been articled to Simpson and Rackham.

Dearest Roger:

I did not imagine when we separated in the street, on the day of your departure from Norwich, that we should not have met again. I had intended to have come and seen you off, but happening to dine at Mr. Barron's, and got [*sic*] into discourse, and the hours slipt past me unawares.

I have been for the last fortnight laid up with that detestable complaint which destroys my strength, impairs my understanding and will in all probability send me to the grave, for I am now much worse than when you saw me last. But *nil desperandum est*, if ever my health mends and possibly it may by the time my clerkship is expired, I intend to live in London, write plays, poetry and abuse religion and get myself prosecuted, for I would not for an ocean of gold remain any longer than I am forced in this dull and gloomy town.

I have no news to regale you with for there is none abroad, but I live in the expectation of shortly hearing from you, and being informed of your plans and projects; fear not to be prolix for the slightest particular cannot fail of being interesting to one who loves you far better than parent or relation or even than the God whom bigots would teach him to adore, and who subscribes himself.

Yours unalterably

George Borrow[1]

In this mood, having sent off his trunk in advance, he travelled up to London himself, on 2 April, armed with letters of introduction and his bundles of manuscripts.

Few men or women have been more determined than Borrow was to lead a literary life, by whatever means, for he remained in London, translating, compiling, composing, editing, for as long as it was physically possible for him to do so, and though circumstances forced him to leave in 1825, he returned in 1829 to renew exactly the same Grub Street life, even though full success still eluded him. People have been critical of this period of Borrow's life, the first period in London, which extended off and on from 1824 to 1833. Was he some type of egomaniac, they have implied, a foolish fellow who thought that by translating obscure Danish and Welsh poets, but not translating them well, he could earn his living by his pen? Should he not have settled down to a normal life in the profession for which he had been trained? Questions of this kind are beside the point. Borrow could have been a solicitor: he chose to be a writer. Not all writers enjoy instant success. Many have to survive arduous and lengthy apprenticeship, as did Borrow. In any case, what is success for a writer aged twenty-one? It is publishing his first articles or his first book. If this results in a handsome series of cheques so much the better, but such a person does not think he has failed if he remains penniless. A rereading of Keats' letters, written just a few years earlier, would remind anyone sceptical about this, if an example were needed, that Borrow was not alone in dissociating money and literature, even though he earnestly hoped to earn his living with his pen. So in good spirits he moved into Roger Kerrison's lodgings, began to explore London for the first time and very soon called on Sir Richard Phillips, to whom William Taylor had written a letter of introduction.

Sir Richard Phillips was a fifty-seven-year-old publishing entrepreneur, originally from the Midlands, who had made a fortune at the beginning of the century, gone bankrupt, started again and again prospered, though more modestly. William Taylor's letter struck a chord, reminding him of his more successful days, and he was willing to do his old acquaintance a favour if he could. He had exploited other young literary enthusiasts long before George Borrow turned up on his doorstep in Tavistock Square. If the youngster was to have any chance at all, it would have to be an outside chance. His own affairs were not so rapidly expanding that he could have found a plum job for him even had he wished, much of his business at this time being the production of low-cost, low-risk, one-volume popular reference books such as *A Million of Facts* and *A Chronology of Public Events Within the Last Fifty Years from 1771 to 1821*. Officially, Sir Richard had retired from his commercial engagements and removed from his 'late house of business in New Bridge Street', as Borrow remembered in *Lavengro*. He did, though, find Borrow a job of sorts, the collecting, transcribing, editing and sometimes translating and re-writing of those famous legal cases which, on the analogy of the French equivalent called *Causes célèbres*, were eventually published in six volumes as *Celebrated Trials and Remarkable Cases of Criminal Jurisprudence, from the Earliest Records to the Year 1825*,[2] and which later in life Borrow sometimes referred to as the *Newgate Lives and Trials* as he did in *The Romany Rye*. Borrow said in *Lavengro* that, of the various bits of hack-work he did for Sir Richard Phillips, the compilation of the *Celebrated Trials* was the most congenial, even though he was expected to add to the collection of legal cases by spending his own money on such extra items as he might find on the bookstalls. He became absorbed in the details of several of the cases, became interested in the characters involved and often sympathised frankly with those whom the law found guilty. As he said:

The trials were entertaining enough, but the lives — how full were they of wild and racy adventures, and in what racy, genuine language were they told! What struck me most with respect to these lives was the art which the writers, whoever they were, possessed of telling a plain story. It is no easy thing to tell a story plainly and distinctly by mouth; but to tell one on paper is difficult indeed, so many snares lie in the way. People are afraid to put down what is common on paper, they seek to embellish their narratives, as they think, by philosophic speculations and reflections; they are anxious to shine, and people who are anxious to shine can never tell a plain story. 'So I went with them to a music booth, where they made me almost drunk with gin, and began to talk their flash language, which I did not understand,' says, or is made to say, Henry Sims, executed at Tyburn some seventy years before the time of which I am speaking. I have always looked upon this sentence as a masterpiece of the narrative style. It is so concise and yet so very clear.[3]

The work of compilation was not mechanical day-labour, for if the labour was severe enough, Borrow was very conscious (as he put this six-volume book together) of stylistic matters that affected his own style directly. He remarks in the Preface that as to the French *Causes célèbres*, 'more persons praise this work than have read it; for it is altogether Gallic – light, frothy, prolix, and sentimental – and in no way adapted to the chastened taste and matter-of-fact curiosity of English readers'. The development of Borrow's own prose style, directed as it was by the early but then continuous influence of Defoe, was much affected by his immense labour on the *Celebrated Trials*. His own style was restrained, economic, terse and uncluttered; he was the right man for the job and the job was a useful one for him.

Incidentally, although it is not possible to prove conclusively that Borrow wrote the Preface to *Celebrated Trials*, it contains sentences that constitute a strong hint that he had a hand in it, sentences like the following: 'Murders, under forms of law, are nevertheless the worst of crimes. Examples of punishment may deter the solitary individual, but retributive justice is rare in regard to those who commit murders in ermine, and under sanction of legitimate authority.'[4] Of course, he tinkered with a sentence here, a paragraph there, and often rewrote whole sections of a report when obliged to do so by the existence of multiple sources.

While Borrow slaved away at the *Celebrated Trials*, an undertaking that by itself would have taxed the power of most of us, he had plenty of other things to do, both for Sir Richard Phillips and on his own behalf. He had already published in *The Monthly Magazine* a number of verse translations from German, Dutch and Danish, as well as a brief essay on 'Danish Poetry and Ballad Writing';[5] indeed these translations were the basis of his introduction to Phillips, who despite many fluctuations of fortune had managed to retain the ownership of the magazine from his more prosperous days at the beginning of the century. Borrow continued to publish his translations in *The Monthly Magazine* throughout 1824 and 1825, no doubt dipping into the large store that he had brought with him from Norwich. Of special note, because a major enterprise deriving from one of the principal interests of his life, was the nine-part essay on 'Danish Traditions and Superstitions' that was published between August 1824 and November 1825.[6]

Roughly at the time Borrow arrived in London, Phillips launched a new magazine called *The Universal Review*, or *The Oxford Review* as Borrow referred to it in *Lavengro*, apparently for the financial benefit of his newly-married son, who was to be a sort of sleeping partner while the editor and Borrow did most of the work. Borrow's share of the work was reviewing a wide selection of books, but he did not enjoy the work; he thought that books of merit did not require to be reviewed – 'they can speak for themselves' – and that books of no merit did not require to be reviewed either – 'they will die of themselves, they require no killing'.[7] If the reviewing of books like Oehlenschlager's *Samlede digte* or *The Devil's Elixir: from the German of Hoffman* caused Borrow any anxiety, his typically bland account in *Lavengro* concealed the fact.

If I am asked how I comported myself, under all circumstances, as a reviewer – I answer, – I did not forget that I was connected with a review established on Oxford principles, the editor of which had translated Quintilian. All the publications which fell under my notice I treated in a gentlemanly and Oxford-like manner, no personalities – no vituperation – no shabby insinuations; decorum, decorum was the order of the day. Occasionally a word of admonition, but gently expressed, as an Oxford undergraduate might have expressed it, or master of arts. How the authors whose publications were consigned to my colleagues were treated by them I know not; I suppose they were treated in an urbane and Oxford-like manner, but I cannot say; I did not read the reviewals of my colleagues, I did not read my own after they were printed. I did not like reviewing.[8]

This little magazine only lasted for five issues, so despite his saying that the plan for *The Universal Review* was that a notice should be written for every new book received, his job in this department cannot have been particularly onerous, especially because his bibliography reveals, though *Lavengro* glosses over the fact, that he himself chose the books he felt like writing about, notably the possibly influential (for Borrow), *Narrative of a Pedestrian Journey through Russia and Siberian Tartary from the Frontiers of China to the Frozen Sea and Kamtchatka* by Captain John Dundas Cochrane, R.N., a stirring account of a recent journey in which the author describes innumerable adventures of the road, beginning with his being attacked, robbed, stripped naked and abandoned in a forest on the first day. Just the sort of book to appeal to that lifelong admirer of Defoe and future Bible Society agent in Russia.

In addition to his work on the *Celebrated Trials* and his preparation of reviews, articles and translations for *The Monthly Magazine* and *The Universal Review*, Borrow was also asked to translate into German his employer's own book, *Twelve Essays on the Proximate Causes*, an absurd request but one that it was impossible to refuse, since Taylor had recommended him for his knowledge of German. Borrow said it was the obscurity of Phillips' English which prevented his translating this work to their mutual satisfaction. Sir Richard thought otherwise but soon realised that the task was beyond the powers of his young assistant and gave it to someone else.

That first lonely, arduous winter in London confirmed the cast of Borrow's mind, as perhaps he remembered when he later said that most people acquire their character by the time they are twenty-five, after which they scarcely change. He had become a resolute person, the elements of whose existence remained unresolved. If we wonder where this gifted, eccentric writer is to be placed, historically, in the overall scheme of things, the answer must be that despite himself, that is by his very nature rather than by choice, he at an early age joined the ranks of those for whom moral ambivalence was more of a fact than moral certainty, if only because a strong awareness of their own dislocated sensibility made it impossible for them to believe fully in the actuality of what happened around them. This is not to say that he lacked self-assurance. One part of the young Borrow was gregarious, inquisitive, outward-going. He went to prizefights, bear pits, taverns, galleries. He made many acquaintances, and *Lavengro* makes clear how much he enjoyed his first explorations in London. But another important part of this young man was essentially private, secretive, withdrawn, and these two parts of him were never reconciled, except in his books, creatively. In this he was blood brother to the Romantic poets and also a not-too-distant cousin of those late nineteenth-century anti-bourgeois artists and writers, who became preoccupied with the iconography as well as with the painful, puzzling, psychological fact of detachment from the day-by-day. So what Borrow discovered within himself, as he thought about his own life, was akin to much of Pater, and Gissing characters like Godwin Peak in *Born in Exile*, and characters in Chekhov. His whole *oeuvre* is in fact an anticipation of the moral dislocations of decadent literature.

Roger Kerrison reported in Norwich that Borrow was so agitated, whether from loneliness, or frustration, or overwork, that he feared for his sanity, feared he would commit suicide, and when Borrow refused to return 'home' to Norwich, Kerrison moved away to new lodgings, alarmed by the wild, uncontrollable, or at least uncontrolled, forces that beset his friend's mind. In all likelihood, Borrow had a number of severe fits. Reasonably enough he made heavy weather of his condition and a manuscript note has survived from this period, which simply reads: 'Dear Roger Come to me immediately I am I believe dying.' He had rejected outright the bourgeois comforts of Norwich but never having had to manage by himself was probably unprepared for the experience, though in *Lavengro* plain loneliness and anxiety were translated into interesting formulations that constitute a type of sharply defined, wrily exposed self-knowledge.

Mine was an ill-regulated mind at this period. As I read over the lives of these robbers and pickpockets, strange doubts began to arise in my mind about virtue and crime. Years before, when quite a boy, as in one of the early chapters I have hinted, I had been a necessitarian;[9] I had even written an essay on crime (I have it now before me, penned in a round boyish hand), in which I attempted to prove that there is no such thing as crime or virtue, all our actions being the result of circumstances or necessity. These doubts were now again reviving in my mind; I could not, for the life of me, imagine how, taking all circumstances into consideration, these highwaymen, these pickpockets, should have been anything else than highwaymen and pickpockets; any more than how, taking all circumstances into consideration, Bishop Latimer (the reader is aware that I had read Foxe's *Book of Martyrs*) should have been anything else than Bishop Latimer. I had a very ill-regulated mind at that period.[10]

When Borrow said that he had an 'ill-regulated mind' he used the phrase literally. He meant he did not know what to believe in, so that consequently he did not know, either, what to do with himself. Throughout his life he was able to hobnob with 'robbers and pick-pockets' because he lacked the evangelical zeal that would have allowed him or made him wish to judge them, but at the same time, because he lacked a moral centre himself, and realised this, he was often tormented by the impossibility of doing anything with conviction. This was why he said, in a passage deleted from *Lavengro*, that everything a person does is from a selfish motive. 'The wish for salvation itself springs from a selfish motive and no-one has a right to blame another for selfishness provided the selfishness does not infringe upon the comforts and welfare of others.'[11] These are the words, of course, of a socially detached ego that is contemporary to J. S. Mill. In *Lavengro* as published, he was more circumspect and interesting.

My own peculiar ideas with respect to everything being a lying dream began also to revive. Sometimes at midnight, after having toiled for hours at my occupations, I would fling myself back on my chair, look about the poor apartment, dimly lighted by an unsnuffed candle, or upon the heaps of books and papers before me, and exclaim, – 'Do I exist? Do these things, which I think I see about me, exist, or do they not? Is not everything a dream – a deceitful dream? Is not this apartment a dream – the furniture a dream? The publisher a dream – his philosophy a dream? Am I not myself a dream – dreaming about translating a dream? I can't see why all should not be a dream; what's the use of the reality?' And then I would pinch myself, and snuff the burdened smoky light.[12]

Though not in the least suicidal (his reflections on London Bridge notwithstanding) he questioned the utility of his own existence, as a person well might who was living in London by himself, his own masterworks still fifteen years or more ahead of him, as yet unimagined, unanticipated.

They say that light fare begets light dreams; my fare at that time was light enough; but I had anything but light dreams, for at that period I had all kinds of strange and extravagant dreams, and amongst other things I dreamt that the whole world had taken to dog-fighting; and that I, myself, had taken to dog-fighting, and that in a vast circus I backed an English bulldog against the bloodhound of the Pope of Rome.

The importance of these passages from chapter 36 of *Lavengro* will become more and more obvious as Borrow's story unfolds. If it is hazardous to attribute to a twenty-two-year-old hack writer who, when not labouring over a vast editorial task, was spending his time exploring London and no doubt enjoying himself, the vast troubles of Victorian self-consciousness, moral ambivalence and incipient hypocrisy, which is the outward form of an internally fractured sensibility, it can nonetheless be said that he was never able to extricate himself from the imaginative predicament that he first analysed during that first period in London.

Borrow was meanwhile incredibly busy during that London winter of 1824–5. He continued to work at his own translations, particularly from the Welsh, did a little reviewing, collected more and more material for the *Celebrated Trials* and prepared for the press his translation of *Faustus: His Life, Death and Descent into Hell* in the version of

Friedrich Maximilian von Klinger, which he had probably made in Norwich in 1822 or 1823, either from the first German edition of 1791, as seems likely because of the powerful influence of William Taylor, or conceivably from the French translation published in Amsterdam in 1798, as suggested by Clement Shorter. It had been announced as a forthcoming publication in the July 1824 issue of *The Monthly Magazine*, and since it seems unlikely that he would have had time to translate 250 book-pages in two or three months, it may be assumed that he brought the work with him in an almost complete state. *Faustus* appeared in the late spring of 1825, with a preface dated April 1825.[13] Borrow may have been briefly enthusiastic about this lurid and sensational Gothic production, and so were a few reviewers. The book scarcely made an impact on the public, however, and at least one library (that of the Norfolk and Norwich Literary Institution) immediately 'disposed' of its copy (his derogatory interpolations about Norwich were not appreciated there), while according to Knapp, the author later told the publisher that he was willing to take thirty copies in place of the publisher's final payment, which is not to say that the publisher, Simpkin and Marshall, intended at this point to make a payment of any kind. Though it might be charitable to suppose that the labour of translating this worthless book was part and parcel of Borrow's learning the language in Norwich, it will be seen that a second edition was put out in 1864, which is a hint, at least, that Borrow had not completely sloughed it off.

Brief mention must also be made of two other publications that over the years came to be associated with Borrow, though it now seems certain that he had little or nothing to do with them. The first is a book called *Tales of the Wild and the Wonderful*, which was printed in Edinburgh by Hurst, Robinson and Co., for T. and A. Constable in 1825 and dedicated by the anonymous author to 'Joanna Baillie, as a Slight Tribute of Admiration to her Resplendent Talents'. Although this book has long been associated with Borrow, it was in fact the work of Mary Diana Dods and had nothing to do with Borrow at all.[14] The other book was *Memoirs of Vidocq*, which was published in 1828 but which some early biographers believed Borrow must have worked on during his first spell of time in London, Clement Shorter in fact including in the Norwich Edition of Borrow's works passages that he thought were indubitably Borrow's. Borrow got to know Vidocq, the famous French criminal turned chief of police, during the twenties and kept up the acquaintance for at least twenty years, but there is no firm evidence that he had a hand in the publication of the English translation of the *Memoirs*, which is now attributed to William Maginn. It is scarcely possible that Borrow could have tackled yet another substantial work during his first London year.

Borrow describes in *Lavengro*, though, how he did one final piece of work in order to pay his bills and leave. The necessity for this was forced upon him when he realised one morning he only had a few shillings to his name. He could not remain in London. He did not wish to remain in London. While out walking the streets wondering what to do, he saw a notice in the window of a printer's shop or a book-seller's offering £20 for a story or a novel, which Borrow promptly decided to write. Buying bread for his final weekend with his last 18*d*. and having already in his possession pen, ink and paper, as well as candles, he determined to closet himself away and go 'doggedly to work'.

What though would his story be about? In *Lavengro* he pretends to consider various possibilities – Jemmy Abershaw? Harry Sims? – but he rejects each of them. No doubt he did indeed run his mind over the vast store of material he had at his disposal because of his recent scavenging through libraries and bookstalls while compiling the *Celebrated Trials*. At any rate, there follows that section of chapter 55 of *Lavengro* which for a hundred years or so gave rise to so much speculation about what it might have been that Borrow wrote. After dismissing a number of possible subjects, he says:

I want a character for my hero, thought I, something higher than a mere robber; some one like – like Colonel B——. By the way, why should I not write the life and adventures of Colonel B——. of Londonderry, in Ireland?

A truly singular man was this same Colonel B—— of Londonderry, in Ireland; a personage of most strange and incredible feats and daring, who had been a partisan soldier, a brave – who, assisted by certain discontented troopers, nearly succeeded in stealing the crown and regalia from the Tower of London; who attempted to hang the Duke of Ormond, at Tyburn; and whose strange eventful career did not terminate even with his life, his dead body, on the circulation of an unfounded report that he did not come to his death by fair means, having been exhumed by the mob of his native place, where he had retired to die, and carried in the coffin through the streets.

Of his life I had inserted an account in the *Newgate Lives and Trials*; it was bare and meagre, and written in the stiff, awkward style of the seventeenth century; it had, however, strongly captivated my imagination, and I now thought that out of it something better could be made; that, if I added to the adventures, and purified the style, I might fashion out of it a very decent tale or novel. On a sudden, however, the proverb of mending old garments with new cloth occurred to me. 'I am afraid', said I, 'any new adventures which I can invent will not fadge well with the old tale; one will but spoil the other.' I had better have nothing to do with Colonel B——, thought I, but boldly and independently sit down and write the life of Joseph Sell.

This Joseph Sell, dear reader, was a fictitious personage who had just come into my head. I had never even heard of the name, but just at that moment it happened to come into my head; I would write an entirely fictitious narrative, called the *Life and Adventures of Joseph Sell, the Great Traveller*.

I had better begin at once, thought I; and removing the bread and the jug, which latter was now empty, I seized pen and paper, and forthwith essayed to write the life of Joseph Sell, but soon discovered that it is much easier to resolve upon a thing than to achieve it, or even to commence it; for the life of me I did not know how to begin, and, after trying in vain to write a line, I thought it would be as well to go to bed, and defer my projected undertaking till the morrow.[15]

These words constitute one of those characteristic Borrovian deceptions that will be discussed at greater length in chapter 5. When Borrow wrote his 'Joseph Sell' passage in 1843, he knew perfectly well that the story he had sold to the bookseller had not been called *Life and Adventures of Joseph Sell, the Great Traveller*, but by concealing the identity of the work he insisted, as it were, upon the autobiographical importance of his having written it, without encouraging the reader of *Lavengro* to think about it, the work, rather than him, the author. Because no work entitled *Life and Adventures of Joseph Sell* has ever been discovered, generations of scholars have tried to decide whether or not Borrow was telling the truth, some believing that since he rarely told the truth there was no reason to believe his story about Joseph Sell, and others believing that since he always told the truth this particular passage in *Lavengro* had to mean something.[16] Because of Borrow's unwillingness to tell the simple truth and his preference for embroidering fact in a way calculated to deceive, the Joseph Sell problem, though it only stems from a single week during his Grub Street period, can be seen as representative of the enigma of his whole life, since it forces anyone interested in Borrow into that dream world, already referred to, where the boundaries of truth and fiction become uncertain, the world which he himself wrote about in the same early section of *Lavengro* and to which he referred in that book's full title. He was himself perfectly clear about the boundaries between truth and fiction: at that time, in 1825, he simply wanted to sell some work in order to pay his bills.

What Borrow called the *Life and Adventures of Joseph Sell, the Great Traveller*, was in fact the *Life and Adventures of the Famous Colonel Blood*.[17] This is a twenty-four-page booklet, with a chocolate-brown paper wrapper, which has pasted in between the front cover and the titlepage a brightly-coloured folded illustration showing in five panels Colonel Blood himself and four scenes from his life. The title-page is given here because Borrow's authorship of the work has not previously been established.

LIFE AND ADVENTURES/OF THE FAMOUS/COLONEL BLOOD,/WHO/SEIZED ON THE PERSON OF THE/DUKE OF ORMOND,/AND/CONVEYED HIM TO TYBURN,/WITH THE INTENTION

OF PUTTING HIM TO DEATH ON/A *Common Gibbet,*/And who afterwards, in the disguise of a Priest, with several of his/daring Associates, obtained admittance into the/TOWER OF LONDON,/WHICH THEY ROBBED OF THE CROWN, BALL, SCEPTRE,/ AND OTHER REGALIA;/BUT WHO WAS AFTERWARDS PARDONED BY KING CHARLES II./ WHO SETTLED ON HIM A HANDSOME PENSION FOR LIFE./[double short rule]/ *London:*/PRINTED BY AND FOR HODGSON AND CO./NO. 10, NEWGATE STREET/[short rule]/*Sixpence.*

An important feature of this booklet is the paper cover, on the front and back of which is printed the list of other works in the same series.

The identity of 'Joseph Sell' is established by one of the surviving *Lavengro* autograph manuscripts, specifically by volume II of the substantial though incomplete manuscript in the Library of the Hispanic Society of America in New York. This part of the Hispanic Society's manuscript dates from the winter of 1843–4 and for the matter to be clear the extremely important subject of how Borrow wrote *Lavengro* must be briefly anticipated. During that particular winter period Borrow was rewriting the first part of *Lavengro* by copying, but also supplementing and expanding, an earlier version of an autobiography, which it can be shown he had in front of him, while from each new sheet as he completed it his wife made a fair copy that several years later would be sent to John Murray. When a new page was so heavily corrected that Mary Borrow could not read it, or when talk between scribe and writer resulted in further emendation, Borrow copied out the undecipherable or troublesome part on a scrap of paper, which was then pinned to the page in the appropriate spot. A few of the pins have survived. Other scraps of paper with pin-holes are collected together at the end of the manuscript. Interestingly, the all-important paragraph in chapter 55 (quoted above), which begins 'This Joseph Sell, dear reader, was a fictitious personage . . .' was an addition of this kind. In other words, the whole paragraph was a correction, an afterthought. The preceding sentence was also an addition, though made on the page itself rather than on a fresh slip of paper, showing that Borrow brought himself right up to this point before sitting back in his chair and deciding to make a change.

In the same manuscript, all other mentions of 'Joseph Sell' are corrections: that is, where in chapter 55 the name 'Joseph Sell' occurs it has been written over a deleted 'Colonel B——'. This means that when Borrow first wrote chapters 55 and 56, whether before or after his spell of work for the Bible Society, he was simply recollecting first, that before leaving London in 1825 he had written a work with 'Colonel B——' in the title and, secondly, that he did not change the name until he set to work again in 1843, buoyed up by the immense success of *The Bible in Spain* and by John Murray's enthusiasm for the proposed autobiography.

The British Library's attribution of 1825 to the undated *Life and Adventures of the Famous Colonel Blood* tends to confirm that this was indeed the work to which Borrow referred, but more telling still is the fact that when Borrow wrote about Colonel Blood in 1825 he had in front of him his copy of 'Thomas Blood, Generally called Colonel Blood who stole the Crown from the Tower of London', which he had edited for Phillips' *Celebrated Trials*, vol. II, pp. 348–54, the verbal parellels being obvious at a glance even though the booklet was an expansion and not just a reproduction of the same material in *Celebrated Trials*. Perhaps Borrow in 1843 thought it prudent to conceal the fact that he had filched material from the anthology and presented it as his own. At all events, 'Joseph Sell', whether fictitious or not, was a name adopted to conceal the simple truth about Borrow's 'Colonel Blood'.

Although in *Lavengro* Borrow implies that he learnt by chance a certain bookseller was looking for stories, the list of other publications, whether planned or already published – that is, the list on the front cover of *Life and Adventures of Colonel Blood* – contains items that would surely have been of interest to him, like:

> The Atrocious Life of Ali Pacha
> History of Jack Ram, the Robber
> Life of Tarpin, the Highwayman [*sic*]
> Life and Adventures of Colonel Jack
> Life of Wolfe, the Robber
> Hoggart, the Murderer [*sic*]
> Mother Shipton's Prophecies
> Irish Freebooter: the Life and Adventures of Humphrey Kynaston
> History of Jane Shore
> Universal Dream Book
> Bamfylde Moore-Carew

Borrow was an admirer of Defoe; he wrote about Haggart the murderer, in *Lavengro*; he had a lifelong interest in gypsy language and in what he, too, called 'cant'; and he was fascinated by bohemians and criminals. *The Life of Bamfylde Moore Carew ... to which is added, a dictionary of the mendicant's cant phrases* is the sort of book that might have influenced Borrow, had he seen it. It is also the sort of book he might have written. The same applies to other books on the list. Borrow tells us in *Lavengro* that when he went back to the bookseller to receive payment for *Colonel Blood*, 'it was not long before I learned that the work had already been sent to press, and was intended to stand at the head of a series of entertaining narratives, from which my friends promised themselves considerable profit'. This suggests that although other works in the series were named on the cover of *Life and Adventures of the Famous Colonel Blood*, not all of them, and perhaps not one of them, had yet been published. Because the list looks like one Borrow himself might have prepared, perhaps while having tea with his 'friends', the bookseller and his wife, there remains the possibility that Borrow made later contributions to the series, or independently wrote other 'narratives' of the same general character as 'Colonel Blood', although no such work has yet been reliably identified.

As to the general character of *Life and Adventures of Colonel Blood*, Borrow himself described in *Lavengro* what he did. He rejected the possibility of writing about Harry Sims or Jemmy Abershaw because 'both, though bold and extraordinary men, were merely highwaymen'. Borrow said that for his story he wanted a 'character', meaning a colourful personality who had been involved in unusual exploits, whether legal or illegal. He said, too, that he found the stiff and awkward seventeenth-century style of the account in *Newgate Lives and Trials* (as he called the *Celebrated Trials*) 'meagre and bare': 'if I added to the adventures, and purified the style', he said, 'I might fashion out of it a very decent tale or novel'. His mind was flooded, however, with a superfluity of material, a difficulty he only resolved late that night. 'At length I got out of the difficulty in the easiest manner imaginable, namely, by consigning to the depths of oblivion all the feebler and less stimulant scenes and incidents, and retaining the better and more impressive ones.'[18] The book as published is indeed a straightforward narrative of the more startling events of Thomas Blood's career; his part in the attempted insurrection in Dublin in 1663; his setting himself above the law by openly 'courtmartialling' an enemy in a London tavern; his presence at the Pentland Rising in 1666; his bold rescue of a friend, Captain Mason, from an armed guard on the Great North Road; his almost successful abduction of the Duke of Ormond in broad daylight in a London street, his seizure of the Crown Jewels in 1671 and his arrest; his subsequent pardon by Charles II; and years later, his fatal clash with the Duke of Buckingham over reciprocal accusations of sodomy. Many of these episodes had not been used in *Celebrated Trials*, so Borrow must have gone back to his original source material for the 1825 publication.

While there is no internal evidence that securely links this strongly written narrative to George Borrow, there are many passages reminiscent of lively and colourful passages in *The Bible in Spain*. Borrow when telling a tale was nearly always seductively, deceptively specific, as was his master, Defoe. Here, for example, Blood's chief accomplice in the attempt to kidnap and hang the Duke of Ormond was 'Richard Holloway, a tobacco cutter in Frying-pan-alley in Petticoat Lane', which is the sort of detail that reminds one of how often in Borrow's other works a telling phrase leaves the reader no option but to accept Borrow's reconstruction of supposedly 'true' events. When Blood and a different set of accomplices entered the Tower of London, with the assistance of a keeper they had hypocritically befriended,

they threw a cloak over the old man's head, and clapped a gag into his mouth, which was a great plug of wood, with a small hole to take breath at. This was tied on with waxed leather, which went round his neck. At the same time they fastened an iron hood to his nose, that no sound might pass from him that way [an embellishment, this, which is not in the original].

They also hit him on the head a couple of times with a mallet, but finding that he still resisted, 'they gave him nine or ten strokes more upon the head with the mallet, and stabbed him in the belly'. Anyone could have written this, of course, but it is a powerful anticipation of the mature writing of *The Bible in Spain*. The vigorous, uncluttered, unpretentious style that was to serve Borrow so well in that book he utilised here. And, as he said himself, it is not within everybody's power to tell a simple tale well, as Borrow did during his last weekend in London before setting out for Salisbury.

This 'Joseph Sell' episode is important for an understanding of Borrow because it provides a model for the interpretation of other events in his life. He wrote a story about Colonel Blood but disguised it with the name of Joseph Sell; other proper names throughout Borrow's work will be disguises of the same kind, particularly in *Lavengro*. Secondly, he romanticises his account of how the story was written and published. There obviously had to be a bookseller or printer, but was Borrow really paid £20 and did he take the best part of a week to write the story, which as printed amounted to only twenty-four pages?

In *The Romany Rye* Borrow seems to be recollecting this episode from a different vantage point when he says: 'Whilst I reflected on the grisly sufferings I had undergone whilst engaged in writing the *Life of Sell*, I shrank from the idea of a similar attempt'[19] – but only 'seems' because this passage, too, is part of the reconstruction of his own past, as is his later insistence that *Joseph Sell* was an 'original work'. No doubt he did suffer. No doubt his sufferings were grisly. Nonetheless, of his own literary method he could reasonably have used the same language as one of his mentors: 'I have dealt in similitudes' was the quotation Borrow knew was on the titlepage of *The Pilgrim's Progress*. Borrow habitually and consciously dealt in similitudes.

While the ardent Borrow enthusiast will not rest until the figure of £20 can be independently corroborated, until it can be demonstrated that the bookseller excised much of what Borrow had given him, until the bookseller himself is identified and, in short, until every detail of the 'Joseph Sell' story has been investigated, the general reader of Borrow will surely feel that he is getting to know a writer whose creative transformations have an essential authenticity ('Joseph Sell' was not pure fiction), an authenticity that is not invalidated by the memory that transposes, refurbishes, rearranges and selects detail in a way that is consistent with how Borrow *feels* about whatever he allows himself to recollect. This is not an interweaving of fact and fiction, since, although there are uncompromising concealments, few details are merely made up. The snag is, though, that the detection of the actual truth behind the detail provided by Borrow himself, exciting though the process of detection may be, tends to be of antiquarian rather than biographical or critical interest, at least to anyone fascinated by Borrow's own major works. The man as he existed in his own imagination, as necessarily in his reader's, would not survive an analysis that purported to show that Borrow never remembered anything as it had actually happened, since such an analysis would have the effect of discounting Borrow's books for the sake of a truth about the author that was independent of them. Few of us are happy when what we see in one way is represented in a different light by someone else. The truth about oneself that is inconsistent with one's own feeling of self only rarely becomes a type of self-knowledge that can be utilised; but whether this in a general way is correct or not, Borrow seems to provide an example of someone who exists chiefly, significantly, in often mysterious transformations of experience which lack application in the ordinary world of buying and selling, working and playing, creating and destroying, loving and hating. Throughout *Lavengro* there are examples of the same type of manipulation of fact as we have seen in the 'Joseph Sell' episode, it being in the nature of this manipulation that George Borrow for better or worse exists both for persons fascinated by his life and for the reader who loves his books.

The nature of Borrow's perception of reality is most obviously significant when the chief source of information about a particular period of his life is his own books. This is the case in 1825-6, a period which, if the narrative is to be trusted as the 'Joseph Sell' story makes us feel it should, contains some of the most crucial events of Borrow's life, but about which we know very little except from *Lavengro* (and the opening chapters of *The Romany Rye*). Borrow says that, having finished 'Joseph Sell', he sent his belongings back to Norwich, travelled by coach to a town near Salisbury (probably Amesbury) and then for the next few months lived on the road, having a series of adventures that he recounts with considerable *élan* and vividness. Through what was left of the first night out of London, Borrow walked to Stonehenge, explored both it and nearby Roman earthworks, and walked down into Salisbury, where he spent a few days.

From Salisbury he said he travelled west at the rate of 20 to 25 miles a day towards the Welsh border; met a tinker called Jack Slingsby, together with his family, treated them to beer in a pub, and from Slingsby bought his pony, cart and tinker's equipment; resolved to earn his living for a while by means of the tinker's craft; met some gypsies; chatted with a gypsy girl and was nearly killed by her grandmother, who sent Borrow a poisoned cake; and was saved from death by an itinerant Welsh preacher and his wife. After several days of religious and other talk with the Welsh preacher, Borrow met his old gypsy pal, Jasper Petulengro, near the Welsh border and with him turned back into the Midlands, eventually setting up camp in a place called Mumper's Dingle in Staffordshire and, with Jasper (as he describes in *The Romany Rye*), visiting the fair at Tamworth, where with Jasper's £50 he bought the horse that later carried him across the country into Lincolnshire. First, though, Borrow had that violent fit already referred to (in the previous chapter), then had the fight with the Flaming Tinman which, in the period of Borrow's fame, all school-children knew and which many critics praised as one of the best fights in English literature, at least to that point in time. Borrow had camped in the quiet dingle, well away from the traffic of the world. He was recovering from his fit, sitting by himself. To the dingle came the rival caravan of the Flaming Tinman and his two companions, his wife and a younger woman who looked taller and stronger even than Borrow himself. This was the very same fellow who had so terrified Jack Slingsby that he had sold Borrow his pony and cart. The Flaming Tinman now tried to treat Borrow in the same way, for he wanted his territory and refused to share it.

That Borrow took to the road, lived on next to nothing and travelled over a large part of England has never been seriously doubted, for his narrative has the ring of truth to it. That he adopted, at least for a brief period, the trade of tinker, consistent as that was with his love of Norse literature; that he met on the road a large number of interesting characters, such as the superstitious, retired silk-mercer; that he worked for a while as a hostler or postillion, a job his knowledge of horses might easily have got him; and that he made a magnificent, often moving life story from a set of anecdotes richly coloured by his own personality, love of freedom and dislike of cant – none of this has been called in question, though to summarise it all here must necessarily deprive it of its vitality, for *Lavengro* must be read for its special qualities to be appreciated. The questions raised are, of course, legion. Who was the Welsh preacher? Who was the silk-mercer? Where was Mumper's Dingle?[20] Did the journey really take place immediately after Borrow's period in London? Can an itinerary be reconstructed from the few references that seem definite? Was the journey as charmingly unmotivated as Borrow in his high bohemian style persuades us to suppose? The list of questions would be a long one because each detail in *Lavengro* has the same enigmatic quality. But most readers will decide that these very details, though enigmatic, nonetheless convince and seem authentic – not least that fight with the Flaming Tinman which led to Borrow's getting to know the woman called in the book Isopel Berners. The fight assumes extra significance when one realises that Borrow never at any other time represents himself as being dependent upon another human being. Isopel Berners helped him survive the fight and then, with a fierce, right-handed blow she called a Long Melford, to win it. In this way begins an account of a friendship, an account that is continued into *The Romany Rye*, that has delighted generations of readers, while intriguing and frustrating anyone impatient for the full story.

'Isopel Berners' has the same status in the Borrow story as 'Joseph Sell', except that in this case the code has not yet been cracked. Ivor Evans thought that he had correctly identified her from the parish records in Long Melford church as Elizabeth Jarvis, born on 25 July 1803, the illegitimate daughter of the Elizabeth Jarvis who died at the age of thirty-seven on 31 August 1805, but this identification has been challenged.[21] Whatever her real name, Isopel Berners was evidently a real person in Borrow's life. That the two were powerfully attracted to each other is perfectly obvious, despite the assumed *naïveté* of Borrow's description of how she stayed in her 'tabernacle' while he stayed in his tent. Why else would she have remained with him? Why else would he confess in *Lavengro*, which was copied out by his new wife in the 1840s, that many years earlier he had made a proposal of marriage? The memory of Isopel Berners was even then, nearly twenty years later, extremely strong. He had known few other women. He had known no other woman well. There must remain a strong presumption, though as yet unprovable, that when Isopel Berners left, he followed, but whatever sexual or intimate personal life they may have had together remains concealed, although even later, in *Wild Wales*, Borrow did allow a gypsy character to ask: 'I say, what's become of the young woman you used to keep company with?'[22] Furthermore, in *The Romany Rye* Borrow says that he had thought of 'marrying Isopel, of going with her to America, and having by her a large progeny, who were to assist me in felling trees, cultivating the soil, and who would take care of me when I was old',[23] remarks that constitute part of the flimsy evidence that allows Borrovians to debate the question of whether Borrow ever travelled to North America. His telling a friend in 1845 that he was 'thinking of going to America and settling in Texas'[24] did not mean that he had not previously been there. But this is by the by since, whether he followed Isopel Berners or not, his meeting her in 1825 was obviously a high point of his life and too important to conceal completely when he began to write and rewrite his autobiography in 1843, even though it might have been prudent for him to have done so.

We now enter, in this account of the years between his father's death and his departure for Russia, what came to be known as the 'veiled period', because Borrow adamantly refused to say anything about it when his publisher later wanted from him a full, detailed and chronologically coherent autobiography. If *The Romany Rye* is to be trusted, he travelled eastward across England to the Horncastle horse-fair in Lincolnshire, where he sold his horse. Though real places are not named, he seems then to have walked to Boston and King's Lynn, having on the way the encounter with a press-gang that is described in the last two pages of *The Romany Rye*. That was probably in the late autumn of 1826, though it may have been later. We know, too, that he soon, in 1826, went to Norwich, because it was from Norwich that he corresponded with his London friend, the poet Allan Cunningham, about the Preface to Borrow's book *Romantic Ballads*, which he published in 1826. It will be seen that at some point later in 1826 he went to London. Where he went then is not at all clear, though there are many theories.

First, though, a word about *Romantic Ballads*, which was published by S. Wilkin of Norwich. The full title was *Romantic Ballads, translated from the Danish and Miscellaneous Pieces*. Ostensibly, this book was published by subscription, though it is impossible to ascertain how many of those people named as subscribers at the end of the book actually paid for it. That Borrow, in collaboration of course with the bookseller–publisher who kept the list, had taken a few years to collect subscriptions is indicated by the fact that in 1826 at least one of the subscribers, Thurtell, had been dead for two years. When Allan Cunningham, early in 1826, agreed to write a preface, he asked Borrow to give him as clear an idea of the book as possible, since he had never even seen it, let alone read it. Borrow replied as follows:

As you wish to be better acquainted with the characters of the ballads I am publishing, I will endeavour to accommodate you.

They are not all ancient, because I have interspersed them with translations from Oehlenslaeger; but you will find among them four genuine *Kæmpe Viser*: that is to say, 'Heroic Ballads,' and several old ballads about love and witchcraft, etc. The strict *Kæmpe Viser* in the old Danish are in number fifteen. I have translated them all, and am now publishing four of the best, viz. *Svend Vonved*, *The Tournament*, *The Triple Murder*, and *Grimmel's Vengeance*.[25]

Unfortunately, this selection of translations from the much larger body of work that Borrow had taken to London was not well received, indeed was scarcely noticed. When Borrow had disposed of as many copies as possible in Norwich, including of course the subscription copies of half a guinea each, he sent the others to London so that Allan Cunningham could help him find a new publisher. Wise quoted an excerpt from Cunningham's letter on this subject: 'Taylor will undertake to publish the remaining copies. His advice is to make the price seven shillings, and to print a new titlepage. I advise the same.'[26] Borrow did as he was advised with some copies, but others he passed on to Wightman and Cramp, who likewise inserted a new titlepage, with the result that the first edition of *Romantic Ballads* actually exists in three states, all of them dated 1826. The publication was very far from being the great success for which Borrow had hoped.

Though Borrow had written to Cunningham from Norwich about the London issues of *Romantic Ballads*, he must have gone to London himself during the summer, at least after 13 May 1826, which is the date of his last known letter to Cunningham. In all probability it was then that he wrote to, and perhaps went to see, Benjamin Haydon for the last time. John Borrow had taken his brother to see two Haydon paintings that were showing at the Society of British Artists in Suffolk Street in April 1825. Soon after they had visited Haydon himself, so that John could arrange for Haydon's commissioned portrait of the former mayor of Norwich. On that occasion, Borrow asked Haydon to subscribe to *Romantic Ballads*, while Haydon asked Borrow to sit for one of the figures in what he called 'a Cabinet Picture of Pharaoh dismissing Moses and Aaron'.[27] From Haydon's journals, which trace the stages of composition of this painting, it can be seen immediately that Borrow could not have sat for Haydon before leaving London in 1825, even if he had a peep at the painting in an early phase, as reported in *Lavengro*. Haydon in fact painted 'Pharaoh Dismissing Moses' while Borrow was on the road. But there has survived an undated letter from Borrow to Haydon, which was addressed from '26 Bryanston Street, Portman Square' and which reads as follows:

Dear Sir, I should feel extremely obliged if you would allow me to sit for you as soon as possible. I am going to the South of France in a little better than a fortnight, and I would sooner lose a thousand pounds than not have the honour of appearing in the picture.[28]

Because this letter was found in Haydon's journal between two dated pages, which made Haydon's granddaughter confident that *its* date must have been 6 June 1825, she so reported to Knapp, but it seems just as likely that the letter was later moved to that date because Borrow was known to have been in London at that time and that he actually wrote it when he returned to London in 1826, but before he knew that Haydon had finished the painting during his absence. If that were the case, it would be easy to believe that Borrow was in London, however briefly, during the second part of 1826 as other evidence shows was probably the case.

How precisely Borrow spent the next three years has never been determined, although there are a few clues of an inconclusive kind. One of these concerns his saying that he saw the horse Marshland Shales at the Norwich horse-fair in 1818 when he was still a boy, whereas the famous horse was only sold in 1827. Was this just a lapse on Borrow's part? Is he accidentally revealing that he was in Norwich at that time, while giving the impression that he was elsewhere? Similarly, Knapp referred to Mrs Borrow's account books where he said two sets of entries in 1827 were in George Borrow's hand, specifically entries for September and October 1827. Do these two wisps of evidence suggest that, wherever Borrow had been during the preceding twelve months, he visited Norwich at least briefly? Presumably so.

Interesting inquiries have been made recently into the records of the two libraries Borrow might have used while he lived in Norwich. He is not listed as a member of the Norwich Public Library, although as both William Simpson and William Taylor were associated with it he may have in some way obtained permission to use it while articled to Simpson. On the other hand, Borrow was elected a member of the Norfolk and Norwich Literary Institution on 19 November 1822, paying his first subscription for a two-year term, which would have expired some months after Borrow had moved to London. Important as a guide to Borrow's whereabouts between 1825 and 1830 are the Literary Institution's cashbooks and lists of temporary subscribers. These show that Borrow took out temporary, one-month subscriptions on the following dates: 30 January 1826, 17 March 1826, 17 April 1826, 12 August 1826, 27 January 1827, 22 April 1827, 27 December 1827, 22 March 1828 and 25 November 1828. Although Borrow could have been in Norwich without having a library subscription, the spread of dates presumably means that he was without regular employment during this period, whether in Norwich or elsewhere. The dates also suggest that although Borrow was often away from Norwich he was Norwich-based. Most important of all, they pinpoint fairly precisely the four periods when he might have been travelling overseas: that is, during May, June and July 1826; from mid-September to Christmas 1826; from May 1827 at least until the beginning of September; and from late April to late November 1828. It is a fair presumption, surely, that Borrow was travelling during these periods away from Norwich.[29]

Evidence of a different kind is that one has no knowledge of any literary activity between the autumn of 1826 and the autumn of 1829, which is in itself striking given the energy of the man and the amount of literary work he had done in the years prior to the publication of *Romantic Ballads*. If he had spent all or part of the time writing, one would have expected this fact to have been mentioned in letters, whereas no letters have survived from this period, and one would also have expected him, later, to have attempted to publish what he had written. The fact that there is no trace of literary work during this three-year period itself suggests strongly that he was otherwise engaged.

He himself said that he went to France, as we have seen, and there seems to be no good reason to disbelieve this. Many people have been sceptical, however, chiefly because, had they believed that, they would also have had to believe that he had been to the other places he claimed to have visited. Innumerable other hints of foreign travel are scattered through Borrow's works. In *The Zincali* he said he had seen the gypsies of various lands, 'Russia, Hungarian and Turkish', as well as the 'legitimate children of most countries of the world'.[30] In the same book, he recalled encountering some Hungarian gypsies one night while warming himself against a kiln in Genoa. In *The Bible in Spain* he mentions having been in Bayonne, Madrid, the South of France, and indeed says that he had visited 'most of the principal cities of the world'. Throughout *The Bible in Spain* he drops many hints about his earlier travels. 'I have heard the ballad of Alonzo Guzman', he says, 'chanted in Danish, by a hind in the wilds of Jutland.'[31] At another point in the book: 'I have lived in different parts of the world, much amongst the Hebrew race, and I am well acquainted with their words and phraseology.'[32] When he visits Gibraltar, he says he has been there 'several times before'. When he meets Colonel Napier in Seville and is asked where he learnt 'Moultanee', he replies: 'In Moultan'. When he gets a job in Portugal, Andrew Brandram, in a letter of introduction says: 'With Portugal he is already acquainted and speaks the language.' If none of this can be corroborated, none of it can be safely disregarded. Given the extent and intensity of his interest in Danish literature, for example, it is scarcely credible that he would not at some point have explored the shores of the Baltic and the North Sea. Given his lifelong interest in the gypsies, it is easier to believe that he visited Hungary during this period than that he did not, as indeed it will be seen in chapter 8 there must be a strong presumption that he did. Given the casual or accidental nature of some of the references listed above, it seems wiser to suppose that much was being concealed than that a little was being invented. On the other hand, the evidence is not conclusive either. When Knapp suggested that Borrow went to Paris, Bayonne, Madrid and Pamplona, where he was arrested, the evidence for the speculation, that is, the evidence that has survived, seems too flimsy. Similarly, there is no firm evidence to confirm the tantalisingly suggestive hint that he visited Havana. On the other hand, the manuscript of *The Zincali*[33] provides a few clues of a more reliable kind. For example, one of the passages Borrow deleted reads as follows:

It will perhaps not be amiss to afford some account of the Rommany as I have seen them in other countries, for there is scarcely a part of the habitable world where they are not to be found; their tents are alike pitched on the heaths of Brazil and the slopes of the Himalayan Hills and their language is heard at Moscow and Madrid, in the streets of London and of Stamboul.

On balance, the fact that Borrow deleted from the manuscript all mention of Brazil and India probably increases the likelihood that he had been there. If so, one might tend to be less sceptical about his other passing references to places he said he had visited. And this is not an isolated instance, for the manuscript corrections to the passage about the Constantinople merchant also suggest, if a little more remotely, that Borrow had been in China and, of course, Constantinople, as well as India. When one remembers the American plantation owner whom Borrow met in Gibraltar, the sequence of places – Louisiana, Havana, Brazil, China, India, Turkey – begins to suggest rather strongly a world tour, whether a voluntary one (by working his passage perhaps) or involuntary (by being 'pressed' in the Navy) and since he says in *Lavengro* that Isopel Berners went to North America, it seems unlikely that he himself would have set off in an easterly direction. A future biographer may discover conclusive proof that Borrow was in, say Brazil, in 1826 or 1828, assuming overseas travels to have been interrupted by the time he reappeared in Norwich in 1827. If that happened, something of a vast biographical significance might emerge, since Borrow would presumably only have expunged those years with such thoroughness because he had something of importance to conceal, such as a period in prison, or a marriage, or a reunion with Isopel Berners. As it is, we must assume that had Borrow been in England between 1826 and 1829, someone would later have remembered the fact, but that in as far as he went to great pains to conceal his activities, the act of concealment must itself be taken as evidence of a major biographical event that threw a shadow over the rest of his life. As far as we know, he never once told anyone the truth about those years.

We do not recover firm ground until Borrow turns up in London once again in the late autumn of 1829.

One sign of Borrow's return was his activity on behalf of his brother, about whom a little must now be said, even though John Borrow plays only a minor part in the life of his famous brother. It will be remembered that John returned to Norwich from Paris at the time of his father's death in 1824. How he spent the next two years is not completely clear, though from a hint or two it seems he remained in Norwich. First, he continued to exhibit in Norwich exhibitions. Secondly, he safeguarded his position in the West Norfolk Militia by attending those training-camps on which the continuation of his allowance of 2s. 6d. a day depended, his last training-camp being that held between 12 October and 8 November 1825.[34] Thirdly, he acted on behalf of the Norwich City Council in arranging that Benjamin Haydon should paint the portrait of Robert Hawkes, a recent mayor. And, fourthly, he got to know a woman called Elizabeth Cooper, who lived about 5 miles from Norwich in the village of East Carleton. John Borrow and Elizabeth Cooper had two children, but did not marry. As a result, the Overseers of the Poor in East Carleton applied for and obtained a magistrates's order directing John Borrow to pay 3s. a week towards the upkeep of each child, maintenance payments that were made up to, but not after, March 1828. Before that, though, John had followed Allday Kerrison, brother of George's friend Roger, to Mexico, where he got a job first with the Real del Monte Company in Guanajuato, then later with the Anglo-Mexican Company and the United Mexican Company, all of them mining enterprises. John's letters from Mexico are mostly of a practical nature, reveal little of the real person and certainly tell one little about John's feelings for his mother and his brother. Because he remained in Mexico for a longer period of time than the extended period of leave granted by the commanding officer of the West Norfolk Militia, John's 'disembodied allowance' of 2s. 6d. a day lapsed. That was in March 1828. In other words, John supported his children for as long as he received his Militia allowance and ceased to do so when he could no longer claim it.

In 1829, George Borrow began to apply himself to the problem of recovering from the authorities as much of John's 'disembodied allowance' as possible, presumably because he had learnt from his mother either that she herself was supporting Elizabeth Cooper's children or that they were unsupported. Though John signed a sort of affidavit giving George the right to act on his behalf, so that the money could be paid directly to Mrs Borrow, he neglected to say that his leave had terminated in 1828. Consequently, when Borrow tackled the Army in order to recover John's pay, he thought that the authorities owed money for the full period from 1826 to 1830, provided John could show that he had permission for missing such training-camps as had been held while he was out of the country. He therefore committed himself to a protracted negotiation which, in the event, took more than two years. The affair took time, partly because even when the power of attorney arrived, in June 1830, he still had to wait until the authorities accepted its validity, and partly because the relevant authorities were numerous. The commanding officer had to indicate formally whether or not leave had been granted; the paymaster had to calculate how much money was owing to Lt John Borrow for the period for which he had been granted leave; the Army Pay Office had to reimburse the paymaster for the same sum if it could be demonstrated that payment had been legally made; and the War Office had to satisfy itself that Lt Borrow still existed, though abroad, that he had done his duty by his regiment, that the affidavit requesting continued payment, though drawn up abroad, was valid, and that that document giving power of attorney to George Borrow of Willow Lane, Norwich, could be accepted, despite the fact that it seemed not to have been signed by John Borrow himself but only stamped by a Mexican official. A further complication was introduced when Borrow took the liberty of saying that his brother was on his way home and would therefore be able to attend the next Militia exercises, though he knew this was not the case. Eventually, though, the matter was settled. A cheque for arrears of £148 was paid in January 1830, the allowance was declared forfeit on 25 December 1830 because of non-attendance at training, and a final cheque to cover the period up to 24 December was then issued. Though Borrow wrote to Sayer, the West Norfolk Militia paymaster, in September 1831 and later, in May 1833, tried to reopen the case, from the point of view of the Army the file was closed.

We do not know whether Elizabeth Cooper was given the money that Borrow obtained by his persistent, often impudent badgering of the Army authorities, although a Borrow entry in his mother's account book – 'Mr. Lloyd for John' – suggests that perhaps she did. While the episode is important, because it confirms Borrow's whereabouts from the end of 1829 to the end of 1831, and while the letters provide amusing examples of Borrow being cantankerous in order to get his own way',[35] not much light is shed on relationships within the family. John Borrow had existed to date in the form of an unreliable collage of what early biographers chose to preserve before disposing of the evidence

54

they had in front of them. Thus Knapp quoted those parts of John Borrow's letters which seemed to show his brotherly love and concern. Clement Shorter summarised those pages in Knapp, giving prominence to parts that showed 'intelligence, great practicality, and common sense' – as he thought. So fulsome does his account become that he allows himself to say at the end of it that *Lavengro* contains no happier pages than those concerned with this 'dearly loved brother' and to lament, also, that John had not lived to provide nephews and nieces 'to soften the asperity' of Borrow's later years.[36] If Knapp knew about John Borrow's children and chose to conceal the fact we would have an interesting example of a prudish critic recreating the Victorian period in his own image, but it is more likely that he did not know, his attitude being more determined by the feeling that brothers *ought* to like each other. What the 'disembodied allowance' business does not show is that there existed strong, loving feelings between the brothers, least of all on John Borrow's side, for he seems to have acted cynically throughout. George, for his part, was in Russia when he heard that his brother had died of cholera on 22 November 1833, supposedly on the eve of going to a new job in Colombo, after a period of unemployment, and, though it was natural that he should wish to console his mother, his letter of condolence to late twentieth-century ears somehow lacks conviction, is overdone and, even allowing for differences of convention, fails to give assurance of a strong personal tie between the two brothers.

MY DEAR, DEAR MAMMA – I have received your melancholy letter, which has given me the severest stroke I ever experienced. It quite stunned me, and since reading its contents I have done little else but moan and lament – though doing so is of no use. O that our darling John had taken the advice which I gave him nearly three years since, to abandon that horrid country and return to England! though it is probable that that would not have saved him; for I think from his departing so suddenly that his constitution was undermined and gave way at once. Peace be to his soul! a nobler, better, kinder being never walked God's earth. Would that I had died for him! for I loved him dearly, dearly. Perhaps his was the best lot, for the pain he felt is nothing to the pangs which torment me when I think of him. Thank Heaven, his sufferings, if he suffered at all, were short. It is a great consolation to think that he did not lie long languishing on a bed of sickness, with scarcely any one to assist him.[37]

If it seems ungenerous to question Borrow's feelings, it can with safety be said that John Borrow had not played a significant part in his brother's life, except to the extent that much earlier he had talked with him about painters and painting.

Meanwhile, Borrow was once again occupied with that evergrowing pile of verse translations. He was determined to see them published. He had always been determined to publish them. He was to remain determined throughout the rest of his life. Back in London late in 1829 he once more went to work. He tried at the same time to find other things to do, whether on a regular or irregular basis. In December 1829 he wrote a long letter to the Highland Society to inform its members that he would be glad to prepare for them an anthology of Highland verse. He tried to think of ways by which he might obtain a position in the British Museum. Still on his mind was the possibility of foreign appointments, preferably government appointments. People who have to cast about to find a means to use their talents, whether just for the sake of earning a living or for the sake of earning a living in a congenial and interesting way, sometimes proceed openly, sometimes secretly. It was natural for Borrow to search out employment of some kind. Probably we only know a few of the possibilities he had in mind, a few of the things he thought about, a few of the desperate remedies to which he tried to resort, and consequently it seems unfair to attach unnecessary weight, in retrospect, to this or that venture, for what determined literary aspirant in his mid-twenties has not cast about for employment in exactly that way? His return to London showed that he was resolute and in no department of his life was he more resolute than in that which concerned verse translation. It had been and continued to be an immense labour. The world simply had to know about it.

In this mood, Borrow renewed his acquaintance with Dr John Bowring, whom he said he had met at the house of William Taylor and who had just returned from Denmark. So, at least, Borrow claimed in *The Romany Rye*, when he recollected that Bowring uttered 'the most desperate Radicalism that was perhaps ever heard, saying, he hoped that in a short time there would not be king or queen in Europe, and inveighing bitterly against the English aristocracy'.[38] Yet this is one of those occasions on which Borrow's supposedly infallible memory is not completely to be trusted, since had Borrow met Bowring in William Taylor's house in 1821 there would have been no need for Taylor to write the letter of introduction to Bowring dated 1824 which is now preserved in the library of the University of Iowa. Then again, there is no record of Borrow having met Bowring during 1825, which perhaps suggests, though this is a speculation, that if the two translators met in Norwich it must have been in 1829. In *Lavengro*, Borrow gave the date incorrectly and injected his account with the venom he felt for Bowring after Bowring deserted the Radical cause and began to vote Whig. None of this, though, could be anticipated in 1829. In 1829, Bowring was thirty-seven, but his diplomatic and political career was still before him: he had published books of translations and on the face of it seemed, like Borrow, to be concerned mostly with literature, though

after 1832 he was to seek favour with the new Government, thus starting a new career that resulted in his becoming M.P. for Bolton in 1841.
Borrow told him of two of his projects: his translation of the *Death of
Balder*, 'Ewald's most celebrated production', and his *Kæmpe Viser*,
that is, his collection of early Danish verse in translation, which he had
left in Norwich with William Taylor. Bowring had found rooms at 5
Millman Street; Borrow had taken up residence at 17 Great Russell
Street. The two enthusiasts soon had their first meeting, then continued
to see and write to each other regularly until the autumn of 1830. The
Death of Balder may have been shown to publishers and rejected: there
is no way of telling. Borrow and Bowring may have talked about it;
if so, Bowring's opinion is lost to us. The manuscript was shelved, and
only published after Borrow's death when it was found by Webber
amongst Borrow's papers and published by Jarrolds of Norwich.[39] The
Kæmpe Viser was different, because here was something that both of
them knew about and on which they might therefore collaborate. Here,
surely, was someone in whom Borrow could have confidence. Bowring
had been in Russia in 1820; in 1822, according to his own account, he
had been arrested in Calais, charged with aiding the anti-Bourbon
faction in France; in 1824 he had helped Jeremy Bentham establish
The Westminster Review; and, though in the late twenties he worked
for Charles Villiers on behalf of the Government (not the Villiers
whom Borrow later knew as British Minister in Spain), he was, when
Borrow first knew him, a young polyglot who had not yet fully declared himself in public life, or who had not yet got close enough to a
public career to make anything like a declaration important. He was
interesting, but safe, and his publications by themselves showed that his
literary interests were genuine and extensive.

So at least thought Borrow, who first mooted the scheme in a letter
to Bowring at the beginning of December.

I trouble you with these lines for the purpose of submitting a little project of
mine for your approbation. When I last had the pleasure of being at yours, you
mentioned, that we might at some future period unite our strength in composing a kind of Danish Anthology. You know, as well as I, that by far the
most remarkable portion of Danish poetry is compressed in those ancient
popular productions termed *Kæmpe Viser*, which I have translated. Suppose we
bring forward at once the first volume of the Danish Anthology, which should
contain the heroic and super-natural songs of the *KV* which are certainly the
most interesting; they are quite ready for the press with the necessary notes,
and with an introduction which I am not ashamed of.[40]

The second volume would consist of 'Historic songs and the ballads
and romances'; the third of 'modern Danish poetry', commencing with
Morten Borup's 'Ode to the Birds'; and the fourth, of the poems of

'Ölenslager', including his 'Aladdin'. What did Bowring think about this? Bowring thought it was a good idea, though he must have realised straight away that Borrow had left little room for a contribution from himself.

There followed a period of activity and excitement. Bowring thought they should aim for three rather than four volumes; so be it, said Borrow. Borrow thought they should advertise their project in order to cut out the competition, 'for I am terribly afraid of being forestalled in the *Kæmpe Viser* by some of those Scotch blackguards who affect to translate from all languages, of which they are fully as ignorant as Lockhart is of Spanish'. Bowring agreed and went to see a publisher (unidentified) who expressed interest. In January, Borrow prepared a 'prospectus' or advertisement for the volume, which he sent to Bowring for his approval. Borrow accepted Bowring's revision. 'I approve of the prospectus in every respect', he said; 'it is business-like, and there is nothing flashy in it.'[41] He had borrowed some books from Bowring and from one of them was translating '3 longish *Kæmpe Visers*'. Was Bowring, incidentally, aware of Oehlenschlager's 'St. Hans Aftenspil?' And if Bowring now had a publishing contact, would he ask the foreign editor if he had any interest in Borrow's reviewing Tegnér or in a 'good article on Welsh poetry?' Later in the month, Borrow was obliged to 'decamp', as he put it, when the duns descended on 17 Great Russell Street, but he escaped with his belongings, moved to 7 Museum Street, and kept going. They had the prospectus printed by an old Norwich acquaintance, Richard Taylor of Red Lion Court, continued to see each other, and continued to exchange books. Borrow was briefly happy. 'Thorlakson's Grave-Ode is superlatively fine, and I translated it this morning, as I breakfasted.'[42] Meanwhile, Bowring was out and about. He spoke to people in the British Museum about Borrow and would rejoice, he said, 'to see you *niched* in the British Museum'.[43] He went up to Cambridge – would he enlist the support of a few dons, said Borrow, for their book? And would Bowring write to the King of Greece to see if Borrow could get a job with him? He would want to go in a military not a civil capacity, he coolly informed his friend: 'I am uneasy to find myself at four and twenty drifting on the sea of the world, and likely to continue so.'[44] Wise after the event we may presume to think that Borrow should have got himself a regular job and worked at his Danish translations on Sundays. We may see more clearly than he did at the time that his friendship with Bowring was an unequal one. The point is that Borrow was happy to know someone who shared his enthusiasm for Scandinavian literature, happy to be working at it, happy to be obsessed by it. This is shown in many ways, not least by the fact that he exposed his thoughts and plans more to Bowring than to anyone else at this period, which perhaps explains the violence with which he repudiated Bowring some twenty years later, when this secretive man felt mortified that he had been so open and frank.

The correspondence between Bowring and Borrow probably only reveals part of Borrow's activities during the early part of 1830. Bowring had introduced Borrow to the distinguished Danish scholar, Grundtvig, for whom he did some transcription and translation. In the spring, he wrote a long review article of two Danish publications: *Den Danske Digtekunsts Middelalder fra Arrebo til Tullin fremstillet i Academiske Forelaesinger holdne i Aarene, 1798–1800* and *Dansk-norsk Literaturlexicon, 1818*. This forty-page article appeared in *The Foreign Quarterly Review* in June.[45] It is important as a major effort on Borrow's part and because it contained sixteen of his own translations. It also shows that he was familiar with the editorial work of Rahbek and Nyerup, the scholars who edited the first of these two volumes under review, and who also edited the *Kæmpe Viser* of Anders Sorensen Vedel. In addition, Borrow translated, presumably during the early part of 1830, the work of the Welsh poet, Ellis Wynn, of which he said in 1860, when he published it, that it had long existed in manuscript. Associated with this translation was the essay on Welsh poetry which he had mentioned to Bowring and which the foreign editor had decided he did not want. Borrow still had with him the translation of the *Death of Balder* and it must be assumed that while in London he continued to look for a publisher for it. All these translations and associated papers will be referred to at greater length in the final chapter of the present book, for Borrow devoted his later years to further attempts at getting them published and in part succeeded. In 1830, he did not succeed. Though he continued to work at the proposed *Songs of Scandinavia*, as the surviving manuscripts show, the project fell through. Bowring and Borrow drifted apart. Literary fame had eluded him once again. He was exhausted from overwork. He fell ill. And in September he returned to Norwich.

Although the precise dates of meetings and decisions cannot be ascertained, it seems likely that Borrow remained in London only for as long as the affair of John's allowance justified his doing so. Perhaps he even lived on part of the £148 that had been paid in January 1830 in the belief that he could extract more. He had written to Bowring from Museum Street on 14 September, at the same time returning some of Bowring's 'Bohemian' books:

I am going to Norwich for some short time as I am very unwell, and hope that cold bathing in October and November may prove of service to me. My complaints are, I believe, the offspring of *ennui* and unsettled prospects. I have thoughts of attempting to get into the French service, as I should like prodigiously to serve under Clausel in the next Bedouin campaign.[46]

No more came of this last idea than of any of the others that he had shared with Bowring. Between September 1830 and November 1832 he spent much of his time in Norwich and, in as far as none of his literary work can be associated with this period, it may be assumed that he found some way in Norwich by which to earn his living, though which way that was has never been discovered. He could not avoid being interested in the politics of the Reform Bill period; he may, as Knapp said could be inferred from the Appendix to *The Romany Rye*, have indulged in occasional journalism; and he certainly wrote the article on the 'Origin of the word "Tory"' (though not necessarily *in propria persona*), which was published in the *Norfolk Chronicle*, as well as various drafts for articles on the differences betwen the Tories and the Radicals, one of which, incidentally, contained the ominous prediction that the three parties (Tory, Whig and Radical) 'must at no very distant period subside into two great hostile masses between whom there is a physical and moral necessity that war to the knife be carried out until victory shall declare with one or the other'.[47] But when in September 1831 he wrote the last of those pre-Russian letters to Bowring (which Clement Shorter later purchased), he did not say what he was doing, or indeed whether he was doing anything. He was sorry Bowring had been unsuccessful in his approaches to the Belgian authorities on his behalf. He was grateful for Bowring's offer to help him towards an Army commission if he could afford it. He more had in mind, though, making his knowledge of Persian and Arabic available to the Government in some Eastern appointment. In short he tried to leave the way open for future correspondence, but told Bowring very little, except that if he went into the Army at all it would be into the Militia rather than into a regiment of the line, because the latter would cost £500. The period of intimacy was over and, after the frenzy of the months in London, he had gone back into his shell.

Interestingly, though, he did tell Bowring in a postscript that he had lately been wandering about Norfolk and that the 'minds of the peasantry are in a horrible state of excitement'. He had heard men and women in the fields saying that 'not a grain of corn they were cutting should be eaten, and that they would as lieve be hanged as live'. Someone had told him in the street on the day he wrote the letter 'that twelve corn stacks are blazing within twenty miles of his place'. 'I am afraid', he concluded, 'that all this will end in a famine and a rustic war.'[48] In another letter, of 12 January 1831, he said: 'I have been endeavouring to the utmost of my ability to check radicalism and disaffection, to seize upon machine breakers and to bring them to condign punishment.'[49] (These machine-breakers came to trial in Norwich later that month at the Quarter Sessions.) Like many Englishmen before and since he was aware of political events in which he apparently could not or would not participate, except when forced to do so. He knew about hunger, exploitation, unemployment and civil disorder and his later writings show a great sympathy, not only with the great heroes of Nordic legend, but also with workers, peasants, gypsies, migrant labourers, and even vagrants and thieves. But somehow, in a Defoe-like transformation, the misfit who had left Norwich five years earlier to contribute to a Radical magazine had moved to the right, though still without a position in the world that would have allowed the establishment to recognise him as one of its own. Perhaps he was too individualistic to have been a member of a left-wing movement, had that been possible, too detached from other peoples' lives to have felt in any genuine way the need for democratic association in pre-Reform Bill years. So he inclined against that political change that might have saved England from later class dissension.

As the question is, or will shortly be, Tory or Radical, we say Tory! and advise every honest man to say so too. The chief reason for Toryism, a reason sufficient by itself, is that within it are comprised love of country and pride of country. Not the least reason against Radicalism, if the only one a sufficient one – is that love of country and pride of country constitute no part of it.[50]

Borrow's Englishness and love of England are not to be doubted; despite his cosmopolitan interests, his travels, his knowledge of other languages, he remained throughout his life, immensely, the patriot. At the same time, perhaps his failure to resolve the conflict between his rural, East Anglian Tory instincts and his Radical impulses associated with his first-hand knowledge of rapidly changing, and for many people deteriorating, social conditions was part of that larger lack of integrity, that larger difficulty he had in making a unified sense of the various parts of his life which was so alarmingly, interestingly exposed when he wrote his major books. Before that, however, he was to spend a few years in Russia.

3

Russia: 1833–1835

The story is told in the *History of the British and Foreign Bible Society* of a Russian colonel who, having purchased a Bible in Balaklava, asked how it was possible to sell the volume at so low a price. Mr Melville, the Society's agent, explained the nature and objectives of the Bible Society, adding that the scriptures were now read, 'thanks to its labours and God's blessing', in 150 tongues. 'Oh, Britain', exclaimed the amazed colonel, 'thou are rightly called great! When will Russia be like thee?'[1] In such terms, the Bible Society in London thought about itself.

The Society was committed to the then-fashionable, middle-class missionary task of putting into the hands of everyone who would accept it an accurately translated copy of the Bible. For this high-minded, if ultimately ambivalent, purpose, the Society – like the other nineteenth-century Protestant Societies, particularly the American and the German – was prepared to go to great lengths, paying large sums of subscription money for translations into what were then little-known languages and supporting full-time agents in the field, often in the most remote parts of the world. Whether the Society existed to salve the British Evangelical conscience or whether it represented a sincere, profoundly felt desire to share the benefits of civilisation with barbarians, there can be no doubt about the energy of its officers. Appendix III of the Society's official history shows that up to 1853 18 millon copies of the Bible were distributed in the United Kingdom alone. The Society was fearless in its evangelical and missionary zeal; almost 3 ½ million copies in French were circulated, for example, while for Asia, which is of immediate concern in this chapter, there had been translations into 20 languages, including Chinese, Persian, Mongolian, Syriac, Bengali, Turkish and Arabic.

The distribution of more than half a million copies of the Protestant Bible in Asia in the first part of the nineteenth century had not proved simple, which by itself explains the importance of the Society's outpost in St Petersburg. The St Petersburg Agency, as it was called, which had opened early in the century, then for political reasons closed again, had reopened in 1828 and until 1840 remained the administrative centre for the Society's work in Asia, both for the Society itself, on whose behalf it distributed 350,000 Bibles 'in languages spoken from the Rhine to the interior of China, and from the Kola Peninsula to the Islands of Greece',[2] and for the American Bible Society, which from time to time provided funds for campaigns in particular countries, notably Livonia and Esthonia. Particularly important in the minds of the London committee members because of what was to become something of an obsession with China, an obsession which closely affected Borrow, were the two activities of two missionaries operating through St Petersburg, Mr Swan and Mr Stallybrass, who found time to have printed there a Mongolian version of the Bible and organise the distribution of copies: 'Buriat converts carried them far and wide among the Tartar hordes; and though no direct intercourse was allowed with the millions within the Chinese frontier, the books still found their way to many of those who understood the language in that land of darkness.'[3] It was during this period, the 1830s, that Borrow first became involved in the work of the British and Foreign Bible Society.

A terse official summary of the Society's interest is given in *Letters of George Borrow to the British and Foreign Bible Society*, where apparently without humour or irony the editor comments on the imperialist function of the Russian colony in Peking during the eighteenth century. One of the Russians with whom Borrow later found himself working had spent twenty years in China before returning to a job in the Asiatic Department of the Russian Foreign Office in St Petersburg. This was Stepan Vasilievitch Lipotsev (1773–1841), who in 1821 had agreed to translate and have printed the New Testament into Manchu, 'the official language of the Chinese Court and Government'.[4] He had done this, had been paid £560, had in 1822 produced a small edition of St Matthew from a fount typecase manufactured at the Society's expense, had stored the 550 copies in the vaults of Sarepta House (the St Petersburg office of Asmus, Simondsen and Co., the Society's German bankers), and had sent two copies of the complete manuscript to the Society in London in 1826, where they gathered dust in the editorial superintendent's office. Lipotsev had also told the Bible Society about a translation into Manchu of 'a considerable part' of the Bible that had been prepared much earlier by a Jesuit called Puerot. But there had been no opportunity at that time for anyone associated with the Bible Society to inspect or assess this earlier translation. As to the one for which the Society had paid, the 550 copies of St Matthew were destroyed in the flooding of the Neva in 1824, and the type damaged, and so, because it seemed that nothing further could be done, the whole matter was shelved.

So matters rested until 1832, when Mr Swan, while passing through St Petersburg on his way back to his mission at Lake Selinginsk, unexpectedly came across two copies of Puerot's version, both in private hands. Though one of the owners, a Dr Veschechofsky, was only prepared to part with his manuscript for a sum the Society considered exorbitant, the other was in the possession of the Holy Synod of the Russian Church, whose officials gave permission for a transcription. Since Swan was the only competent person available to transcribe this manuscript, he remained in St Petersburg at the Bible Society's expense in order to make the most of the unexpected opportunity. In this way it came about that the committee members in London once again began to think about printing a Manchu translation. They had the makings of a complete translation: Lipotsev's translation of the New Testament, held in London, and when it was finished Swan's transcription of Puerot's translation of the Old Testament and part of the New. Could anything be done with this material? And if so, should it be done in London or St Petersburg? The Society was not in the least daunted by the prospect of producing in St Petersburg, where it was banned, an edition of the Bible in Manchu for distribution in China, where it was not wanted. But was there anyone available to do the actual work for them? The Rev. Swan could not: he was not a full-time agent of the Society and in any case the future of Christianity among the Buriat Mongols in the region south of Lake Baikal depended upon his returning to Selinginsk. Nor could Lipotsev: now almost fifty years old, he had responsible positions in the Russian Foreign Office which by regulation precluded other work. Exactly at their moment of decision, so God or Providence decreed, the committee members were made aware of the existence of George Borrow, the ideal man for the job: that is, someone who would not be put off by the absurdity of the task but, on the contrary, would be excited by the prospect of unusual undertakings in remote places.

Borrow was introduced to the Bible Society in a letter dated 27 December 1832 from the Rev. Francis Cunningham, Vicar of Lowestoft, who for some years had been a staunch supporter of the Society. Borrow, said the Rev. Cunningham, is 'a person without university education, but who has read the Bible in thirteen languages. He is independent in circumstances, of no very exactly defined denomination of Christians, but I think of certain Christian principle.'[5] Borrow's Christianity remained conveniently ill-defined throughout his life: indeed, leaving aside questions of routine observance (for many good-hearted souls found it appropriate during the nineteenth century to repress their scruples about going to church), it is doubtful whether in any real sense he was a Christian at all. Of this, more later. The Rev. Cunningham had in his letter described Borrow as 'of the middle order in Society, and a very produceable person'. The committee members were interested. A person who could read the Bible in thirteen languages was exactly what they needed, particularly if he was 'produceable'. What more suitable agent could there be for civilising the Chinese by means of a Manchu Bible manufactured in St Petersburg than an anti-social young Englishman in his late twenties, to whom the Vicar of Lowestoft had been introduced by chance?

Story has it that Borrow walked from Norwich to London to meet the officials of the Bible Society. According to his own manuscript notes for an autobiography,[6] he made the 112 mile journey in 27 hours, spending only 5½d. on the way, and going straight to the offices of the Society, where he simply waited on the doorstep until someone arrived. These incidentally were the steps of the Society's first house in Earl Street, not those of the present Bible House on Queen Victoria Street. The officials who first met him were impressed by his robust good health and his size, something that seemed always to work in his favour. Within a few days, he met members of the General Purposes Committee, including the Rev. Jowett, the literary superintendent, was interviewed, was given some sort of examination to test his knowledge of languages, including Arabic, and on 4 January was lent books from the Society's library so that he could come to terms with Manchu. These books included Amyot's *Dictionnaire Tartare–Mantchou François* (Paris, 1789–90), L. Langlès *Alphabet Mantchou* (Paris, 1807), and a copy of the previously published edition of St Matthew's Gospel. While the Society began to deliberate over what it should do about a possible Manchu version, as yet uncommitted to having the work done in London or in St Petersburg, Borrow was given £10 to cover his expenses and sent back to Norwich to learn the language. Borrow lost no time in telling Francis Cunningham that the expedition had been a success. The committee had defrayed his travel and accommodation expenses in 'the most handsome manner'. He had nothing to complain of, he said, and then added – with that strange and, it was to turn out, characteristic ambivalence of manner that would surely have made anyone but a clergyman distrust him –

and I hope, Sir, that I shall have the benefit of your prayers for my speedy success, for the language is one of those which abound with difficulties against which human skill and labour, without the special favour of God, are as blunt hatchets against the oak.

A reasonable place to stop? Not so for George Borrow, whose thoughts were running ahead of him as he wrote:

and though I shall almost weary him with my own prayers, I wish not to place much confidence in them, being at present very far from a state of grace and regeneration, having a hard and stony heart, replete with worldly passions, vain wishes, and all kinds of ungodliness.

Won't this be more than the Vicar of Lowestoft can stomach? Should Borrow not stop? Not he.

So it would be no wonder if God to prayers addressed from my lips were to turn his head away in wrath and in lieu of cleverness were to send stupidity, dimness of vision in lieu of sharp sightedness, and in every case that which is contrary to what I pray for. Therefore, Sir, I hope you will not be offended if I recommend this point particularly to your recollection.[7]

There might be some hope for George Borrow if God and the Rev. Francis Cunningham devote their best energies to his redemption. Meanwhile, he himself was delighted to be acknowledged as a 'philologist', so set to work with the same enthusiasm as he had always felt when tackling a new language.

Evidently he enjoyed himself. Only a month later, he wrote to the Jowett to say that he could already translate Manchu and 'am perfectly qualified to write a critique on the version of St. Matthew's Gospel, which I brought with me into the country'.[8] Lest there be any doubt about this, he treated Jowett to a paragraph on the infelicities of the original translation, especially the translator's improvisations from the Greek where, according to Borrow, there was a perfectly good Manchu word he might have used. This is in Borrow's letter of 10 February 1833, with its very pleasant tongue-in-cheek first sentence: 'I have just received your communication, and nothwithstanding it is Sunday morning and the bells with their loud and clear voices are calling me to church, I have sat down to answer it by return post.' Borrow's attitude to the Bible Society during the spring of 1833 was both positive and discriminating. He liked learning a new language, so he worked hard, and in March coolly reported that 'if I had a Grammar, I should in a month's time be able to read a Manchu translation of Jonah'.[9]

He had mentioned to the committee members two other interests with which they might be able to help on a *quid pro quo basis*. These were his brother, then in Mexico, whom he thought the committee might like to employ in some capacity or other, perhaps as translator of the Bible into Mexican, and the gypsies, into whose language he himself — with a little help and encouragement — could translate the Gospel according to St John. For this purpose he would need money to pay elderly gypsy informants, for 'the gypsies are more mercenary than the Jews'.[10] It is interesting to notice that Borrow had talked about gypsies at his very first set of meetings with Andrew Brandram, who was one of the two joint secretaries of the Society at that time, that Borrow came to the conclusion that their interests were compatible, his and Brandram's, if the price of having a chance to learn more about gypsies was to say he would rescue them from ignorance of religion and morality, and that according to Borrow it was Brandram himself who suggested he should prepare a gypsy vocabulary. The eminently respectable and august Bible Society committee thus provided a pretext and later an opportunity for gypsy studies which to that point had eluded him. Meanwhile Borrow was able to report in March that his work was proceeding 'at full gallop'. Finally, in a letter dated 9 June 1833, he told Jowett: 'I have mastered Manchu, and I should feel obliged by your informing the committee of the fact, and also my excellent friend Mr. Brandram.'[11]

By this time one of the Society's agents, a Dr Pinkerton, had reported from St Petersburg that the restrictions imposed by the Holy Synod, which had led to the ban on a Mongolian New Testament some years earlier, had been relaxed so that there might after all be some point in again applying for permission to proceed with the manufacture of a Bible in translation. Dr Pinkerton also confirmed that Lipotsev was alive and in St Petersburg. That the Society wanted to proceed in some way or other, though how precisely had yet to be determined, is clear from the fact they had asked an associate called John Hattersley to learn Manchu as well as Borrow. Dr Pinkerton's report reassured the committee, so much so that, anticipating the final outcome, Jowett wrote to tell Borrow about these most recent developments. 'Might not Mr. Borrow be invited to proceed to St. Petersburg, to assist in the work and to profit by the opportunities which would then be afforded him for acquiring a greater proficiency in this very important language?'[12] And would Borrow tell Jowett his feelings about this idea in time for the decisive committee meeting in July? Borrow's reply was thoroughly characteristic of him. A job was a job.

What you have written has given me great pleasure, as it holds out hope that I may be employed usefully to the Deity, to man, and myself. I should be very happy to visit St. Petersburg and to become the coadjutor of Mr. Lipotsev, and to avail myself of his acquirements in what you very happily designate a most singular language, towards obtaining a still greater proficiency in it. I flatter myself that I am for one or two reasons tolerably well adapted for the contemplated expedition, for besides a competent knowledge of French and German, I possess some acquaintance with Russian, being able to read without much difficulty any printed Russian book.[13]

The adventurer who had been willing to work in London was positively eager to go to St Petersburg.

The General Purposes Committee met at Bible House on 5 July, decided to ask Borrow to go to St Petersburg and presented the proposal on the 22 July to the General Committee of the Society, when it was immediately approved. Mr Jowett had already told Borrow by letter of what the sub-committee intended to recommend.

It is recommended to the General Committee that your services be engaged for one year, to proceed to St. Petersburg, to assist Mr. Lipoftsoff [*sic*] in the editing of such portions of the Manchu Testament as we may choose to print (Luke and Acts have been resolved upon already), if the Government shall consent to the work being executed there; if not, to assist Rev. Wm. Swan in transcribing and collating the MS version of a large part of the Old Testament in the language, and to avail yourself meanwhile of all the facilities which may offer for correcting and perfecting your acquaintance with the Manchu. The Society, it is proposed, shall pay your expenses to and fro, and a salary, while employed by them at the rate of £200. per annum, to cover all other expenses.[14]

The committee members had in mind that William Swan would need to be released from the chore of transcription, that Borrow, if he was to help at all, might as well be sent immediately and that in any case he should get there before winter set in. Mr Jowett therefore asked Borrow to hold himself in readiness and at the same time warned him about the impropriety of his, Borrow's, letter.

There is occasionally a tone of confidence in speaking of yourself, which has alarmed some of the excellent members of our Committee. It may have been this feeling, more than once displayed before, which prepared one or two of them to stumble at an expression in your letter of yesterday...It is where you speak of the prospect of becoming *useful to the Deity, to man, and to yourself.* Doubtless you meant *the prospect of glorifying God;* but the term of expression made us think of such passages of scripture as Job 22:2; 35:7 and 8; Psalm 16:2 and 3.[15]

Borrow on this occasion, as on later occasions, adopted a pragmatic attitude to employment. The prospect of glorifying God was not in his mind, his reasons for accepting the Society's offer being entirely personal. The Society wished him to go to St Petersburg on what was quite obviously a speculative venture; he for his part liked the idea of going to Russia, but for reasons which had little to do with the spread of Christianity amongst peoples who did not want it. He regarded himself as an independent person entering into a contract, kept his religious opinions to himself and, when interviewed by the editorial sub-committee on 29 July, unhesitatingly agreed to abstain 'from mingling himself with political or ecclesiastical affairs during his residence in Russia'.[16] The Society needed Borrow's egotism and were prepared to pay £200 a year for it, for who else would have accepted such a daunting assignment? Armed with letters of recommendation and a manuscript copy of Lipotsev's Manchu version of the New Testament, Borrow sailed from London on 31 July 1833 bound for Hamburg, from where he would travel by land to Lubeck and then by sea again to St Petersburg.

Actually, Borrow was exhausted, physically and emotionally drained by recent events, despite his outward composure, and at the end of a three-day voyage, the only Englishman in a medley of Germans, Swedes and Danes, he was carried off the ship at Hamburg in what he described as a fit of delirium and deposited in a hotel called the *König von Engeland*, where a doctor gave him forty drops of laudanum, had his head swathed in wet towels and sent him to bed. Borrow calmly told Jowett that, though he had been seriously ill on board ship, he had not come close to the slightest harm, 'for the Lord took care of me through two of His instruments, Messrs. Weil and Valentin, highly respectable Jews of Copenhagen, who had been my fellow-passengers, and with whom I had ingratiated myself on board, in our intervals of ease, by conversing with them about the Talmud and the book Sohar'.[17]

Borrow reported that the doctor's treatment worked, that he slept all day and woke in the evening 'perfectly recovered and in the best spirits possible', that he visited and then the next day dined with the British Consul, Mr H. Canning, and that he intended to leave on the 6th to be at Lubeck in time to catch the steamboat for St Petersburg on the 8th. Like many travellers before and since he became fascinated by the experience simply of being in Hamburg. He had already told Jowett, in his letter of 4 August, of his first exploration of Hamburg, where 'no observer can fail to be struck with the liveliness and bustle which reign in this emporium of continental Europe, worthy to be compared with Tyre of old and our own Liverpool', and where 'little can be said in commendation of the moral state of this part of the world, for rope dancers were displaying their agility in the park today, and dancing saloons, which I am informed are most infamous places, are open to the public this evening'.[18] Were these the sentiments of a new lay missionary who could readily identify with the Bible Society? Or the first reaction of a still relatively unsophisticated young man from Norwich whose experiences in Russia were to broaden his outlook? Or was he once again being ironical at Jowett's expense when he allowed himself to continue his letter in a vein he knew would be acceptable to the recipient? 'England with all her faults has still some regard to decency, and will not tolerate such a shameless display of vice on so sacred a season, when a decent cheerfulness is the freest form in which

the mind or countenance ought to invest themselves.' This was the
Hamburg that was to become a symbol of corruption and vice for
Victorians like George Eliot and W. P. Frith, both of whom became
as fascinated by the place as Borrow was in 1833. Having told Jowett
that his next letter would be from St Petersburg, he did not write again
to the Bible Society from Hamburg. It was in this manner that Borrow
invariably managed his private life.[19] He eventually left Hamburg on 7
August, travelled by road through Lubeck and reached the port of
Travemünde on the 8th.

The St Petersburg Borrow visited in 1833 was a city of half a million
people, with sizeable German, French and English communities and,
to an unprepared outsider, an amazing ethnic mixture in the population
as a whole. From an English point of view, it was a thriving and
important Baltic port: of the thousand or so foreign ships that visited St
Petersburg each year in the late 1820s, about half were English.
There was an English church, built in 1754 and reconstructed in 1815,
and two clubs — The English Club, with a membership restricted to
English, Germans and Russians, and the Commercial Club, on the
English Quay, a meeting-place for English travellers, which had a good
collection of English books. When Borrow arrived, there was an
English colony of about 1,500 people, only a third the size of the
German community but still an adequate presence as far as a new-
comer was concerned.

Many travellers had described the arrival in St Petersburg by sea,
though whether Borrow himself knew what to expect when he sailed
from Travemünde on the paddle-steamer *Nikolai* at the beginning of
August is doubtful. 'The beauty of the entrance to St. Petersburg cannot
easily be paralleled', said a near-contemporary German traveller.

First, the magnificent Cronstadt, with its harbour full of countless ships, its
docks without end, its remarkable towers and works, rising in wonderful
strength and beauty out of the depths of the open sea, strikes us with admiration. A little further we pass the beautiful palace of Peterhof, with its delightful
gardens, its pleasant park, its fairy-like buildings. After several hours' sail
upstream, and after passing the splendid building appropriated to the mining
school, we reach the majestic English quay, where the steamer stops, just
opposite to the Exchange.[20]

This was the arrival as Borrow, like all other travellers, must have
experienced it. He surrendered his passport at Cronstadt, from where
it was passed on to the military governor of St Petersburg and to the
Imperial Chancery. In exchange, he was given a transit paper, which
required him to register with the police within three days and obtain
a residence permit. He would need a certificate from the chief of police

before he could leave.[21] There is no record of Borrow having had the troubles with customs officials that had marred the arrival of so many other travellers. It was only later that his credentials were challenged.

How could he fail to be struck, this romantic traveller, by the St Petersburg that he now began to get to know? A few years later, Elizabeth Rigby described the view that Borrow would have seen from the Admiralty Tower, the magnificent city 'with its oriental spires and domes, and many tributary islands' which lay 'couched low beneath us, while as far as the eye could reach, spread a naked waste of land and water, each equally flat, and dotted sparingly as possible with signs of life'.[22] Borrow was excited by these vast tracts, for he was already dreaming of Kiatchka far to the East and in all probability had read accounts of that fabulous distant city. But St Petersburg itself he immediately described as 'the finest city in the world', sending Jowett a glowing account of the Nevsky Prospect, 'floored with small blocks of wood shaped diagonally' and the broad and rapid, as yet unbridged Neva, which 'runs through the centre of this Queen of Cities'.[23] Glanville, four years earlier, had been surprised 'in witnessing most of the principal streets thronged with people of all ranks and degrees; many of them intent on business – others in search of pleasure', and this, the activity in the summer streets, would have been part of Borrow's first impressions too, so different from anything he had previously experienced were the things he saw now: the ceaseless activity on the Neva and the canals; the pleasure boats, the ferries, the barges bringing supplies from the country; the floating fish-markets moored to the quays from which fresh fish could be netted on request; the vast open market on Sieurnaïa, which was three times the size of Leicester Square; the iron shelters outside public buildings where fires would blaze on winter nights for coachmen, servants and passers-by; and the street vendors, the girls bringing milk from the country in earthenware jars carried on their heads and covered with birchbark, and the purveyors of all kinds of drink, for 'spirituous liquors are the rage amongst the lower classes'.[24] One doubts that it would have taken Borrow long to discover the flea-market, what Glanville called 'a kind of rag fair', which was opposite the Bank of Assignats, teeming with male Armenians, Greeks, Tartars, Calmucks and Russians and, notably, 'sellers of kvass, sbitine, gingerbread, horseflesh, and a peculiar sort of black cabbage soup, thick and nasty, of which the people are fond'.[25] Yet, whatever his reaction to this splendid city with its impressive buildings on either side of the river and its bustling street life, he lost no time in reporting to Jowett, in his first letter, that the 'lower orders of the Russians are very willing to receive Scriptural information, and very willing to purchase it if offered to them at a price which comes within their means'.[26] As usual Borrow's sympathies were strongly with what he here called the 'lower orders' and hardly at all with the bourgeois and aristocrats on whom other writers had naturally focussed their attention. Borrow had not the slightest desire to gain access to the society of formal dinner parties and receptions though, since it was by and large the rich not the poor who travelled from England to Russia, for tourist books to be addressed to them was natural enough. Borrow avoided the bourgeois like the plague, vastly preferring, in Russia and on all his other travels, the company of ordinary working people, gypsies, vagrants, labourers and even criminals, who in Borrow's estimation were at least not contaminated by gentility. Ordinary Russians, Borrow told his mother, were 'the best-natured people in the world, and though they do not know as much as the English, they have not their fiendish, spiteful dispositions and if you go amongst them and speak their language, however badly, they would go through fire and water to do you a kindness'.[27] Borrow was a confirmed democrat. The St Petersburg he quickly got to know was the city of the majority of its citizens, not the aristocrats but the peasants, 'the most prominent features of whose character are love of warmth and hatred of exertion'.[28] The political tendencies that had begun to show themselves in Norwich were thus strongly reinforced in St Petersburg, as he himself, though not in any sense a political activist, probably realised, for he was later to say: 'Russia is doomed eventually to effect a revolution in the political world, perhaps in the literary.'[29] At all events, Borrow evidently felt at ease in St Petersburg, for he told Mr Gurney:

Notwithstanding I had previously heard and read much of the beauty and magnificence of the Russian capital, I confess that which I have beheld has surpassed my expectation. There cannot be a doubt that it is the first city in Europe, being pre-eminent for the grandeur of its public edifices and the length and regularity of its streets. The princely and rapid Neva, a river of the width of the Thames, intersects it, and on each side of this river there is a superb, granite-faced quay, which affords one of the most delightful walks imaginable.[30]

Later on in life, in *Wild Wales*, he was to say: 'If I had my choice of all the cities in the world to live in, I would choose St. Petersburg.'[31]

This despite his initial experience of Russian hotels, which then as now sometimes took the travellers by surprise.

Short of a forest cavern, a foreigner could hardly meet with anything more uninviting and unpleasant than the aspect of one of these caravanserais, or with anything more dismal than its arrangement and distribution. He is ushered into ill-lighted rooms, betraying a sad want of the careful and cleansing hand of a tidy hostess; and where the elegance of the furniture is by no means so great as to make amends for its extreme scantiness. The absence of anything like a bed particularly strikes him.

In such terms a contemporary visitor described the St Petersburg hotels, the Russian ones that is.[32] The attendance was 'execrable', the whole experience a 'purgatory'. In such a hotel Borrow stayed for his first two weeks.

Quickly making contact with Mr Swan, Borrow began to help him with the transcription first of the Manchu Old Testament and then of the New. This exacting work was to continue for several months. He had a letter of introduction to Prince Alexander Galitzin, whom he immediately went to visit. He also went with Swan to see both Schmidt and Lipotsev. Isaac Schmidt, whose translation of the New Testament into the 'Lingua Calmucco–Mongolica' had been published at the Bible Society's expense in St Petersburg, was at this time a member of the Russian Board of Censors, which licensed books for publication. He encouraged Swan and Borrow (this was in August 1833, of course, just after Borrow's arrival) to believe that there would be no serious obstacle to their proceeding with the plans to print a Manchu translation of the Bible. He would look into the matter himself. Lipotsev, now busy with other work, was surprised to learn that the Bible Society intended to incorporate his own translation into a new Manchu Bible, but promised to help Borrow as best he could, particularly with the business of finding manuscripts and printed books in Manchu, which he said were plentiful. It turned out that Lipotsev, by then in his late sixties Borrow thought (actually sixty), was unable to help Borrow to the extent that the Bible Society had expected; he remained friendly but was indifferent to the fate of his translation, probably realising, because he had lived in China, the foolishness of the whole enterprise.

Borrow had carried with him from England a letter from John Venning of Norwich, to his son, James, and through the good offices of a friend of the Vennings, a Mr Egerton Hubbard, found bed and board at 221 Galernoy Ulitza, a street that over the years had become familiar to English visitors in need of lodgings. In this place, popularly known as the Maison Chabot, he remained during the three months devoted to the transcribing of Puerot's manuscript, and he worked hard at a difficult task, for Swan reported to Jowett that 'I willingly bear witness to his diligence in transcription. I have collated with him all he has done, and hope he will succeed in the objects of his visit.'[33] Certainly the task was an onerous one. Borrow transcribed Nehemiah, Job, Daniel and Jonah from the Old Testament and the Acts and the first fourteen chapters of St Matthew. Scarcely any wonder, then, that the Bible Society committee in London did not hear from Borrow for four months, indeed – and not for the last time – had to write to him immediately after Christmas to find out what he was doing. 'Resolved that Mr. Borrow be requested by the Superintendent to make a fresh report on the merits of Lipotsev's Manchu version of the New Testament, and on the expediency of seeking from the Russian Government permission to print the whole.'[34] By that time, indeed at the beginning of December, roughly when Mr Swan left St Petersburg, Borrow had moved to cheaper lodgings where he could cook for himself and live more freely.

Few people will have had the experience of learning, from scratch, how to manufacture an eight-volume leatherbound work in a foreign country in a language that in that place was scarcely known. Yet this was Borrow's task. He had to find a printer who would not baulk at the Manchu characters. He had to find a supply of paper adequate for the proposed eight volumes in an edition of a thousand copies. He had to find both type and compositors. He had to know enough about how things were done in Russia to avoid paying outrageous sums of money unnecessarily. And he had to obtain formal permission from the Russian Government before the work could be undertaken at all. Swan's departure, presumably when the chore of transcription was over or almost over, and Jowett's letter of 2 January 1834 together constituted the spur that pricked him into action, though in the middle of his first St Petersburg winter he was literally still getting to know the city in which he had lived for only four-and-a-half months. People have expressed doubts about Borrow's language skills. At this stage in his life, Borrow had a working knowledge of about a dozen languages, including French and German, both of which were used extensively in St Petersburg in certain circles. He frequently told people, however, that contrary to popular opinion in England, French and German were not enough. To live and work with Russians one needed to speak Russian: Lipotsev, for example, spoke neither French nor German. Probably an educated and experienced man like Lipotsev found Borrow's Russian rather trying, yet Borrow's knowledge of the language seems to have been adequate for most practical purposes, or maybe already somewhat more than adequate. At the same time – that is, during the winter of 1833–4 – Borrow was paying 6s. a week to one Ali Makisha, a Tartar, who taught him Manchu, which Borrow now described as

one of those deceitful tongues, the seeming simplicity of whose structure induces you to suppose, after applying to them for a month or two, that little more remains to be learned, but which, should you continue the study a year, as I have studied this, show them to you in their veritable colours, amazing you with their copiousness, puzzling with their idioms.[35]

Borrow described his teacher as 'very simple and ignorant'. Still, he had lived in Pekin for twelve years and from this kind of person it was in Borrow's character to learn as easily as from a university teacher. So he at least knew the language well enough to answer Jowett's questions about the adequacy of Lipotsev's translation. Borrow's knowledge of French, German, Russian and Manchu might not have satisfied degree-level examiners, but, if we say that he had a good working knowledge of all four languages, we mean something very much more than the tourist's superficial knowledge of idioms and phrases. His knowledge was adequate for the task in hand, a task that involved fairly complex dealings with a variety of people.

Borrow did not find Lipotsev and Schmidt particularly helpful when it came to the business of getting permission to proceed. Instead, he personally petitioned Mr Bludoff, Minister of the Interior, at the same time enlisting the support of the Hon. Mr Bligh, 'His Britannic Majesty's plenipotentiary at the Court of Russia', whose work over the dinner table and behind the scenes proved so influential that Borrow recommended to Jowett that the Bible Society should thank him formally, which Lord Bexley, the Society's newly-elected chairman, later did. There was presumably no reason for the Russian Government to feel threatened by the mere printing in Manchu of a thousand copies of the Bible which the Bible Society intended to ship to England: nonetheless, because the Russian control of publication was so strict, it was a considerable achievement on Borrow's part to have been able to proceed positively and, at the same time, diplomatically. Headstrong and eccentric though Borrow often was, he was also capable of canny and circumspect behaviour, as the men back in the Bible House now began to realise. Borrow satisfied the Minister of the Interior, whom he met at least twice, that the 'Manchu version was not intended for circulation nor calculated for circulation in any part of the Russian Empire, but in China and Chinese Tartary solely'.[36] He accepted the proposed working arrangement that he should act as editor while Lipotsev, in his official capacity, should be the censor required by Russian law. And, having no option in the matter, he merely submitted to the judgement of the Director of Worship, whose approval was also needed. Despite long hours waiting in bureaucrats' offices and the frustration of not knowing how the proposal was being received, Borrow was at last instructed to call at the Asiatic Department and on 20 January was able to tell Jowett that 'permission had been granted to print the Manchu scripture'.[37] Borrow gave Mr Bligh full credit but prudently told Jowett that it was 'thanks to the Lord' that permission had been granted.

Now he could turn his mind to the practical matters of manufacture. He had to deal successively with the translated and transcribed text itself; with the type (was there an adequate supply of type in St Petersburg for a large book?); with the paper (could he find an adequate supply at a reasonable price?); with the printer (was there in fact a printer who would not shy away from such a formidable task?); with the process of manufacture, particularly the task of proof-reading the work of compositors unfamiliar with the language; and finally with the binding and shipment. Someone who had lived in St Petersburg for many years, who was fluent in both Russian and Manchu, and who had experience in manufacturing books — who was, in short, a publisher – might well have managed more easily than Borrow. But he had to find out how to do everything as he did it. So the months passed. Meanwhile, through the early months of 1834, as his project gradually became a reality to him, he dreamed again of Kiatchka, which he would visit on foot and use as his base for the distribution of Bibles once the task of making them was over. The ancient city on the borders of Russia and China had a strong grip upon his imagination – and what was to prevent his going there? When he read Captain Cochrane's account of the foot-journey he had made across Russia a few years earlier his imagination had been kindled by Cochrane's many adventures, for Borrow was invariably excited by stories of the solitary individual resolutely looking to his own survival in adverse circumstances. Cochrane, for Borrow, was simply another character out of Defoe. He had described Kiatchka (or Maimatchin) as a caravan or border town through which the Russians imported teas, cottons, nankeens, silks, satins and (strangely) rhubarb, while in exchange the Chinese took the furs of foxes, sables, river- and sea-otters, wild cats, beavers and millions of squirrels. 'Here were the limits of two mighty empires', said Cochrane, and described the activity of the old town and its market: 'a small, ill-built mud town, with four narrow mud-paved streets, running at right-angles; containing during the fair from twelve to fifteen hundred men and boys, for the female sex are prohibited'.[38] Borrow wanted to go there. Though just beginning to think about how to get the Manchu Bible printed, he told Jowett it would be pointless for the Bible Society to distribute the book along the Chinese coast, supposing this were possible, first because no one there understood Manchu and, secondly, because of 'the dislike entertained there of the English'. On the other hand,

about five thousand miles from St. Petersburg, on the frontiers of Chinese Tartary, stands the town of Kiatchka, which properly belongs to Russia, but the inhabitants of which are a medley of Tartars, Chinese and Russians...This town is the emporium of Chinese and Russian trade, Chinese caravans are continually arriving and returning, bringing and carrying away articles of merchandise...There would not be any difficulty in disposing at a low price of any quantity of Testaments to the Chinese merchants who arrive thither from Pekin and other places and who would be glad to purchase them on speculation.[39]

Borrow would go there himself:

Were an agent for the Bible Society to reside at this town for a year or so, it is my humble opinion, and the opinion of much wiser people, that if he were active, zealous and likewise courageous, the blessings resulting from his labours would be incalculable. It would be by no means a difficult thing to make excursions into Tartary and to form friendships among the Tartar hordes, and I am far from certain that with a little management and dexterity he would be unable to penetrate even to Pekin, and to return in safety, after having examined the state of the land.[40]

Not satisfied with the novel experience of St Petersburg itself, Borrow spent many winter nights dreaming of vast expeditions into the interior. For why should he not make such a journey? He was without fear, was prepared to walk, and had an insatiable curiosity about almost every race except the Anglo-Saxon.

Jowett stalled, politely. Borrow had not yet finished his work in St Petersburg, so there was time for further exchanges on the subject of Kiatchka. And Borrow himself was indeed at last genuinely engaged in the work for which he was being paid, though the preparations themselves were to take the first four months of 1834.

There was first the question of the translation, about which Jowett had asked for a report. Borrow diplomatically manoeuvred Lipotsev to the side, because he was 'to all appearances perfectly indifferent to the fate of his excellent translation, caring nothing whether it be published as a powerful instrument to open the closed eyes and soften the hard hearts of the idolaters of China and Tartary, or whether it be committed to the flames, and for ever lost to the world'.[41] Lipotsev would be useful to the Society, if willing, but Borrow was the editor, so communications should be addressed to him. In the event, Lipotsev and Borrow worked together on the text of the New Testament, so Borrow was able to report, in April, that Lipotsev had made 'an immense number of alterations in his translation, all of which are excellent improvements'.[42] The editor believed he had in hand an adequate, complete and internally consistent translation of the New Testament; it was this that he eventually had printed. Having spent so many hours transcribing the Old Testament from Puerot's version, he needed to know the Society's wishes. But the Puerot was not compatible with Lipotsev's New Testament, according to Borrow, and there would in any case be a delay because Jowett had not yet received the transcript that Swan had sent back to England in the care of an English merchant called Merrilies. Though Borrow devoted time to the problems of the Old Testament translation, as he reviewed it in the spring of 1834 while waiting of Jowett's instructions, it eventually had to be put aside, which was just as well, in as far as printing the New Testament proved to be difficult enough.

While the question of what exactly should be printed was being settled, Borrow turned his attention to the problem of type. There were only two sources of type, one set belonging to the Society, the other to Baron Schilling, whom Borrow had already come to know reasonably well. The report to Jowett on this matter was sufficiently incisive for it to be quoted verbatim. In the vaults of Sarepta House, the Bible Society's bankers,

is a chest containing Mandchou characters, belonging to the Bible Society, which I shall cause to be examined for the purpose of ascertaining whether they have sustained any injury from rust during the long time they have been lying neglected; if any of them have, my learned friend Baron Schilling, who is in possession of a small fount for the convenience of printing trifles in that tongue, has kindly promised to assist us with the use of as many of his own as may be necessary. There is one printing office here, where they are in the habit of printing with the Mongolian character, which differs but little from the Mandchou; consequently the Mongolian compositor will be competent to the task of composing in Mandchou.[43]

The Society was in luck, for the type proved to be usable, yet the accounts show that additional type had to be made at a later stage, while the availability of suitable compositors depended upon his finding a printer who would accept the undertaking at a not too exorbitant cost. This, then, was his next task.

The University Press, recommended by Schmidt, turned out to be too expensive, at least it was too expensive according to Borrow, who perhaps, though, had other reasons for preferring a smaller firm, with whom he would be able to work in a less formal way. Borrow sent Jowett both bids, rather quaintly urging that the people of his choice, 'being young beginners, and not having very much to do' were more likely to give the work their full attention. The bid from Schultz and Beneze read as follows:

In respect to the printing of the New Testament in the Mandchou language, the undersigned oblige themselves to undertake the printing of the said work. In the first place, as the Bible Society, and in particular their agent Mr. Borrow, think fit to furnish the printers with the necessary types and papers, the under-signed offer to supply the sheet consisting of four pages with composition, clean and black printing, at the rate of 25 roubles, paper currency, for a thousand copies; for two thousand copies, five additional roubles assignats, so that the same sheet, only by a greater edition, amounts to 30 roubles assignats; thirdly for 3000 copies in the above proportion, 35 roubles. Fourthly, we promise during the interval of a certain period to supply at the rate of three sheets per week.

SCHULTZ & BENEZE[44]

Jowett had little option but to accept Borrow's advice.

Borrow now had the text he would use, the type he thought would be adequate and the printer. Next he entered into a little flurry of activity to guarantee himself an adequate supply of paper, which he said had to be better than ordinary paper but not as expensive as what the Society had previously used. Here he presented himself to Jowett as a practical man of business zealous to reach a good bargain for the Society's sake; asked Jowett to authorise the renting of a room for the large amount of paper that would be required (450 Russian reams at 280 sheets a ream); requested the transfer of funds to the Society's bankers, Messrs Simondsen and Company, so that the paper could be secured by cash payment; hired a calesh, so that he could visit as many paper manufacturers as possible, in order to beat down the price; and enlisted the help of two friends, so that the work would be done as efficiently as possible. Borrow enjoyed these expeditions to Peterhof and the other unspecified places where paper was made. Spring had arrived. The skis had been taken off the carts and carriages. The ice was melting and the police had their annual duty of restraining people from their winter habit of crossing the icy Neva on foot. Like everyone else, Borrow was glad to be released from the confinements of winter. 'I must inform you', he told Jowett at the end of April, 'that I also employed two agents, and we three going various ways have ascertained that the necessary paper may be procured for between 30 and 40 roubles per ream, paper of as good a quality – nay, better than that on which the Gospel of St. Matthew was printed, and that for which 100 roubles were demanded at Peterhof.'[45] Between 28 April and the beginning of October, a period of five months, the Society heard from Borrow only once. That was towards the end of July when he sent two brief notes, one concerning the readiness of the type, the other the confirmation of a deposit that had to be paid for the paper.

In the spring of 1834 Borrow had done no more than prepare the ground for the printing of the Manchu New Testament: the manufacture of the edition only began after Borrow moved in August. He had persuaded the Bible Society to pay a year's rent in advance for the extra space needed for the storage of paper and books, acquired suitable accommodation at the Maison Pehl on Gorókhonaïa Ulitsa, and very sensibly moved there himself, together with his servant. Borrow appears not to have kept track of his own correspondence. He seems not to have written to his employers between 27 August 1833 and 20 January 1834; he then wrote spasmodically during the period of preparation, as it were; then he again ceased all communication during August and September 1834. Naturally, people wanted to know what he had been doing. Mr John Jackson sent him by hand a letter on behalf of the Society, with the implication that Borrow could not be reached by normal means, while Mr J. Tarn, the under-treasurer, asked Borrow to account for the funds he had received during his first year in St Petersburg. Jackson got nowhere. 'I am exceedingly sorry you should have had the trouble of writing to me to no purpose', was the gist of Borrow's reply.[46] Tarn received an account of Borrow's journey from London to St Petersburg, though of course not for the extra time Borrow had spent *en route*.[47] Jowett also wrote anxiously to Borrow at the beginning of October, for 'it should also be considered that the Society lives in the public estimation, not merely by the final effects which it produces, but by the knowledge of its difficulties, trials, hopes (not to say its prudent and Christian measures), as detailed in the periodical reports of its Agents and Correspondents'.[48] He needed a progress report. He wanted the assurance the work was 'accelerating'. He had to satisfy the members of the committee who had now begun to ask: 'What is Mr. Borrow doing?'

To this letter, Borrow wrote a characteristically spirited reply. Were he not a Christian, he said, he would be proud to tell the committee what he had been doing the previous two-and-a-half months. He had found the type in the bankers' vaults 'on the floor trampled amidst mud and filth', so had the type cleaned and more made. He taught the compositors the Manchu alphabet in 'a few days' but they still made so many mistakes that Borrow had to oversee the work himself: but he got round this. 'Two rude Esthonian peasants, who previously could barely compose with decency in a plain language which they spoke and were accustomed to, have received such instruction that with ease they can each compose at the rate of a sheet a day in Mandchou, perhaps the most difficult language for composition in the whole world.' The paper began to arrive, at first erratically and of uneven quality. 'Now those who reside in England, the most civilized and blessed of countries, where everything is to be obtained at a fair price, have not the slightest idea of the anxiety and difficulty which, in a country like this, harass the foreigner who has to disburse money not his own, if he wish that his employers be not shamefully and outrageously imposed upon.' Borrow seems to have forgotten the letter he wrote about paper in the spring, because he now says that he got a friend of his, Hasfeld, to introduce him to a printer, Mr Pluchard, who in effect guaranteed

Borrow a supply of paper at the trade rate of 25 roubles per ream. But this arrangement had been satisfactory only in part: Borrow needed a supply of paper that arrived with sufficient regularity for the compositors to be steadily employed. He therefore arranged for an alternative supply through the good offices of his friend, Baron Schilling, who spoke to one of his own friends, State-Councillor Alquin, who owned a paper factory. The printing had begun. Everything was in control. Borrow had been reduced to a skeleton, he said, was working up to thirteen hours a day but was resolved 'to do or die'. Would the committee have preferred complaints? Would a detailed account of the difficulties he had had to overcome have been 'a communication more suited to the public?' Should he have returned to England when he found that, instead of assisting Lipotsev, he himself had to assume responsibility for the entire enterprise? His letters to his private friends 'have always been written during gleams of sunshine, and traced in the characters of hope'. Should he have written 'distressing and perplexing letters' to the committee, instead of slaving away in 90 degrees of heat, sparing neither himself nor his money, and indeed using the latter to bribe people to work 'whom nothing but bribes would induce to do so?' 'Commend me to our most respected committee', he says towards the end of the letter. 'Assure them that in whatever I have done or left undone, I have been influenced by a desire to promote the glory of the Trinity and to give my employers ultimate and permanent satisfaction.'[49]

This is indeed a fine letter, one of the best that Borrow ever wrote, very rhetorical, very assured in tone, and, as Herbert Jenkins said, very impressive in its simple manliness and restrained dignity. Though it does not tell us how Borrow really spent August and September 1834, or where he was, it certainly had its effect. The committee was impressed, wanted to reimburse Borrow for his expenses (even the bribes) and thought that the small amount of pother was justified for its having given rise to such a full account of the work of one of its agents in the field. The letter was circulated. The Rev. Francis Cunningham saw a copy. So did Mrs Clarke at Oulton Hall. It was referred to at Bible meetings. Though the letter was about the labour of manufacturing a book, it was received as the witness to Christian vocational work abroad, and as such had an impact upon Borrow's future that went far beyond his period in Russia, as will be seen.

This letter was followed by a second, dated 13 October, in which Borrow concluded his account of work in progress, at the same time giving some small indication of how he himself thought about it. He sends a testimonial written by Lipotsev about himself, yet cannot manage more than a few hurried lines because he is busy with proofs and begrudges 'every moment that is not devoted to my Maker or to my great undertaking'.[50] He had settled the business of how the books would be bound: Baron Schilling's binder had been persuaded to do the work. He promised that the complete New Testament would have been printed and bound by the following May. But he was too busy to write, so they might not hear from him again until Christmas.

Meanwhile, though he knew that he was being pressed by the Society to give a convincing account of himself, there were two matters on his mind that he felt obliged to write about. The committee was perhaps not aware that there were upwards of 3,000 Tartars in St Petersburg, most of whom could read and write the Turkish dialect that they spoke, though 'not one Testament is at hand suited to their understandings'.[51] Borrow said he had formed many acquaintances among these singular people.

Notwithstanding the superstition and fanaticism of these men, I am much attached to them; for their conscientiousness, honesty and fidelity are beyond all praise. They stand in strong contrast to the lower orders of the Russians, a good-natured, lowly, vicious, wavering race, easily excited, easily soothed; whilst the former are sedate, sober, temperate beings, with minds like Egyptian granite, from which it is no easy matter to efface an impression once made.

It was typical of Borrow that he should so readily identify with the migrant *khality* who lived in Grafsky Lane and thereabouts; the fact of ethnic community, not just the idea of it, fascinated him throughout his life. Perhaps, too, he was giving the Bible Society a strong hint about a future area of activity for himself.

But the other matter was as important to him. Borrow had a strong sense of the futility of his own daily work, or at least of the likelihood of that work being wasted unless the Bibles he was manufacturing could be distributed. 'If you wish for readers you must seek them among the masters of Pekin and the fierce hordes of desert Tartary; but what means do you have for introducing them to Tartary or Pekin?' The Bible Society's only recourse, he said once again, was for George Borrow to be sent to Kiatchka. How else achieve the conversion of the Tartar hordes!

Inevitably, the first half of 1835 had to be devoted to the manufacture of the remaining volumes, Borrow being kept steadily busy with the daily chores of composing and proof-reading. Minor emergencies became a commonplace of existence. When one of the compositors fell ill, he actually succeeded in finding another, a man who had worked for the Bible Society ten years earlier. When Lipotsev, in his capacity as censor, objected to something in proof, Borrow would argue the point but often patiently reprint. When he miscalculated the amount of paper needed, off would go a letter to Mr Tarn, the under-treasurer, justifying the additional expenditures. To this, in the spring, was added responsibility for supervising the binding, which was done volume by volume by Baron Schilling's binder. Borrow was therefore extremely busy, heavily engaged in a task that many would have found quite beyond their powers. He was also restless, cramped in mind by the Russian winter and by his own anomalous position.

Throughout the winter, he had continued to work at his translations, including a few extraordinary new ventures. One of these involved the proposal to the Prayer Book and Homily Society that he should trans-late three homilies into Russian and the second homily (St Luke) into Manchu. He was actually authorised, by the secretary of the Society, C. R. Pritchett, to spend £12 on an edition of 500 copies of the second homily, though Pritchett stipulated as a condition that the translation should be checked for accuracy – 'especially that Dr. Morrison of Canton should be requested to submit copies to the inspection of Manchu scholars as he shall see fit' – and that 'the plan of submitting copies in letters of gold to the inspection of the highest personages in China should probably be deferred'.[52] These translations, however, have not been traced, so Borrow must have abandoned the scheme.

Another new venture was translation from Russian and yet another, translation from Turkish. His Russian translations, no doubt mostly the work of the winter of 1834–5, will be discussed as a group at the end of this chapter; they are important as an early serious engagement with Russian literature by an English writer, albeit a writer whose interests were ideologically restricted, not representative. As to his translations from Turkish, it seems likely that his version of *The Pleasantries of the Incredible Mulla Nasrudin*[53] must date from this period, though admittedly the evidence is conjectural. It has already been mentioned that Borrow had probably been in Turkey before going to Russia. He was to go again in 1844, after publishing *The Bible in Spain* and in the middle of writing *Lavengro*. But if he had translated this book before 1832, he would probably have mentioned the fact, while it remains difficult to know where in England he would have obtained a copy of it. On balance, therefore, it seems reasonable to keep in mind the possibility that all his Turkish translations were made during the long Russian nights, while his mind filled once again with plans for further travels, particularly along the routes so long ago followed by the Vikings.

It was not only with plans for further travel that his mind was filled. He received a letter from a Mrs Ropes, in England, and in reply said that her letter was 'a great comfort in this cold, strange city', that he had been 'unwell and much occupied' and that his mind was in 'a very dark and melancholy state'. To Mrs Ropes, at least, he was prepared to say that his unhappiness could be 'attributed to my having been early cast upon the world with no-one to cheer or counsel me: I am confident that most of my errors may be traced to that cause'; and also that, he hopes, 'God will give me the desire to seek him, which, we are told, is the finding of him.'[54] During Borrow's last Russian winter, God did not oblige. Even when fully occupied, Borrow was lonely and sick at heart, literally not knowing what to do with himself and impatient for the more active life for which he seemed suited. The fluency and vigour of *The Bible in Spain* show, if this needs to be shown, that Borrow was to the highest degree articulate, yet *The Bible in Spain* was published in 1842, and in 1835, in St Petersburg, Borrow's loneliness and frustration were exacerbated by his not having a language to express his emotions, his psychological needs, his thoughts about himself. He did not continue to describe his mental state in terms of an alienation from God because he believed in God but because that was the only language available for describing his emotions at all. Like other Victorians, Borrow referred to emotional, sexual, psychological, essentially private matters in religious phraseology – of necessity; or at least apparently of necessity, for when he came to write *Lavengro*, Borrow discovered that this strategy was not after all adequate for him. In 1835, however, the harsh experience of *Lavengro* could not be anticipated, so Borrow simply had to struggle on as best he could.

Life in St Petersburg was in any case not all struggle. He made many friends in Russia, male friends, chief among whom was John Hasfeld, a Dane who worked at the Danish legation or was associated with it in some way. Hasfeld met Borrow in the latter's first lodgings on Galernoy Ulitza, as he recalled years later when the house was pulled down to permit construction of a bridge. They had in common, first and foremost, a real love of Danish literature. They spent many hours talking about languages and books. They, together, made other friends, something that Borrow, the solitary, seldom did. The extent to which they shared their time in St Petersburg is indicated by Borrow's not reacting against Hasfeld when he recalled the details of the days when they first met: Borrow's singing so much, their reading *Till's Owl Glass* together, Borrow's pike soup.

Do you remember the time when you lived on that dish for more than six weeks, and came near exterminating the whole breed? And the pudding that accompanied it, that always lay hard as a stone on the stomach? This you surely have not forgotten. Yes, your kitchen was delicately manipulated by Mahmoud, your Tartar servant, who only needed to give you horse-meat to have merited a diploma.[55]

When Borrow was ill during his first autumn in St Petersburg with a fever followed by a violent attack of the 'horrors' – 'I had never had it so bad as then' – Hasfeld nursed him back to health, this beginning in a solid, practical way one of the few genuinely deep friendships of Borrow's life, a friendship later sustained not only by Hasfeld's helping Borrow with his Bible Society work, but also by Borrow's writing to Hasfeld from Spain and by his inviting him to visit England, which he did. There seems no way of determining whether Hasfeld accompanied Borrow on his expeditions, for example to Novgorod and Moscow, though it is difficult to suppose that he did not. It is equally difficult to suppose that, given Borrow's lifelong interest, they were never together in Denmark. (In August 1834 perhaps?) When Borrow left Russia, Hasfeld gave him as a parting gift an ancient coin, a Jewish shekel. Did he keep it with him, Hasfeld later wondered? 'Do you ask whether I retain your parting gift?' replied Borrow.

Why at this moment I hold it clenched in my left hand, and many times in the sandy plains of La Mancha and Castille, among the olive and orange groves of Andalusia, amidst the wild mountains of the Asturias, and the dusky thickets of the ever verdant Galicia, I have gazed upon it, till tears blinded my eyes, as it reminded me of happier times and a better land.[56]

While it is no part of the purpose of the present book to denigrate the work of the previous biographers, who must have believed that they were circumscribed by contemporary standards, there are times, too many of them maybe, when it is difficult to retain one's composure. In this instance Professor Knapp paused at volume 1, p. 217, to write the stunning sentence: 'I must here pause at the dawn of a new year – 1835.' He then said: 'The Russian autograph letters in my possession, running from July 5th 1833, to September 9th, 1835, number forty-nine.' From this total he treats his reader to extracts from thirteen, some of which were letters addressed to him. He then says he will 'make a few extracts from Hasfedt's [sic] Danish letters to Borrow', meaning letters Hasfeld wrote after Borrow left St Petersburg. There are eight such abstracts. Although Knapp said that he gave the papers he used for his *Life, Writings and Correspondence of George Borrow* to the Library of the Hispanic Society in New York, they are not there now. Since he threatened to destroy documents that were not consistent with the view of Borrow he wished to present, it may be reasonably supposed that he did so in this case. Equally, since some of the letters between Borrow and Hasfeld that have turned up in St Petersburg concern subjects like Hasfeld's womanising and visits to brothels, it may be assumed that at least some of the letters Knapp suppressed related more to the private lives of the two friends than to Borrow's work of the Bible Society. In other words, Knapp deliberately placed himself between his reader and Borrow's day-to-day life by destroying the record of it. While this must mean that Borrow did not lead the sort of life of which Herbert Jenkins, for example, would have approved, in as far as Jenkins thought of Borrow as the perfect missionary, it is extremely frustrating to know that Borrow and Hasfeld were close friends and yet not know how they spent their time together, how they amused themselves, what they read, where they went at the weekend, and so on, and, of course, not least what they said to each other about Borrow's work. This is just one example of many. Taken together they mean that only by painstaking research over the years will it be possible to put together a more detailed picture of Borrow's daily life. Meanwhile at least we know that it was with John Hasfeld that he got to know people like Nikolai Gretch, the grammarian, so that his life was not quite as melancholy as he reported it was in letters to people like Mrs Ropes in England.

By 20 June, the printing of the eight volumes was finished and, while the remaining two volumes were being bound, Borrow went to Moscow. Characteristically, Borrow included a brief account of his Moscow visit in his final report to the Bible Society, an account that is here reproduced *verbatim*, because it is the only record that has survived of that particular expedition.

At the termination of my editorial task, having little to employ myself upon whilst the two last volumes were undergoing the process of binding, I determined upon a journey to Moscow, the ancient capital of the Russian Empire, which differs widely from St. Petersburg in appearance, structure, and in the manners, habits, and opinions of its inhabitants. I arrived there after a journey of four days. Moscow is by far the most remarkable city it has ever been my fortune to see: but as it has been frequently described, and with tolerable correctness, there is no necessity for me to enter into a particular account of all that presented itself to my observation. I ascended the celebrated tower of Ivan Veliké, situated within the walls of the Kremlin, from the top of which there is a glorious view of Moscow and of the surrounding country, and at the foot of which, in a deep hole in the earth, is the gigantic bell which weighs 27,000 poods, or eight hundred and seventy thousand pounds. I likewise visited the splendid church of the Kremlin, and had much conversation with the priest who is in the habit of showing its curiosities to strangers. He is a most intelligent and seemingly truly pious person, and well acquainted with English spiritual literature, especially with the writings of Bishops Taylor and Tillotson, whom he professed to hold in great admiration; though he asserted that both these divines, great men as they undoubtedly were, were far inferior writers to his own celebrated countryman Archbishop Teekon, and their productions less replete with spiritual manna – against which assertion I felt little inclined to urge any objection, having myself perused the works of the great Russian divine with much comfort and satisfaction, and with which I can only regret [that] the devout part of the British public are up to the present moment utterly unacquainted.

As one of the principal motives of my visit to Moscow was to hold communication with a particular part of its population, which from the accounts I had received of it had inspired me with the most vivid interest, I did not fail shortly after my arrival to seek an opportunity of accomplishing my work, and believe that what I have now to communicate will be of some interest to the Christian and the philosopher. I allude to the people called Zigani or Gypsies, or, as they style themselves, Rommany, of which there are several thousands in and about Moscow, and who obtain a livelihood by various means. Those who have been accustomed to consider these people as wandering barbarians, incapable of civilization and unable to appreciate the blessings of a quiet and settled life, will be surprised at learning that many of those in Moscow inhabit large and handsome houses, appear abroad in elegant equipages, and if distinguishable from the genteel class of the Russians [are] only so by superior personal advantages and mental accomplishments. Of this singular phenomenon at Moscow the female Gypsies are the principal cause, having from time immemorial cultivated their vocal powers to such an extent that, although in the heart of a country in which the vocal art has arrived at greater perfection than in any other part of the world, the principal Gypsy choirs in Moscow are allowed by the general voice of the public to be unrivalled and to bear away the palm from all competitors. It is a fact notorious in Russia that the celebrated Catalani was so filled with admiration for the powers of voice displayed by one of the Gypsy songsters, who, after the former had sung before a splendid audience in Moscow, stepped forward and with an astonishing burst of melody ravished every ear, that she tore from her own shoulders a shawl of immense value which had been presented to her by the Pope, and embracing the Gypsy compelled her to accept it, saying that it had been originally intended for the matchless singer which she now discovered was not herself. The sums obtained by these performers are very large, enabling them to live in luxury of every description and to maintain their husbands in a princely way. Many of them are married to Russian gentlemen; and every one who has resided for any length of time in Russia cannot but be aware that the lovely, talented, and domesticated wife of Count Alexander Tolstoi is by birth a Gypsy, and was formerly one of the ornaments of a Rommany choir at Moscow as she is now one of the principal ornaments of the marriage state and of illustrious life. It is not, however, to be supposed that all the female Gypsies in Moscow are of this high, talented, and respectable order; amongst them are a great number of low, vulgar, and profligate females who sing in taverns, or at the various gardens in the neighbourhood, and whose husbands and male connections subsist by horse-jobbing and such kinds of low traffic. The principal place of resort of this class is Marina Rotche, lying two versts from Moscow, and thither I drove, attended by a valet-de-place. Upon my arriving there the Gypsies swarmed out from their tents and from the little tracteer or tavern, and surrounded me. Standing on the seat of the calèche, I addressed them in a loud voice in the dialect of the English Gypsies, with which I have some slight acquaintance. A scream of wonder instantly arose, and welcomes and greetings were poured forth in torrents of musical Rommany, amongst which, however, the most pronounced cry was: ah kak mi toute karmuma – 'Oh, how we love you,' for at first they supposed me to be one of their brothers, who, they said, were wandering about in Turkey, China, and other parts, and that I had come over the great pawnee, or water, to visit them. Their countenances exactly resembled those of their race in England and Spain, brown, and for the most part beautiful, their eyes fiery and wildly intelligent, their hair coal-black and somewhat coarse. I asked them numerous questions, especially as to their religion and original country. They said that they believed in 'Devil' which, singularly enough, in their language signifies God, and that they were afraid of the evil spirit, or 'Bengel'; that their fathers came from Rommany land, but where that land lay they knew not. They sang many songs both in the Russian and Rommany languages; the former were modern popular pieces which are in vogue on the stage, but the latter were evidently very ancient, being composed in a metre or cadence to which there is nothing analogous in Russian prosody, and exhibiting an internal character which was anything but European or modern. I visited this place several times during my sojourn at Moscow, and spoke to them upon their sinful manner of living, upon the advent and suffering of Christ Jesus, and expressed, upon my taking a final leave of them, a hope that they would be in a short period furnished with the word of eternal life in their own language, which they seemed to value and esteem much higher than the Russian. They invariably listened with much attention, and during the whole time I was amongst them exhibited little in speech or conduct which was objectionable.[57]

A few words must now be said about Borrow's interest in Russian literature, an interest that was made manifest in a number of publications, both in St Petersburg and later in England. Lady Eastlake was to dismiss St Petersburg as a city in which nothing of literary or intellectual significance was likely to occur. 'Here, it is absolute *mauvais genre* to discuss a rational subject – mere *pédanterie* to be caught upon any topics beyond dressing, dancing and a *jolie tournure*. The superficial accomplishments are so superficialized as scarcely to be considered to exist – Russia has no literature, or rather none to attract a frivolous woman; and political subjects ... exist not.'[58] What she called her reluctant conclusion was that 'Russia is the country where the learned man wastes his time, the patriot breaks his heart, and the rogue prospers.'[59] Part of the problem, of course, was the distraction of cosmopolitan taste: the cultural languages were (for many people) French, German and English, not, to any significant extent, Russian. Glanville noted that the 'official' cultural journal was the *Journal de St. Petersbourg, Politique et Littéraire*, which appeared three times a week. 'This paper, written in the purest French, frequently contains articles of great interest on literature, the fine arts, and some judicious remarks on theatricals.'[60] In the same way, university lectures were for many years given only in German. In as far as the French, German and English communities had been in the ascendant in St Petersburg for a hundred years or so, while the ruling class of Russians found it convenient and politic to speak a language that differentiated them from their compatriots, demotic literature – and the indigenous arts in general – were by that measure retarded. Impossible to imagine George Borrow having any sympathy with a genteel cosmopolitan literary awareness, least of all one which reinforced an unacceptable political system. His sympathy would obviously be for folk literature and, to the extent to which he could get to know it, the literature of the Russian peoples themselves.

This natural sympathy, which had already been expressed in Borrow's work on Scandinavian and Norse literature, was in St Petersburg stimulated by Nikolai Ivanovitch Gretch and his son Alexis, both of whom became good friends and strong admirers of Borrow. Nikolai, a scholar of the Russian language, was Imperial Librarian and the author of an important Russian grammar. Glanville had remarked on Gretch's key position as an advocate of things in some sense Russian, saying: 'An instance of the earnest desire existing in the highest quarters . . . to improve, and also to render more familiar the use of their native language, may be found in the encouragement given to Professor Greitsch.' His son, Alexis, was editor of the *Severnaya pchela* (*The Northern Bee*), a journal that later published several favourable notices of Borrow and his work. According to Academician M. P. Alekseyev, there is little evidence to show that Borrow got to know very many writers but he was welcomed by the Gretchs, whose 'salon' he attended fairly frequently. The later correspondence between Borrow and his Danish friend, Hasfeld, shows that they both knew Nikolai extremely well (in old age Hasfeld married his daughter), so in all likelihood this friendship was the means by which Borrow became acquainted with Russian literature.

A. G. Cross has pointed out that Borrow's translations from the Russian 'present a remarkable ideological' unity.[61] Borrow himself said:

That the character of a nation is best distinguishable by the general tone of its poetry has been frequently remarked and is a truth which does not admit of controversy...In most instances the writer in the selection of pieces of this little work has been guided by a desire of exhibiting what is most characteristic of the people to whose literature it belongs.[62]

Cross puts it in this way:

In *The Zincali* he reiterated this view in connexion with the songs of the Russian gypsies, believing that 'a collection of these songs, with a translation and vocabulary, would be no slight accession to literature, and would probably throw more light on the history of this race than anything which has yet appeared' (I, 10). This approach to poetry, so characteristic of the post-Herder generation, determines Borrow's selection of poems – and prose; his translations from Russian, published in his lifetime or left in manuscript, present a remarkable 'ideological' unity. He deliberately avoids all poetry which lacks local colour or elements of folk or tribal psychology. Thus, his Pushkin is not the Pushkin of aristocratic Petersburg, of high society or salon culture with its sacrifice of the national for the general; his Pushkin is the author of 'Chornaya Shal', Zemfira's song from *Tsygany*, 'Rusalka' ('The Mermaid') and 'Talisman'. Translations of the first two poems appeared in *Targum*, together with a poem on the Cossacks by Boris Fyodorov and an ancient ballad entitled 'The Cossack', translated from Ukrainian; the other two poems were published with translations of an old Russian song, a Ukrainian ballad and Mickiewicz's 'The Renegade'. In addition Borrow left the first draft of a complete translation of *Tsygany* and translated extracts from *Ruslan i Lyudmila*. They manifest Borrow's instinctive sympathy for free, nomadic peoples, his 'philo-Bohemianism', as Sutherland Edwards put it, his romantic love of the exotic East and his reverence for folk-song and folk-lore; they are poems full of colour and drama, magic and passion. But for all that, although they are in the main translations from Russian, they are a strange misrepresentation of Russia and of her poet, Pushkin. Only of 'Rusalka' and the prologue to *Ruslan* may we say 'Tam Rus'gu pakhnet'; elsewhere it is the Southern Pushkin in evidence, the Russian equivalent of Hugo of *Les Orientales*. Both 'Chornaya shal' and Zemfira's song are based on Moldavian, not Russian folk songs, and their enormous success both in Russia and abroad is attributable to their Romantic character rather than to their 'Russianness'.[63]

This opinion, representing as it does the most extended attempt yet to assess Borrow's attitude to Russian literature as he knew it, obviously deserves discussion, since 'Russianness' is such a vague concept, while Borrow's preference for the non-metropolitan may preserve his place with the angels. As to the facts, there are essentially three groups of translations, those published in St Petersburg, those published in England at a much later date, and those that remained unpublished at Borrow's death.

In St Petersburg, Borrow had printed two small books, both issued in an edition of 100 copies from the printing house of Schultz and Beneze, where the Manchu Bible had also been printed. The first of these was *Targum. Or Metrical Translations from Thirty Languages and Dialects*, which, according to a note in Borrow's handwriting which Knapp pasted into Mrs Borrow's copy, now in the Library of the Hispanic Society, was approved for publication by the Russian censor on the 23 April 1835, printed by 31 May and sewn (but not bound) by 21 June, perhaps just a few days before Borrow left for Moscow. It seems probable, although no precise record has survived, that not only *Targum* but all the Russian translations were made before this date. This means in effect that they were done during 1834, when Borrow was coming to have a better sense of the language but before the final heavy spell of work on the Manchu Bible. Borrow's second publication in St Petersburg was a little chapbook of just fourteen pages called *The Talisman. From the Russian of Alexander Pushkin, With Other*

Pieces, which was also published in 1835. Borrow never met Pushkin, but left copies of both *Targum* and *The Talisman* for Hasfeld to present to him on Borrow's behalf. Pushkin acknowledged this gift by adding a note to one of Hasfeld's letters to Borrow: 'Alexander Pushkin has received with profound gratitude Mr. Borrow's books and sincerely regrets that he had not the honour to be personally acquainted with him.'[64]

Borrow later published three Russian folk tales, which he had translated in 1834, reworked in the late 1850s and presumably intended for the volume announced as forthcoming in the advertisements included in the first edition of *The Romany Rye*. *Emelian the Fool* was the first of three Russian tales to be published by Borrow in 1862 in the magazine *Once a Week*. It was followed by the *Story of Tim* and *The Story of Yvashka with the Bear's Ear*.[65] In 1913 Thomas J. Wise published variants of the three tales in small private editions. From an analysis of the two sets of manuscripts, Wise established that his manuscripts represented the original translations prepared by Borrow during his stay in St Petersburg. As Cross pointed out, the 1862 versions of the Russian folk tales reveal Borrow's careful stylistic revision and are markedly superior; it is regrettable that the earlier versions, rejected by Borrow, were nonetheless included in the Norwich edition of his work. Borrow claimed of *Emelian the Fool* that 'from whatever source the *Story of Emelian* may have sprung, the manner in which it is wrought is essentially Russian, and from it, as here rendered, the English reader may form a better idea of the way of life, and the feelings of the Russian mujiks, or peasantry, than from a dozen books of travel in Russia'. Borrow did not succeed in getting these stories published in book form during his lifetime. His democratic tendencies made him more interested in the Russian peasant than in the upper classes, though back in England his assessment was to be a cautious one. When he wrote in 1862 of the Russian peasant he referred to his 'love of warmth and hatred of exertion, though when he chooses to get up and rouse himself, he is capable of very great things, can outwit the tchort himself, bear hunger and fatigue better than any man, and contend even with the Briton at the game of the bayonet'.[66]

By the end of July, Borrow was able to tell the Bible Society that the New Testament was on its way to London. 'I herewith send you a bill of lading for six of the eight parts of the New Testament, which I have at last obtained permission to send away, *having paid sixteen visits to the House of Interior Affairs*.'[67] Red tape absurdly delayed the despatch of the remaining two volumes, but eventually, at the beginning of August, they too were shipped off. As far as one can tell, the Bible

Society was pleased with Borrow's work in Russia, for in its official report for 1835 it was noted that 'Mr. G. Borrow . . . has in every way afforded satisfaction to the Committee', 'while the devoted diligence with which he has laboured, and the skill he has shown in surmounting difficulties, and in conducting his negotiations for the advantage of the Society, justly entitle him to this public acknowledgement of his services'.[68] As for the edition itself, Hasfeld appropriately called it 'a beautiful edition of an oriental work – that is printed with great care on a fine imitation of Chinese paper, made on purpose'.[69] The whole operation had cost the Society £2,600, so it was fortunate that they were able to dispose of one or two copies before realising that other strategies would have to be adopted were the Far East to see the Light. Borrow himself returned to England in mid-September, stayed in London until he had written his report and then travelled on to Norwich, having been away for just over two years.

The first visit to Spain:
November 1835–September 1836

After travelling for another full day over the rocky, trackless country-side, Borrow at nightfall came with his guide to a small village of about six or eight black huts and in one of these *Chozas* had bacon and eggs by the family hearth, then 'lay down on the boards' of the hayloft, watched 'the gleams of the fire through the interstices of the floor', listened to the murmur of voices, 'dozed, started, dozed again', and dropped into a profound sleep from which he was only roused 'by the crowing of the second cock'.[1] The next day was one of the most important of his life.

For several weeks he had been travelling by horse, mule and on foot, over extremely difficult terrain, towards the north-west extremity of Spain, whose 'savage coast' he had already seen at close quarters when the ship on which he had travelled from England was almost wrecked. 'Yes', he exclaims, 'this is indeed Spain – stern, flinty Spain – land emblematic of those spirits to which she has given birth.' Two years had passed since Borrow's imagination had been stirred by the first sight of this savage coast, which now he was within an ace of reaching overland. It was 'a beautiful autumnal morning' when he and his guide set out again. Borrow was impatient. After walking at 'a rapid pace along rough bridleways and footpaths, admidst furze and brush-wood', they took directions from a shepherd boy, turned north-west, and quickly reached a rise of land, from which point there was suddenly a view of a 'long and irregular line of lofty and precipitous coast'. Borrow says of this moment that he had 'arrived at such a place as in my boyhood I had pictured to myself as the termination of the world, beyond which there was a wild sea, or abyss, or chaos'. Filled with excitement at having reached the end of the world, he cries out disarmingly:

Such is the grave, and such are its terrific sides; those moors and wilds, over which I have passed, are the rough and dreary journey of life. Cheered with hope, we struggle along through all the difficulties of moor, bog, and mountain, to arrive at – what? The grave and its dreary sides. Oh, may hope not desert us in the last hour – hope in the Redeemer and in God!

Whatever the connection between these pious thoughts and his boyhood dreams, Borrow pressed on, descended the hill, 'again lost sight of the sea amidst ravines and dingles, amongst which patches of pine were occasionally seen', came to a village on the side of an inlet, took fresh directions from a drunkard in a bar, and 'striking across a sandy peninsula at the back of the town, soon reached the shore of an immense bay, the north-westernmost end of which was formed by the far-famed cape of Finisterre, which we now saw before us stretching far into the sea'. The day was perfect, the sea calm, and as they walked along the beach towards the famous headland 'the waves which broke upon the shore were so tiny as scarcely to produce a murmur'. Borrow's response to the place was characteristically intense, passionate and direct. He 'sped along the deep winding bay'. His mind as he walked filled with 'strange recollections'. It was on this very beach that,

according to the tradition of all ancient Christendom, Saint James, the Patron Saint of Spain, preached the Gospel to the heathen Spaniards. Upon this beach had once stood an immense commercial city, the proudest of all Spain. This now desolate bay had once resounded with the voices of myriads, when the keels and commerce of all the then known world were wafted to Duyo.

But the ancient city of Duyo, when Borrow reached it, had been reduced to five or six 'ruined houses'. The experience struck to the heart of his being, for nothing more moved him than the reality of a vast historical perspective in which past cultures were recollected, not as history-book generalisation, but as sets of individuals in particular places doing particular, sometimes even heroic, deeds. It was to renew this sense of the past transcending the present that he had travelled so far.

They walked on. The journey had exhausted Borrow. Dysentery, too, had severely weakened him. Now he found the going difficult under the midday sun. 'My boots were torn, my feet cut, and the perspiration streamed from my brow.' Though the guide seemed unaffected by the heat, Borrow reeled and staggered, felt faint and, less than halfway up the ascent from the beach to the headland, had to be carried to the shade of a crude boundary wall, where the guide revived him by fanning him 'with great assiduity' with his enormous hat. After a long rest, Borrow struggled to the top and at length stood 'at a great altitude between two bays, the wilderness of waters before us'. One of his most deeply rooted ambitions had at last been achieved, as though to fulfil himself in his own terms he needed this solitary experience in a brutally harsh, exceptionally remote place. He stayed on the headland for about an hour.

Of all the ten thousand barks which annually plough those seas in sight of that old cape, not one was to be descried. It was a blue shiny waste, broken by no object save the black head of a *spermaceti* whale, which would occasionally show itself at the top, casting up thin jets of brine. The principal bay, that of Finisterre, as far as the entrance, was beautifully variegated by an immense shoal of *sardinhas*, on whose extreme skirts the monster was probably feasting. From the other side of the cape, we looked down upon a smaller bay, the shore of which was overhung by rocks of various and grotesque shapes,

a notoriously fearful place in bad weather, says Borrow,

when the long swell of the Atlantic pouring in is broken into surf and foam by the sunken rocks with which it abounds.

When in the extravagant language of his youth, the language of Romanticism, he says that 'on all sides there was grandeur and sublimity', he means that he was profoundly moved by the experience and by the exceptional beauty of the scene. But when they walked down to the nearest village, Borrow quickly found a house in which to stay, had a simple meal and flung himself onto 'a rude and dirty bed' where, exhausted, he fell asleep.

Borrow's own account of this important day is so graphic that it would be pointless to try to improve upon it. 'I was soon asleep', he says,

but my slumbers were by no means tranquil. I thought I was surrounded by difficulties of various kinds, amongst rocks and ravines, vainly endeavouring to extricate myself; uncouth visages showed themselves amidst the trees and in the hollows, thrusting out cloven tongues, and uttering angry cries. I looked around for my guide, but could not find him; methought, however, that I heard his voice down a deep dingle. He appeared to be talking of me. How long I might have continued in these wild dreams I know not. I was suddenly, however, seized roughly by the shoulder, and nearly dragged from the bed. I looked up in amazement, and by the light of the descending sun I beheld hanging over me a wild and uncouth figure; it was that of an elderly man, built as strong as a giant, with much beard and whisker, and huge bushy eyebrows, dressed in the habiliments of a fisherman; in his hand was a rusty musket.

Borrow was under arrest. Pulled violently from his bed and into the street, he was marched through an excited and 'vociferating' crowd of villagers, and pushed into the presence of the *alcalde* or local magistrate, under suspicion of being none other than Don Carlos, the Pretender, himself. 'I was aware, for the first time', he says, 'that I had indeed committed a great imprudence in coming to this wild place, and among these barbarous people, without being able to assign any motive which could appear valid in their eyes.'

So it happened that on this hazardous journey, at more or less the furthest point from his base in Madrid, Borrow found himself hustled

into a long, low store-room in the house of the *alcalde*, where a committee of villagers awaited him, while his guide, who had been arrested
too, stood to one side guarded by 'two stout fishermen . . . one with a
musket and the other with a boat hook'. His appearance on this expedition into the wilds was, as he himself on another occasion
acknowledged, by no means calculated to instil confidence. On his head,
he wore an old Andalusian hat which, 'from its condition, appeared
to have been trodden underfoot'. His 'nether garments' were 'by no
means of the finest description' and were covered with mud. He had a
beard of several weeks' growth.[2] And he had left Madrid with both his
'trusty cloak', which 'had perhaps served a dozen generations', and
the 'excellent fur *shoob*' that he had brought with him from Russia; so
that evening as the sun went down he might have been wearing either,
or both.

The magistrate had never before interrogated such an unusual
character. Could he prove that he was not Don Carlos or 'Don Calros',
as his questioner put it? Yes, he had a passport. But the passport was
in a foreign language – French? Yes, he was an English visitor, come
to see Finisterre. Was his hunchback guide, Sebastian, not in fact the
hunchback nephew of Don Carlos, the *Infante* Don Sebastian? No.
Don Sebastian and Borrow's servant might both be hunchbacks but
obviously Borrow himself did not look like a Spaniard and in any case
was nearly a foot taller than the Pretender. 'That makes no difference',
said the *alcalde*. 'You of course carry many waiscoats about you, by
means of which you disguise yourself, and appear tall or low according
to your pleasure.' Even if the two were not the Pretender and his
nephew, they must obviously be Carlist spies and therefore should be
shot. Immediately. The guard at the door demurred, said that he knew
an Englishman when he saw one, having sailed in English ships, eaten
English biscuits, and stood by Nelson when he was killed. This was
an Englishman and should not be shot. The *alcalde* became violently
incensed. 'He is no more an Englishman than yourself', he exclaimed;

If he were an Englishman would he have come in this manner, skulking across
the land? Not so, I trow. He would have come in a ship, recommended to some
of us, or to the Catalans. He would have come to trade – to buy; but nobody
knows him in Finisterre, nor does he know anybody, and the first thing,
moreover, that he does when he reaches this place is to inspect the fort, and to
ascend the mountain, where, no doubt, he has been marking out a camp.
What brings him to Finisterre, if he is neither Calros nor a *bribon* of a
faccioso?

Particularly telling in the mind of the magistrate was the obvious truth
that no one in his right mind would climb the mountain merely for the

sake of doing so; he had lived in Finisterre for forty years without ever having found it necessary to put himself to so much trouble. He therefore stuck to his idea that, whatever Borrow was up to, he should be shot for it.

From what was fast becoming an extremely disagreeable, even dangerous, situation, Borrow was rescued by the presence of mind of his guide who explained to everyone present that 'the English have more money than they know what to do with, and on that account they wander all over the world, paying dearly for what no other people care a groat for'. In any case, he could prove that Borrow was speaking the truth by conversing with him in English. This he proceeded to do, without revealing to his captors that the only English words he knew were 'knife' and 'fork'. Sufficient doubt was introduced into the minds of the locals by this strategy for them to resolve to send Borrow on to the head magistrate at Corcuvion, provided he would bear the cost of the escort but they baulked at letting go the guide, who obviously was not English.

'And now, fellow, who are you, and what is your master?'
Guide: 'I am Sebastianillo, a poor broken mariner of Padron, and my master for the present is the gentleman whom you see, the most valiant and wealthy of all the English. He has two ships at Vigo laden with riches. I told you so when you first seized me up there in our *posada*.'
Alcalde: 'Where is your passport?'
Guide: 'I have no passport. Who would think of bringing a passport to such a place as this, where I don't suppose there are two individuals who can read? I have no passport; my master's passport of course includes me.'
Alcalde: 'It does not. And since you have no passport, and have confessed that your name is Sebastian, you shall be shot. Antonio de la Trava, do you and the musketeers lead this Sebastianillo forth, and shoot him before the door.'

Now it was Borrow's turn to intervene. In his characteristically cool manner, he said that 'if they shot the guide, they must shoot me too', for it would be a singular cruelty and barbarity to take away the life of 'a poor unfortunate fellow who, as might be seen at the first glance, was only half-witted'. So the Antonio de la Trava who was to have been executioner became the escort to take not Borrow alone but Borrow with his guide, back along the beach to Corcuvion, with such halts to permit him to swallow 'pan after pan of wine' at Borrow's expense that it was well after dark when they arrived at the house of the *alcalde mayor*.

Here Borrow was in luck. The official was a liberal, newly arrived from Madrid. Not only that, but he prided himself on being educated, being familiar with the works of 'the most universal genius', Jeremy Bentham.

Myself: 'You doubtless, sir, possess the English language.'
Alcalde: 'I do. I mean that part of it which is contained in the writings of Baintham. I am most truly glad to see a countryman of his in these Gothic wildernesses. I understand and appreciate your motives for visiting them: excuse the incivility and rudeness which you have experienced. But we will endeavour to make you reparation. You are at this moment free – but it is late; I must find you a lodging for the night. I know one close by which will just suit you. Let us repair thither this moment. Stay. I think I see a book in your hand.'
Myself: 'The New Testament.'
Alcalde: 'What book is that?'
Myself: 'A portion of the sacred writings, the Bible.'
Alcalde: 'Why do you carry such a book with you?'
Myself: 'One of my principal motives in visiting Finisterre was to carry this book to that wild place.'
Alcalde: 'Ha. Ha! How very singular. Yet, I remember. I have heard that the English highly prize this eccentric book. How very singular that the countrymen of the grand Baintham should set any value on that old English book!'

Borrow did not tell the magistrate what he later told his readers; that since he had nearly been shipwrecked on this extreme point of the Old World, he thought that 'to convey the Gospel to a place so wild and remote might perhaps be considered an acceptable pilgrimage in the eyes of my Maker'; and that though he was only carrying one copy of the New Testament, the fact

far from discouraging me in my projected enterprise, produced the contrary effect, as I called to mind that, ever since the Lord revealed himself to man, it has seemed good to him to accomplish the greatest ends by apparently the most insufficient means; and I reflected that this one copy might serve as an instrument for more good than the four thousand nine hundred and ninety-nine copies of the edition of Madrid.[3]

Borrow's attitude on this as on other occasions was uncomplicated and pragmatic. He gave his one copy of the New Testament to Antonio de la Trava, together with 'a gratuity', and accepted the good meal that was prepared by the *alcalde's* maid. He sincerely hoped, he said, in his blandest manner, that he would have a chance to 'acquaint the world with the hospitality which I have experienced from so accomplished a scholar as the *Alcalde* of Corcuvion'.[4]

The 'eccentric book' was the New Testament in the Spanish version of Father Felipe Scio de San Miguel (without notes or commentaries of any kind), recently reprinted in Madrid in a special edition prepared by Borrow for the Bible Society. Borrow was once again working for the British and Foreign Bible Society – had been doing so since November 1835, nearly two years before his journey to Finisterre. On this particular expedition, and probably habitually, he carried with him a notebook or journal, though he has the villagers of Corcuvion fail to discover it when they searched him for weapons. He also wrote occasionally, very occasionally, to his long-suffering employers in London. From these two sets of documents, his notebooks and his letters, were later to come the book that made him famous overnight, *The Bible in Spain*. The story of this in many ways bewildering metamorphosis is the subject of these Spanish chapters, which concern the whole period of his 'Peninsula' years, that is, the period from 1835 to 1842, a period that includes his first two years in Oulton Cottage, where he wrote *The Bible in Spain*.

When Borrow returned from St Petersburg to London in September 1835, his stock with the secretaries of the Bible Society was high simply because he had succeeded in achieving his, or rather their, objective, in circumstances they knew from other people to have been extremely difficult. Borrow had brought the edition back with him, which was what they wanted. They naturally wondered whether the services of this redoubtable character would be retained for any other mission. This possibility was particularly in the mind of Andrew Brandram, who from 1823 to 1850 was one of the Society's secretaries. Whereas from Russia, Borrow had written principally to the Rev. Joseph Jowett, because Jowett was the Society's editorial superintendent, his future dealings were to be chiefly with Brandram, there growing up between the two men a quite remarkable relationship, starting from Brandram's vicarious appreciation, from the security of his London office, of Borrow's adventures, as he called them, but over the years developing into something more complex, as will be seen. In Stoughton's *History of Religion in England* there is a good description of this Andrew Brandram, which was later quoted by Canton in his history of the Bible Society. 'To eminence in learning', Stoughton said,

he conjoined a masculine mind, an uncompromising spirit, active habits, strong affections, and devoted piety. I think I see him now, with the appearance of a country gentleman, portly in figure, honest in countenance, with a loose coat, a large hat, a thick neckcloth, and a bag of papers in his hands, entering a committee room before the commencement of a meeting, with an open hand to return friendly grasps, given by friends waiting for his arrival.[5]

This was the man with whom Borrow now had to deal. Were they a match for each other? Would the urbane but essentially tough-minded secretary be able to control his agent without offending him and would Borrow submit to being just an agent if managed by such a man as Andrew Brandram?

Borrow had told Jowett that he was prepared to be the Society's agent in China, but in 1835 this was impractical. He went to Norwich to see his mother, the Clarkes and other friends, while the Society's committee considered what might be done. Eventually he wrote a letter from his mother's house, evidently referring to a conversation that had occurred earlier in London, to say that he 'should be most happy to explore Portugal and Spain, and to report upon the possibility of introducing the Gospel into those countries, provided that the plan has not been given up', adding that he was 'weary of doing nothing' and was 'sighing for employment'.[6] This crossed with a letter to Borrow from Andrew Brandram stating that the committee had decided to send Borrow to Portugal but that he, Brandram, had misgivings. 'I had in imagination set you down in Oporto . . .' and his heart quailed. 'Favour us with your thoughts', he said: 'Experimental agency in a Society like ours is a formidable undertaking.'[7]

Brandram's attitude, perhaps not shared by other members of the Society, was frankly experimental. In as far as the Society's aim was to let the New Testament work for itself by ensuring that it was available, in the right languages and in modern translations, to as large a part of the world's population as possible, Brandram had no reservations about distributing it in Portugal or Spain, despite the powerful, obvious presence of the Roman Catholic Church. If an individual had in his hand the word of God, he would himself know the truth, whatever anyone else might say to him. In the case of Portugal and Spain the problems, as perceived by Evangelical philanthropists in England, were not the activities of the other Church, but the backwardness and illiteracy of the greater part of the population. These were problems Brandram was quite prepared to tackle, if the means proved to be at hand.

The immediate cause of his hesitation was the political confusion that had prevailed in the Peninsula, particularly in Spain, since the end of the war. Ferdinand VII, who had been restored to the throne in 1814 with the support of British military power, had at first agreed to govern within the terms of a liberal constitution, the Constitution of 1812, but had rapidly reverted to the autocratic type of rule that made him a virtual dictator. Under this regime, in a set of moves that are as familiar now as they were then, the nobility was exempted from taxation; the monasteries were restored; the Jesuits returned to Spain; the Inquisition was formally re-established; liberal politicians were persecuted and often executed.[8] His first 'reign of terror' resulted in the secession of the Spanish colonies in South America,[9] and in the Revolution of 1820, which re-established the Constitution and restored to the Liberal Party its political independence. But only for a brief period of time, because in 1823 a French army of 100,000 men invaded Spain, restored Ferdinand as absolute monarch, and occupied the country for the next four years, those liberals who survived the new period of persecution being forced overseas or into the hills to join the ever-increasing bands of guerillas. While there is no need here to retell the history of Spain between 1814 and 1815, enough must be said for the situation in 1835 to be intelligible. By his fourth wife, Maria Christina of Naples, Ferdinand VII had a daughter, Isabella, in October 1830, a daughter who by 'Pragmatic Sanction' was immediately declared to be heir to the throne, Don Carlos, Ferdinand's brother, thus being excluded or being at least significantly demoted in the line of succession. When Ferdinand died in 1833, Isabella was proclaimed Queen, with her mother Doña Christina as regent. Thus came into existence the Carlist and Christino parties, which in 1835 were still in open hostility with one another. Don Carlos had travelled to Northern Spain by way of Portugal, England and France and round him rallied the Basques and the representatives of the absolutist and ultra-clerical party throughout Spain. Against him were rallied not only the supporters of Isabella and the supporters of the Constitution of 1812, in a new alignment, but also the small British, as it were 'peace-keeping', force that had been sanctioned and sent to Spain by the Foreign Secretary, Lord Palmerston, in 1835. Thus when Borrow and Brandram were discussing in London whether anything useful might be done in the Peninsula, England and Spain were officially allies, but Spain itself was in a state of civil war. Few people in England knew much about the political issues; what had been reported in the *Times* and the *Morning Chronicle* were the massacres and the torture and execution of prisoners. In such circumstances was it sensible to go to Spain? Was it sensible even to go to Portugal?

Borrow's reply to Brandram established the tone of future communications. He 'approved' of the plan. So did 'all the religious friends' he had talked with. He was willing to go to Spain despite the danger, especially to investigate the possibility of introducing the Bible to 'institutions of infantine education'. 'I will moreover undertake, with the blessing of God, to draw up a small book of what I have seen and heard there.' Then, on his return from Spain and Portugal, he would edit the Armenian Testament. While doing that, 'I may be acquiring much vulgar Chinese from some unemployed Lascar or stray Canton-man whom I may pick up upon the wharves; and then – to China.'[10] Borrow was telling Brandram plainly that he wanted at all costs to go abroad again and that he was thinking of writing a book based upon his experiences. He did not tell the secretary that he was a devoted Christian who could only find fulfilment in life by being a missionary. Brandram, already knowing and understanding Borrow as a person better than the committee members to whom he reported, was prepared to experiment. He saw that Borrow was not a convinced Christian but this fact did not matter to him. A strange friendship began, based upon a mutual perception of a shared pragmatism. Neither man was a fool. Far from it. Each was perfectly prepared to conduct his life within the constraints of Victorian social convention without feeling in the least uncomfortable about the accommodation. How much each of them understood this later becomes apparent, though neither man was much bothered by any tiresome urge to be explicit. On 6 November 1835, Borrow sailed for Portugal on the *London Merchant*, with a mandate to inquire on behalf of the British and Foreign Bible Society as to the possibility of its starting operations there. The Society had, in every sense, appointed a free agent.[11]

Because events occur later on during Borrow's stay in the Peninsula that require discriminating interpretation, to say the least, it is worth underlining the extent of the Bible Society's trust in its agent, as expressed, for example, in Andrew Brandram's letter of 4 November 1835 to the Rev. E. Whitley, who was already in Portugal. In it Brandram says that there is some prospect of Borrow going eventually to China, but that meanwhile, since he already knows Portugal and speaks the language, he is being sent there with 'no specific instructions' to find out what, if anything, can be done on the Society's behalf; that he will 'direct his attention to schools'; and that if circumstances prove propitious he will also go to Spain.[12]

With Borrow on the *London Merchant* on his way to Lisbon, a word can be said about the sources of information on which any account of his years in Portugal and Spain must be based. The chief of these is Borrow's own extremely persuasive best-seller, *The Bible in Spain*, the racy style of which left many readers, perhaps most readers, with the impression that not much had been left unsaid on the subject of what it was like to be an Englishman in Spain during a period of civil war. This vividly written personal document must be supplemented by the earlier book, *The Zincali*, which Borrow wrote in Seville towards the end of his visit and published soon after his return from Spain. Almost as important as these two books, even when taken together, are Borrow's letters to his employers as edited by T. H. Darlow and published, in 1911, as *Letters of George Borrow to the British and Foreign Bible Society*. These are the letters that Borrow borrowed back from the Society and had before him when he was writing *The Bible in Spain*. Borrow said of *The Bible in Spain* that, though it was written in a solitary hamlet in a remote part of England, it was 'founded on certain journals' that he kept while in Spain: it indeed has the ring of truth that derives from directly related detail and the first-person narrative of stirring events. It will be seen, though, that only fragments of these journals have survived.[13] As to Borrow's correspondence with the officers of the Bible Society, Darlow says unambiguously that 'nothing has been omitted' and that 'each document is here printed *in extenso*, without alterations or omissions'.[14] Early biographers of Borrow, and notably Knapp, did not know that Borrow's letters to the Bible Society had survived. When they were discovered, and then used by Herbert Jenkins as the basis for a new biography,[15] it was immediately noticed and confirmed that Borrow had in fact done what he had said he would do, that is, used his letters to the Bible Society as the basis for large sections of *The Bible in Spain*. Or at least there were sections in the two books that were identical. Of course, no one would ever wish to ignore or belittle such a wealth of documentary evidence, particularly because when Knapp set himself the uninspiring task of checking Borrow's itinerary in Portugal and Spain against his collection of Borrow's receipts, bills, tickets, hotel accounts and so on – and he said that he had collected 'everything' – he found on the level of reported fact nothing whatsoever in Borrow's reports to challenge. Borrow had been where he had said he had been and Knapp did not inquire about, or at least did not write about, the omissions and the periods of silence.[16]

All this means that, on the basis of a large body of fact that is not in dispute, any new account of Borrow in Portugal and Spain must essentially be an act of interpretation. What Borrow did is of great interest: what that means is of greater interest. Certainly the narrative that derives from the books mentioned above can be filled out, sometimes in a quite significant manner, by documents, especially letters, which were not available to early biographers. Certainly a sharper focus can be achieved if the well-intentioned distortions of early writers like Knapp are discounted. Nonetheless, there seems no alternative to a two-part procedure in which *The Bible in Spain* and *Letters to the Bible Society* are first accepted as authentic, primary documents for the sake of mapping out what Borrow did and are then not necessarily accepted as authentic, both because of the selectiveness of Borrow's remarks about himself and because of glaring omissions and evasions. Borrow's manner at this stage in life was positive and urbane. Can a man whose manner is positive and urbane be trusted? Not in this instance – not completely, that is. Incidentally, Borrow made three separate expeditions to Spain – from November 1835 to September 1836, from November 1836 to September 1838 and from December 1838 to April 1840. It will be seen that the three stays in Spain were very different from each other.

By 10 November 1835, the *London Merchant* was passing Cape Finisterre. 'I found myself off the coast of Galicia, whose lofty mountains, gilded by the rising sun, presented a magnificent appearance.' The following day, in rough weather, a sailor who had dreamt that he would fall off the mast and drown fell off the mast and drowned. 'Truly wonderful are the ways of Providence!' said Borrow, setting the tone for much of *The Bible in Spain*. Two days later he was disembarking at Lisbon, much irritated by customs officers who insisted upon examining his baggage 'with most provoking minuteness'. Borrow very much disliked being examined by anyone for any purpose, least of all with minuteness. He heartily wished himself back in Russia, a country where he had left, he said, 'cherished friends and warm affections'. Having been robbed in the customs house, he found 'dirty and expensive' lodgings after a long and tiring search, then hired a Portuguese servant, 'it being my invariable custom, on arriving in a country, to avail myself of the services of a native, chiefly with the view of perfecting myself in the language', soon making himself intelligible, not in what he calls the normal English fashion of putting the hands in the pockets and fumbling them lazily there, 'instead of applying them to the indispensable office of gesticulation', but by opening his mouth wide and making 'much noise and vociferation'. With these important matters settled, he immediately began to explore the 'huge ruinous city', concentrating initially on its principal sights and monuments but not forgetting that he was supposed to be looking at schools.

Before long, however, he began to plan little expeditions out of Lisbon, which plans he justified by the idea that it would be wrong for him to base his idea of Portugal on a city 'so much subjected to foreign intercourse'. He actually liked foreign intercourse a lot but he was also itching for travel, itching for new experiences, itching to be on the road. 'Curiosity is the leading feature of my character',[17] he said, so off he went to satisfy it, full of energy, full of resolve, for ever on the look-out for novelty, for something he might do that no one else had done, but also deeply sensitive to the history of place and always aware, if he did not know its full history, or was mistaken about it, of the sense of the human events associated with where he was, however startling might be the contrast between the past he imagined and the present he observed. Although some of his early descriptions have a Gothic or Romantic Period quality about them, the writing is always so direct, or always seems so direct, that despite the period language it has the veracity of an eyewitness account, is in fact the type of writing he said he had learnt from Defoe. His first expedition was to Cintra, a few miles from Lisbon. Here is what he said about it.

My first excursion was to Cintra. If there be any place in the world entitled to the appellation of an enchanted region, it is surely Cintra; Tivoli is a beautiful and picturesque place, but it quickly fades from the mind of those who have seen the Portuguese Paradise. When speaking of Cintra, it must not for a moment be supposed that nothing more is meant than the little town or city; by Cintra must be understood the entire region, town, palace, *quintas*, forests, crags, Moorish ruin, which suddenly burst on the view on rounding the side of a bleak, savage, and sterile-looking mountain. Nothing is more sullen and un-inviting than the south-western aspect of the stony wall which, on the side of Lisbon, seems to shield Cintra from the eye of the world, but the other side is a mingled scene of fairy beauty, artificial elegance, savage grandeur, domes, turrets, enormous trees, flowers, and waterfalls, such as is met with nowhere else beneath the sun. Oh! there are strange and wonderful objects at Cintra, and strange and wonderful recollections attached to them. The ruin on that lofty peak, and which covers part of the side of that precipitous step, was once the principal stronghold of the Lusitanian Moors, and thither, long after they had disappeared, at a particular moon of every year, were wont to repair wild *santons* of Maugrabie, to pray at the tomb of a famous *Sidi*, who slumbers amongst the rocks. That grey palace witnessed the assemblage of the last Cortes held by the boy-King Sebastian, ere he departed on his romantic expedition against the Moors, who so well avenged their insulted faith and country at Alcazarquibir; and in that low shady *quinta*, embowered amongst those tall *alcornoques*, once dwelt John de Castro, the strange old viceroy of Goa, who pawned the hairs of his dead son's beard to raise money to repair the ruined wall of a fortress threatened by the heathen of Ind; those crumbling stones which stand before the portal, deeply graven, not with 'runes,' but things equally dark, Sanscrit rhymes from the Vedas, were brought by him from Goa, the most brilliant scene of his glory, before Portugal had become a base kingdom; and down that dingle, on an abrupt rocky promontory, stand the ruined halls of the English millionaire, who there nursed the wayward fancies of a mind as wild, rich, and variegated as the scenes around. Yes, wonderful are the objects which meet the eye at Cintra, and wonderful are the recollections attached to them.[18]

That this is a set-piece is perfectly obvious. Its appropriateness in the first pages of *The Bible in Spain* comes from the fact that Borrow is still a tourist, unaffected by the type of dramatic event he was to experience during the next four years. The reader of *The Bible in Spain* sees Cintra as Borrow said he saw Cintra when he first went there. The passage, though, is not part of Borrow's first letter to Andrew Brandram in which he reports that he arrived in Lisbon safely, that he had difficulty in finding a place to stay but had at last found a lodging which was 'dark, dirty and exceedingly expensive, without attendance', and that after 'discourse with people on all occasions' he had come to the conclusion that 'in Lisbon carelessness for religion of any kind seems to prevail'.[19] In that letter he told Brandram that he had visited both Cintra and Mafra in the course of a journey of about a hundred miles. He also told him that in Cintra he had had a useful talk with three priests about the deplorably low standard of popular education that prevailed in Portugal, just as he had already talked with people in Lisbon about religious education in the orphanage at the Convent of San Geronymo. After Cintra he went to Colhares where he visited the village school and was told that, long before the children had learnt to read, they were taken away by their parents to work in the fields. It was therefore quite impossible for them to read the Bible. After Colhares, to Mafra, where he looked at another small school. Then back to Lisbon where he met a Mr Wilby, a friend of the Society, with whom he talked about 'the best means of causing God's glorious Gospel to be read in Portugal'.[20] All this is a reminder that, while Andrew Brandram would have been, indeed was, perfectly satisfied by Borrow's first reports of his activities in Portugal, not least because of the enjoyment he always derived from Borrow's inclusion of 'adventures' and descriptions of dangerous journeys, the modern reader of Borrow cannot help but be intrigued by the difference between the artificially made world of Borrow's letters to the Bible Society and the artificially made world of his later book, *The Bible in Spain*. Was he already writing a book of his own, parts of which he worked up as reports to the Bible Society, or was he at first primarily concerned with religious education, only later realising that what he had written in his journal would be a good basis for a book? In his selection of places worth a visit, which were entirely of his own choosing, did he have primarily in mind the pleasures of satisfying his own curiosity, as when he visited the ancient convent library at Mafra, which next to the Escurial, he said, was the most magnificent edifice in the Peninsula, or were the episodes of this kind incidental to the main task of discovering whether the Portuguese were religious or not? The assessment of Borrow's ambiguous tone, an ambiguous tone that is expressed even at the very beginning of *The Bible in Spain*, must ultimately depend upon a reading of that book itself. Certainly anyone who reads it with pleasure today, a hundred years after Borrow's death – and who could resist its immense charm if it were generally available? – must baulk at his being described as a devoted missionary.[21] If Borrow was a missionary in any sense of the word at all, he was one much devoted to satisfying the predilections of his own ego.

His next journey of exploration was to the town of Evora, some 70 miles due east of Lisbon. He set out on 6 December with a small bundle of some twenty New Testaments and two Bibles. As always, he describes his own journey with great animation, starting with a perilous 12-mile crossing of the Tagus to Aldea Gallega, which he undertook in a small boat manned by a 'wild-looking lad' because he was unwilling to wait for the delayed ferry crossing. With the tide against them, but the wind in their favour, they 'sprang along at a wonderful rate', the waves crested with spray and the little boat pitching and tossing as though totally out of control. 'In a little time I had made up my mind that our last hour was come; the wind was getting higher, the short dangerous waves were more foamy, the boat was frequently on its beam, and the water came over the lee side in torrents.'[22] In fact, by the time they reached the far shore the boat was swamped and Borrow drenched to the skin. That night Borrow did not sleep. He was given a room in the inn over the stables next to the pigsty: 'the hogs grunted, the mules screamed and the *almocreves* snored most horribly', so he was glad to start his journey to Evora at four in the morning, in the bright moon-light and in piercing cold. With an old man and a young boy as guides, Borrow passed over the sandy, desolate land, was overtaken by five or six armed horsemen, who, however, simply went on their way, and at dawn met an old man who told stories about the atrocities committed by bandits and robbers until Borrow could stand no more and 'rode on considerably in front'. After another hour-and-a-half of travel across 'savage, wild, broken ground covered with *mato* or brushwood', they came to the ruins of an old inn, which the guide said used to be the headquarters of the 'celebrated robber Sabocha' and which was still frequented by 'banditti'. Indeed the ashes of the fire were still warm and Borrow left a New Testament and some tracts for the 'sons of plunder'. After riding on in the now hot sun, they were joined by a party of horsemen, in whose company they eventually reached the village of Pegoens, much to Borrow's satisfaction, for in the whole of Portugal, he says,

there is no place of worse reputation, and the inn is nicknamed *Estalagem de Ladroens*, or the hostelry of thieves; for it is there that the banditti of the wilderness, which extends around it on every side for leagues, are in the habit of coming and spending the money, the fruits of their criminal daring; there they dance and sing, eat fricasseed rabbits and olives, and drink the muddy but strong wine of the Alemtejo.

At this remotely situated inn he had fried rabbit with a delicious gravy 'and afterwards a roasted one, which was brought up on a dish entire; the hostess having first washed her hands, proceeded to tear the animal to pieces, which having accomplished, she poured over the fragments a sweet sauce'.[23] Borrow ate heartily of both dishes, and ended his meal with figs from the Algarves and apples. So onwards through the afternoon to the village of Vendas Novas, where Borrow for once spent a night in a clean bed 'remote from all those noises so rife in a Portuguese inn'.

Borrow was now beginning to enjoy himself. He was away from the city, away from gentility and convention, in search of banditti, robbers, guerrillas, the ordinary people of the land, and in particular the Moors, or traces of Moorish influence; though later he was forced to admit that throughout his wanderings in Portugal he saw nothing of 'that most singular people'.[24] He waxed eloquent about a hill called Monte Almo in a manner once again characteristic of his early, uninhibited tourist style.

A brook brawls at its base, and as I passed it the sun was shining gloriously on the green herbage, on which flocks of goats were feeding, with their bells ringing merrily, so that the *tout ensemble* resembled a fairy scene; and that nothing might be wanted to complete the picture, I here met a man, a goat herd, beneath an *azinheira*, whose appearance recalled to my mind the Brute Carle, mentioned in the Danish ballad of Swayne Vonved[25]

– this last because the man had an otter and a wolf by his side and two or three 'singular looking animals' peering from the top of a bag that he had on his back. The way of seeing, or at least the way of writing, that involved the eighteenth-century aesthetic of a *tout ensemble*, an arranged view or prospect, together with the Wordsworthian distanced or outsider's notice of the strange single figure of the old man, was typical of 'early' Borrow. This was how he had been brought to think about landscape. This was how life could be viewed. It was, of course, remarkable that a thirty-two-year-old Englishman from Norwich should have travelled across a robber- and bandit-infested wasteland during a civil war but, having done that, he necessarily described what he saw, intelligently, in the idiom of his age.

This account of his trip to Evora he *did* send to the Bible Society. He was not concerned about the language he used, nor did he imagine that it was anybody's business, even his employer's, to question his decision to go to a particular place at a particular time, however unintelligible that decision might be, but, for all that, he included a small diatribe, just to give balance to his account of the journey. About the type of people he was meeting he said:

I have always found in the disposition of the children of the fields a more determined tendency to religion and piety than amongst the inhabitants of towns and cities, and the reason is obvious – they are less acquainted with the works of man's hands than with those of God; their occupations, too, which are simple, and requiring less of ingenuity and skill than those which engage the attention of the other portion of their fellow-creatures, are less favourable to the engendering of self-conceit and self-sufficiency, so utterly at variance with that lowliness of spirit which constitutes the best foundation of piety. The sneerers and scoffers at religion do not spring from amongst the simple children of nature, but are the excrescences of over-wrought refinement; and though their baneful influence has indeed penetrated to the country and corrupted man there, the source and fountain-head was amongst crowded houses, where nature is scarcely known. I am not one of those who look for perfection amongst the rural population of any country – perfection is not to be found amongst the children of the fall, wherever their abodes may happen to be; but, until the heart discredits the existence of a God, there is still hope for the soul of the possessor, however stained with crime he may be, for even Simon the magician was converted. But when the heart is once steeled with infidelity, infidelity confirmed by carnal wisdom, an exuberance of the grace of God is required to melt it, which is seldom manifested; for we read in the blessed book that the Pharisee and the wizard became receptacles of grace, but where is there mention made of the conversion of the sneering Sadducee, and is the modern infidel aught but a Sadducee of later date?[26]

As to the danger inherent in expeditions across wild territory, Borrow said that he had experienced none. In any case, 'when threatened by danger, the best policy is to fix your eye steadily upon it, and it will in general vanish like the morning mist before the sun'.[27]

Borrow stayed in Evora for a week, talking with anyone he happened to meet, but without a plan of action and perhaps without any need of one. Both *The Bible in Spain* and the *Letters to the Bible Society* are full of accounts of random encounters, most of them vividly told. Occasionally, Borrow meets someone whom he continued to know throughout his time in Portugal and Spain, yet this is rare, because while travelling he preferred the anonymity of the traveller, so much so, indeed, that most of the people he met failed to appreciate that he was an agent of the British and Foreign Bible Society. As to his responsibilities in that regard, he would sit for a few hours each day by the fountain in Evora and talk about the New Testament with anyone who would listen, while at other times, he rode about the area on a mule 'for the purpose of circulating tracts' and also 'dropped a great many in the favourite walks of the people of Evora, as I felt rather dubious of their accepting them had I proffered them with my own hand, whereas, should they be observed lying on the ground, I thought that curiosity might cause them to be picked up and examined'.[28] There were no reports from Portugal, after Borrow's visit, of renewed spiritual life in Evora as a result of these casual distributions. In fact, Borrow found the Portuguese ignorant, superstitious and backward. Between the lines of his reports and descriptions, it becomes clear that he disliked them. He returned to Lisbon by retracing his steps, arrived on 19 December, picked up his desultory tourist ways, and was only lifted from the doldrums by sudden, and in the end important, encounters with two quite separate groups of people, both more interesting to him than the Portuguese peasant. These were the Jews of Lisbon and the gypsies of Badajoz.

Here were experiences much more to Borrow's taste. Of course, anyone on earth might reasonably be perplexed by the task that Borrow had been set or had set himself, for to test the social, political and religious climate of a country with a view to civilising it by means of the New Testament was, if taken seriously, an immense undertaking, as Brandram and his colleagues in London fully appreciated. It is fairly obvious, also, that anyone faced with such a task would have to tackle it in his own way, for nothing would have been gained had Borrow's instructions been detailed and specific. Nonetheless, he appears to have made no attempt whatsoever to contact literate people in Portugal, whether traders, civil servants, merchants, shopkeepers, students or educated or semi-educated women, who might at least have been interested in the Protestant proposition that it made sense to read the Bible in a good translation and come to terms with it, or respond to it, in a direct and personal way. It would have been extremely difficult for a complete stranger to make such an attempt, least of all quickly and without a thoughtfully prepared and long series of letters of introduction. But Borrow had no inclination to become acquainted with the educated or semi-educated bourgeois. If he met someone by chance on his travels, well and good. He would not or could not search such people out. This was not just because it would have required more effrontery than even Borrow possessed to gain a foothold in institutions where he might be heard. It was because, in Portugal as elsewhere, he entirely lacked any sense of community, any desire to relate to other people *en masse*. He lacked a social sense. Having been brought up on the road, he had had whatever social inclinations that remained knocked out of him in Norwich. For better or worse, his only interest in humanity in the mass consisted of an insatiable curiosity about sub-cultures, migrants and the dispossessed. This was consistent with his sense of the world being an unstable place for most people and peoples, but it was also consistent with his own habits, since he knew little about those minorities who had contrived to abstract themselves from the seething chaos of existence by means of the artificial establishment of a stable 'society', whereas he knew a lot about people who had to survive as best they could without very much help from other people. When he saw a group of Jews in Lisbon dressed in 'a red cap, with a blue silken tassel on top of it, a blue tunic girded at the waist with a red sash, and wide linen pantaloons or trousers', it was therefore in character for him to introduce himself into their midst and pronounce a *beraka* or blessing. He explained:

I have lived in different parts of the world, much amongst the Hebrew race, and am well acquainted with their ways and phraseology. I was rather anxious to become acquainted with the state of the Portuguese Jews, and I had now an opportunity. 'The man is a powerful rabbi,' said a voice in Arabic; 'it behoves us to treat him kindly.' They welcomed me. I favoured their mistake, and in a few days I knew all that related to them and their traffic in Lisbon.[29]

It no more bothered Borrow to pass himself off as a rabbi than it bothered his first biographers to call him an excellent missionary.

However strongly Borrow may have wished to be acquainted with the Jews of Lisbon, his meetings with them were not successful, or at least they were so successful that he dismissed them as ignorant and primitive, and not as interesting as he had hoped. Borrow's comments, with an irony of such remote application that to discuss it at this point would be premature, would certainly not pass muster in 1981 in a western world so determined to rid itself of racist sentiments and racist practices. Having listened to the stories of Barbary Jews about their corrupt teachers and synagogues, he says:

How well do superstition and crime go hand in hand! These wretched beings break the eternal commandments of their Maker without scruple; but they will not partake of the beast of the uncloven foot, and the fish which has no scales. They pay slight regard to the denunciations of holy prophets against the children of sin, but they quake at the sound of a dark cabalistic word pronounced by one perhaps their equal or superior in villainy; as if, as has been well observed, God would delegate the exercise of his power to the workers of iniquity.[30]

Maybe some of the strength of feeling in these remarks, though nothing by comparison with what Borrow often allowed himself to say about Popish priests, derived from the fact that he had developed a partiality for the 'lombo or loin' of the gallant swine of the Alemtejo when broiled in the live embers of a fire, 'especially when eaten with olives'. Some of the feeling, but not much of it, for he had much stronger remarks to make about the Jews of Lisbon in a passage that concluded chapter 5 of the first edition but was excised from later editions.[31]

I found them a vile, infamous rabble, about two hundred in number. With a few exceptions, they consist of *escapados* from the Barbary shore, from Tetuan, from Tangier, but principally from Mogadore; fellows who have fled to a foreign land from the punishment due to their misdeeds. Their manner of life in Lisbon is worthy of such a goodly assemblage of *amis réunis*. The generality of them pretend to work in gold and silver, and keep small peddling shops; they, however, principally depend for their livelihood on an extensive traffic in stolen goods which they carry on. It is said that there is honour among thieves, but this is certainly not the case with the Jews of Lisbon, for they are so greedy and avaricious that they are constantly quarrelling about their ill-gotten gain, the result being that they frequently ruin each other. Their mutual jealousy is truly extraordinary. If one, by cheating and roguery, gains a *cruzado* in the presence of another, the latter instantly says, 'I cry halves,' and if the first refuse he is instantly threatened with an information. The manner in which they cheat each other has, with all its infamy, occasionally something extremely droll and ludicrous.[32]

Whatever hope Borrow may have had of finding in the Jews of Lisbon an alternative life-style with which he could identify was thus quickly frustrated. It was now late in December and surely time for him to be making his way to Madrid.

On 1 January, well wrapped up in his Russian *shoob* against the 'truly terrible' cold, he left Lisbon, again crossed the Tagus, this time by *felook*, hired mules for his journey and, in the boy who looked after them, acquired a companion for the first part of the expedition. 'He was short, but exceedingly strong built, and possessed the largest head which I ever beheld upon mortal shoulders; neck he had none, at least I could discern nothing which could be entitled to that name. His features were hideously ugly, and upon addressing him I discovered that he was an idiot.'[33] As always Borrow's pen makes memorable the simple events of the difficult journey. When he is threatened by the huge, snarling mastiff of a shepherd, he stoops down until his chin is level with his knees and looks the dog full in the eyes, 'for no large and fierce dog or animal . . . will venture to attack an individual who confronts it with a firm and motionless countenance'.[34] When he fails to gain admittance to a convent where the nuns – or anyway, the women inside – merely titter at him through the grilled windows, he nonchalantly eats their cheesecake, the speciality of the convent, in a café in the town square. When a company of soldiers jeer at him as he passes them on the road, he merely laughs at them – 'but it would have been more prudent of me to have held my peace, for the next moment, with bang-bang, two bullets, well aimed, came whizzing past my ears'.[35] Had he at all in mind his own childhood and upbringing when he said of this episode: 'Oh, may I live to see the day when soldiery will no longer be tolerated in any civilized, or at least Christian country'?[36] If Borrow on this first journey from Lisbon to Madrid had moments of panic, moments when he was flustered and put out of countenance, these are not revealed. At Estremoz, near the frontier, he stayed at an inn that was terrible enough even before a drunkard rode wildly into the kitchen and then, having stabled his horse, so irritated and insulted the company that a fight almost broke out.

The fellow, enraged at this contempt, flung the glass out of which he was drinking at the Spaniard's head, who sprang up like a tiger, and unsheathing instantly a 'snick and snee' knife, made an upward cut at the fellow's cheek, and would have infallibly laid it open, had I not pulled his arm down just in time to prevent worse effects than a scratch above the lower jaw-bone, which, however, drew blood.[37]

With incidents of this kind occurring daily, he made his way to Elvas, and so to the frontier, where he shouted, in ecstasy, '*Santiago y cierra España*', as he forded the stream.

Borrow stayed three weeks in Badajoz, instead of travelling on to Madrid immediately as he had intended. This was because in Badajoz he came across his first large settlement of gypsies. In *The Bible in Spain* he makes no secret of the fact that he had little to do with Spaniards, whom he found haughty, reserved and hostile to strangers, and that he felt more at ease with the gypsies, whose way of life he perfectly understood. Just as he passed himself off as a rabbi in Lisbon, now he allowed himself to be mistaken for a gypsy, lived in the gypsy encampment and was soon good friends with those individuals he names and describes in *The Bible in Spain*. For all his bravura, Borrow had now been away from England for two months, had struggled to find his feet in Portugal, without much help, and was now glad to be able to relax and take stock of things. He was after all as much at home in a gypsy encampment as anywhere else. It was here, as he said himself, that as well as 'preaching the gospel', he began to mull over a possible book on the Zincali or Gitanos of Spain and at the same time began to translate into Spanish Gypsy portions of the Gospel according to St Luke. Although at this stage, in January 1836, no decision had been made by the Bible Society about whether the main 'experiment' should be in Portugal or in Spain, it is interesting to notice that, even before he reached Madrid, Borrow already had in mind ideas for the books that were eventually published as the translation called *Embeó e Majaró Lucas* (1837) and the anthology called *The Zincali* (1840). As a matter of fact, from Badajoz, he sent Brandram a package of papers consisting of a translation of the fifteenth chapter of St Luke, together with 'specimens of the Horrid Curses in Use Among the Spanish Gypsies', with a request that the Bible Society should give financial backing to the St Luke, which, after the 'specimens' were printed and inspected, it did.[38] Borrow felt his own literary motives were compatible with the work he had to do for the Bible Society. He divided his time, judiciously, between the two.

Borrow's first visit to Madrid was no more than a lengthy reconnaissance. At some point, though precisely when is uncertain, Borrow discussed with Brandram the possibility of doing in Spain what he had already done in Russia, that is producing a New Testament for distribution on the Society's behalf, with the important difference that this one would be intended for the country in which it was produced. This was something he knew to be within his capability, whereas he had no desire either to proselytise or to be what the Bible Society called a 'colporteur', that is, a distributor. As in St Petersburg, the problem initially was to obtain official permission to proceed. Because Bibles without notes or commentaries were banned in Spain, whereas it was only a Bible, or at least a New Testament, *without* notes and commentaries that the Society could endorse and have any desire to distribute, the likelihood of obtaining permission was very slight indeed. Furthermore, the officials who ostensibly had the authority to approve or not approve a request that a new edition of the New Testament should be printed were for the most part powerless, since the aristocracy, the monarchists, the Carlists and especially the Church continued to behave as though the Constitution did not exist, as indeed they were in part obliged to do during the civil war. Decisions were not made constitutionally but behind the scenes – when, that is, they were made at all. Very few Cabinet ministers were in a position to disregard the wishes of the Church. Very few had any inclination to do so. In any case, most Spaniards of any standing or intelligence, as well as those without intelligence, naturally thought they could get on perfectly well without the British and Foreign Bible Society. Consequently, when Borrow arrived in Madrid in February 1837 and acquired lodgings – an 'immense' sitting-room and a tiny bedroom – at 3 Calle de la Zarza,[39] the direct approach to the Government, which was the only approach he could think of to make, was almost bound to be rebuffed. As Borrow said himself: 'Notwithstanding I entertained a hope of success, relying on the assistance of the Almighty, this hope was not at all times very vivid.'[40]

It has already been mentioned that England's relationship with Spain had, while Borrow was there, a special character because of the temporory importance to the Government in Madrid of the British expeditionary force. Consequently, when Borrow went to see the Prime Minister, Don Juan Alvarez de Mendizabal, whom he described, incidentally, as a 'huge athletic man' with a florid complexion, fine and regular features, an aquiline nose, and splendid white teeth, it was not really to be expected that he would be given a straight yes or no. The Prime Minister had no intention of saying yes, yet it was diplomatic not to say no. He did point out that ever since coming to power, he had been pestered by English Evangelists and that only the previous week on his way to a Cabinet meeting he had been waylaid by a hunchbacked fellow who told him that Christ was coming. 'What a strange infatuation is this which drives you over lands and waters with Bibles in your hands.'[41] Mendizabal dealt with Borrow in a time-honoured way. 'Come again whenever you please, but let it not be within the next three months.' Borrow, reasonably enough, took the instruction literally.

During the early part of 1836, Borrow browsed about Madrid, recording in his diary for later use in *The Bible in Spain* just a few of the things that happened to him. He watched the public execution by garrotting of two murderers. He met Benedict Mol for the first time – an old Swiss soldier on a wildgoose chase, supposedly for buried treasure in the north of Spain.[42] And he witnessed the public disturbances caused by the Revolution of La Granja, actually being present when the old general, Quesada, made a courageous stand on behalf of the old order in a crowded square and later the same day seeing his dismembered hand used to stir the drinks of celebrating revolutionaries. By and large, though, it was a frustrating time, made more so by the fact that he ran out of money and had to make an emergency appeal to Brandram. In *The Bible in Spain* he said that he had come to be a great admirer of the ordinary Spaniard, who, he said, was in fact extraordinary, despite his ignorance, whereas he mingled little with society, which was just a way of saying that he did not try to gain access to Spanish society, or that, if he tried, he failed. As usual his own words are eloquent. There need be no apology, on this as on so many other occasions, for letting Borrow speak for himself.

I have visited most of the principal capitals of the world, but upon the whole none has ever so interested me as this city of Madrid, in which I now found myself. I will not dwell upon its streets, its edifices, its public squares, its fountains, though some of these are remarkable enough; but Petersburg has finer streets, Paris and Edinburgh more stately edifices, London far nobler squares, whilst Shiraz can boast of more costly fountains, though not cooler waters. But the population! Within a mud wall scarcely one league and a half in circuit, are contained two hundred thousand human beings, certainly forming the most extraordinary vital mass to be found in the entire world; and be it always remembered that this mass is strictly Spanish. The population of Constantinople is extraordinary enough, but to form it twenty nations have contributed – Greeks, Armenians, Persians, Poles, Jews, the latter, by-the-by, of Spanish origin, and speaking amongst themselves the old Spanish language; but the huge population of Madrid, with the exception of a sprinkling of foreigners, chiefly French tailors, glove-makers, and *perruquiers*, is strictly Spanish, though a considerable portion are not natives of the place. Here are no colonies of Germans, as at Saint Petersburg; no English factories, as at Lisbon; no multitudes of insolent Yankees lounging through the streets, as at the Havannah, with an air which seems to say, 'The land is our own whenever we choose to take it;' but a population which, however strange and wild, and composed of various elements, is Spanish, and will remain so as long as the city itself shall exist. Hail, ye *aguadores* of Asturia! who, in your dress of coarse duffel and leathern skull-caps, are seen seated in hundreds by the fountain sides, upon your empty water-casks, or staggering with them filled to the topmost stories of lofty houses. Hail, ye *caleseros* of Valencia! who, lolling lazily against your vehicles, rasp tobacco for your paper cigars whilst waiting for a fare. Hail to you, beggars of La Mancha! men and women, who, wrapped in coarse blankets, demand charity indifferently at the gate of the palace or the prison. Hail to you, valets from the mountains, *mayordomos* and secretaries from Biscay and Guipuzcoa, *toreros* from Andalusia, *reposteros* from Galicia, shop-keepers from Catalonia! Hail to ye, Castilians, Estremenians, and Aragonese, of whatever calling! And lastly, genuine sons of the capital, rabble of Madrid, ye twenty thousand *manolos*, whose terrible knives, on the second morning of May, worked such grim havoc amongst the legion of Murat![43]

This was all very well, yet did little, of course, for the cause of the Bible Society. As the months passed, Borrow kept the business of an edition in the official mind as best he could; the British Minister, George Villiers,[44] began to intercede more actively by talking to Cabinet ministers; Borrow actually got the Ecclesiastical Board to consider his petition, though its members subsequently deferred to the Government; the Government fell and with the new Government of Isturitz, which came to power in May 1836, there seemed more chance – more chance, that is, not of good government but of Borrow getting his way. Isturitz himself put Borrow off by referring him to his secretary, who in turn referred endlessly, if *The Bible in Spain* is to be trusted, to the pro-hibitions of the Council of Trent,[45] but through Isturitz's friend and Cabinet colleagues, Antonio Alcalá Galiano, and his Minister of the Interior, the Duke de Ribas, Borrow began to make a little progress, at least in getting his position understood. In the end, after a covert tussle that had lasted more than four months, the Government temporarily succumbed to British pressures and on 9 June 1836 Villiers wrote to Borrow the following letter:

I have had a very satisfactory conversation with the Duque de Ribas, in which I hope I convinced him of the advantage not only of permitting but of encouraging the publication of the Bible.

I trust you will not experience any further difficulty, but pray command my services if you require them.[46]

Borrow did not require them, for Villiers wrote to him again on 23 June 1836:

I have had a long conversation with Mr. Isturitz upon the subject of printing the Testament, in which he showed himself to be both sagacious and liberal. He assured me that the matter should have his support whenever the Duque de Rivas brought it before the Cabinet, and that as far as he was concerned the question *might be considered as settled*.

You are quite welcome to make any use you please of this note with the D. de Ribas or Mr. Olivar.

I am, Dear Sir,

yours faithfully,

George Villiers[47]

The second letter allowed Borrow to write home to Brandram on 7 July 1836:

The affair is settled – thank God!!! and we may begin to print whenever we think proper.

He added:

Perhaps you have thought I have been tardy in accomplishing the business which brought me to Spain; but to be able to form a correct judgement you ought to be aware of all the difficulties which I have had to encounter, which I shall not enumerate; I shall content myself with observing that for a thousand pounds I would not undergo again all the mortifications and disappointments of the last two months.[48]

Whereas Brandram, on receiving this letter in London, took it as the beginning of the Society's work in Spain, Borrow behaved as though his task was over. 'I am not aware that there is any great necessity for my continuance in Spain', he said. There were loose ends to be gathered up; that was all. Would Brandram have the president thank the British Minister for his help? Would he not also transmit a vote of thanks to His Excellence Antonio Alcalá Galiano? Would he accept Dr Usoz, Borrow's friend, as a subscribing member of the Society? Would he send more money? The treasurer sent Borrow cash. Brandram had the letters of thanks written and sent off. But he also told Borrow 'you may now consider yourself under marching orders to return home as soon as you have made all the requisite arrangements'.[49] A few of Borrow's activities in Madrid had alarmed Brandram and his colleagues, so consultation, they thought, was now necessary.

The second visit to Spain:
November 1836–September 1838

Borrow's arrival back in London on 3 October 1836 marked the beginning of a new, important phase of his work in Spain. To this point he had been finding his feet, discovering, albeit in his own idiosyncratic way, what was possible. Now it was up to Andrew Brandram and his colleagues to decide, on the basis of Borrow's reports, what action, if any, they wanted to take. They had two agents in Spain, Borrow and Lt Graydon, a retired naval officer who devoted many years of his life to the Society's cause. Graydon's operations were based upon Barcelona, so the question was whether anything could be done in the rest of Spain, Brandram having no difficulty in deciding that, since his two agents were men of such very different characters, he ought to insist upon a division of territory that would keep them apart.

Borrow's position when he met Brandram in London was a strong one. He had contrived to live in Madrid during a period of incredible political and military unrest. He had had direct dealing with two Governments, having seen both Prime Ministers. He had won the support of the British Minister, George Villiers. In the circumstances, all this amounted to a fairly solid achievement. Brandram recognised it as such. Now Borrow told him that, although the Spanish Government's approval of the plan to print a New Testament was only verbal, Villiers had instructed him by letter that there was no obstacle to his proceeding with the manufacture of it, if the Society wished. Borrow was prepared to return to Madrid, though he had reservations about doing any work himself except that of seeing the new edition through the press. These reservations he expressed, as he had done previously, by letter; in his opinion, the labour of distributing the New Testaments once they had been manufactured, could well be taken over by people of lesser talent, though if his going back to Spain depended upon his having a hand in distribution he was prepared to compromise. He was willing to serve the Society, but did not conceal the fact that he had ambitions of his own. He was keen to have the Bible Society support the publication of the Gospel according to St Luke both in 'Gypsy' and in Basque, Borrow and Brandram were large, forceful, determined men of character, not given to mincing their words. Borrow did not conceal from Brandram that, in addition to the books mentioned above, he had in mind to write a book of his own and that, if he travelled about Spain in order to distribute the New Testament, it would be partly for his own purposes. Brandram, on his side, who was after all experienced in handling a great variety of agents with a great variety of temperaments, saw that Borrow, with his considerable talent, could do *something* for the Society and did not expect him to do everything. He therefore sent him back to Spain. He had little to lose, or so at least he thought. The Society had a well publicised, well established policy of political non-involvement, which meant that the significance of gross intrusions into other people's affairs was not always apparent to its officers. Later historians might suppose that the simultaneous presence in Spain of the Bible Society and British troops was not a coincidence, that the Bible Society had indeed a political function and that the pressure George Villiers brought to bear upon the Government of Isturitz was a measure of the power of the Evangelical Movement in England. Brandram would have disagreed. *He* only wished people to have a New Testament in their hands, so that they could decide matters for themselves. Brandram could therefore use Borrow provided Borrow stayed out of politics.

To be on the safe side Borrow acquired a passport, then sailed on the steamship *Manchester* for Lisbon and Cadiz. Typically Borrow says next to nothing in *The Bible in Spain* about the crucial discussions he had had in London but he does describe the voyage in characteristically vivid terms, for the ship was unseaworthy, his cabin an airless hole, the captain a novice and the other passengers mostly invalids on their way to convalescence in Portugal and Madeira. Though almost drowned in the immense storm they encountered off Finisterre and struck down by a water-cask that had broken loose and crushed the foot of the helmsman, Borrow described the ordeal that brought him so close to death with his usual economy and *sangfroid*, always the observer of a scene even when one of the characters in it.

What continues to be of considerable interest is the unhibited way in which Borrow describes what happens to him as he begins this, his second visit to Spain. Or at least what continues to be of interest is the uninhibited way in which he appears to describe faithfully what actually happens to him. It soon becomes clear from Borrow's actions when he reaches Madrid that he has come back to Spain with a positive plan of action. The Bible Society members expected to hear about its implementation. Borrow knew that whatever he wrote in his letters Brandram invariably read aloud to the assembled committee. Despite this, his reports continued to be much more those of the traveller than of the missionary – Brandram had probably encouraged him in this, for the obvious reason that Borrow's adventures were more interesting than his thoughts about religion – and they continued to be so phrased as to make any alert reader fully aware of Borrow's ambivalent position. His description of his journey from Cadiz to Madrid actually constitutes a cameo portrait of the man, not least in his successful avoidance of the explicit while being explicit would appear to any casual reader to be his main purpose.

When he landed in Cadiz, he obtained accommodation in a 'species of cockloft' at the French hotel in the Calle de la Niveria, later the Hôtel de Paris, which he said was popular because of the excellence of its table. Borrow, though, did not take the opportunity provided by this good hotel to enjoy a few days' leisure in the company of the educated, well-heeled people who were also staying there, as well he might have done after a long, dangerous and fatiguing voyage. Avoiding the cosmopolitan middle-class travellers in the hotel, he instead went the rounds of the coffee-houses, where everyone was talking about a political situation that had greatly deteriorated during Borrow's relatively brief absence. In one of the coffee-houses 'no less than six orators were haranguing at the same time on the state of the country, and the probability of an intervention on the part of England and France'.[1] What was his opinion, someone unexpectedly asked, and Borrow's reply is revealing: 'As I did not wish to engage in any political conversation, I instantly quitted the house, and sought those parts of the town where the lower classes principally reside.'[2] It is true that Borrow had been specifically instructed to stay out of politics. It is true, too, that while in Cadiz he had an informal chat with a bookseller about the demand for Bibles. But it is also clear that he habitually felt ill-at-ease with mannered middle-class people of whatever nationality, blaming them not himself for his inability to get on with them, their 'gentility', that is to say, the inherent artificiality of their lives, constituting an ever-present barrier that he refused to cross, whereas he was more relaxed in the company of what he here calls 'the lower classes', presumably because they inhabited a plain, more earthly world and presented no challenge to his ego. Yet when he 'entered into discourse with several individuals' he found them ignorant. He spoke with them. They were unable to speak with him. Borrow was not really at home in either world.

After dealing with a violent bout of an illness he at first feared was cholera by administering in large doses a mixture of oil and brandy, he sailed for Seville on 24 November on the river-steamer *Betis*, characteristically noting – for was he not still searching out the elusive Moorish element in Spanish life? – that the Guadalquivir was originally the Wady el Kebir and that it was 'impossible to move along this river without remembering that it has borne the Roman, the Vandal and the Arab'.[3] In Seville, he found a room in the Posada de Toreo and did the sights, visiting the cathedral, with its Moorish tower, La Giralda, the Alcazar – also Moorish – of course, and the amphitheatre, where he forced his way through 'the wild fennel and brushwood' into its neglected recesses and remained until he had 'sated' his curiosity. As always in Borrow, a detail is enough to hold the event in the mind, even though no attempt is made to record *all* the events of his two weeks in Seville. Here it is the half-eaten carcass of a horse: 'upon it with lustrous eyes, stood an enormous vulture, who, as I approached, slowly soared aloft till he alighted on the eastern gate of the amphitheatre, from whence he uttered a hoarse cry, as if in anger that I had disturbed him from his feast of carrion'.[4] Important for a book Borrow was to write in Seville between two and three years later were his first visits to the suburb called Triana, on the other side of the river, a suburb which he said 'is inhabited by the dregs of the populace, and abounds with Gitanos or Gypsies'.[5]

Borrow did not have an entirely solitary existence in Cadiz and Seville. In Cadiz, he renewed his acquaintance with an English business-man called John Wetherell, with whom he explored the city. In Seville, he ran into Baron Taylor, an old friend whom Borrow praised highly in *The Bible in Spain*, evidently seeing in him a kindred spirit whether they met 'in the street or the desert, the brilliant hall or amongst Bedouin haimas, at Novogorod or Stamboul'.[6] Meanwhile, Borrow was telling Brandram by letter about the difficulties of the situation. The way to Madrid was 'beset with more perils than harassed Christian in his route to the Eternal Kingdom' – a typical Borrow irony. Com-munication between Seville and Madrid was at a standstill. Carlist armies were on the rampage.

The three friends, famine, plunder, and murder, are playing their ghastly revels unchecked; bands of miscreants captained by such – what shall I call them? – as Orejita and Palillos are prowling about in every direction, and woe to those whom they meet. A few days since they intercepted an unfortunate courier, and after scooping out his eyes put him to death with most painful tortures, and mangled his body in a way not to be mentioned. Moreover, the peasantry, who have been repeatedly plundered by these fellows, and who have had their horses and cattle taken from them by the Carlists, being reduced with their families to nakedness and the extreme of hunger, seize in rage and desperation upon every booty which comes within their reach, a circumstance which can awaken but little surprise.[7]

Even within the cities, people were divided among themselves, suspicious, angry, fearful, so much so that Borrow had to tell a fellow guest in a house disrupted by Carlist and anti-Carlist feeling:

My good man...I am invariably of the politics of the people at whose table I sit, or beneath whose roof I sleep; at least I never say anything which can lead them to suspect the contrary; by pursuing which system I have more than once escaped a bloody pillow, and having the wine I drank spiced with sublimate.[8]

The dangers were real and Borrow's ability to survive them quite remarkable.

After fourteen days in Cordova, 'a mean, dark, gloomy place', where Borrow found it convenient to be mistaken for a Carlist, he proposed to travel the 300 miles to Madrid on horseback and with a guide. This, he explained calmly, was because he did not know the route. If he had known the way, he would have gone on foot by himself, 'dressed as a beggar or a Gypsy', but because the route lay through the 'dismal and savage mountains of the Sierra Morena' where he would 'inevitably be bewildered, and perhaps, if not murdered, fall a prey to the wolves',[9] he would have to incur the expense of animals and guide, if he was to go at all. Despite his graphic description of the dangers involved, he had no intention of giving up or even of delaying. He estimated that the journey should take five weeks. If after a further lapse of time, Brandram had not heard from him, would Brandram himself go to Norwich to break the news to Borrow's mother? This letter, dated 5 December 1836, affected the Bible Society's committee as Borrow no doubt anticipated that it would. A letter was sent from London instructing Borrow to abandon his plans. This communication, if he received it, Borrow ignored. Brandram had known that he would. As he said in a later letter, 'my own feeling was that, while I could not urge you forward, there were peculiarities in your history and character that I would not keep you back if you were minded to go [*sic*]'.[10] Borrow had left Cordova on 20 December.[11] He managed to survive the hazards of the route, reached Aranjuez on Christmas Day – 'where he got into the house of an Englishman and swallowed two bottles of brandy'[12] – and Madrid itself on 26 December, thus completing according to plan a journey that few people either in Spain or in London would have considered possible.

It would be tempting to allow Borrow to tell the whole story of his time in Spain by means of extensive quotation from *The Bible in Spain* but this is impossible for many reasons, some of which have been given already. *The Bible in Spain*, great book though it undoubtedly is, does not tell the whole truth; it will be discussed later in this chapter as a great book that tells part of the truth. In any case, as Borrow's difficulties as an agent of a Protestant Society attempting to initiate a campaign in a Catholic country became more and more intense, and it will be seen that his position deteriorated very rapidly, the discrepancies between the various accounts of his time in Spain become more noticeable, so that whereas one must trust his report of a difficult journey over a mountain range, because he was the only person there, or at least was the only person interested in giving an account of what happened, when it comes to his time in Madrid one must read between the lines, to get behind Borrow's own story, if possible, even when that story is not untrue. His arrival in Madrid on Boxing Day 1836 was certainly a turning-point. Before that date, everything he had done in Spain consisted essentially of exploration, reconnaissance, familiarisation, but once in Madrid for the second time it was essential that he should devote his energies to the Bible Society's interests, since these had now been clearly defined.

He took rooms at 16 Calle de Santiago and settled down to a four-month period of intensive work on three closely related printing-projects: the manufacture of a new edition of the New Testament in the Spanish version originally prepared by Father Felipo Scio de San Miguel, of the Gospel according to St Luke in Spanish Gypsy, and of the same Gospel in Basque. Having already done this sort of thing in St Petersburg, Borrow proceeded confidently, and was soon involved in the detailed work of production, as described in his letter to Brandram dated 14 January 1837.[13] He got George Villiers to confirm that, despite a change of government, there was no need for him to obtain official permission once again. He asked for and obtained the assistance of an Irish banker called O'Shea, in order to purchase paper at a good price from the 'paper manufactories of the south'. His old contact in the only English press in Madrid having moved to a new job, he negotiated with a Mr Borrego for the printing of 5,000 copies in a single-column edition. And he enlisted the help of a friend called Dr Usoz to help with the proof-reading, Borrow having got it into his head that, if the Bible Society were to authorise the establishment of a branch office in Madrid with Dr Usoz as secretary, Dr Usoz could assume responsibility for the distribution of the Bibles that were being manufactured, leaving Borrow free to explore other parts of Spain. Though not much is known about Borrow's day-by-day life in Madrid during this four-month period, it seems that his personal involvement in the making of a Spanish New Testament was by no means as great as it had been in the making of the Manchu Bible in St Petersburg. He had more time at his disposal and much of this he devoted to the Gypsy and Basque translations of the Gospel according to St Luke.

It will be remembered that he had started to translate Luke into Spanish Gypsy while in Badajoz, as part of his own attempt to come to terms with the language. The translation was by no means the casual experiment that at first glance it might appear to be: he placed great store by it and later in life treated it as one of his principal philological achievements. While in London, he had asked Brandram for the Bible Society's support, so in his letter of 27 February he said that his translation was ready for the press, implying that Brandram had already given the project his tacit approval. This approval was confirmed by the committee, which authorised 'Mr. Borrow to print 250 copies of the Gospel of St. Luke, without the vocabulary, in the Rummanee dialect, and to engage the services of a competent person to translate the Gospel of St. Luke by way of trial in the dialect of the Spanish Basque'.[14] Actually 500 copies were printed – but not until the following year.

The Basque Luke, which Darlow specified was 'in the Guipuzcoan dialect of Basque, with an admixture of Biscayan',[15] was translated for Borrow by a Basque doctor called Oteiza, whom Borrow paid £8. This was printed in the early part of 1838, when Borrow was in the thick of his dispute with the Spanish authorities.

Borrow was perfectly prepared to spend the first four months of 1837 seeing these books through the press, or, in the case of St Luke, preparing them for the printer, so to this extent he was a loyal servant or officer of the Bible Society that employed him. At the same time, he was making plans of his own for a long expedition to north-west Spain, an expedition which he had had in mind for many months and which had much more to do with his own proposed book than with the circulation of the scriptures. The New Testament was ready for circulation by 1 May 1837 or shortly before that. Borrow told Brandram that he had prepared a circular to advertise its existence and, on 29 April 1837, 'that some hundreds of our books have been placed in the hands of a bookseller at Madrid'.[16] Meanwhile, Borrow had told Brandram that he himself preferred not to remain in Madrid and one wonders whether this was partly because he anticipated the trouble that the publication of a New Testament without notes or commentary was bound to cause. 'What is to be done with the volumes when the work shall have passed through the press?' he therefore asked Brandram. 'As I am sure you will feel at a loss to give a satisfactory answer', he continued, coolly, 'allow me to propose the only plan which appears feasible.'[17] He had mused over this plan, he said, 'when off Cape Finisterre in the tempest, in the cut-throat passes of the Morena, and on the plains of La Mancha'. He would go himself into the wildest

parts of Spain, taking 1,200 copies with him to be distributed as he went
along and to be left in some of the principal towns. To do this, he only
needed the committee's approval and the money to buy a couple of
horses. Would the committee give its approval? Incidentally, he had
already bought one of the horses – 'an exceedingly strong, useful animal'
– for £11 7s.

One wonders, over the gap of years, whether any member of the
committee was alerted by this mention of a horse to the stirring within
the mind of its agent of something essentially un-Biblical. For Borrow
a horse meant travel, freedom, an escape from society. Interestingly,
however, the committee was distracted from a consideration of Borrow's
motives by his mention of the 'wild people of the wild regions I intend
to visit'. 'Could these wild people read?' asked Brandram dubiously.
Could not Borrow restrict his work with wild people to excursions of
two or three days at a time? Borrow was sufficiently experienced to
know how to answer such a question. He would visit villages and
towns as well as remote and secluded glens. 'True it is that such a
journey would be attended with considerable danger, and very possibly
the fate of St. Stephen might befall the adventurer; but does the man
deserve the name of a follower of Christ who would shrink from
danger of any kind in the cause of Him whom he calls his Master?'[18]
Brandram wrote back immediately to say that Borrow could have his
horses, that the expedition was approved and indeed, Borrow could do
exactly as he wished, except in the matter of Dr Usoz, since forming
branch offices was outside the Society's usual course. So shortly after
delivery of the Bible from the printers, instead of distributing it in
Madrid and in the surrounding districts, as it might have been expected
he would have done, Borrow prepared for what was going to prove the
most difficult, dangerous and exhausting journey of his career.

He had his second horse by this time, 'a black Andalusian stallion
of great size and strength ... but unbroke, savage and furious'.[19] It
was by the sight of Borrow on this magnificent steed that many people
remembered him, years later, when all other aspects of their meetings
with him in Madrid had been forgotten. Borrow, as he told his friend,
Hasfeld, also had a servant who would go with him at least part of the
way, an old soldier who had some good points 'yet in many respects
a more atrocious fellow never existed'. Borrow's description of this
servant probably tells us more about Borrow himself than the man he
had chosen as his companion. 'He is inordinately given to drink, and
of so quarrelsome a disposition that he is almost constantly involved
in some broil. Like most of his countrymen, he carries an exceedingly
long knife, which he frequently unsheaths and brandishes in the faces

of those who are unfortunate enough to awaken his choler.'[20] Only the other day, Borrow continued, he had to rescue from this violent fellow a man whom he was threatening to kill for having burnt a red-herring. But he was honest and knew the country and so was 'a very suitable squire for an errant knight, like myself'.[21] (These almost unavoidable comparisons with Don Quixote always amused Borrow). The servant, though, proved unsatisfactory and was dismissed. He was replaced by a Greek called Antonio Buchini, who stayed with Borrow until the middle of 1839. Having sent 500 copies of the New Testament to Corunna to await his arrival, or having made arrangements for them to be sent, to await his arrival, he left Madrid in May bound for Finisterre, on a journey designed if not destined to satisfy his deepest longings.

As Borrow sets out, it is important to notice that whereas he devoted almost the entire second volume of *The Bible in Spain* to this journey, he seems only to have written to Brandram a few times, specifically on 7 June, 5 July, 20 July, 23 August, 15 September and 29 September. That makes seven letters in roughly six months. Anyone who compares these letters with the account in *The Bible in Spain* will immediately notice that they were incorporated almost *verbatim* into the book and were in a sense written for it, being largely descriptive and not much concerned with Bible Society business. He will see, too, that whereas Borrow never entirely forgets that he is an agent of the Society, his references to his work for it become infrequent and perfunctory. Furthermore, the letters to Brandram are mostly about the first part of the journey, when he had the New Testaments he had brought with him still to dispose of, while he says much less about the return journey even though a large part of *The Bible in Spain* is devoted to it. This is where the questions that have already been mentioned about the discrepancies between *The Bible in Spain* and *Letters of George Borrow to the British and Foreign Bible Society* are most noticeable, as is the fact that there is much that Borrow leaves unsaid. Was he on this long expedition the devoted missionary who had suppressed his reservation about being a colporteur in order to do what Brandram wished? Or did he merely find it convenient to play missionary in order to justify the journey?

Certainly he did not neglect his duties entirely. Having disposed of five copies of the New Testament during the four-day journey to Salamanca, he did there what he later did in other towns and cities, that is, put an advertisement in 'the official bulletin of the place', had the same advertisement printed as a broadsheet on posters, and at the same time made the rounds of the booksellers, leaving them with such copies as they were willing to accept. He did this in Valladolid, Astorga, Lugo, Santiago, Corunna, Longoria and no doubt other places as well. By mid-July he had disposed of the stock he had taken with him and had to wait until he got back to Corunna before he could renew the work. Because his remarks are, characteristically, dry and laconic, it is sometimes difficult to interpret their tone. Of his stay in Valladolid, he says: 'I believe the whole number disposed of during my stay amounted to fifteen so that my visit to this dark corner has not been entirely in vain, as the seed of the gospel has been sown, though sparingly.'[22] In Lugo, the Lord had 'deigned to favour' his efforts and he disposed of thirty copies in a single day. In Santiago he sold between thirty and forty through a bookseller who had 'taken up the cause with an enthusiasm which doubtless emanates from on high'.[23] And from Corunna he reported, as we saw at the beginning of chapter 4, that he had 'carried the Gospel to the extreme part of the old world, having left a Testament in the hands of Antonio de la Trava, an ancient mariner of Finisterre'.[24] Although copies were undoubtedly given away in other parts of Spain, Borrow specifically states that none were given away on this particular expedition but that, on the contrary, he received between 10 and 12 *reals* for each copy, which was just below cost. The financial implications of this statement will be discussed later, but on the face of it, Borrow was doing exactly what his employers expected of him. Or was he? Was it not rather the case that he found it easy to introduce into his letters the kind of remark that is quoted above and that the Bible Society's policy of merely putting Bibles, or in this case New Testaments, into people's hands, without commentary, argument, explanation or any type of proselytising was extremely convenient, since he had no intention of doing anything other than dispose of his stock? There is no evidence whatsoever that Borrow had any interest in the salvation of souls, even his own. No doubt this was because he saw at first hand that the Spaniards of the north-west, whom he customarily dismissed as, at best, rogues, were beyond redemption and because in the villages he visited the priests were in complete control. He does not say in so many words that priests made life difficult for him on his travels but since, when he later returned to England, his outright hatred of Roman Catholicism had been powerfully reinforced, it seems likely that the high feeling derived from encounters on the road, which affected him directly, as opposed to his later encounters with the authorities in Madrid, which, though disagreeable and inconvenient, were not exclusively personal. This supposition is supported by the fact that, although Borrow spent several weeks in Salamanca, Valladolid and Santiago, he for the most part moved rapidly through the countryside, even mysteriously, very much like the bandits, beggars and gypsies whose identities he sometimes adopted as a disguise for reasons of safety. Had Borrow's first readers not been predisposed to take for granted the sincerity of any agent of the Bible Society, they would no doubt have seen that Borrow's own account of his time in Spain was at best ambivalent, at worst – from a religious point of view – distinctly suspect. Perhaps this does not matter, though: it is largely its ambivalent tone that makes *The Bible in Spain* such good reading.

Good reading it is, particularly this second volume about his expedition to Finisterre.

Having indulged himself hugely, as well as having completely exhausted himself, for he had had dysentery continuously during the final two months, which in turn caused eye-trouble that he called ophthalmia, Borrow when he reached Madrid on 31 October 1837 immediately turned to the task of making available to the public the store of New Testaments that had remained virtually untouched during his absence. So began the most turbulent period of Borrow's time in Spain. He remained in Madrid, concentrated on his job and responded to the opposition of the Spanish authorities with the greatest possible determination. The authorities had not interfered with the essentially private enterprise of the printing of the New Testament: to see it openly distributed was another matter. Powerful opposition from Church and state was inevitable, even if it at first worked in a subterranean way. Borrow knew that conflict was inevitable and he was by no means the man to withdraw from it.

On the contrary, on 17 November he rented a shop at No. 27 in the Calle del Principe for 8 *reals* a day,[25] placed above it a large painted sign that read 'Despacho de la Sociedad Biblica y Estranjera', put bright yellow signs and advertisements in the window and hired placard-bearers to walk in the streets outside. Soon everyone knew about this novelty in the heart of the city, though some were surprised that, despite the shop's name, you could buy only New Testaments there but not Bibles. To the committee in London the scheme afforded 'no little merriment', Brandram balancing this, however, with the hope 'that it may not be prejudicial'.[26] But it was. The Bible Society, from the official Spanish point of view, was now giving itself too much freedom, its two agents, Borrow and Graydon, acting so energetically that their presence could no longer be ignored. Representations had already been made by the authorities to George Villiers to halt the practice of giving New Testaments away, because this was a propaganda exercise different in kind, they thought, from the type of voluntary purchase that indicated a desire on the part of the buyer.

Both Borrow and Graydon had obviously given Bibles and New Testaments away; both assured Brandram that the numbers were very small. Brandram asked Borrow to explain this to Villiers. Meanwhile, an increasingly difficult situation was made more critical by a letter prefixed to a pastoral from the Bishop of Valencia, designed as an answer to Graydon's advertising placards. When Borrow saw the Bishop's letter he wrote one himself about the role of the Bible Society and the inadequacies of the Catholic Church, which was printed in the newspaper *El Español*, thus bringing the controversy out into the open. In the course of all this, Borrow became petulant about Graydon. He disliked having a rival, accused him of not understanding the political scene in Madrid and complained to Brandham. Graydon was stirring up trouble and should be recalled! Graydon, who was far more efficient than Borrow in the work of distribution, had similar feelings about his colleague.

While the Borrow–Brandram–Graydon correspondence was in progress, the priests 'swooped'.[27] Borrow had got a bad reputation for himself not only by opening the shop, but also, the authorities said, by consorting with gypsies. How religious could that person be who regularly brought gypsy women to his house? The Church made representations to the Political Governor of Madrid, who on 15 January 1838, ordered the whole stock of New Testaments to be seized. He also issued an order, dated 12 January, that no further Testaments were to be sold.

Borrow's report to Brandram, in a letter dated 15 January 1838, was characteristic. He had been apprehensive about the change of Government, 'the present head of the Cabinet, Ofalia, being one of the most furious bigots in Spain'.[28] Villiers probably would not help much 'having opposed with all his power the accession of Ofalia to the premiership'. But 'I still have great confidence in myself.' He had been 'advised' to erase the Bible Society's name from the shop, but would not:

I am not a person to be terrified by any danger, when I see that braving it is the only way to achieve an object. The booksellers refused to sell my work; I was compelled to establish a shop of my own. Every shop in Madrid has a name. What name should I give mine but the true one? I was not ashamed of my cause nor my colours. I hoisted them, and have fought beneath them not without success.[29]

This to Brandram. Despite what he says, he of course also had talks with George Villiers, who on the eve of Borrow's departure for Finisterre had shown himself to be an ally by having his secretary, Southern, order a number of New Testaments for British consulates throughout Spain. Villiers at first tried to resolve the matter informally but eventually had to ask Borrow to prepare a statement about the work and purposes of the Bible Society for presentation to Count Ofalia. This Borrow submitted, in Spanish,[30] on 23 February, together with the following covering letter to Villiers:

I take the liberty of forwarding the paper which you did me the honour of requesting me to draw up, and in which I have stated the intentions of the Bible Society in respect to Spain. You will increase the obligations which you have already conferred upon me by presenting it to Count Ofalia.

Should his excellency still prove unwilling to sanction the sale of the New Testament, I shall be happy to obtain an assurance of not being interrupted in the sale of my other two little books, St. Luke in Gitano and Basque, against which I do not conceive that any objection can reasonably be brought.[31]

From this point on, Borrow's position in Madrid steadily deteriorated and, as it did so, there occurred the first difficult passage in the relationship between Borrow and Brandram. Had Borrow not behaved rashly, Brandram allowed himself to wonder. Rashly? Not at all. 'I have been almost incessantly engaged in negotiations with Count Ofalia.'[32] Villiers had said that Ofalia had the '*anima*' of a mouse, and when Borrow went to see him, he described his as 'a dusky, diminutive person ... with false hair and teeth, but exceedingly gentlemanly manners', who, despite his manners, was terrified of the clergy and had no intention of acceding to Borrow's requests. Borrow affected to believe he was being victimised merely because, being in Madrid, he was the person nearest at hand. He picked little quarrels, or differences of opinion, with Brandram, not only about Graydon, but also over a Mr Rule who, Borrow said, was duplicating his work in the south and over a M. Marin, an impecunious turncoat Catholic priest, whom Rule had sent to Madrid so that Borrow could look after him. Borrow was definitely ruffled. His Gypsy Luke had come out, Ofalia had inspected it and in the Spanish papers it had been called, according to the translator, 'a great accession to the literature of Spain', but Brandram 'never had the urbanity to acknowledge the receipt'[33] of it. 'Should he return to England?' Borrow asked. 'Not yet', replied Brandram,[34] still attributing the cause of the problem more to Borrow's eccentric character than to the situation itself. At the end of April, the stock of Borrow's Gitano and Basque Luke, which he kept in the shop, was confiscated by the police, forcing Villiers to protest vigorously, on the grounds that the Civil Governor, Don Ramon Cambon, had not banned the sale of these two books when Borrow had sent him copies. Perhaps, though, the Spanish police, who had been watching Borrow for some time, had a more complete knowledge of Borrow's character and life-style than had Villiers. Borrow, realising this, had meanwhile taken the precaution of removing from the shop, under cover of darkness, a good stock of the three books he had been trying to sell there.

On 1 May, while Borrow was having breakfast, his landlady ushered in 'a mean-looking fellow, about the middle stature, with a countenance on which knave was written in legible characters'.[35] He said that he came from the political chief of Madrid, that he had to tell Borrow that his covert activities had been observed, that he had authority to search the apartment and that he had a mind to do so, poking about with his stick in a heap of papers on a chair and irritating Borrow by asking if they were Gypsy papers. 'I instantly determined upon submitting no longer to this behaviour, and taking the fellow by the arm, led him out of the apartment, and then still holding him, conducted him downstairs from the third floor in which I lived, into the street, looking him steadfastly in the face the whole while.'[36] This happened so quickly, that his visitor left his sombrero on the table; so Borrow sent it down to him 'as he stood in the street staring with distended eyes at the balcony of my apartment'.

That was Borrow's account as he recollected the affair when he wrote *The Bible in Spain*. The account of Pedro Martin de Eugenio, read as follows:

Madrid, 30th April, 1838.

OFFICIAL REPORT OF THE POLICE AGENT OF THE
LANGUAGE HELD BY MR. BORROW

Public Security. – In virtue of an order from His Excellency the Civil Governor, I went to seize the copies entitled the Gospel of St. Luke, in the Shop Princes Street No. 25, belonging to Mr. George Borrow, but not finding him there, I went to his lodgings, which are in St. James Street, No. 16, on the third floor and presenting the said order to Him He read it, and with an angry look threw it on the ground saying, that He had nothing to do with the Civil Governor, that He was authorised by His Ambassador to sell the Work in question, and that an English Stable Boy, is more than any Spanish Civil Governor, and that I had forcibly entered his house, to which I replied that I only went to communicate the order to Him, as proprietor as he was of the said Shop, and to seize the Copies in it in virtue of that Order, and He answered I might do as I liked, that He should go to the House of His Ambassador, and that I should be responsible for the consequences; to which I replied that He had personally insulted the Civil Governor and all Spain, to which He answered in the same terms, holding the same language as above stated.

All of which I communicate to you for the objects required.

PEDRO MARTIN DE EUGENIO.[37]

Already predisposed to accept the report of the agent, the Civil Governor of Madrid, Diego de Entreña, had little option but to treat this whole episode seriously, since the authorities behind the scenes had decided that the Bible Society's activities could no longer be tolerated. Borrow knew this and moved into 'a celebrated French tavern in the *Calle del Caballero de Garcia*, which as it was one of the most fashionable and public places in Madrid, I naturally concluded was one of the last where the corregidor would think of seeking me'.[38] That night a party of officials searched his house, so the next day Borrow visited Villiers at the embassy, told him what had happened, and was advised to remain as Villiers' guest till the storm blew over, because, even though the civil authorities were acting beyond their powers, Borrow might be put to considerable inconvenience if he left the refuge of the embassy. Leave it he did, however, and was immediately arrested.

Borrow later claimed that the 'prospect of incarceration' had not alarmed him, because 'an adventurous life and inveterate habits of wandering' had made him adaptable to situations of every kind. In any case, he had been thinking of visiting the prison for some time, indeed had actually applied to do so, 'partly in the hope of being able to say a few words of Christian instruction to the criminals, and partly with a view to making certain investigations in the robber language of Spain'.[39] Refused permission before, he now found himself after all in the Carcel de la Corte where, in a section of the prison reserved for political prisoners, he was allowed to make arrangements for furniture, food, drinks and books to be brought in and to receive visitors who, if *The Bible in Spain* is to be believed, arrived in an endless stream. These visitors included Mr Southern, Sir George Villiers' secretary.

Lively and persuasive as Borrow's own account of his imprisonment still is, it must now be read in conjunction with other documents not available, perhaps fortunately, to the first readers of *The Bible in Spain*. Borrow always did exactly as he wished. His egoism was not threatened by imprisonment, because he did not believe he had committed a crime and because he knew Villiers would take care of things. Whether in his prison cell he felt those normal pangs of fear, anxiety, even guilt, that would afflict most people is not known: there is no evidence that he did. On the contrary, he decided to seek redress for his unlawful arrest, to this end making it known that he would not leave prison until the Spanish authorities had climbed down. His arrest had caused a minor international incident, a partial record of which is enshrined in official correspondence between Sir George Villiers and Count Ofalia, between Villiers and Palmerston, and between Villiers and both Borrow and Graydon, correspondence that can be reconstructed from letters in the Clarendon Papers in the Bodleian, the Public Record Office, and the Library of Bible House. Ofalia pointed out that, while he hoped nothing would disturb good relations between Spain and Britain, the distribution of Bibles or Testaments that lacked notes and commentaries was illegal in Spain, that this applied both to Bibles imported from abroad and those manufactured in Spain, that both Borrow and Graydon had disregarded official direction on the matter, and that, though British subjects, they had to be made to see that the same laws as applied to Spaniards applied also to them, even though the Civil Governor might have gone beyond his powers in actually putting out a warrant for Borrow's arrest. Villiers could not, and probably did not wish to, disagree. From the point of view of both the Spanish Prime Minister and the British Ambassador it was simply a matter of finding a way to smooth things over without loss of face. That Sir George Villiers did not wholly identify himself with what Borrow represented as a just cause is made sufficiently clear by a despatch to Viscount Palmerston, dated 5 May 1838, in which he said: 'This disagreeable business is rendered yet more so by the impossibility of defending with success all Mr. Borrow's proceedings.'[40]

Borrow always claimed that, while he himself had behaved diplomatically in Madrid, the Society's other agent, Graydon, had wrecked their chances of success by flouting authority. Graydon's career had in fact been quite similar to Borrow's. Since his first reconnaissance in 1834, he had encountered the same problems in the east of Spain as Borrow had in the west. The books he had imported and placed with a Barcelona bookseller were impounded. It was illegal to import books that were on the Index. Like Borrow, he therefore printed a New Testament and from his base in Barcelona tried to distribute it. As with Borrow, Graydon's vehement anti-Catholic feelings were significantly reinforced by his experience of Spanish life and particularly by his experience of the Church. He came to realise over the years that the Church was too strong in Spain to be much concerned with the covert activities of one or two foreigners, that though the Bible Society was impressed by his distribution figures the Church was not, and that only a more open confrontation would bring to the public's attention the fact that in a Christian country the Bible was not generally available. He therefore decided upon roughly the same line of action as Borrow. He travelled south, distributing Bibles as he went. He attacked the Roman Catholic Church in newspaper articles. And he advertised his presence with placards. The Church authorities caught up with him when he reached Malaga on 24 April 1838. On that day, the Bishop of Malaga censured him for illegally selling in Malaga Bibles that were incomplete – that is, that lacked the Apocrypha. A jury decided that there were grounds for legal action and Graydon was taken into custody. When he was brought to trial on 8 May (when Borrow, incidentally, was still in prison), the prosecutor demanded a six-year sentence 'for subversive activity'. Now, although Graydon was acquitted by a jury vote of eleven to one and the Bishop, in an unrelated political intrigue, arrested a few days later, it is fairly clear from the almost simultaneous arrest of the Society's two agents that the Spanish Government had decided to bring their activities to an end. Villiers understood this perfectly, even if Borrow did not, because of course Villiers was involved in both incidents. At the same time, the discrepancy between what actually happened and Borrow's account of the incident in *The Bible in Spain* is probably to be explained by the fact that Villiers did not feel obliged to reveal to Borrow the explicit nature of his verbal agreement with Ofalia.

This agreement was that the two Englishmen would be released if Villiers would guarantee that their activities would cease. Villiers instructed W. P. Mark, British Consul in Malaga, to advise Graydon that the British Government could offer him no further protection unless he agreed to obey the law of the land. Borrow was released from prison or at least, when presented with a face-saving arrangement, agreed to leave. Villiers wrote to him on 22 May, giving him the same advice as he had already given Graydon. The following day Villiers and Borrow called on the Archbishop of Toledo, who had headed the Church's commission of inquiry into the activities of the Bible Society.[41] In *The Bible in Spain* Borrow affected not to understand the purpose of this visit: clearly it was arranged by Villiers so that the Bishop would have some assurance that the troublesome but not really important affair was now over. On 25 May, Villiers wrote to Ofalia to give him, too, that assurance. Because the Ambassador had considered the episode to be potentially serious, he had kept the Prime Minister, Palmerston, informed of what was happening, so copies of the correspondence were sent to the Foreign Office, which in turn later had copies sent to Bible House, where they can still be examined. At this point, Villiers must have felt that he had been successful in containing a dangerous situation.

Andrew Brandram learnt of Borrow's arrest from *The Times*. Because the crises in Madrid and Malaga had come to a head so suddenly, and because Sir George Villiers had had to act quickly, there was a time-lag between events in Spain and the Bible Society's knowledge of them. 'We are grieved to learn from the public papers that you have been imprisoned', wrote Brandram on 15 May – after Borrow had been released – 'and shall be all anxiety to hear from you'.[42] Before he had received Borrow's first letter from prison, which though despatched on 11 May, refrained from giving a detailed report on what had occurred, for somehow Borrow knew that there had been a full account in *The Times*, Brandram had written a second time to say he 'could not but feel assured that you had done nothing wrong from the fact that you would not quit the prison when the doors were set open for you'.[43] He could not say very much because he still did not know what had happened. Just as Brandram, when he wrote his second letter, was unaware of the action Villiers had been obliged to take, so Borrow was unaware of the seriousness of Graydon's predicament and therefore continued to behave as though Graydon's indiscretions in Malaga were the cause of Borrow's difficulties in Madrid. In his letter to Brandram immediately after his release from prison, a letter in which he naively announced that whatever he in future did for the Society in Spain would have the 'sanction of the Government', not realising that behind his back a deal had been made that ensured he would do very little at all, he openly attacked Graydon in terms one hopes he later came to regret.

I shall not make any observation of this matter further than stating that I have never had any other opinion than that he is insane – insane as the person who for the sake of warming his own hands would set a street on fire. Sir George said today that he, Graydon, was the cause of my *harmless* shop being closed at Madrid and also of my imprisonment. The Society will of course communicate with Sir George on the subject: I wash my hands of it.[44]

Communicating directly with Sir George Villiers was exactly what Andrew Brandram had no wish to do, because the Society avoided any type of political involvement. At a meeting of the full committee on 25 May, there was a 'long conversation' about 'the Society's concerns in Spain with especial reference to the actual situation of its agents there', but the matter had to be deferred until the next meeting for lack of information. Before that next meeting, held on 28 May 1838, Lord Bexley attempted to obtain the details of what had happened in Madrid and Malaga from the Foreign Office, but without success, because the Under-Secretary, Mr Backhouse, was not available. On the agenda was Borrow's disclaimer, which had been published in the *National Courier*, a disclaimer that had apparently been received only on the day of the meeting though published in Madrid on 17 May. Although this letter to a newspaper was part of the face-saving operation, Borrow was presumably sincere when he said that the design of the Bible Society was 'the propagation of the word of Christ in all countries, separated wholly from the forms of discipline of the Church, [which are] matters of secondary consideration, which have tended to keep up in the hearts of the Christians unhappy and malignant feuds'.[45] But this perhaps important document was for the moment of secondary importance to the committee, which had to wait until Bexley ascertained the facts not from the Society's agents but from the Foreign Office. As soon as the facts were known, both agents were recalled.[46] Graydon, understanding how serious his position had been, travelled back to England by way of Marseilles; Borrow prevented by his egoism from understanding why he had been released from prison, and perhaps not really knowing how it had happened, left Madrid and went into hiding in Villa Seca, at the house of his Madrid landlady's husband, 9 leagues from Madrid.

Both Borrow and Graydon had been told that there was nothing to prevent them remaining in Spain, indeed that there was nothing to prevent their representing themselves as agents of the Bible Society, provided they refrained from printing, selling and distributing un-authorised versions of the Bible and provided they tried a little harder to get on with the Catholic clergy. Unfortunately, Borrow continued for a couple of months to misunderstand his position. In his report to the Bible Society, of which he gave Villiers a copy,[47] he once again blamed Graydon for 'various writings' that contained passages 'insulting to the Government and the Ecclesiastical authorities in Spain'. This was on 3 June. He appears not to have realised that Brandram and others took exception to his attacks on Graydon and, in the correspondence through-out June, there is a petulant and self-righteous tone, which can only be justified by the possibility that Villiers had been 'genteel' in his remontrances instead of plainly having Borrow on the carpet. So in the stifling midsummer heat, Borrow continued the illicit distribution of New Testaments in La Mancha, believing himself to be on the side of the angels. This situation continued at least until 23 July when Borrow wrote to Brandram the letter that Herbert Jenkins said 'showed a dignity and calmness of demeanour that had been lacking from his previous letters'.[48] This letter was chiefly about the closing-down of Borrow's 'depots' at Oviedo, Pontevedra, Salamanca, Santiago, Seville and Valladolid, which Brandram, whom Borrow had so far told little of a specific kind, hardly would believe possible, but in it Borrow allowed himself the following paragraph:

It appears from your letters that the depots in the South of Spain have escaped. I am glad of it, although it be at my own expense. I see the hand of the Lord throughout the late transactions. He is chastening me; it is His pleasure that the guilty escape and the innocent be punished. The Government gave orders to seize the Bible depots throughout the country on account of the late scenes at Malaga and Valencia – I have never been there, yet only *my* depots are meddled with, as it appears! The Lord's will be done, blessed be the name of the Lord.[49]

Jenkins may have considered that this showed a 'calmness of de-meanour', but Andrew Brandram did not. For a second time he told

The second visit to Spain

Borrow to return to England. If Borrow was to continue to work for the Society, the members of the committee '*must*' see him. This letter was endorsed by a resolution passed at a General Council meeting on 6 August: Borrow was to be instructed to return to England 'without delay', and Brandram did so instruct him.

Both letters reached Madrid, however, after Borrow, accompanied by Antonio and Juan Lopez (his newly-employed assistant), had left on yet another expedition into the country. In his account of his expedition in *The Bible in Spain*, there is as great an emphasis upon the selling of Bibles as in any other part of that book. At the same time, Borrow made no bones about the fact that he was on the run. He went first to Aranjuez, to which place he had forwarded 'a large supply of books'. He stayed there three days, 'found a vast deal of poverty and ignorance amongst the inhabitants', and experienced what he called 'some opposition'. He wanted to travel on from there past Ocaña into Carlist territory, 'to conceal myself for a season amongst its solitary villages'. But in Ocaña Lopez was arrested and 200 copies of the New Testament seized by the local authorities. Assured by a messenger that Lopez would be released, Borrow galloped back to Madrid with Antonio. That he could not remain in Madrid was obvious. He therefore set out again, to La Granja, Segovia, Abades and Labajos, where Lopez was again arrested. This frantic attempt by Borrow not to accept defeat, not to obey Brandram's directive that he should return to England, not to face up to the reality of what had occurred, naturally began to tell upon him. He got Lopez out of gaol but fell ill himself, exhausted amongst other things by the terrible heat of that particular summer. Characteristically, he does not tell the reader of *The Bible in Spain* about the tension that existed between his employers and himself but simply ends the account of his second period in Spain by saying 'Change of scene and air was recommended; I therefore returned to England.'[50] Borrow's statement of expenses, submitted when he reached Earl Street, show that he travelled overland by way of Saragossa, Bordeaux, Paris and Boulogne. Since he wrote his last letter to Brandram from Madrid on 19 September, it is likely that he reached London only at the end of the month; indeed when later he said he arrived on the last day of August he may simply have made a mistake and meant, rather, the last day of September.

Seville and Tangiers:
December 1838–April 1840

While in England, Borrow divided most of his time between London, where he stayed in the Spread Eagle at Gracechurch Street, and Norwich, where he visited his mother, as well as a number of his friends. With his fate in the balance, the Bible Society tried to put him to work, asking him, for example, to go, of all places, to Colchester, presumably to talk about his work in Spain, but he refused, writing a note from the Spread Eagle to say that he was 'feverish and ill', adding that he wished he were still in Spain, 'for I cannot see that my coming over was at all necessary; it has discomposed me in many points, and has been a source of much expense and loss of time'. In a characteristic lapse into self-pity, he told Jowett that he had not a single friend or acquaintance in this 'huge gloomy town'.[1] He was lonely, disorientated, idle. He had left Spain without a full understanding of the political situation there, as it affected his work, and in London was not convinced that the conditions in which he would have to live in the Spain of 1839 were very much different from those he had experienced and coped with in the Spain of 1837. Besides, because he wished, was indeed determined, to return, he was not inclined to take seriously any of those obstacles to further work which were now perceived more clearly by the Bible Society committee. The committee had not said that he was being recalled for good, so he pointed out that he would *have* to return to Spain to put his, as well as the Society's, affairs in order. As to England itself, he later told his friend, Luis de Usoz:

I must confess that England is little to my taste; for, notwithstanding its advance in civilization and the marvellous public works that call the travellers' attention on every side; in spite of the fact that one can travel there at the rate of twenty Spanish leagues an hour, and that you have peace, tranquillity and justice. Still I must say I prefer poor distracted Spain, and prize its bright sun above all the arts and civilization of England, especially for a person like myself, gloomy by nature and averse to a climate of fog and rain.[2]

Bible Society accounts show that Borrow stayed at the Spread Eagle from 1 to 4 October and from 17 to 25 October, so it may have been during the intervening period that he went to visit his mother in Norwich.

At all events, with his future still undecided, he went not only to Norwich, but also to visit Mrs Mary Clarke and her daughter, Henrietta, at Oulton Hall, just outside Lowestoft. Knapp thought that Borrow had first met the Clarkes through mutual friends, the Batemans.[3] He had certainly known them at least since 1832, for in one of her letters Mrs Clarke later referred to his having 'left his couch' to visit them at Mutford Lock in that year. While Borrow was in Russia, she had kept up with his news by reading his letters to Francis Cunningham, including a copy of Borrow's much-discussed reply to the Bible Society's query: 'What is Mr. Borrow about?'[4] Cunningham had represented Borrow to her as 'one of the most extraordinary and interesting individuals of the present day',[5] which was no less than the truth, though perhaps not in the sense that Cunningham intended. The thoughts that stirred in Mary Clarke's mind as she read of this local hero's exploits are not recorded but may easily be guessed, for by some inner compulsion she was preparing, unwittingly, for the same experience as liberated Miriam Baske in Gissing's novel *The Emancipated*. Mrs Clarke was the widow of Lt Henry Clarke, whom, as Mary Skepper, she had married on 26 July 1817. Henry Clarke, however, had died within a year of their marriage, on 21 March 1818, so their child, Henrietta, was born in the home of her parents, where mother and child had lived ever since. Not much has survived from this long period of widowhood, to indicate how she lived, whom she knew, what she thought, except a souvenir book, now in the Norfolk Record Office, which, consisting as it does mostly of verses copied out in a very youthful hand, tells us nothing of the joys, discontents, anxieties or thoughts of her interior life during the time she was bringing up her daughter. That she was religious in an orthodox way may be assumed from her friendship with clergymen and her attendance at Bible meetings. If it must be supposed that her life was relatively stable, if uneventful, while she lived with her parents, this stability had been placed in jeopardy at roughly the same time Borrow had returned from Russia. Her mother, Ann Skepper, died in September 1835, just before one of Borrow's visits to them, a visit that became one of condolence and family talk. Then on 5 February the following year her father died, bringing about that complex legal situation which is at the heart of the Borrow story. Mr Skepper's will specified that his son, Breame Skepper, should inherit Oulton Hall and the 300-acre estate, while his daughter should inherit Oulton Cottage with its octagonal summerhouse and live on an income that derived from a mortgage on the Hall. Presumably Mr Skepper senior, if somewhat casual in the making of these arrangements, thought that his estate would continue to support both his son and daughter quite adequately, since it had done so to date, but he reckoned without the animosity that had built up over the years between his daughter and his daughter-in-law. It was also impossible for him to anticipate that his son, Breame Skepper, would himself die not much more than a year later on 22 May 1837, aged only forty-two. When this happened, it rested with the two women to put their affairs in order, if they could. Mrs Clarke was in the cottage with her young daughter, Henrietta, now aged nineteen. The cottage and its grounds were part of the Oulton Hall estate. Mrs Breame Skepper was in the Hall with her six young children. At stake was the ownership of the Hall and its estate. Both women wanted it.

No record has survived of the no doubt heavily charged conversations that occurred between daughter and daughter-in-law. Whether Mrs Skepper chose freely to leave the Hall or whether she was forced to conclude that only by leaving it would she get its full value is not clear. She put it on the market, though, and soon sold it to a Mr Joseph C. Webb for £11,000. Knapp said that, though the sale was agreed, it 'was not carried into effect'.[6] This was because of the intervention of Mary Clarke, who had her solicitor purchase back the mortgage on the Hall so that she became, as Henrietta told Clement Shorter, 'mortgagee in possession'.[7] This meant that she had, at least for the time being, blocked the sale, which promptly became the subject of a Chancery suit initiated by the unfortunate purchaser. Because Mrs Breame Skepper and her children were still in the Hall, the two women remained at loggerheads, which was how Borrow found them when he visited Oulton in the latter part of 1838, about a year-and-a-half after the death of Mrs Skepper's husband. Mrs Clarke was absolutely determined to keep possession of what had always been her home. How could it not be *her* property? How could her father have wished her to lose it? The sun-tanned, weather-beaten essentially pragmatic traveller and the polite, church-going stay-at-home together quickly hit upon a scheme that would solve their problems and make life better for both of them. While not everything that occurred in the winter of 1838 can be reconstructed, it can safely be supposed that Borrow heard a full account of Mrs Clarke's problems and that, as a solicitor himself, he was quite capable of assessing them. Naturally enough, they kept their plans to themselves; the implications for Borrow of Mrs Clarke's sense of property only came to be felt many years later; but it may be mentioned here and now when Borrow said that marriage was 'by far the best way of getting possession of an estate', he was not only referring to himself.

By whatever means, Borrow persuaded the General Purposes Committee of the Bible Society that he should return to Spain. It has often been suggested that the committee members, against their better judgement, simply succumbed to his persuasiveness, his charm, his directness of approach, his general manner. This seems plausible. Knapp was the first to offer this explanation when he said that Borrow's differences with Andrew Brandram were resolved 'under the spell of his personal presence',[8] though this is not to say that the committee expected Borrow to stay in Spain for very long. They obviously knew that in the current political climate the Society's work there could not be continued, were not in the least disposed to flout what amounted to an instruction from the Foreign Office, and presumably had decided to place some limit on their agent's travelling expenses, instead of allowing him to make his own rules as he had done on his trip to Finisterre.[9] On the other hand, Borrow had left the Society's property and papers at various locations; he had, or could say he had, unfinished business of his own; and he had an expectation of employment, which some committee members were not inclined to deny to an agent who had been in prison on the Society's behalf. At any rate, he had his way, though at the eleventh hour, left by coach for Falmouth on 21 December, having missed *The Thames* when it sailed from London on the 20th; embarked on the 23rd; and, after an uneventful voyage, reached Lisbon on 29 December and Cadiz on 31 December, coolly picking up the narrative in *The Bible in Spain* with the words 'I again visited Spain', as though nothing of consequence had occurred while he was in England, whereas he had in fact, while there, formed a very distinct idea of what he now intended to do, that is, what he intended in the immediate future. Interestingly he still felt free to write to Hasfeld in his old manner.

It is however my firm intention, provided I am preserved, as soon as I shall have accomplished all in my power in Spain and have cleared the way for others, to turn my undivided attention to the North East when we shall perhaps meet again. In a word I purpose to return to Russia whence, having studied Mongolian and Chinese for a year or two at Saint Petersburg or Moscow, I shall pass on into remotest Scythia perhaps even as far as the 'Great Wall,' beneath whose shadow I should have no objection to spend the remaining years of my singular life, amongst wandering herdsmen and hunters discoursing with lamas and shamans.[10]

This letter, written on the very eve of his departure, could mean that he planned to put a great distance between Norfolk and himself, it could mean that he did not yet see the scope of the business in which he had been caught up, or it could mean that discrepancies between what he said to one person and what he said to another did not bother him. He had always wished to go to China. At least in that he was sincere.

Back in Spain, Borrow devoted much of the next four months to the Bible Society's affairs, as he interpreted them. His accounts show that he stayed in Seville from 3 to 13 January;[11] from Seville he wrote the first of several important letters to Mrs Clarke, as will be seen. Then, collecting material for his book as he travelled through Andalusia, he went once again to Madrid; called upon George Villiers, by this time Lord Clarendon; was reunited with his former Greek servant, Antonio, being amazed, said this pathologically reserved, inhibited individual, to find himself 'encircled in a person's arms'; took up temporary residence in his former lodgings; and bought himself a magnificent horse, called Sidi Habismilk, for 'what is a missionary in the heart of Spain without a horse?'[12] It need not be supposed that the British Minister neglected to remind Borrow that the circulation of the Bible without notes was still banned, though in his usual dry manner Borrow, in *The Bible in Spain*, merely says that Clarendon told him, 'amongst other things', about the seizure of books at Ocaña.[13] Presumably this was Borrow's way of saying that the British Minister instructed him not to cause trouble by circulating the New Testament in defiance of the law, while he in turn told Clarendon that he was in Madrid only to wind up the Society's affairs and to protect its property. The method adopted for this, though, may have ruffled Clarendon's temper. From the village of Villa Seca, where he had once taken refuge, Borrow employed a new assistant, an old peasant called Vitoriano and bought him a horse. Then, with his new colporteur he engaged in a short, sharp campaign to dispose of his remaining stock of New Testaments, including those he had left in Madrid unbound, but now had bound (thus giving that edition a further state).

First he tried the villages around Madrid. Presumably to reduce the possibility of arrest, he and his assistants travelled separately, with Borrow himself disguised as a white-haired old man, 'dressed in the fashion of the peasants of Segovia, namely, I had on my head a species of leather helmet or *montera*, with a jacket and trousers of the same material'.[14] Despite the relative isolation of the villages and the surprise factor that derived from the basic improbability of people travelling yet again through bandit-infested territory to dispose of New Testaments, an improbability that at first worked in Borrow's favour, the campaign lasted for only two months, because the authorities soon got wind of this latest flouting of the law and arrested Vitoriano when he arrived with his stock of books at the tiny village of Fuente la Higuera. For what occurred during this expedition to the villages outside Madrid between mid-January 1839 and mid-March, one has only Borrow's own account in *The Bible in Spain*. He was still smarting from the conversations he had had in London. He would not be a failure. He would dispose of the stock of New Testaments as agreed. This, specifically, was the justification for being in Spain at all. Well, then, his third visit would be fully justified, that is to say, all the Testaments would be disposed of, after which he would be free to do as he wished. Even a man as determined as Borrow undoubtedly was could not, however, keep a campaign of this kind going for very long and in *The Bible in Spain* he gave his own account of how he was baulked.

Providence, however, which had hitherto so remarkably favoured us in these rural excursions, now withdrew from us its support, and brought them to a sudden termination: for in whatever place the sacred writings were offered for sale, they were forthwith seized by persons who appeared to be on the watch; which events compelled me to alter my intention of proceeding to Talavera, and to return forthwith to Madrid.

I subsequently learned that our proceedings on the other side of Madrid having caused alarm amongst the heads of the clergy, they had made a formal complaint to the government, who immediately sent orders to all the alcaldes of the villages, great and small, in New Castile, to seize the New Testament wherever it might be exposed for sale; but, at the same time, enjoining them to be particularly careful not to detain or maltreat the person or persons who might be attempting to vend it. An exact description of myself accompanied these orders; and the authorities, both civil and military, were exhorted to be on their guard against me and my acts and machinations; for, as the document stated, I was today in one place, and tomorrow at twenty leagues' distance.[15]

Borrow had planned to complete his business in Madrid by mid-April or by the end of April at the latest. This is clear from the fact that he had written to Mrs Clarke to suggest she should join him there.

Though it seems not to have attracted very much attention, this letter is extremely important for a number of reasons. It shows that Borrow himself took the initiative in getting Mrs Clarke and her daughter to travel out to Seville. It shows that he did this almost immediately, so that, however loud his talk about disposing of Testaments, he in fact planned his time in Seville well in advance. And it shows that he was prepared to represent himself as a sincere Christian to Mrs Clarke, while making what in Lowestoft terms must have been an extraordinary proposal, or would have seemed extraordinary had it not been broached, at least in general terms, on some earlier occasion. It is a long letter, the first part of it being devoted to a description of Borrow's work (he is only going to Madrid, he says, to collect a stock of Testaments) and of Seville, its streets, its houses, the cathedral, the Alcazar.

I must however proceed no further at present in describing the remarkable objects of Seville as there are other matters which I must touch upon, and which relate immediately to yourself. Respecting your question as to what quarter I would advise you to direct your cause, as soon as your affairs have been arranged to your satisfaction, I beg leave to answer that I do not think that yourself and Miss Hen could do better than to come out to Seville for a time, where you would be far out of the reach of the malignity of your ill-wishers, you might live here with the greatest respectability, tenant one of the charming houses which I have just described, and enjoy one of the finest climates in the world. Therefore you had better give this point your very serious consideration. I do not think that Colchester or Edinburgh would please you half so much as Seville where you would find a few excellent and worthy families, long established in Spain, and following with great success the pursuits of commerce.[16]

This is the crucial part of a crucial letter, the rest of which is devoted to business advice, except for the last paragraph, which concludes the letter on a note of finely contrived religiosity. Henrietta, Borrow says, should 'continue to collect as much money as possible towards affording spiritual instruction to the Spanish Gypsies'. He, for his part, is about to publish 'a work which I hope will prove of no slight spiritual benefit to these unhappy people'. Of course, he intended no such thing.

Whether Mary Clarke would have gone to Seville had she known that Borrow was only nominally working for the Bible Society, was not himself religious, was not writing a religious book, had not in mind a plan of the 'greatest respectability' and indeed intended to use the time for his own purposes, must be open to doubt, though Borrow was by now a well-practised religious hypocrite not likely to trouble her with arguments on points of doctrine or church observance. It is also difficult to know whether she acceded to Borrow's advice for her own sake or for Henrietta's: later events show that Henrietta was deeply attached to Borrow and in 1838, at the age of twenty, she must have desired to have a man in her life, a husband even, at least as strongly as did her mother.

Further correspondence followed while Borrow was in Madrid, having to do with the things Mrs Clarke and her daughter would need in Seville.

I smiled – nay, laughed outright – when you informed me that your counsellor had advised you against taking a house and furnishing it. Houses in Spain are let by the day: and in a palace here you will find less furniture than in your cottage at Oulton. Were you to furnish a Spanish house in the style of cold winterly England, you would be unable to breathe. A few chairs, tables and mattresses are all that is required, with of course a good stock of bedlinen. During the whole of the summer and autumn the people of Seville reside in

their patios over which an awning is hung. A very delicious existence it is –
a species of dream, of sunshine and shade, of falling water and flowers.

Bring with you, therefore, your clothes, plenty of bedlinen, etc., half a dozen
blankets, two dozen knives and forks, a mirror or two, twelve silver table
spoons, and a large one for soup, tea things and urn (for the Spaniards never
drink tea), a few books, but not many – and you will have occasion for nothing
more, or, if you have, you can purchase it here as cheap as in England.[17]

Knapp said that it was the Chancery proceedings that 'compelled Mrs.
Clark to disappear for a while',[18] an explanation which, though vague,
seems often to have been accepted as sufficient. Perhaps it is putting the
matter a little strongly to say that only marriage could save Mrs Clarke,
or at least save her property, and that the only person she could think
of to marry was George Borrow; nonetheless a strong compulsion was
obviously at work within her when she thought of, or agreed to, the
scheme by which she and her daughter would set sail for Seville leaving
her business affairs unresolved in England. As for Borrow, if he did
not fully anticipate the outcome of Mary Clarke's impending visit, he
certainly had the visit itself in mind as he hurried to finish his work in
Madrid. He also thought that, if he quickly completed the labour for
which he had been employed, he would then be free of obligation and
responsibility to the Society, even though he might continue to receive a
salary from it. Within him, too, a strong compulsion was at work: a
book was waiting to be written, a book he had now had in mind for at
least two years.

In mid-March, he abandoned his country campaign and turned his
attention to Madrid itself, where he could pursue his labours in com-
parative secrecy amongst the crowds and where he would offer the New
Testament from house to house 'at the same low price as in the
country'.[19] Borrow describes this crash programme for the disposal of
his remaining stock in his usual laconic fashion:

Having an extensive acquaintance amongst the lower orders, I selected eight
intelligent individuals to co-operate with me, amongst whom were five women.
All these I supplied with Testaments, and then sent them forth to all the parishes
in Madrid. The result of their efforts more than answered my expectations.
In less than fifteen days after my return from Naval Carnero, nearly six hundred
copies of the life and words of Him of Nazareth had been sold in the streets and
alleys of Madrid: a fact which I hope I may be permitted to mention with
gladness and with decent triumph in the Lord.[20]

As part of this new campaign, he had bound those copies, already
referred to, that he had left in sheets in Madrid. These, too, were
distributed, both by his 'eight intelligent individuals' and by those new
acquaintances whom he mentions in *The Bible in Spain*, the ecclesiastic,
the Marquis and the enormously rich, elderly gentleman of Navarre –

until the inevitable once more occurred. Borrow was summoned in the middle of the night by an ancient police agent, a white-haired hobgoblin, Borrow said, with eyes that sparkled in the dark like those of a ferret, to appear before a magistrate or *corregidor*; accused of ordering Antonio to steal back a box of Testaments the authorities had impounded; taxed once again for his impudence in presuming to return to Spain to overturn the religion of the country; and threatened with prison, where Borrow, in the lively conversation reported in *The Bible in Spain*, said he would be happy to go, since the 'most polite society of Madrid was to be found there'; and 'as I am at present compiling a vocabulary of the Madrilenian thieves, I should have, in being imprisoned, an excellent opportunity of completing it'.[21] Borrow extracted himself from this particular predicament by promising to return the Testaments to the authorities. 'I am a man of peace', he said, 'and wish not to have any dispute with the authorities for the sake of an old chest and a cargo of books, whose united value would scarcely amount to forty dollars.'[22] It was all very well to adopt a sensible and diplomatic tone years after the event: at the time he realised he had been taking incredible risks, was genuinely in danger, and could do no more. 'By the middle of April', he later told the reader of *The Bible in Spain*, 'I had sold as many Testaments as I thought Madrid would bear: I therefore called in my people, for I was afraid to overstock the market, and to bring the book into contempt by making it too common.'[23] Unfortunately there is no record of what Andrew Brandram thought of this extraordinary remark.

Brandram did, however, comment on Borrow's account of his return to Seville. Vitoriano was paid off. His horse was sold for just a little less than Borrow had paid for it. Borrow said goodbye to Maria, his Madrid landlady, for what he thought would be the last time. Then he sent Antonio with the two horses and their baggage in one of the 'convoys' that were often formed to give security from bandits, while he himself travelled in the mail coach, despite the fact that on its previous trip the mail had been ambushed by six mounted robbers, four of the six soldiers guarding it murdered, their corporal shot in the head at close range while tied to a tree, the courier robbed and stripped (though not killed because the robbers knew him) and the coach burnt. As usual, Borrow gives a vivid visual account of this episode. When they passed the tree to which the corporal had been tied 'the ground around was still saturated with blood, and a dog was gnawing a piece of the unfortunate wretch's skull'. As usual he drew attention to the danger and risk by underplaying it, for 'we travelled all the way without the slightest incident', he said, 'my usual wonderful good fortune accompanying us'.[24] In fact, the only incident he chose to recollect was his second meeting with the 'prophetess' of Marzanares. None of this was to Brandram's taste.

> As you request to hear from us I sit down to write at once, and shall make a few remarks on your last two letters. I scarcely know what to say. You are in a very peculiar country; you are doubtless a man of very peculiar temperament, and we must not apply common rules in judging either of yourself or your affairs. What, e.g., shall we say to your confession of extreme superstitiousness? It is very frank of you to tell us what you need not have told, but it sounded very odd when read aloud in a large Committee. Strangers that know you not would carry away strange ideas. The report of your successes in Madrid followed in the next paragraph, and made us forget the superstition.
>
> But to return to your first letter. In bespeaking our patience there is an implied contrast between your own mode of proceeding and that adopted by others – a contrast this a little to the disadvantage of others, and savouring a little of the praise of a personage called number one.
>
> Your second letter has something of the same kind in it and leads me the more to make the remark. Perhaps my vanity is offended, and I feel as if I were not esteemed a person of sufficient discernment to know enough of the real state of Spain, and was therefore unreasonable in expecting large immediate good to result from your journeys; and that all this rendered it necessary for you to enlighten my somewhat dull mind.
>
> Bear with me now in my criticisms on your second letter. You describe your perilous journey to Seville, and say at the beginning of the description: *My usual wonderful good fortune accompanying us*. This is a mode of speaking to which we are not well accustomed; it savours, some of our friends would say, a little of the profane. Those who know you will not impute this to you. But you must remember our Committee room is public to a great extent, and I cannot omit expressions as I go reading on. Pious sentiments may be thrust into letters *ad nauseam*, and it is not for that I plead; but is there not a *via media*?
>
> We are odd people, it may be, in England; we are not fond of prophets or 'prophetesses.' I have not turned back to your former description of the Lady whom you have a second time introduced to our notice. Perhaps my wounded pride had not been made whole after the infliction you before gave it by contrasting the teacher of the prophetess with English Rectors.[25]

This letter Borrow received only late in May for it was written on the 22nd. It shows, of course, that the relationship between the two men was deteriorating rapidly, but before Borrow had to respond to it he had been able to busy himself with other matters.

When precisely Borrow reached Seville is uncertain, thought it must have been towards the end of April, for he says that when he took up his abode there Antonio arrived 'within a few days' with the horses. In *The Bible in Spain* he speaks as though he is merely transferring from one theatre of action to another, says that he still has Testaments to sell and intends to distribute them, and generally gives the impression, at least at first, that his work for the Bible Society was to continue.[26] In reality, he knew it would not. There was no possibility whatsoever that the local authorities would overlook further attempts to sell Testaments. A description of Borrow had been widely circulated. Local officials had been given strict instructions to arrest him if necessary and later events show that he was under police survelliance. He knew very well that he had no recourse but to protect the Society's property if he could and, as instructed, ship it out of the country. This he did. At the same time, his intentions were beginning to be more clear. He had enrolled the assistance of a friend in Seville to gather material for a Gypsy vocabulary and in Madrid he had employed a scribe, a Mr Yuda, to copy passages from library books.[27] Obviously he intended to work on his own book as soon as he could settle to it. Another indication of interest is in his report of accounts. Knapp reproduced a 'Financial Statement of George Borrow from December 21, 1838, to April 16, 1839', in order to show, he thought, that Borrow had not overspent or been wasteful, as many people later said had been the case. Since Knapp did not consult the Bible Society's records, what he saw must have been an account sheet drawn up by Borrow for the Society. Perhaps it was a copy that Borrow retained. At all events, the terminal date is important. Evidently, if Knapp is to be believed, Borrow thought that *something* had terminated on 16 April and that 'something' was obviously the sale of Bibles and Testaments, which are enumerated in summary fashion. At this point, one is only noting that date that Knapp and Borrow gave to his financial report: the accounts themselves are revealing in other ways and will be discussed later. The third indication of what Borrow had in mind is the fact that, although he put up in the Posada de la Reyna when he arrived in Seville, he soon rented the two-storey house at 7 Plazuela de la Pila Seca, which he describes so graphically in *The Bible in Spain*. Assuming that he was in residence there at least by early May, he had only a short period by himself, for Mary and Henrietta Clarke embarked on the *Royal Tar* on 7 June and reached Seville eleven days later. So began a new phase of Borrow's life in Spain, a phase that had nothing whatsoever to do with the Bible Society. Borrow was now thirty-six and in his prime, very fit, very good-looking and as urbane as ever. Mary Clarke was forty-three, Henrietta twenty-one. The three of them set up house in a secluded little square in a quiet part of Seville, where they lived together until the following March, while Borrow wrote *The Zincali*. Andrew Brandram was not informed of this arrangement. As far as Borrow was concerned, it was none of Brandram's business.

Borrow had towards Spain a tourist or what is not infrequently called a 'colonial' attitude. He did not like Spaniards very much, but the fact did not bother him unduly since he had no wish to understand Spain in its own terms, no desire to adapt to an alien way of life except for reasons of convenience, and no inclination to commit himself in friendship to anyone he met, the few exceptions to this last statement being the exceptions that proved the rule, since although, for example, he wrote in warm terms to his old Madrid friend, Dr Usoz, at this time in Italy, it will be seen that it was Usoz who later had to remonstrate with Borrow for his derogatory remarks on the Spanish character. Both Antonio and Maria Diaz had a strong affection for Borrow, which to a large extent was returned, but he no more regarded them as equals than he did the gypsies, thieves, travellers and reprobates whom he caused to people the pages of *The Bible in Spain*.

Knapp quoted at length from the account given by Lt Col Elers Napier in *Excursions along the shores of the Mediterranean*, both because Napier gave a physical description of Borrow at exactly the time he returned to Seville from Madrid — Borrow was a 'tall, gentlemanly-looking man, dressed in a *zamarra*' with hair 'so deeply tinged with the winter of either age or sorrow, as to be nearly snow-white' — and because Napier was amazed to hear Borrow, within a short period of time, talk English, French, German, Greek, Italian and Hindee, as well as Spanish and Spanish Gypsy. What Napier also recorded was Borrow's total unwillingness to say anything about himself. Borrow did not even reveal his name, though the day after their meeting Borrow and Napier went on an expedition together. Nor did Borrow reveal what he was doing in Seville. Which is hardly surprising. Would Borrow tell a total stranger that, while employed by the British and Foreign Bible Society, he was about to set up house with a widow and her daughter of marriageable age without himself being married to either woman? The Napier episode is characteristic of the way Borrow preferred to live. He was secretive by nature. He still kept himself to himself. When in *The Bible in Spain* he describes some event, perhaps something that happened on the road, or an interesting character whom he met by chance, the writing is so direct and vivid that the reader feels the power of a unique personality and is won over to it, momentarily forgetting that after all he is not being told very much. When, by contrast, Borrow describes a place, the reader feels the extent to which Borrow is the 'outsider' detached from what he is describing, as in this eloquent if rather quaint apostrophe to Seville.

O how pleasant it is, especially in springtide, to stray along the shores of the Guadalquivir! Not far from the city, down the river, lies a grove called Las Delicias, or the Delights. It consists of trees of various kinds, but more especially of poplars and elms, and is traversed by long shady walks. This grove is the favourite promenade of the Sevillians, and there one occasionally sees assembled whatever the town produces of beauty or gallantry. There wander the black-eyed Andalusian dames and damsels, clad in their graceful silken mantillas; and there gallops the Andalusian cavalier, on his long-tailed thick-maned steed of Moorish ancestry. As the sun is descending, it is enchanting to glance back from this place in the direction of the city: the prospect is inexpressibly beautiful. Yonder in the distance, high and enormous, stands the Golden Tower, now used as a toll-house, but the principal bulwark of the city in the time of the Moors. It stands on the shore of the river, like a giant keeping watch, and is the first edifice which attracts the eye of the voyager as he moves up the stream to Seville. On the other side, opposite the tower, stands the noble Augustine convent, the ornament of the faubourg of Triana, whilst between the two edifices rolls the broad Guadalquivir, bearing on its bosom a flotilla of barks from Catalonia and Valencia. Further up is seen the bridge of boats, which traverses the water. The principal object of this prospect, however, is the Golden Tower, where the beams of the setting sun seem to be concentrated as in a focus, so that it appears built of pure gold, and probably from that circumstance received the name which it now bears. Cold, cold must the heart be which can remain insensible to the beauties of this magic scene, to do justice to which the pencil of Claude himself were barely equal. Often have I shed tears of rapture whilst I beheld it, and listened to the thrush and the nightingale piping forth their melodious songs in the woods, and inhaled the breeze laden with the perfume of the thousand orange gardens of Seville:

kennst du das land wo die citronen bluhen?

The interior of Seville scarcely corresponds with the exterior: the streets are narrow, badly paved, and full of misery and beggary. The houses are, for the most part, built in the Moorish fashion, with a quadrangular patio or court in the centre, where stands a marble fountain, constantly distilling limpid water. These courts, during the time of the summer heats, are covered over with a canvas awning, and beneath this the family sit during the greater part of the day. In many, especially those belonging to the houses of the wealthy, are to be found shrubs, orange trees, and all kinds of flowers, and perhaps a small aviary, so that no situation can be conceived more delicious than to lie here in the shade, hearkening to the song of the birds and the voice of the fountain.[28]

Borrow's description of his house is another example of this. He said 'it stood in a solitary situation, occupying one side of a small square', that it was built 'in the beautiful taste of Andalusia, with a court paved with small slabs of white and blue marble', that in the middle of this court was a fountain, the water of which played into an octagonal basin, and that the house itself was 'large and spacious'. From this house Borrow would ride out into the country in the evening.

It is here that the balmy air of beautiful Andalusia is to be inhaled in full perfection. Aromatic herbs and flowers are growing in abundance, diffusing their perfume around. Here dark and gloomy cares are dispelled as if by magic from the bosom, as the eyes wander over the prospect, lighted by unequalled sunshine, in which gaily painted butterflies wanton, and green and golden Salamanquesas lie extended, enjoying the luxurious warmth, and occasionally startling the traveller, by springing up and making off with portentous speed to the nearest coverts, whence they stare upon him with their sharp and lustrous eyes. I repeat, that it is impossible to continue melancholy in regions like these, and the ancient Greeks and Romans were right in making them the site of their Elysian fields. Most beautiful they are, even in their present desolation, for the hand of man has not cultivated them since the fatal era of the expulsion of the Moors, which drained Andalusia of at least two thirds of its population.[29]

Then in his usual direct, unaffected way Borrow describes what occurs one evening after his return from such a ride.

It is eight o'clock at night. I am returned from the Dehesa, and am standing on the sotea, or flat roof of my house, enjoying the cool breeze. Johannes Chrysostom has just arrived from his labour. I have not spoken to him, but I hear him below in the courtyard, detailing to Antonio the progress he has made in the last two days. He speaks barbarous Greek, plentifully interlarded with Spanish words; but I gather from his discourse, that he has already sold twelve Testaments among his fellow labourers. I hear copper coin falling on the pavement, and Antonio, who is not of a very Christian temper, reproving him for not having brought the proceeds of the sale in silver. He now asks for fifteen more, as he says the demand is becoming great, and that he shall have no difficulty in disposing of them in the course of the morrow, whilst pursuing his occupations. Antonio goes to fetch them, and he now stands alone by the marble fountain, singing a wild song, which I believe to be a hymn of his beloved Greek church. Behold one of the helpers which the Lord has sent me in my Gospel labours on the shores of the Guadalquivir.[30]

Characteristically, he does not participate in the conversation beneath him. He listens, represents himself as the observer of the scene and indulges himself, typically, in a little irony. So he was always. So he was, at least, until Mary Clarke arrived.

When Mrs Clarke arrived, Antonio was sent back — on 1 July – to his wife in Madrid, a wife by this time very anxious, according to Maria Diaz, for news of her husband.[31] A new regime had begun and Borrow began to understand the full implications of the situation he had created for himself.

In England, Andrew Brandram could not understand the situation Borrow had created for himself, because he did not know about it, but he did know that something of an unorthodox kind was on foot, so he wrote to Borrow on 29 July, ordering him back to London. The committee's resolution, as forwarded by Brandram, was certainly clear enough:

That, since it appears that the object of Mr. Borrow's present mission to Spain is nearly attained, by the disposal of the larger part of the SS [Spanish Scriptures] which he went out to distribute, he be requested to take measures for selling the remainder, or leaving them in safe custody, and that he then do proceed to this country – [32]

To make this doubly clear he had sent a copy to John Brackenbury, the British Consul in Cadiz. Meanwhile, Borrow had independently decided to go from Seville to Cadiz, not as the first stage of a return trip to England, but to make arrangements on the way with Charles Phillips, HM Consul in Bonanza and with John Brackenbury in Cadiz for the shipment to London of the remaining stock of New Testaments. After a brief overnight stop at Bonanza and San Lucar, Borrow reached Cadiz on 2 August, before Brandram's letter had arrived. As happened throughout his life with all sorts of people, he immediately fell into a good relationship with the British Consul, giving a vigorous account once again of how he had been thwarted in his work for the Bible Society, how few men could have achieved what he had achieved, how his good work had been undermined by the foolish and presumptuous behaviour of Lt Graydon, and how even now he bitterly regretted the termination of his work in Spain, if termination it actually was. Brackenbury believed him. He knew nothing of Borrow's former dealings with the Bible Society. He had not yet received the letter of recall – that is, his copy of it. In his own home, he found himself with a famous traveller who turned out to be as interesting as he had very likely heard would be the case, a man whose company he immediately enjoyed. He therefore helped Borrow with the shipment of books, as was his duty, then beyond the call of duty, wrote Brandram the letter that is reproduced below, a letter that certainly clarifies Borrow's position at that time, if not quite in the way that Professor Knapp supposed.

British Consulate, Cadiz, Sept. 19th, 1839.

MY DEAR FRIEND – I have had great pleasure in making the acquaintance of Mr. George Borrow – very great. He did me the kindness to dine here and spend the day with us, preceding his departure, and promised to revisit us on his return from Tangiers.

I furnished Mr. Borrow with a letter to my friend Mr. Drummond Hay, Her Majesty's Agent and Consul General for Morocco, from whom I have received the most agreeable accounts of Mr. Borrow.

What a subject of sorrow is the order recently issued to prevent the further distribution in this country of the Holy Scriptures without note or comment! and how much is that sorrow augmented by the apprehension that this inhibition was assuredly accelerated, if not absolutely occasioned, by the indiscretion of some of those who entered Spain for the avowed object of circulating the Scriptures, and of others who, not being Agents of the British and Foreign Bible Society, were nevertheless considered to be connected with it, as they distributed your editions of the Old and New Testaments. Our objects were defeated and your interests injured, therefore, when the Spanish Government required the departure from this country of those who, by other acts and deeds wholly distinct from the distribution of Bibles and Testaments, had been infracting the Laws Civil and Ecclesiastical.

Previously to these proceedings, the circulation of the Word of God was not only an legal act, but was one countenanced by the Government itself. All Authorities, therefore, Foreign and Domestic might co-operate in furtherance of this blessed undertaking without fear, without reproach. But how has the fine gold become changed! This Government which co-operated with us, is now arrayed against us. The Circulators of the New Testament (some of them) have been removed from the Kingdom; the copies which were printed by permission in Spain, to be circulated throughout its unhappy Provinces, have been collected and sent to England, and neither Spanish Authority nor Foreign Consul may now distribute the New Testament without knowingly violating the Law and incurring the penalties of the transgresison. And as if it were to augment my personal mortification, I have been called upon officially to attest the transmission to England of the remaining copies of those which were in Mr. Borrow's hands.

This duty I discharged reluctantly. The Bills of Loading were enclosed to Mr. Jackson, from whom I must require the Certificate duly attested by the Spanish Consul General in London of the landing of the two boxes.

I retained three copies of the New Testament and three copies of St. Luke's Gospel in the Gipsy Language, one of each for H.E. the Governor [Capt.-General], the Political Chief [Civil Governor], and myself.

That our severe disappointments are derivable from the indiscretions of those who, in the distribution of the Holy Scriptures in Spain, have acted in opposition to the advice and judgment of others who knew the habits and propensities of the Spaniards better than themselves, and by whom they were warned of the consequences of entering into religious controversies founded on the Doctrine and Discipline of the Established Religion of this country – *I have no doubt whatever*. The Agents of the B. and F. Bible Society in Spain should neither be Sectarian Ministers of the Gospel, who, by teaching and preaching, strive to make Proselytes, nor should they be distributors of Tracts, nor private individuals who consider it to be their duty to combat on Spanish ground the errors of Popery – but the distributors should be wholly unconnected with the discharge of any other religious occupation, conforming themselves as strictly as possible to the letter and spirit of their instructions issued by their Principals; they should never be lured into controversy with the Papist, but endeavour by God's assistance to be as wise as serpents and harmless as doves towards the Roman Catholicks themselves.

These opinions, so often heretofore expressed by me, are concurred in, I am happy to say, by Mr. Borrow, who has an intimate knowledge of the Spanish character, and whose zeal and judgment have gone hand in hand throughout this Province – I am (etc.),

'J. M. BRACKENBURY'[33]

Although in *The Bible in Spain* Borrow said that he was taking some of the New Testaments that had been impounded in Spain for distribution in Africa, he had no authority to do so. He did no further work for the Bible Society. He did not at this stage tell Brackenbury about Mary and Henrietta Clarke. He did not make it clear that he was going to Africa to satisfy his curiosity and for the sake of his book. Nor did he say then what he said later, that he had to 'flee into Barbary'.[34]

Presumably Brackenbury was at a later stage a little perplexed that Borrow did not obey the letter of recall to London with great promptness, but he had no reason to meddle officiously in what did not concern him, so remained good friends with Borrow till the end. There was in any case little time for debate, because Borrow, who had long dreamed of a trip to the 'Barbary Coast', on 4 August boarded the steam-packet to Gibraltar *en route* to Tangiers.

Borrow went to Tangiers to gather material for his book about gypsies and gypsy life, to ascertain whether at some much earlier point in time gypsies had crossed over from Spain to Africa and to see for himself whether there were gypsies there, or rather hear for himself, for he said in *The Zincali* that the absolute test would be the retention of key words that all gypsies used whatever the country they happened to inhabit. The British Consul had arranged accommodation for him in the house of one Joanna Correa, where he said he spent six weeks. Some of his remarks in *The Zincali* imply that he was advised or decided for himself that to explore the land in the same free way as he had explored Spain was much too dangerous. He did not suppose the gypsies could have penetrated very large areas of hinterland because they would 'have quailed before the Africans, who, unlike most other people, engage in wars, from what appears to be an innate love of the cruel and bloody scenes attendant on war'.[35] Borrow must also have quailed, for his readers were not treated to stories of adventurous expeditions into the interior. He browsed through his days, explored the city, continued to work at his book, and met as usual a number of unusual people. It cannot be supposed that Borrow's decision to spend six weeks in Tangiers, or longer, just six weeks after Mrs Clarke had arrived in Seville was not related to talks they had had with each other, or at the very least to Borrow's embarrassment at having created a situation that could not be resolved in his normal style, which was to avoid having intimate relationships with people by moving away from them. Going to Tangiers was an attempt to evade or at least postpone the issue, but an attempt doomed to failure, because having himself told Mrs Clarke to come to Seville he could not reasonably go into hiding in Africa and leave her to her own devices. Or perhaps he could have done so, but on reflection chose not to. If Borrow stayed with Joanna Correa in Tangiers for six weeks, he would have left on about 20 September. He was back in Seville by the 25th, having stayed with John Brackenbury in Cadiz on the way. Knapp had in his possession a receipt showing that Mrs Clarke cashed a bank draft in Gibraltar on the 13th. This means, not that they missed each other as Knapp thought,[36] but that she calculated the six-week period from the time Borrow left Seville and went to meet him in Gibraltar at what she thought was the right time. Obviously, Mrs Clarke was not a casual tourist: she went to Gibraltar because she wanted to be with Borrow, because it was not part of her plan to live by herself in Seville, because the question of what they should next do was unresolved – or, in short, because she wanted him. But she had to wait while Borrow spent those days in the inn at Tarifa that are so graphically described in *The Zincali*.[37]

In Borrow's account of this period in *The Bible in Spain* one sees clearly how un-autobiographical he was prepared to be when writing about his own travels. When he left Seville at the beginning of his journey to Tangiers, he went to Bonanza where he took a 'cabriolet' along the beach to San Lucar.

This place is famous in the ancient novels of Spain, of that class called Picaresque, or those devoted to the adventures of notorious scoundrels, the father of which, as also of all others of the same kind is Lazarillo de Tormes. Cervantes himself has immortalized this strand in the most amusing of his smaller tales, *La Ilustre Fregona*. In a word, the strand of San Lucar in ancient times, if not in modern, was a rendezvous for ruffians, contrabandistas, and vagabonds of every description, who nested there in wooden sheds, which have not vanished. San Lucar itself was always noted for the thievish propensities of the inhabitants – the worst in all Andalusia. The roguish inn-keeper in Don Quixote perfected his education in San Lucar. All these recollections crowded into my mind as we proceeded along the strand, which was beautifully gilded by the Andalusian sun. We at last arrived nearly opposite to San Lucar, which stands at some distance from the waterside. Here a lively spectacle presented itself to us: the shore was covered with a multitude of females either dressing or undressing themselves, while (I speak within bounds) hundreds were in the water sporting and playing: some were close by the beach, stretched at their full length on the sand and pebbles, allowing the little billows to dash over their heads and bosoms; whilst others were swimming boldly out into the firth. There was a confused hubbub of female cries, thin shrieks, and shrill laughter; couplets likewise were being sung, on what subject it is easy to guess – for we were in sunny Andalusia, and what can its black-eyed daughters think, speak or sing of but *amór*, *amór*, which now sounded from the land and the waters.[38]

This is the style of much of *The Bible in Spain* of course; this is its manner, its tone, its appeal. It has the ring of authenticity to it, seems to derive directly from actual experience and is uncluttered with artificial phrases or pedestrian comment. So the reader goes with Borrow to the Consul's house where he chats for two hours with the assembled womenfolk – in Spanish 'which flexible and harmonious as it is . . . seems at times quite inadequate to express the wild sallies of their luxuriant imagination';[39] to the house at Bonanza where he must wait for the morning ferry and where his sleep was broken by the snores of his host and 'by cats, and I believe rats, leaping upon my body';[40] to Cadiz where John Brackenbury was dealing with a mutinous sailor whose captain had called him 'a lazy, lubberly Greek';[41] to Trafalgar by steam-packet – 'impossible for an Englishman to pass this place without emotion';[42] and finally to the bay of Gibraltar where Borrow took up position on the prow 'with my eyes intently fixed on the mountain fortress, which, though I had seen several times before, filled my mind with admiration and interest'.[43] Even in this final part of *The Bible in Spain*, the narrative carries the reader along, providing him with little cause to hesitate. Borrow sits outside his inn talking with whoever will talk with him; and he waits for a boat, he admires the British soldiers, explores the batteries and the caves, and hobnobs with a plantation owner from Carolina, who pretended – or was it pretence? – that he began the day by flogging a few slaves and who amused Borrow by saying, when asked how he liked the excavations in the Rock: 'Liked them? You might just as well ask a person who has just seen the Niagara Falls how he liked them – like is not a word, mister.'[44] The occasional diatribe scarcely disrupts the flow of the narrative. 'Oh England!' he exclaimed after watching a parade of troops,

long, long, may it be ere the sun of thy glory sink beneath the wave of darkness! Though gloomy and portentous clouds are now gathering rapidly around thee, still, still may it please the Almighty to disperse them, and to grant thee a futurity longer in duration and still brighter in renown, than thy past! Or if thy doom be at hand, may that doom be a noble one, and worthy of her who has been styled the Old Queen of the waters! May thou sink, if thou dost sink, amidst blood and flame, with a mighty noise, causing more than one nation to participate in thy downfall! Of all fates, may it please the Lord to preserve thee from a disgraceful and a slow decay; becoming, ere extinct, a scorn and a mockery for those self-same foes who now, though they envy and abhor thee, still fear thee, nay, even against their will, honour and respect thee![45]

And so to Tangiers. Bread and cheese for lunch during the crossing – and a bottle of cognac to prevent sea-sickness. For supper a mess of pickled tomatoes.

Perhaps he wrote letters to Mary Clarke from Gibraltar which he consulted when he came to write *The Bible in Spain*, but he did not write to her from Tangiers and therefore did not say much about it later, because he lacked his normal documentary source of information. In *The Bible in Spain* he hardly devotes more space to Tangiers than he had already devoted to Gibraltar. This by itself is a clue to the muddle he was in. Only by staying in Spain could he expect his employment with the Bible Society to continue and, whether, as he had hinted to Mrs Clarke, he rented the house in Seville by the day, or, as seems more likely, for a year, it was in it that he planned to write the book called *The Zincali*, which was what he in fact did. On the other hand, when he returned to Seville from Tangiers, he found there was the, for him, unusual necessity of explaining his intentions to other people: to John Brackenbury, to Mrs Clarke, to the local authorities, and to Andrew Brandram, who on 1 November sent him a further letter of recall. As to Mrs Clarke, Borrow by November had either offered or agreed to marry her, perhaps the latter, for it was Mary Clarke who wrote to Borrow's mother to inform her of their engagement. If, in Seville, people assumed that Mary Clarke already was Mrs Borrow, the mistake was not corrected, because it was easier to allow this natural conclusion than to enter into explanations of the basis on which they were living together. By this device, Mary Clarke protected her daughter, though what Henrietta thought about their *ménage* in Seville has never been revealed. What Ann Borrow thought about it is not clear either. She wrote back a cryptic note, hardly a letter of congratulations, in which she said that, though she knew nothing of it, she was not surprised; that she had much to say – did she mean about the family? – but could not write; and that she hoped and trusted that 'each will try to make the other happy'.[46] A Protestant marriage was impossible in Spain. When, in the New Year, Borrow received a further letter from Andrew Brandram instructing him to return to England – the letter dated 10 January – Borrow exchanged notes with John Brackenbury in a correspondence designed to ascertain with absolute certainty that marriage, for example a consular marriage, was impossible, which Brackenbury confirmed, but since he was free throughout the winter of 1839–40 to obey Brandram's instruction and leave Spain on the monthly packet from Cadiz, so putting himself in a position to marry, it must be assumed from this long delay that he did not wish to do so. He could have returned to England in November and, by doing so, remained in good standing with the Bible Society. He chose to remain in Seville. Mary Clarke, who was also free to leave, also chose to stay. Whether they at this stage shared or did not share an ardent desire to spend the rest of their days together, they were apparently not embarrassed by the situation they made for themselves.

Knapp quoted, but dismissed as irresponsible gossip, a sentence from an unpublished biography of Borrow by a Norwich solicitor called Arthur Dalrymple, who said: 'At this time the widow of a merchant living at Mutford or Oulton near Lowestoft in Suffolk, found him out, having travelled over half Europe in search of him, and took possession of him, and upon her income of £300 or £400 per annum, with what his writings have produced, he has lived ever since.'[47] This, of course, was just an ungenerous way of stating one of the important matters George Borrow and Mary Clarke had to discuss that winter.

As to the local authorities, they remained hostile, suspicious and on the alert. Borrow was still under police surveillance. His continued presence in Seville was a mystery to them requiring an explanation, which was never forthcoming. If he was not distributing Protestant Testaments, what was he doing? Was he a newspaper correspondent? Was he a spy? And who were the women who lived with him? Not members of his own family, of course: that they knew from the passports that had to be presented whenever foreigners established residence. In November, Borrow's own residence status was called in question. According to Knapp, when Borrow attempted to recover his passport from the *alcalde de barrio* or mayor, the official pointed out that his residence permit was invalid because unsigned. Borrow had at first sent his servant, Felipe, but then went to the Mayor's office himself, where there was the inevitable altercation. Mrs Clarke heard about this by note.

My Dear Mrs. Clarke, – Do not be alarmed, but I am at present in the prison, to which place the *Alcalde de Barrio* conducted me when I asked him to sign the passport. If Phelipe has not already gone to the Consul, let Henrietta go now and show him this letter. When I asked the fellow his motives for not signing the Passport, he said if I did not go away he would carry me to prison. I dared him to do so, as I had done nothing; whereupon he led me here. Yours truly, George Borrow.[48]

Borrow's third spell of imprisonment in a Spanish gaol lasted for only thirty-odd hours, time enough, though, for the local police to raid and search his house. Either incensed or pretending to be incensed by this episode, Borrow, as soon as he got out of prison, attempted to obtain redress, that is attempted to establish with the authorities that he was wrongfully imprisoned and had a right to remain in Spain. Referred to Madrid by Brackenbury but unable to obtain satisfaction by letter, Borrow went himself to Madrid on 3 January 1840 and eventually received from the Hon. G. S. Jerningham, Secretary to the Embassy, a brief note indicating that the matter had been put to the Minister of State, from whom a reply had been received 'in a satisfactory tone'. What had Borrow had to say, one wonders, to protect his residence status? That he was or was not still working for the British and Foreign Bible Society? Presumably he did not say he was. At all events, he returned to Seville on 9 January and settled down once again to the writing of *The Zincali*, having written to Brandram from Madrid to say that he would bid adieu to the shores of Spain 'in a very short time'.[49]

Perhaps from Borrow's point of view the first three months of 1840 *was* a very short time. By the time Brandram wrote to Brackenbury to find out what Borrow was up to, Brackenbury was able to reply that

Borrow had asked him to book a passage back to London on the first sailing after 1 April. This turned out to be the Peninsular Steam Navigation Company's *Royal Adelaide*, which put in at Cadiz on 3 April 1840. Borrow closed up his house in Seville, sold his other horse to Brackenbury, then embarked by tender together with his servant, his horse, Sidi Habismilk, and Mary and Henrietta Clarke. After brief stops at Lisbon, Oporto, Vigo and Falmouth, they reached London on 16 April and repaired to the Spread Eagle in Gracechurch Street. Borrow's Spanish years were over.

Borrow met Andrew Brandram and also the General Purposes Committee on 20 April. Unfortunately, no records of such meetings have survived: there are records of resolutions passed at such meetings, but no minutes. It may be assumed, however, that Borrow had to make a report on his work since he was last in England, on the state of affairs in Spain when he left and on the expenses he incurred. His expenses must be discussed here, because they became a subject of controversy and because they throw light on the way in which Borrow handled his affairs during his last period in Spain. Although the evidence is not complete, a general picture can be reconstructed from Borrow's own accounts in Knapp, from papers in the Bible Society's archives, from the Society's ledger and from a Bible Society summary that some officer of the Society was at one stage asked to prepare. Borrow's expense reports were spasmodic. Some ledger entries can be associated with particular items such as paper, horses, fodder, wages, rent and so forth. Many cannot be identified with certainty. Similarly, some credit items can be identified, in particular the five ledger entries for monies received from the sale of Testaments, but since Borrow used such income to cover expenses and often only reported totals, it is difficult to determine exactly what money went where, especially because the officers of the Society preferred to err on the side of generosity and forbearance. It is with these reservations in mind that one attempts to arrive at total figures for salary, expenses, costs and sales.

The 'summary' gives the total charge of Borrow's work in Russia and Spain to have been £4,619 6s. 9d., of which £2,268 6s. 3d. was for translation, printing and manufacture. The ledgers indicate that the cost of manufacturing the New Testament in Spain was £658 4s. 0d. – in other words that the manufacturing costs were much lower in Spain than in Russia, just as one would expect.

In the Bible Society archives there are several reports on sales in Borrow's handwriting, as well as the Society's own records in the form of published accounts, the 'Foreign Accounts Current' books, the ledgers, and a summary of accounts relating to Borrow prepared by

J. G. Watt, the Society's secretary between 1896 and 1899. The relevant ledger entries are dated 11 December 1838; 15 May 1838; 24 November 1838; 6 May 1839; and 30 May 1840, together constituting a total income from sales of £182 2s. 2d. These ledger entries, with the corresponding reports from Borrow, are difficult to interpret: if he in fact sold the New Testaments at 10 *reals* a copy, he would have sold between 800 and 1,000 copies in all; but, because he said he was obliged to give some away and to sell others below cost, it has to be supposed that in some way or another a larger number was disposed of. There appears to be no record of whether Borrow had satisfactory or unsatisfactory discussions in London about the New Testaments that had not been sold or accounted for. Of particular interest are the 'summary' entries of £14 13s. 9d. on 6 May 1839 and £48 12s. on 30 May 1840 because these presumably represent Borrow's answers to the question, put to him either at the meeting on 20 April or subsequently: 'If you stayed in Spain in order to dispose of the stock of New Testaments, despite your recall to London, where is the money you received?' Because the residual stock had been sent back to London before Borrow went to Tangiers, this, or something like it, would have been a perfectly fair question. Brandram obviously knew or soon discovered that Borrow had not remained in Spain for the Society's sake, so the most obvious explanation is that the entries in May 1839 and May 1840 represented an estimate of final sales that had not been, and perhaps could not have been, meticulously recorded, given the hazardous conditions in which Borrow lived and worked. This was better than talking openly about the strong likelihood that Borrow had given away many of the Testaments, because the Society was firmly wedded to the idea that willingness to pay money, however little, for a New Testament was evidence of the individual's desire for it. It was a face-saving device for Borrow as well – one that he could well afford, in so far as the Society had continued to pay both salary and expenses up to his arrival in London.

Borrow had been paid £916 13s. 4d. as salary while in Spain, at a rate of £50 per quarter, but whereas in Russia he had paid many of his own expenses, in Spain he, by agreement, charged them to the Society, to a total of £911 4s. 5d., of which £433 15s. 1d. was incurred between May 1838 and 30 April 1839 and £208 2s. 10d. between 1 May 1839 and 30 May 1840. If there figures are to be trusted, the Society paid Borrow just over £400 during his final year in Spain. The final expense-account payment of £143 9s. 1d. on 30 May 1840 perhaps covered more than the cost of Borrow's own journey from Seville to London, the fare from Cadiz to London being at that time £20. These figures, resting though they do upon an imperfect record of what transpired, seem to show that the Society preferred not to make an issue of the high expenses he had incurred, leaving matters of conscience to be settled by Borrow himself and leaving officers of the Society free to speak their minds on the matter only in the privacy of their chambers. It fell to Andrew Brandram, however, to inform Borrow that there was no prospect of further employment – this in a letter dated 21 April, which notably did not conclude with an expression of thanks for a job well done.

The Society's final official word is to be found in its Annual Report for 1840. G. Borrow, Esq., who had just returned home, had succeeded 'by almost incredible pains, and at no small cost and hazard, in selling during his last visit a few hundred copies of the Bible, and most that remained of the edition of the New Testament printed at Madrid'. Nothing remained for the committee, the report said, 'but to await the opportunity of renewed exertions; and in the meantime, to seek a blessing on the seed already scattered on the plains and in the villages, and along the shores of that land of distraction and woe'.

George Borrow and Mary Clarke were married at St Peter's Church, Cornhill, on 23 April 1840. Henrietta Clarke and John Pilgrim, Mrs Clarke's solicitor, were the witnesses.

The books about Spain

Before Borrow's association with the British and Foreign Bible Society
had begun, Borrow had wanted to be an author. He had been a
translator, an editor, a reviewer and, as he would have put it, a philologist; had contributed his work to London journals and worked for
one of them; had met other literary people while in London; and above
all had found himself persuaded that his *forte* was with words, the
words of many languages, to the extent that a career as a solicitor
seems never to have been considered seriously. In Spain, he had
collected material for a book about the gypsies of Spain. Back in East
Anglia, he immediately set to work to prepare a manuscript that could
be offered to a London publisher. This kept him busy during the period
of adjustment to his new life. It kept him busy, in fact, for the next
four years, the four years that saw the publication not only of *The
Zincali; or, An Account of the Gypsies of Spain* and *The Bible in
Spain* but also of these same books in the one-volume editions that
initiated John Murray's Colonial and Home Library, the series that
made Borrow available to such a wide readership that he achieved
almost instant fame.

'I can remember no period when the mentioning of the name of
Gypsy did not awaken feelings within my mind hard to be described,
but in which a strange pleasure predominated.' So says Borrow on the
first page of *The Zincali*. Throughout his youth he had frequently
come across and spent time with groups of gypsies as his father's
regiment travelled from one part of Britain to another. He had con-
sorted with them on Mousehold Heath and other such places near
Norwich; had met them at horse-fairs and prizefights; had lived with
them, sometimes, and been accepted by them as the companion of
Isopel Berners. He had probably visited and studied the gypsies of
Hungary, as he claimed, for his account is circumstantial enough to be
believed, or at least not dismissed out of hand. He had probably hob-
nobbed with gypsies at the great fair of Dresden. Gypsies were not
permitted in St Petersburg during Borrow's time there, but he had

visited an encampment just outside Novgorod and later a much larger settlement in Moscow. In all these places, he had been accepted by the gypsies, partly because he had taken the trouble to learn their language, which early in life he recognized had constant characteristics irrespective of the country in which it was spoken, and partly because of a scarcely definable feeling of kinship he and many gypsies immediately felt for one another. 'The gypsies themselves', he said on the first page of *The Zincali*, 'account for it on the supposition that the soul which at present animates my body, has at some former period tenanted that of one of their people.'

With so many experiences behind him, the aspiring author must have felt, when he crossed the frontier between Portugal and Spain in 1835, that he had found his proper subject, for he was excited to find gypsies in large numbers, gypsies who had been well-established for several centuries and who welcomed him like a brother. He soon realised that he was in a position to write a book containing material inaccessible to most other people. Because the civil war continued to rage throughout the whole period that Borrow was there, he had often found it safer to be with gypsies than with anybody else, particularly when making a long journey. As Knapp put it: 'The old words and the ancient strategy that had put him at the heart of gypsydom in England, were appealed to now for personal insulation in the maze of hidden dangers in the Peninsula.' Settled in Oulton in 1840 with the gypsy material he had gathered in Seville, Borrow looked back over his years in Spain, pondered this his subject, decided that the book he had in mind had the compelling advantage of combining the two things he knew well, the remoter parts of Spain and a language few other people understood, and went quickly ahead. After Mary Clarke, now Mrs George Borrow, had had the pleasure of devoting the first months of her marriage to the task of preparing a fair copy he got his old friend, John Bowring, to write a letter of introduction to John Murray, the publisher. That was in November 1840, just six months after they settled at Oulton. Obligingly Bowring called it 'a very remarkable book – a book which nobody but himself could have written – about a people with whom no Englishman but himself is acquainted'.[1]

Later that month Borrow travelled up to London with his manuscript, found himself accommodation at 58 Jermyn Street and took his first book round to Albemarle Street. Samuel Smiles, in his *Memoir and Correspondence of the late John Murray*, recalled the tall, athletic gentleman who called on Mr Murray that November. 'Mr. Murray could not fail to be taken at first sight with this extraordinary man. He had a splendid physique, standing six foot two in his stockings, and he had brains as well as muscles, as his works sufficiently show.'[2] As impressed as most people were who met Borrow in person, John Murray sent the manuscript to Richard Ford for an opinion. This was the Richard Ford whose two-volume *Handbook for Travellers in Spain and Readers at Home* John Murray published in 1845. Although Ford recognised that Borrow had incorporated into his account of the gypsies too much second-hand material from relatively worthless sources (the material that had been gathered in Madrid), he liked the book as a whole and recommended acceptance. If Borrow could see his way to saying more about his own experiences, so much the better. Ford became an important force in Borrow's writing and publishing life, at least during these early years at Oulton. Having experienced disappointment enough when he attempted to gain entry to the London literary world in the 1820s, Borrow was keenly interested in the opinions of a man who had the ear of one of the principal publishers. Ford said that Borrow should write about his own experiences rather than reproduce passages from long-forgotten volumes, so Borrow wrote to Murray to say he could 'at any time add two or three more chapters of *personal narrative*'[3] should Murray wish it. Later, when Ford said that there was little public interest in Russia, Borrow refused to write about his time there, as will be seen. There was public interest in Spain according to Ford, so Borrow wrote *The Bible in Spain*. After that, it was Ford who most badgered Borrow for a full account of his own life, so Borrow wrote *Lavengro*. Of a relationship that is difficult to assess, this much can be said, that Borrow in November 1840 was not in the least inclined to disregard the advice of the man who recommended the publication of *The Zincali*, for to whom next would he have turned had Murray turned him down?

John Murray did not turn him down. The publisher's daybook preserves a copy of the letter despatched to Borrow on 23 December 1840:

Mr. Murray having considered what appears to be your wish respecting the publication of your MS on the *Gypsies of Spain*, begs through me to make you the following proposal. He will print at his own cost and sole risk, an edition of 750 copies of your work, and will divide with you the profits when they are sold. After which the copyright remains yours, to do what you like with it.[4]

(The figure of 750, incidentally, can be compared with the 1,500 copies of Scrope's *Salmon Fishing* and the 1,000 copies of the fifth edition of Eyre's *Affghanistan*, both of which appeared in 1840.) If this was no more than the first cautious, not ungenerous move by a prudent publisher, who well knew what such a printing would cost him, the niceties of author–publisher relations did not at this stage worry

Borrow. The offer was promptly accepted; Borrow returned to Oulton a highly satisfied man, since his plan of the last two years had worked; and John Murray began to manufacture the two-volume book immediately after Christmas.

'The two or three more chapters of personal narrative' were not called for, so the book was published in the two parts Borrow had had in mind from the beginning.

The Zincali was by no means the pot-boiler it might at first appear to be when compared with the hugely successful *Bible in Spain* that followed it, for in scope and design it demonstrates that Borrow had in mind a major study of the gypsies and that he went to considerable trouble to bring it off. He attempted a historical but up-to-date account of gypsy settlement in Spain based partly on first-hand observation and partly on a reading, in Madrid, of books that he thought inaccessible and therefore probably interesting to English readers. Part I of the book was to be about the past, Part II about the present. To this account he added a collection of folk literature, mostly consisting of gypsy poems, and a vocabulary or glossary of the gypsy language, including a vocabulary of robber language, all this to confirm his thesis that gypsies wherever they settled were of common stock, that they had a single language with marked but intelligible variations, that they had come, centuries ago, from India, and that their language was rooted in Sanskrit. Perhaps his Grub Street experience inclined him to suppose that a book could be made in this way and that the combination of long quotations with personal narrative would be an asset. He did not yet know that readers who were totally indifferent to questions of philology would be stirred by the narrative and want more of it.

The Zincali is an idiosyncratic not a scholarly book, though it has its plan. In preparation for the main part of the book, which is to be almost exclusively about the Spanish gypsies, Borrow refers in the Introduction to gypsy communities and individiuals whom he had known in other parts of the world. He recalls his long expedition to see the gypsy settlement in Moscow and also the 'appearance of an aged Ziganskie Attaman, or Captain of Zigani, and his grandson, who approached me on the meadow before Novo Gorod, where stood the encampment of a numerous horde'.[5] He recalls the gypsies of Hungary whose 'hovels appear sinks of the vilest poverty and filth', whose 'dress is at best rags', whose food is 'frequently the vilest carrion, and occasionally, if report be true, still worse' but who are very fond of music and 'are heard to touch the violin in a manner wild, but of peculiar excellence'.[6] He recalls the gypsies of England with their dark complexions, oval faces, low foreheads, and small hands and feet. 'They all speak the English language with fluency', he says, 'and in their gait and demeanour are easy and graceful; in both points standing in striking contrast with the peasantry, who in speech are slow and uncouth, and in manner dogged and brutal.'[7] He recalls, too, the gypsies of the east whom he said he came across in Turkey, and one in particular who greatly impressed him because, though a native of Constantinople, 'he had traversed alone and on foot the greatest part of India', spoke several dialects of the Malay and understood the original language of Java. 'From what I could learn from him', says Borrow, as usual emphasising that his information had been gathered at first hand, 'it appeared that his jewels were in less request than his drugs, though he assured me that there was scarcely a Bey or Satrap in Persia or Turkey whom he had not supplied with both.'[8] In this way Borrow establishes himself, within the book, as a reliable informant, a reliability seemingly confirmed by those descriptive passages which made him famous.

I have seen Gypsies of various lands, Russian, Hungarian and Turkish; and I have also seen the legitimate children of most countries of the world, but I never saw, upon the whole, three more remarkable individuals, as far as personal appearance was concerned, than the three English Gypsies who now presented themselves to my eyes on that spot. Two of them had dismounted, and were holding their horses by the reins. The tallest, and, at the first glance, the most interesting of the two, was almost a giant, for his height could not have been less than six feet three. It is impossible for the imagination to conceive anything more prefectly beautiful than were the features of this man, and the most skilful sculptor of Greece might have taken them as his model for a hero and a god. The forehead was exceedingly lofty, – a rare thing in a Gypsy; – the nose less Roman than Grecian, – fine yet delicate; the eyes large, overhung with long drooping lashes, giving them almost a melancholy expression; it was only when they were highly elevated that the Gypsy glance peered out, if that can be called glance which is a strange stare, like nothing else in this world. His complexion – a beautiful olive; and his teeth of a brilliancy uncommon even amongst these people, who have all fine teeth. He was dressed in a coarse waggoner's slop, which, however, was unable to conceal altogether the proportions of his noble and Herculean figure. He might be about twenty-eight. His companion and his captain, Gypsy Will, was, I think, fifty when he was hanged, ten years subsequently, (for I never afterwards lost sight of him,) in the front of the jail of Bury St. Edmunds. I have still present before me his bushy black hair, his black face, and his big black eyes, full and thoughtful, but fixed and staring. His dress consisted of a loose blue jockey coat, jockey boots and breeches; in his hand a huge jockey whip, and on his head (it struck me at the time for its singularity) a broad-brimmed, high-peaked Andalusian hat, or at least one very much resembling those generally worn in that province. In stature he was shorter than his more youthful companion, yet he must have measured six feet at least, and was stronger built, if possible. What brawn! – what legs! – what thighs! The third Gypsy, who remained on horseback, looked more like a phantom than any thing human. His complexion was the colour of pale dust, and of that same colour was all that pertained to him, hat and clothes. His boots were dusty of course, for it was midsummer, and his very horse was of a dusty dun. His features were whimsically ugly, most of his teeth were gone, and as to his age, he might be thirty or sixty. He was somewhat lame and halt, but an unequalled rider when once upon his steed, which he was naturally not very solicitous to quit. I subsequently discovered that he was considered the wizard of the gang.[9]

This is Borrow's manner throughout. In assessing those anecdotes of the writer Don Juan de Quiñones, that for the most part 'are so highly absurd, that none but the very credulous could ever have vouchsafed them the slightest credit', Borrow says of one of them that he himself 'can bear testimony that there is such a forest as Las Gamas, and that it is frequented occasionally by Gypsies', to which he adds: 'It will be as well to observe that I visited it in company with a band of Gitános, who bivouacked there, and cooked their supper, which however did not consist of human flesh but of a puchéra, the ingredients of which were beef, bacon, garbanzos, and berdólaga, or field-pease and purslain.'[10] To determine whether the 'Beni Aros' of the Barbary coast were of gypsy stock he says, characteristically, 'I have occasionally spoken with them ...'[11] In his chapter on the urban gypsies of Madrid, he makes it clear that he is very familiar with 'two dirty lanes, called the *Calle de la Comadre* and the *Callejon de Lavapies*' where they chiefly resided.[12] When he wants to discuss the movement, or possible movement, of gypsies between Spain and North Africa he describes with great particularity the inn at Tarifa. His method, in all those parts of the book that recount his own experiences, is visual, specific, anecdotal and, because Borrow as writer does not try to persuade his reader, he presents himself as essentially urbane and detached, as though to say: 'This is what happened. I was there. I saw what I now describe. Make of it what you will, for I attach no particular importance to it except as a detail in my book about gypsy culture.'

Borrow gives lively accounts of gypsy occupations: 'jockeyism', horse-dealing, horse-stealing; sorcery, confidence tricks, fortune-telling; 'hokkano baro', 'ustilar pastésas' and 'la bar lachi', dancing, begging, theft. He does not sentimentalise, though he does sympathise with gypsies as a persecuted minority group trapped in a never-ending vicious circle of law, which at once singles them out as underprivileged and, in so doing, makes change virtually impossible; 'nor was it probable that they would entertain much respect for the laws which, from time immemorial, have principally served, not to protect the honest and useful members of society, but to enrich those entrusted with the administration of them'.[13] As to these same Spanish laws, Borrow says

on the next page: 'as might be expected, the labourers, who in all
countries are the most honest, most useful and meritorious class, were
the principal sufferers'.[14] So throughout. There is a controlled but
unambiguous democratic sentiment informing the book that absolutely
precludes a patronising disposal, as it were, of the gypsies as a bother-
some people not worth serious consideration. And even though Borrow
asserts that a simple narrative of facts will be far more agreeable and
instructive than commentary or reflection, he allows himself an occasional paragraph that clearly shows where his heart is, as does, for
example, that paragraph on the 'inward monitor' in the concluding
chapter of Part I.

It has been said, that there is a secret monitor, or conscience, within every heart,
which immediately upbraids the individual on the commission of a crime; this
may be true, but certainly the monitor within the Gitáno breast is a very feeble
one, for little attention is ever paid to its reproofs. With regard to conscience,
be it permitted to observe, that it varies much according to climate, country,
and religion; perhaps nowhere is it so terrible and strong as in England; I need
not say why. Amongst the English, I have seen many individuals stricken low,
and broken-hearted, by the force of conscience; but never amongst the Spaniards
or Italians; and I never yet could observe that the crimes which the Gitános
were daily and hourly committing, occasioned them the slightest uneasiness.[15]

Borrow knew that not everyone in the world had an ample house, a
garden, a paddock and a few acres; that not everyone placed at the
centre of existence the laws of property; that not everyone could afford to
do so; that not everyone wished to do so; and that whereas stability of
residence, customs and laws had a great appeal for some, stability of
that kind was unknown to many and unwanted by at least a few. He
did not pity the migrant, scorn the thief, patronise the uneducated, or
scoff at the socially maladjusted. Nor did he write about the gypsies of
Spain as though their continued existence had in some sense to be justified. The stridency familiar to us nowadays in the voices of those who
behave as though minority groups, particularly ethnic minority groups
should somehow conveniently disappear or, more ridiculous still, return
to the place from whence they came, as though the history of mankind
were not one of constant movement and migration, was in Borrow's
narrative absent, for he showed not only that he understood the predicament of the dispossessed, and sympathised with it, but also perceived
those larger cultural affinities and patterns which frequently belie
national boundaries. *The Zincali* is not a completely successful book by
any means – how could it be when weighted down by those lengthy
quotations from dusty tomes? – but its tone is assured, its style convincing and its descriptive passages often lively and entertaining. No

wonder Murray wanted a second book based on Borrow's own experiences, with the spurious erudition omitted.

The complete isolation of Oulton Broad allowed Borrow to find his feet as a writer, difficult though that is to imagine these days when one goes in search of Borrow places near Lowestoft. The roads, the docks, the minor industry, the marinas and the congestion of housing have long come close to obliterating the country backwater where Borrow made his home at a time when the main means of transport was the horse. He fished, rode about his estate, began to get to know his new neighbours (who knowing the Clarke history were not, of course, predisposed in his favour), continued to be interested in horses, his and other people's, yet found there was also still plenty of time for writing and little to distract him from it. Though he desired fame, contact with the literary establishment would have been a distraction; anything that had made him self-conscious, self-critical would have been a hindrance. But there was, in these first few years of marriage, nothing to stop him believing in himself, nothing to call in question his plan of using the security of Oulton Cottage to write about Spain in peace, nothing that might disrupt the spontaneity, energy, essential *naïveté* of his work: no check or challenge. Not yet. His link with the world of letters was almost exclusively by way of John Murray and Richard Ford. Both believed in him. John Murray had declined to have Borrow incorporate much of a personal kind into *The Zincali* because he saw that there was another, quite different book Borrow might write. Murray had talked with Borrow about this before *The Zincali* was published, and therefore before he knew whether the public would like it or not. Ford was soon badgering Borrow for the story of his life, making Borrow believe that it was indeed wanted. As early as February 1841 Ford wrote: 'I am delighted to hear that you meditate giving us your travels in Spain. The more odd personal adventures, the better, the still more so if *dramatic*: that is, giving the exact conversations.'[16] Ford already trusted Borrow as someone whose information about Spain was accurate and authentic, so much so that, during this crucial period of Borrow's writing life, he corresponded with him fairly regularly, not about Borrow's but about his own work, especially for those parts of his *Handbook on Spain* which concerned travel. 'It is so long since I performed one of these grand tours on my *jaca cordobesa*, that I am anxious to have my recollections refreshed by your more recent, and I dare say greater, knowledge and experience in horseflesh.'[17] Borrow enjoyed this. He liked being recognised as the expert he undoubtedly was. He therefore responded to Ford's letters in a positive mood, sent him the information he needed and later read various pages of Ford's *Handbook*, annotated them at Ford's request, and even corrected proofs for one or two sections. This meant that when Ford told John Murray that Borrow's strengths were his spontaneity, the vigour and directness of his writing and his essential honesty in writing about what he himself knew at first hand, so that what the publisher should want above all was the story of Borrow's life, and when John Murray communicated these opinions to Borrow as his own, Borrow quite naturally listened. The publisher's adviser was on his side. So was the publisher. What they wanted he thought he could provide. In May 1841, therefore, he set to work.

It is possible that by this time, the spring of 1841, an essential misunderstanding between author and publisher had become entrenched, though it was not a misunderstanding that was to matter much in these early years of their relationship. In a letter we only know about from Knapp, Ford said enthusiastically: 'How I wish you had given us more about yourself...I shall give you a hint to publish your *whole* adventures for the last twenty years. Would you like me to furnish a few hints? What countries have you been in? What languages do you understand? All this would excite public attention and curiosity and sell the future book.'[18] There were many things Borrow had no intention of revealing. He did not in 1841 have any plan for a book about his 'adventures' of the last twenty years. He was able to respond in a positive way to Ford's enthusiasm for biography only because he thought he could write a second book about Spain based on the letters he had written to the Bible Society. When Ford knew that he was at work on such a book, he said:

I would preface these rambles in Spain with a short *biography* – beginning at the beginning, and touching lightly on every country where I had been; what people I had lived with, what languages I had learnt, and what books I had translated. Do this in a natural manner, as if there was nothing in it. I am sure it will tell. The more curious the biography you put into it, the better.[19]

These letters of Ford's came from Exeter, so Borrow did not have to discuss with Ford face to face any of Ford's ideas or reveal to him what he did not intend to reveal. His own sense of the complexity of his imaginative life remained unstated. He and his wife were excited about the book, the prudently defined limits of which they could clearly see, so the consequences of Ford's not really knowing Borrow very well were postponed for a few years. The remainder of 1841 and the whole of 1842 were devoted to the making of *The Bible in Spain*, while 1843 was devoted to new editions of both *The Zincali* and *The Bible in Spain* culminating in the all-important single-volume editions in the Colonial and Home Library. Borrow was far too busy to worry about those personal matters that so disrupted his life later on.

Borrow had given Andrew Brandram a copy of *The Zincali* when it came out in April. Towards the end of May, he asked Brandram if he could use his letters to the Society for a new book about Spain. 'I wish particularly', he said, 'for those which touch upon my negotiating with the Government.'[20] Brandram had a good look at *The Zincali* to decide whether he should be alarmed or not: then he wrote to Borrow to ask for more information on what he intended, making clear that the operations of the Society should not become the object of public scrutiny. 'Think not', replied Borrow, 'that I purpose introducing the affairs of the Bible Society into my book.' The public only cared for personal narrative. At least that is what Ford said the public cared for. He had learnt his lesson from the public reaction to *The Zincali*.

The public take very little interest in Sanskrit derivations and in Gypsy words; those parts that cost me the labour of years have been received with the utmost indifference, while particular chapters on which I set not the slightest value, as being the result neither of research nor serious reflection have obtained for the work some slight portion of public favour.[21]

By this time Borrow was in London. When he called on Murray he received his confirmation that a book about his travels in Spain would be of interest. No doubt he told Murray that the material already existed. He called on Brandram and convinced him that he should be allowed to consult the letters. He very likely reminded Brandram that he did not need the letters to reveal the Society's secrets to the world, that *The Zincali* was an indication of the sort of thing he found interesting and that Brandram could himself discover from John Murray what kind of book John Murray wanted. It was possibly not difficult for Borrow to persuade Brandram that religion and the affairs of the Society were not his chief concern. At all events, he returned to Oulton with the letters in his possession, set to work immediately and devoted the next six months to the preparation of a first draft of *The Bible in Spain*, writing the occasional letter to Murray by way of reassurance. 'A queer book will be this same *Bible in Spain*', he said in August, 'containing all my queer adventures in that queer country, whilst engaged in distributing the Gospel, but neither learning, nor disquisition, fine writing or poetry.'[22] Fortunately for his future readers he was still under the spell of Richard Ford, as the terms of this letter to Murray clearly show.

Borrow had at hand the notebook from Spain which is now in the Berg Collection of the New York Public Library, those letters to the

Bible Society represented by Darlow's edition of *The Letters of George Borrow to the British and Foreign Bible Society*, probably a few letters to his wife, such as his letters from Seville to Oulton, possibly quite a few letters to him, though there is not much evidence that he made a habit of keeping letters addressed to him in Spain, and that vast collection of bills and receipts which Knapp later said he had purchased, together with a miscellany of papers, many of them no doubt having to do with literature and language. Borrow looked over the Bible Society letters, then honoured his wife with the task of making a fair copy, while he himself concentrated on the links between the parts. He wisely avoided using those bills and receipts to reconstruct his comings and goings in Spain with precision. If he had the chance to determine where exactly he had been and when, which inns he had stayed at, whom he had seen, he did not take it. Nor did he attempt either to convert his original letters to Brandram into a sort of traveller's guide, or to clarify matters of fact that an intelligent reader looking for consistency might have thought vague. The Bible Society's letters already said about as much as he was prepared to divulge, so he built the rest of the book around them, so much so that, when his new friend Dawson Turner asked him for part of the manuscript, Borrow was only able to give him that section of the book which concerned his trip to Gibraltar and Tangiers – that is, the partial manuscript now in the Library of the Hispanic Society[23] – the rest only existing as a totality in Mrs Borrow's fair copy. Whether Borrow would have been able to write *The Bible in Spain* from scratch, without utilising his letters, is doubtful. Not only did they represent the means by which the book was made, so that Ford, when he saw it, was able to tell John Murray that Borrow's writing had strengthened, but they represented also a means by which Borrow could retain an authentic connection with his own past and thus bring himself to reveal it. The letters allowed him to say about Spain only what he had been prepared to say when he was dramatising his experiences for Brandram's benefit. If his wife, as she copied away, occasionally, or even often, raised her head from the page to ask: 'George, this is so interesting: what happened next?' or 'what happened *after* you left . . . wherever it was?' there are no hints in *The Bible in Spain* as to what George's answer might have been. The method of composition virtually ensured that *The Bible in Spain* would not be a startlingly revealing type of autobiography. Presumably Borrow understood this perfectly well.

Although Borrow (in his days with Phillips) had had plenty of experience of making long books and remembered how time-consuming and all-engrossing the work could be, and although he had recently laboured over the manuscript of *The Zincali*, he was not prepared for the task of having to satisfy his publisher about the detail of his new book, part of which he despatched to London at the end of 1841. Murray pointed out innumerable minor errors and wanted to know how long the complete book would be. As to what he called the 'trifling mistakes' Borrow calmly blamed his country 'amanuensis'. As to length, he said: 'Each volume will consist of from 460 to 480–90 pages of highly interesting matter of which I have more than a sufficiency',[24] thinking here, not of the three-volume book that *The Bible in Spain* became, but of a two volume book like *The Zincali*. Just over a week later, he wrote again to say that he had corrected 700 consecutive pages and had about 200 still to correct. 'I do not think there will be a dull page in the whole book, as I have made one or two very important alterations; the account of my imprisonment at Madrid cannot fail I think of being particularly interesting.'[25] Alterations? Alterations to what? This could mean that Borrow was making alterations to the fair copy as his wife passed it to him, but more likely that Murray had sent the manuscript back with the request that it should be tidied up. This would explain Borrow's letter of 22 February in which he told Murray that he was sending volume I to London by the night mail and described the contents of volume II, indicating by this that Murray had not yet seen it all.[26] Not surprisingly, the author was beginning to feel the strain of eight months work on the manuscript. Perhaps he had worked on it only intermittently at first: by the time he had forced himself to attend carefully to the detail of the fair copy he became nervous and crotchety, and so apprehensive about how the book would be received that he began to be unreasonably cantankerous with John Murray, telling him, almost as soon as he had sent the whole book, that he could not accept the same terms as for *The Zincali* and that Murray had better send the manuscript back to him by the Yarmouth Lowestoft Mail, so that he could take it with him to Constantinople 'whither I am going next autumn'.[27]

Murray, though, had already sent the manuscript to Ford for an opinion, so nearly two months passed before there could be any further discussion of it.

Because Ford's influence on Borrow extends beyond the shaping of *The Bible in Spain* – because, indeed, it was in many ways Ford's report to Murray that shaped Borrow's subsequent career as a writer – it seems important to give the report *verbatim*.

There are numerous faults in spelling and some in grammar. I have corrected the latter where I have noticed them; but some may have escaped me. These points should be very carefully attended to by the author in carrying the work through the press. The work is written in short sentences; but the copyist has in a vast number of instances run them together. There are also a good many words left blank; these the author must supply. I should recommend also that he should, after all Portuguese, Spanish, and Gypsy words, insert the English of them in Italics, and between brackets.

But the more important points which I would recommend to Mr. Borrow's consideration are the following:—

1st. In the narrative there are at present two breaks — one from about March 1836 to June 1837, — and the other from November 1837 to July 1839. These blank periods should be filled up. It is not at all necessary that this should be done in detail, as the MS. is, I conceive, at present as long as the nature of the subject will well bear. All that is wanting is a rapid sketch of where the author was and what he was doing during the two intervals.

2nd. The work is not finished — the last Section (No. 9) terminating abruptly with the second day of his residence in Tangiers in August 1839; from which place he again proceeds to Spain, and returns to England in April 1840. Some part of this period must be given to terminate the volumes — the more briefly, perhaps, the better.

3rd. At page 56 of Section 3rd and at page 59 of Section 4th, passages are left unfinished, in order to produce an air of mystery. This is taking an unwarrantable liberty with the reader. A Novel writer, or even a writer of Travels, may pretend to be ignorant of things in order to keep them back; but they have no right to conceal what they admit they know. I would recommend that these gaps be filled up.

4th. In the Letter of the 16th August 1837, there is an interesting story of a man stung to death by vipers. I think Mr. Borrow should introduce it into his narrative — and indeed I would recommend him to go carefully over the whole of his Letters, as it is very probable that other points of interest which they contain may have been omitted in the narrative. Some of the most interesting Letters relate to journies not given in the MS.

5th. The Dialogues are amongst the best parts of the book; but in several of them the tone of the speakers, of those especially who are in humble life, is too correct and elevated, and therefore out of character. This takes away from their effect. I think it would be very advisable that Mr. Borrow should go over them with reference to this point, simplifying a few of the turns of expression and introducing a few contractions — *don'ts, can'ts*, etc. This would improve them greatly (!)

6th. This is just one of those books the interest of which would be augmented by the readers knowing something about the writer. I would strongly recommend, therefore, that Mr. Borrow should prefix to his narrative a few pages of preface, telling us very concisely his birth, parentage, and education, and the leading features of his life, especially his connection with the Bible Society, and the engagement under which he proceeded. If he does this in the easy, frank, and lively style in which his narrative is written, I feel convinced that it will tend greatly to the effectiveness and success of his volumes.

7th. I think that a small Map of Spain, showing only its Provinces and principal Towns, with the author's route laid down upon it, would be a judicious addition to the work. It should take in Tangiers.

8th. I do not conceive it necessary or advisable to insert any of the Letters, either in the body of the work or as an Appendix. Some of them are embodied in the narrative. Nor are they requisite as a verification of the facts stated in it. Unlike the *History of the Gypsies*, this MS. in all the more important points, completely authenticates itself.[28]

This report is interesting for several reasons. It shows, first, that Borrow had decided to authenticate the story by sending Murray the Bible Society letters on which it was based, that Ford so much accepted the book that he recommended that the letters should not be included, and that, despite his recommendation, he nevertheless felt that authenticity was a key factor. This was to dog Borrow for the rest of his life. Was it not enough that he had written a supremely interesting book? No. He had also to be sincere. If Borrow was not sincere, if events had not been exactly as he described them, the books would be invalid. Secondly, the report shows that either he or his wife had omitted from the manuscript some of the more interesting episodes. Had Mrs Borrow done this without his knowing? Or had there been a conscious decision that some episodes, such as that about the vipers, were unsuitable? – unsuitable, that is, for the typical reader of Mr Murray's books. The point here was that, if George Borrow had really experienced such disagreeable things while working as a missionary in another country, there was nothing to prevent his telling the reader about them, whereas if he had not been a missionary it would have been inappropriate to mention such things. It was exactly this restriction on his imagination that Borrow was to find so inconvenient when he came to write *Lavengro*. Thirdly, the report repeats Ford's ideas on his pet subject of the author's biography. *The Bible in Spain* turned out to be a good book because the way in which it was written convinced the reader of its authenticity: Ford, however, clung to the naive idea that *The Bible in Spain* was a good book because Borrow was such an interesting character. Maybe as a human being with a regard of decency Ford was on the side of the angels: George Borrow was not on the side of the angels and, as author, knew better than to accept Ford's advice on this point when, unknown to Ford, John Murray showed him the report.

Borrow got to know about Ford's report on his manuscript when he went to see John Murray in May.[29] Borrow so badly wished to see the book published that the question of terms was scarcely an obstacle: he was again offered a half share of the profits, again accepted. In fact, the meetings presumably went quite well, for back in Oulton at the beginning of June, he sent Dawson Turner a cheerful note, together with some tench and a pike 'which I caught this morning in a preserve which I have near Oulton Lake',[30] telling his friend that he expected the book to be out by 1 October. But he found it more difficult to remain calm while revising his book than he had when faced by a band of brigands in Spain: in the one case he just had to fend for himself, whereas he now had to take into account other people's opinions. The strain began to tell. In May, he had told Murray: 'I have been dreadfully unwell since I last heard from you – a regular nervous attack.'[31] Knapp said this was because of a dispute with the Rev. Denniss about their dogs: Borrow says he had caught a bad cough while chasing poachers in the middle of the night: but a 'nervous attack' most likely had a more deep-seated cause – that is, his growing anxiety about his book. The anxiety swirls on the surface of a cranky letter he wrote to Murray at the beginning of July. Had Murray not received the last part of his revised manuscript? Why had Woodfall, the printer, temporarily halted production?

What are your intentions with respect to *The Bible in Spain*? I am a frank man and frankness never offends me. Has anybody put you out of conceit with the book?...Or, would the appearance of the *Bible* on the first of October interfere with the avatar, first or second, of some very wonderful lion or divinity, to whom George Borrow, who is neither, must of course give place?[32]

As badly as he wanted to see his book in print, he had the gall to end this letter with the threat that he would look for a new publisher unless Murray got a move on. Yet another impatient author was behaving as though the manufacture of a book was the labour of a day or two.

Another instance of this anxiety was a letter to Dawson Turner, which amusingly reveals the opposite of what Borrow intended. Turner had wished Borrow good fortune with his forthcoming publication and immediately received the following paranoid reply:

I have no fear at all about the success of the forthcoming...but I am anxious it will add considerably to the number of my enemies. The Pope is very powerful here in England (much more so than in Italy) and I have handled him very roughly. *Nous verrons*! Yesterday our dirty Rector must needs have a fling at me from the pulpit. He preached upon the text 'Blessed are the meek' and took that opportunity to inveigh against those who seek a little vain applause and set themselves up above their neighbours. Poor creature, I suppose he has seen the advertisement to which you allude which causes him to 'shed those tears'. Applause! I seek no applause only a few hundreds to add to our yearly income so that I may occasionally treat my wife with a silver tea urn, teapot, ewer or salver and myself to 'a bit of a blood' and am I to be blamed because Blackwood or the Edinburgh, North American or the Examiner take it into their heads to applaud me? – Basta! This morning I went out coursing and caught nothing: and this afternoon I went to my fish ponds where I netted an enormous pike which I intend to dine upon tomorrow drinking your very good health in a glass of old Madeira.[33]

The two John Murrays, father and son, had ample experience of highly-strung authors. The printing recommenced when they had the complete manuscript in hand; Borrow was sent the proofs during the late summer and early autumn;[34] no more problems were encountered; and *The Bible in Spain* at last appeared, just a few days before Christmas 1842 – though dated 1843. As he too had checked the proofs, Ford had written to Murray in his usual enthusiastic way.

You may depend upon it that the book will *sell*, which, after all, is the rub. It is the antipodes of Lord Carnarvon, and yet how they tally in whatever they have in common, and that is much – the people, the scenery of Galicia, and the suspicions and absurdities of Spanish Jacks-in-office, who yield not in insolence or ignorance to any liberal red-tapists hatched in the hotbeds of jobbery and utilitarian mare's nests...Borrow spares none of them. He hits right and left and floors his man, wherever he meets him. I am pleased with his honest sincerity of purpose and his graphic abrupt style. It is like an old Spanish ballad, leaping in *res medias*, going from incident to incident, bang, bang, bang! hops, steps and jumps like a cracker, and leaving off like one, when you wish he would give you another touch or *coup de grâce*. He has improved as a writer; there are fewer sticking places, less poetry and quotation from ponderous Spaniards. Here and there he has got swamped in that damnable slough – fine writing; but on the whole he has been true to himself and his theme.[35]

Nearly everyone agreed with Ford. The early reviews were excellent. 'This is a most remarkable book', exclaimed *The Examiner*: 'Apart from its adventurous interest, its literary merit is extraordinary. Never was a book more legibly impressed with the unmistakable mark of genius.' The *Athenaeum*: 'There is no taking leave of a book like this.' The *Dublin University Magazine*: 'We have had nothing like these books before ... *The Zincali* was the prize book of last season, and *The Bible in Spain* is likely to be the favourite of the present one. We look to Mr. Borrow with longing expectation for a book on Russia.'[36] These were the early reviews and at Christmas there were only a few shadows on Borrow's landscape. *The Times* wondered whether he was a Christian or not, so he wrote a plain, straightforward letter to say that he had always been a member of the Church of England. Then Murray sent him a batch of reviews, including one by Lockhart in the *Quarterly*, which Borrow called 'very good – very clever – and very neatly done – only one fault to find – too laudatory', and added, ominously: 'I am by no means the person which the reviewers had the goodness to represent me.'[37]

The book certainly did sell. Indeed 1843 was one of the high points of Borrow's life, for though it took him some time to pull himself together, to this end going on a two-week tour of Norfolk on Sidi Habismilk, before long he began to bask in the fame that had come to him overnight, applying himself energetically to the business of preparing new editions of both *The Bible in Spain* and *The Zincali*, which at first just meant correcting proof and writing a slightly different introduction for the second edition of *The Bible in Spain*. Writing to a Mr Sparham, whom he had been to see during his tour of north Norfolk, he anticipated the second would be out on 1 February: 'the book has had a tremendous run: I have just begun another. The booksellers will not let me rest and I must be doing something.'[38] This was not mere puffing on Borrow's behalf, for the letter was not mostly about him, but about Sparham's son and also Borrow's interest in a horse, should it happen to be an animal 'full of blood, bone and spirit'. *The Bible in Spain* had been the talk of the Christmas season. The soul of the Evangelical middle class had been stirred by this frank story of an intrepid missionary who had survived such dreadful hazards in order to distribute the New Testament to a benighted people whose need for it was obviously great. The book, apparently so direct in its method, had penetrated the reader's moral defences. Such exciting adventures, yes, but in such a good cause. Events of the kind reported by Mr Borrow, for a report it seemed to most readers, could not occur, of course, in England, but about Spain it was legitimate to imagine only the worst, blamelessly deriving thrill after vicarious thrill from Mr Borrow's narrative. The two-edged strategy of the book, whether consciously or unconsciously contrived, ensured that it would appeal to two types of reader: the intelligent reader who would enjoy Borrow's irony and dry humour and the less perceptive reader who enjoyed the story and remained oblivious to the irony. Evidently there were many readers of one kind or the other, for John Murray reprinted the three-volume first edition of *The Bible in Spain* three times during 1843, and there were two new printings, as well, of *The Zincali*, which *The Bible in Spain* carried along the wave of success.

John Murray's ledgers show that he and Borrow, in dividing the profits of the three-volume editions of *The Bible in Spain*, did pretty well for themselves. Murray's costs for the first three printings were as follows:

To printing – Woodfall	£169.12.0
Paper	£125.12.6
Advertising	£ 30. 3.7
Stationer's Hall	£ 5.0
Boarding 3,000 copies	£ 81. 5.0

According to Wise the published price was 27s.,[39] though in any calculation based upon these figures one has to have in mind that Murray naturally gave many copies away and may have disposed of others at below the initial price. Borrow received the sums of £226 8s. 5d., £272 15s. 8d. and £260 5s. 3d. respectively on the three printings of 1,000 copies each,[40] making a total of £759 9s. 4d. The ledgers may not record all the monies that passed between publisher and author, but Borrow was in any case quite satisfied, all the more so as the year proceeded, for by Christmas he had received £8 12s. from the first sales of the fourth printing of *The Bible in Spain* and £121 2s. 6d. as his share of the profits from the second edition of *The Zincali*, which had been issued in March and sold by June. Indeed, Borrow was more than satisfied; he was in his seventh heaven. He received a large number of letters of congratulations. He had dinner with the Bishop of Norwich. While in London in May, he had his portrait painted by Phillips. And on 24 June, in a letter to Murray about the proposed fourth printing of *The Bible in Spain*, he allowed himself to say: 'I begin to take a considerable pleasure in making money, which I hope is a good sign, for what is life unless we take pleasure in something?'[41]

Whether John Murray read this letter is unknown, for he died three days later, on 27 June 1843. It will be seen that his death – one widely lamented throughout the publishing world – was one of the most profound significance for Borrow, because it was in 1843 that his mother's illness caused him to have what may have been his first frank talk with her about his own past, talks that in a sense were part of the preparatory work for his autobiography, which he had referred to as early as 1841, which he had mentioned to Murray in February 1843 and which began more and more to concern him as he was buoyed up by the immense success of *The Bible in Spain*. Borrow had perhaps not even realised before March of this year that his mother had known John Murray years ago when they were both young. John Murray had never mentioned this either. Now he was dead, and little time had Borrow to reflect upon it all because John Murray III very promptly effected a revolution in the affairs of his publishing house which directly and immediately affected many authors, but no one more so than Borrow.

While Borrow, in Oulton, was 'getting on capitally' with his autobiography and Woodfall, the printer, was making preparations for the third edition of *The Zincali*, which was to appear in September, John Murray was planning a new business venture which, judging by the speed with which he acted after his father's death, he must have had in mind for some time. The idea was vastly to extend his market by positive moves both in America and in the colonies, this market penetration to be achieved, not by means of the standard multi-volume work that was to remain in vogue in Britain until late in the century, but by a specially designed, cheaper and smaller book, issued either as a paperback in two parts or as a single volume printed in double columns and with a uniform binding. To achieve the desired reduction in unit cost by printing much larger editions than his father would have considered prudent, he took this part of his business away from Woodfall and gave it to William Clowes, so that he could have the benefit of rapid, stereotype mass production by steam press. He tried to achieve a wider distribution of books in Britain by making arrangements with book-jobbers, arrangements of such a speculative kind that his father would no doubt have disapproved of them. In North America, he tried to counter the piracy that remained possible for as long as foreign authors and books were denied the protection of American copyright, by selling either sheets or unbound copies to American publishers who, in effect, acted as co-publishers. What in business terms was a radical innovation, which we can now see was part of the Victorian publisher's response to population growth, was announced to the public in the terms of the advertisement quoted in full below.

Mr. Murray's Home and Colonial Library
Popular Reading for all Classes
Murray's
COLONIAL AND HOME LIBRARY
Published Monthly. Post 8vo, 2s. 6d.,

Printed in good readable type, on superfine paper, and designed to furnish all classes of Readers with the highest Literature of the day, consisting partly of ORIGINAL WORKS, and partly of new editions of POPULAR PUBLICATIONS, at the lowest possible price. It is called for in consequence of the Acts which have recently passed the British Parliament for the protection of the rights of British authors and publishers, by the rigid and entire exclusion of foreign pirated editions.

In order, therefore, that the highly intelligent and educated population of our Colonies may not suffer from the withdrawal of their accustomed supplies of books, and with a view to obviate the complaint, that a check might in consequence be raised to their intellectual advancement, Mr. Murray has determined to publish a series of attractive and useful works, by approved authors, at a rate which shall place them within the reach of the means not only of the Colonists, but also of a large portion of the less wealthy classes at home, who will thus benefit by the widening of the market for our literature: and the 'Colonial Library' will consequently be so conducted that it may claim to be considered as a 'Library for the Empire.'

Mr. Murray's 'Colonial Library' will furnish the settler in the Backwoods of America, and the occupant of the remotest cantonments of our Indian dominions, with the resources of recreation and instruction, at a moderate price, together with many new books within a short period of their appearance in England; while the student and lover of literature at home, who has hitherto been content with the loan of a book from a book club, or a circulating library, may now become possessed of the work itself, at a cost a little beyond that entailed by either of the methods above mentioned.

The series of Works designed to appear in Mr. Murray's 'Colonial and Home Library' will be selected for their acknowledged merit, and will be exclusively such as are calculated to please the most extensive circle of readers.

The series was an instant success, as Borrow, to his immense satisfaction, soon discovered.

Actually Borrow was so satisfied with the sale of the three-volume editions and so preoccupied with the question of an abridged edition of *The Bible in Spain* that was mooted in August, that he at first failed to understand what Murray proposed. Mr Dundas, John Murray's confidential clerk, was sent up to Oulton to explain. This was on 16 September 1843, and presumably Mr Dundas conveyed basically the same offer as is contained in Murray's letter of clarification written when his clerk got back to London. 'I hope you understand that I guarantee you the sum of £160 out of the half share of profits for the 4th edition if it sells, if not out of the cheap edition, and if that does not pay, out of my own pocket.'[42] Borrow had already accepted, though, for after his conversation with Dundas he wrote to Murray to say: 'Therefore you may disburse as soon as you please as I propose buying a blood horse with the plunder.'[43]

John Murray sent Mr Dundas up to Oulton because *The Bible in Spain* was to be the first volume in the new series, and so it was important that his author should understand what was happening. He presumably also wished to be discreetly efficient in the making of these new business arrangements. He told Borrow that he had fixed the price 'at 2/6 the number or part, which is the utmost it will bear'; this after a request from Mrs Borrow (supposedly) that the single-volume of *The Bible in Spain* should be sold at 5s. not 4s. as originally proposed.[44] He also told Borrow that he had given the job not to Woodfall but to Clowes: 'by the steam power and extra exertions of Clowes it will be printed, stitched and delivered in a week's time'.[45] William Clowes was as good as his word, so the first part of *The Bible in Spain* in John Murray's Colonial and Home Library came out late in September. The autumn of 1843 became a busy time both for Borrow and Murray. Borrow had tidied up the text for the one-volume edition and made a few 'alterations', some of them in response to early reviews. He had not been upset by a negative review in the *Banbury Guardian* or, if he had been, worked his feelings out of his system in a letter to Murray. 'I pity the poor emasculated creatures who write in it; they are beneath contempt and must certainly be old ladies or castrati, I should say the latter from the sound of their voices; so let them rail. They know full well that I possess something which they do not.'[46] But when Gladstone objected to the 'strong language' of certain passages, 'particularly the sentence about the Scarlet Lady',[47] Borrow took Murray's advice and omitted them, at the same time making a few other 'alterations', notably to his section on the Jews of Lisbon. These textual changes were presumably for the printing of the one-volume edition, since the second part of the paperback came out in November.[48] Meanwhile, John Murray was also at work. For example, there is a copy of a letter in the daybook dated 25 October 1843 addressed to Perthes, Besser and Hanke, which reads: 'If you should feel disposed to speculate on 100 or 200 copies you shall be charged at the rate of 1/8 each part for cash or if you sent on *Sales or return* at 1/11 each – and in either case 13 copies as 12 will be given you.'[49] The new John Murray had, as it were, put his reputation on the line, so much depended upon his being able to dispose of the relatively large number of copies of a book that had already sold well in three-volume format.

When Knapp wrote his biography of Borrow, he told John Murray that he had glossed over the question of the American piracy in *The Zincali* and *The Bible in Spain* by excising passages from the letter to Borrow from Hasfeld in which Hasfeld gave a detailed account of the proliferation of illegal American editions and also by omitting all mention of Putnam's, the firm that was then publishing Borrow in the States.[50] According to Putnam, this caution was unnecessary. In a letter dated 19 December 1898 George Putnam told John Murray that he had gone through the firm's records, that he was sure that between 1840 and 1855 Putnam's had not published any British books without agreement and that he therefore assumed that his father's arrangements with John Murray in 1843 had been above board.[51] From Hasfeld's letter Borrow had thought that already, by 25 October when Borrow wrote to Murray about it, there had been eight pirated editions of *The Bible in Spain* in Philadelphia alone, a mistake that arose because James Campbell had called his first stereotype printing of *The Bible in Spain* the seventh edition, perhaps because he knew that John Murray's one-volume edition was called the sixth. In other words, there had been two printings of James Campbell's *The Bible in Spain*, the 'seventh' and 'eighth' editions, by the time Hasfeld, who had presumably seen or heard only about the eighth, wrote to Borrow. There had also been the first American pirated edition in the 'New World Extra Series', which Hasfeld, Borrow and Murray probably did not know about at all. In the case of *The Zincali* there had been a single-volume edition by Putman and Wiley in 1842, quickly followed by presumably pirated editions by the New World Extra Series in New York, by Robert Carter in Pittsburg and by James Campbell in Philadelphia. The same modern processes that allowed John Murray to reduce the cost of his books in England allowed Amercian publishers to reproduce them cheaply. With so much hectic activity on the docks of Boston and New York, where in the early 1840s American magazine editors jostled with each other to get copies of new British fiction, it was obviously greatly to Murray's advantage to sell copies of *The Bible in Spain* to Putnam's if he could. Putnam's letters later in the century indicate that this is what happened, though there is no record of such transactions in the John Murray ledgers. John Murray's experiment, at least initially, proved a huge success. As for Borrow, the accident of the Colonial and Home Library being launched at exactly the moment *The Bible in Spain* was one of Murray's most successful books ensured that he continued to enjoy the high public esteem that had been his since the first edition had appeared. Financially he did pretty well, too: the Colonial and Home Library editions of *The Bible in Spain* brought him an income of roughly £650 in the years 1843–7. This was not just an accident, of course. *The Bible in Spain* had established itself as one of the great books of mid-century Britain.[52]

Lavengro:
the 'book which is no humbug'

It was when Borrow turned his attention to the autobiographical work he called *Lavengro* that his eccentricity was most fully exposed. In *The Zincali* he had tried to write a book that reflected a strong personal interest. It was not, however, directly autobiographical. In *The Bible in Spain* he had contrived to write a lively, readable book that seemed autobiographical because so direct and unaffected in its method, though in fact inherently hypocritical. Borrow enjoyed his fame, wanted to write another book, knew that it had to be based on his own experiences and, indeed, had started to write it even before *The Bible in Spain* was published. Almost ten years were to pass, though, before he produced the book that many regarded as his masterpiece, the book familiar to so many generations of school-children and students and one of the classics, one of the books that at one time or another everyone would read. During these ten years, indeed during the fifteen years that preceded the publication in 1857 of *The Romany Rye*, which was the sequel to *Lavengro*, Borrow experienced the full gamut of the author's feelings, from the high elation of confident composition to the deepest despondency about the human being, George Borrow, whom the writer, George Borrow, analysed and revealed.

The struggle with *Lavengro*, that is, not just the book itself, but the agony that it cost Borrow to write it, more clearly shows us, a hundred years after his death, what he was really like, what was going on in his mind, what were his inhibitions, strengths, weaknesses, than anything that occurred on the surface of his life. This troubled interior existence, therefore, is the subject of the present chapter. Although he told his wife that he could only be happy in their little cottage at Oulton and although he still had fits, occasionally severe ones, which might have inclined him to lead a private, home-based life, he was also frequently bored, hankered after the busy, outdoor life that he had known in Spain, felt that he ought to do something with his energies besides writing, and for a while accepted his wife's suggestion that he ought to seek a 'situation'. She said this in a letter when Borrow was up in London negotiating the terms with John Murray in 1843, presumably in part because life in Oulton Cottage was already proving difficult and because George was becoming crankier and more difficult to live with. Borrow was, of course, forty years old when *The Bible in Spain* was published, still employable presumably but without the work experience of thousands of younger, talented men. There was no chance of a job with the Bible Society. He wrote to Lord Clarendon to enlist his support in finding a government job overseas, one in which his knowledge of other countries and other languages could be put to use. Would Clarendon recommend him to Palmerston as a person suitable for the post of British Consul, perhaps in the Far East? 'I am desirous of travelling in various parts of the world. Does your Lordship conceive that Government might be induced to facilitate such a plan?...I should have no objection to a consulship abroad where I could reside with my family.'[1] Clarendon replied that he would be glad to help, but that Palmerston was swamped with requests for preferment of this kind.[2] Nearer home, Borrow decided he wished to be a magistrate. He told stories of poaching, cattle-theft and vandalism, persuaded himself that there were not enough magistrates in his area and that those there were failed to do their duty, and wrote letters to people in high places in order to have himself recommended as a suitable person to be a magistrate in Suffolk. He would have been a suitable person in Suffolk if he had been a well-known, widely respected, wealthy member of a long-established family, which he was not, with the inevitable consequence that all his attempts came to nought. Certainly his pride was injured by these and other rejections, as he regarded them. In fact, people who knew him during the last twenty years of his life said he was mortified, embittered and angry and blamed his immense egoism for this unhappiness, this inability to be satisfied with what he had. Perhaps a hundred years later, in a period of high unemployment when so many talented people fail to find ways of using their talents, we can be more charitable about Borrow's inability to find the situation his wife said he needed. He did try. What else should a man with a 300-acre estate have done at the age of forty? In any case, whatever he and his wife may have said to each other about his being employed, he in fact browsed about the estate, fishing, riding, managing the property, and spent long hours in the summer-house grappling with the problem of *Lavengro*, which was also the problem of himself. An account of the process of composition will make this painfully clear.

Because this chapter will not be concerned with the details of his day-to-day life, which was repetitive and uneventful, but will rather be about the creative process that lies behind the making of *Lavengro*, on the assumption that this will reveal Borrow's essential self, it is worth recalling, first, that while the vitality and charm of *The Bible in Spain* were widely recognised and praised by Borrow's contemporaries, agreement about *Lavengro*'s qualities was reached only after his death. The reason for this is at the heart of the Borrow story. Because his contemporaries were disappointed that he had not written the book they expected, the first thorough-going reassessment of *Lavengro* occurred, not during his lifetime, but between Borrow's death in 1881 and Oliver Elton's *A Survey of English Literature* in 1920, the forty-year period in which the book was established as one of the classics of English prose writing. Not only did Murray and Putnam keep the book in print on both sides of the Atlantic, but some sixteen other publishers also produced new editions, often with introductions that asserted *Lavengro*'s virtue to a public already familiar with it.[3] In an obituary notice W. Elwin said that Borrow belongs 'among the great masters of English literature' and that *Lavengro* had to be regarded as his masterpiece for the 'singular picturesqueness and beauty in his scenes of rural life', his 'graphic power' in portraying character, and the 'force and felicity' with which he depicted nature's charms.[4]

W. E. Henley was one of the first to recollect and note Borrow's distinctive powers. For him Borrow was a 'true adventurer', who had lived so fully and richly as to be 'the envy of some and the amazement of all'. Not only had his life been remarkable, but his writings, too, had qualities that few could match. 'Circumstantial as Defoe, rich in combinations as Lesage, and with such an instinct of the picturesque both personal and local, as none of these possessed, this strange wild man', said Henley, 'holds on his strange wild way, and leads you captive to the end.'[5] For Lionel Johnson, Borrow's appeal was to the 'ancestral nomad', who by reading his books would be 'purified from the stains of civilization',[6] an opinion that is perhaps too sensational to be worth repeating, except that it reminds us, now, that before and after the First World War admirers of George Borrow read his anti-bourgeois works as statements consistent with their own social dissatisfaction. When Knapp's biography appeared in the same year, that is in 1899, an anonymous reviewer in the *Quarterly Review* called Borrow 'a deathless British writer' and said of *Lavengro* that it was 'incomprehensible' that there should have been a gap of twenty years between the first and second edition, for as long as 'British books are read at all, Borrow's will be read'.[7] The important, or at least influential, early editor, F. Hindes Groome agreed with this; for reasons he decided not to discuss, it was 'only since Borrow's death' that

Lavengro won its 'due place of pre-eminence'.[8] In the same way, Edmund Gosse noted that 'since his death the fame of Borrow has steadily increased, and is now firmly grounded on his picturesque and original studies in romanticized autobiography'. For Gosse 'the really vivid chapters of *Lavengro* and *The Romany Rye* have a masculine intelligence, a breadth and novelty of vision, which makes them unique.'[9] And even Thomas Seccombe, in his somewhat negative and patronising introduction to the Everyman edition, conceded that *Lavengro* was 'a great book'.[10]

Most criticism is ephemeral and these little essays, notices, reviews and introductions were as ephemeral as any: they were not based upon any genuine reassessment of Borrow's work, and certainly not on any reassessment based upon new information, but rather represented a strong swing of taste made possible by the fact that the circumstances surrounding the original publication of *Lavengro* had been forgotten or, if remembered, judged unimportant or irrelevant. The swing of taste was genuine, however, in so far as several generations of readers for the first time began to think about *Lavengro* in its own terms, unburdened by the frustrations that had detracted from the pleasure of readers in the 1860s. This was why Oliver Elton called the initial reception of *Lavengro* and *The Romany Rye* 'a classical instance of the follies of criticism'.[11] Anyone who based his judgement on the book itself would have no difficulty, he thought, in seeing how good it was. For many years the general reader agreed.

The difference between the book tens of thousands of readers have seen *Lavengro* to be and Borrow's own thoughts about it, as he struggled with the manuscript between 1842 and 1851, tell one more, biographically, about Borrow's imagination than could any study of his day-by-day life in Oulton. He is interesting because of what happened when he pored over his papers in his retreat, not because of how he behaved as Suffolk squire. There are few work papers, indeed, that do not expose the true character of their author.

It was Borrow himself who drew attention to the fact that several years had passed between his beginning *Lavengro* and its publication in 1851. In the single-page 'advertisement' that preceded the author's preface to the first edition of *Lavengro*, he said: 'The author begs leave to state that *Lavengro* was planned in the year 1842, and all the characters sketched before the conclusion of the year 1843. The contents of the volumes here presented to the public have, with the exception of the Preface, existed in manuscript for a very considerable time.' Why did Borrow make this unnecessary and ill-advised statement, which, if noticed at all, could only give the impression that the author must have had difficulties either in writing the book or in getting it published? And when he said that the manuscript had existed 'for a very considerable period', how long did he mean?

It was, of course, the reception of *The Bible in Spain* that made Borrow feel that to write another book was within his powers. Murray and Ford thought that *The Bible in Spain* had succeeded because Borrow had written in such a lively, direct and spontaneous way about his own experiences. Ford continued to make much of this idea. Borrow had only to do the same again for the success to be repeated, which could hardly be difficult for a man who had travelled on foot throughout Europe and had even visited remote places like St Petersburg. They were far from understanding, Murray and Ford, that *The Bible in Spain* was *not* an honest account of Borrow's life in Spain, that it was far from complete, that it was evasive in its very nature, and that the irony was of such a deadpan quality as to have passed largely unnoticed. Borrow, for his part, allowed success to go to his head. 'I hope our book will be successful', he had told Murray in December 1842. 'If so, I shall put another on the stocks. Capital subject – early life, studies, and adventures; some account of my father, William Taylor, Whiter, Big Ben, etc. etc.'[12] This original idea kept its hold and the following autumn he wrote to Murray once again.

The book which I am at present about will consist, if I finish it, of a series of Rembrandt pictures interspersed here and there with a Claude. I shall tell the world of my parentage, my early thoughts, and habits; how I became a *sapengro*, or viper catcher; my wanderings with the regiment in England, Scotland and Ireland, in which latter place my jockey habits first commenced. Then a great deal about Norwich, Billy Taylor, Thurtell, etc. etc.; how I took to study and became a *lav-engro*. What do you think of this as a bill of fare for the *First* volume? The *Second* will consist of my adventures in London as an author in the year 23, adventures on the Big North Road in 24, Constantinople (!!!) etc. The *Third*, – but I shall tell you no more of my secrets. Whenever the book comes out it will be a rum one and will equal *The Bible*.[13]

This letter satisfied John Murray, because it gave the impression that Borrow was again writing an original book based upon authentic experience, but it could not have satisfied Borrow himself, except as a plausible holding letter to his publisher, because he had as yet no clear idea of what he would put into that third volume. He had been trapped, or had trapped himself, into the appearance of a type of truthfulness that was contrary to his nature, contrary to his habits and, as it turned out, contrary to his desires as well.

This had come about because he had allowed John Murray and Richard Ford to persuade him that his book should be a fully-fledged autobiography. Because Borrow later attempted to obscure this, and because there have been controversies about Borrow's intentions, it is important to note the details of what happened. On 31 December 1842, for example, he told Murray: 'I frequently meditate on the *Life*, and am arranging the scenes in my mind.'[14] By January, his idea had become more definite. 'I meditate shortly a return to Barbary in quest of the *Witch Hamlet*, and my adventures in that land of wonders will serve capitally to fill the third volume of MY LIFE, A DRAMA. By GEORGE BORROW.'[15] He allowed himself to forget, in this letter to his friend, Hasfeld, that he had not had adventures in Tangiers, but had gone there to escape from Mrs Clarke and impending arrest in Seville; also that if he wrote about Tangiers and the Barbary coast whatever he said would have to be consistent not only with the final section of *The Bible in Spain* but also with what he had told Mrs Clarke in private. He had rarely been in the position of not being able to say just anything. Nonetheless, 'I have begun my *Life*', he once again told Murray in February; 'D.V. it shall beat anything I have yet accomplished.'[16] By 13 March he was 'now getting my father into the Earl of Albemarle's regiment, in which he was Captain for many years'.[17] Because he was writing about his own early childhood and because 1843 was such a good year for him that he was lifted out of his habitual melancholy, he still continued to turn a blind eye to the obstacles in his path. 'I have just received a very kind letter from the Secretary of the Bible Society', he reported in April.

They are going to return me all my letters from Russia, which will be of great assistance in the *Life*, as I shall work them up as I did those relating to Spain. The first Volume will be devoted to England entirely, my pursuits and adventures in early life. I must not, however, risk, by over-haste, what reputation I have acquired. The difficulty of writing a book which is no humbug is enormous; and in the *Life* I propose to blend instruction of a peculiar kind with huge entertainment. I think such a book will take and only such a book. The public has of late become 'fly', exceeding 'fly'.[18]

In these terms the correspondence between author and publisher continued through 1843 and indeed on 25 October, in the period of full excitement about the launching of the Colonial and Home Library, he again told Murray: 'LAVENGRO A BIOGRAPHY. I have just been working at a scene. The First Volume will be ready at Christmas.'[19] While he was working at volume I, he could indeed feel confident. He had worked hard throughout the latter part of 1843. He continued to work hard through that winter, the winter of 1843–4. He was, after all, not giving body to letters that already existed, but writing a new book from scratch. It was the first time he had worked in this way. With enthusiasm and confidence he carried himself into volume II, until at some point, and exactly when is not clear, though it was during

1844, he lost whatever sense he may have had of the shape of his book as a whole. It will be seen that by this time he had written parts of *The Romany Rye*, though he had not yet imagined to himself a book with that title – on the contrary, everything he wrote during 1843 and 1844 was supposed to be part of *Lavengro*. But how? For as long as he wrote about his childhood, he was in a strictly private domain: no one, except perhaps his mother, could challenge his account of his early life. When he began to give an account of his London years, on the other hand, he must have realised that he was entering territory of a different kind altogether. Other people had known him during those years and might challenge his account of himself. He broke down, sat powerless in front of his own mass of papers, could not continue.

Although Borrow had discovered that he could not write the book he had originally described, he did not immediately face up to the difficulty. This was partly because he did not want to change his first draft of what is now volume I, or indeed those parts of volume II which were eventually included, and partly because of the continuing influence of Ford, who, having strongly argued the merits of *The Bible in Spain*, became now, as the intermediary between Borrow and John Murray, an equally strong advocate for the proposed autobiography. In 1843, while Borrow was still confident that he could write a three-volume Life, Ford had advised him: 'Now your name is up in the market, anything will go down. Never fear the "rum and the rare"; make the broth thick and slab. Truth is great and always pleases.'[20] Then, when he realised that Borrow was worried about the critics, or when he thought he realised this, he exclaimed: 'How goes the *Biography*! Lay it on thick – *buena manteca de Flándes*. Stick to your own original style and defy the critics.'[21] In January 1844, Ford went to see Borrow in Oulton. How much of the manuscript of *Lavengro* Borrow chose to show Ford on that occasion is unknown, but they certainly had long talks about the book and probably discussed the overall design of it, because just before the visit Borrow told John Murray that he wrote as erratically as ever – 'first sixty pages quite neat and correct, then I become impatient, write in a hurry and the manuscript is full of blotches and alterations'[22] – while after the visit Ford told Murray: 'he is now writing it by my advice'.[23] From what Borrow had been prepared to say, Ford had got it firmly into his head that a chronological account was planned. He knew volume I was to be about Borrow's early life: he thought he knew that volume III was to be about Borrow's continental travels. What then had happened to the years 1826–33? 'I shall be most anxious to hear your own story and recent adventures: but first let us lift up a corner of the curtain over *those seven years*.'[24] Ford's motives were good; he genuinely thought of Borrow as a kindred spirit; and he attributed Borrow's unwillingness to show him parts of *Lavengro*, as they were being written, to the legitimate quirks of an author. He was a good friend and hoped for Borrow's friendship. We can see now, but he could not see then, that he compounded Borrow's problems by enthusiastically looking forward to the book that Borrow was never to write. This being the case it is natural to wonder whether Borrow's not telling Ford that he was on the wrong track is a sign of a frighteningly chilly indifference on Borrow's part to the amicable concern of someone who had already helped him a good deal, or a measure of the fact that Borrow's problems with the writing of *Lavengro* were of a deeply personal kind, representing something much more serious than just the difficulties any author might encounter with intractable material. A possible answer to this is implicit in the rest of the story of how *Lavengro* was written and published.

Borrow had not thought out the latter part of the book, did not know what would be in volume III, did not know whether volume III would be sufficient for what he eventually decided to say, and, while he must have known there were many things he would not wish to write about, whether humbug or not, had not sufficiently come to terms with himself to see that to reveal less than the truth might prove difficult artistically. It was a question of focus. He would avoid his real life by focussing upon 'adventures' because, according to Ford, this was what people wanted. Presumably this is why he recovered his St Petersburg letters from the Bible Society, though he soon realised he could not use them. Presumably this is why he told Murray he 'meditated' a return to Barbary. Until Ford reminded him of the dangers of travelling inland in Africa, he thought he could gather new material there, like a latter-day Captain Singleton. He thought the problem was soluble. He was short of usable material, but could he not acquire new material? In his letter to John Murray, dated 2 October 1843 (quoted above), he even said that in his second volume, he would be in Constantinople. But *why* did he say this? It must be assumed, in the context of his secrecy about volume III, that he must have felt as unembarrassed to mention Constantinople as he was to mention England, Scotland and Ireland, and, as seen already, that was in all likelihood because he had indeed already been in all the places he listed, including Constantinople. It was not, however, known that he had been to Turkey. Even the extremely attentive reader of *The Zincali* could scarcely have deduced this. Murray did not know. Nor did Ford. Nor did Borrow's wife. One can only too well imagine

anyone of them saying that, since Borrow was writing an autobiography, and since what was wanted was lively writing from his
own experience, it was perverse of him to include in his note about
volume II a place that he had never visited. It is the way in which
Borrow met this difficulty that gives one an ominous sense of having
suddenly entered some dark territory of the psyche. Leaving volume II
unfinished and volume III to all intents and purposes unstarted, he set
out for Constantinople.

People who are less than frank about their thoughts and plans
obviously run the risk of misinterpretation. They earn the reputation
for being shifty in their dealings with other people, confuse a love of
privacy with an inveterate habit of often meaningless self-concealment,
and grumble when they are misunderstood. A type of false pride or
egoism would be placed in jeopardy if a person of this literally self-
contained type had to explain himself in the world of common-sense
and plain affection. Borrow was not given to explaining himself.
He did feel misunderstood. So he set out in a crotchety mood, armed
with a bottle of 'homeopathic globules' as antidote for his 'nervous
attacks'. During the winter he had been debilitated by a bad bout of
bronchitis and he wanted to be on the road again. And it was not just
a matter of his general health. Walking in the way he walked, at a
steady five miles an hour through the day, was his un-medical answer
to his recurring fits, which had struck with renewed frequency during
the months he had been working hard at *Lavengro* while at the same
time seeing *The Bible in Spain* through the press. Sometimes the gaps
of time between these nervous attacks had been so long that Borrow
almost breathed easily and felt himself free, so much so that he did not
tell his wife about them before they were married. Obviously, though,
they had talked about his condition by the time Borrow had completed
the first volume of *Lavengro* and, since Mary Borrow had copied out
the whole of *The Bible in Spain*, Borrow could scarcely avoid straining
the relationship further by prevaricating over his reasons for not
immediately finishing *Lavengro*. It was reasonable for her to pester
him about it, but it was as yet impossible for him to state clearly why
he could not continue. When he left Oulton on 27 April 1844 he was,
on one level, indulging in an expedition for the sake of gathering
material for his book; on another level, he was postponing the time at
which he would have to be explicit about himself. The autobiography
would have to wait until he had accumulated experiences appropriate
to it.

The strain of writing the first half of *Lavengro* had been genuine
enough and Borrow was glad to get away from it all. Because this was

his purpose, however, it is difficult to follow his tracks with any certainty, or at least it is impossible to determine, except in one or two instances, what he did when not actually on the move. Mary Borrow told Dawson Turner that he had set out for Vienna by way of Boulogne, Paris and Strasbourg.[25] From Paris he wrote to John Murray to ask him to send books to Vidocq – this was on 1 May – and then travelled directly to Strasbourg, Ulm, Munich, Ratisbon, and from there by steamer to Vienna, where he found lodgings for a month at Mr Guglielmi's at 642 Rothenthurm Strasse at 25s. a week. Borrow told his wife that the scenery in the Black Forest was 'grand and beautiful to a degree'. 'I think I can settle down here for a month tolerably well', he said, 'especially now I have procured a nice lodging, and commence writing a little anew. God grant that I may be successful; perhaps if I am I may yet see better days, and get rid of the thoughts which have so long beset me.' Mary Borrow took the view that his faltering faith (for lack of faith was more than she could contemplate) was responsible for Borrow's profound fits of depression, so in addressing her he would use phrases like 'God grant' that he managed at other times to do without. He was perplexed to be so different from other people, different physically, different socially and different in desire: this had something to do with his actual make-up, which, however, he was unable to fathom. 'You are almost my only comfort here on earth', he told her, 'and without you I should be lost and wild, and my sensations, alas, never deceive me.' The sensation of being socially, personally disorientated was what he meant. Meanwhile, he would go to Hungary after his month's stay in Vienna,

and from thence, when I have spoken with the gypsies, I shall make the best of my way to Constantinople, and then home by Russia. I want, if I possibly can, to compose my poor mind, for it is no use running about countries unless the mind is at rest. I knew that before I left home, but I had become so unsettled and wretched, as you know, that I could not rest or do anything.[26]

The first edition of *The Zincali* has a six-page section on 'The Hungarian Gypsies, or Chingany', which is sufficiently circumstantial for it to convey an impression of authenticity even though there is also a part of it that is historical and derivative. Borrow comments on the country's barbaric feudal system, notes that gypsies for some reason have a freedom denied to the serfs and then says

a toll is wrung from the hands of the hard-working labourers, that most meritorious class, in passing over a bridge, for example, at Pesth, which is not demanded from a well-dressed person – nor from the Chingany, who have frequently no dress at all – and whose insouciance stands in striking contrast with the trembling submission of the peasants.[27]

How did Borrow know this if he had never been to Hungary? Perhaps he knew about the bridge at Pesth from talk in a tavern in London, in the same way as earlier he said Defoe had got to know about central Africa? On the next page Borrow mentions meeting some Hungarian gypsies in Genoa.

Once, during my own wanderings in Italy, I rested at nightfall by the side of a kiln, the air being piercingly cold; it was about four leagues from Genoa. Presently arrived three individuals to take advantage of the warmth, a man, a woman, and a lad. They soon began to discourse – and I found they were Hungarian Gypsies; they spoke of what they had been doing, and what they had amassed; I think they mentioned nine hundred crowns. They had companions in the neighbourhood, some of whom they were expecting; they took no notice of me, and conversed in their own dialect; I did not approve of their propinquity, and rising, hastened away.[28]

Might Borrow have learnt about the toll-bridge at Pesth from some such encounter as this? Possibly, but on the other hand, he says he recognised their dialect as that of Hungarian gypsies, while – and this surely clinches the matter – he had never before mentioned in print that he had been to Genoa. That these pages in *The Zincali* had given him the trouble of having to explain to people how he knew about such things would seem to be demonstrated by the fact that they were omitted from the fourth edition of 1846. In their place he put some of the material he gathered during his trip to Constantinople during 1844, notably the paragraphs on the Wallachian gypsies and what Borrow called a 'Prayer to the Virgin'. This shows that Borrow was keenly sensitive about the charge that his account of the Hungarian gypsies in *The Zincali* was not authentic, even though as a piece of writing it has the ring of truth to it, and that rather than confess he had in fact been to Hungary at an earlier date, he went there again.

While there he did further work on the language of the Wallachian gypsies, work which is contained in a manuscript now in the British Library and which E. O. Winstedt argued did not need to be dismissed as having been completely superseded, as Knapp did,[29] despite the errors of transcription, which were numerous. According to Winstedt, it is not possible to distinguish the dialect that Borrow attempted to record, partly because he made many pure errors, partly because he mixed dialects and partly because he imposed upon what he heard, sometimes imperfectly, the forms of English gypsy speech, which he knew a little better. Some of these errors he introduced into both the revised *The Zincali* and the later *Romano Lavo-Lil*. Obviously Borrow was not a trained linguist: he lacked a method that would have permitted accurate transcription, a method that many of his contemporaries soon acquired in the process of putting the study of languages on a more scientific footing. Borrow was not a scientist but an enthusiastic dilettante – a dilettante, however, who had been to Hungary to see and hear for himself.

After spending time 'in the Steppe of Debreczin',[30] he travelled to Bucharest, where he stayed with the British Consul, a Mr Colquhoun; from there he wrote home to say that he had arrived safely and would stay for a week or two, before continuing.[31] This he did, though for how long is not known precisely: all that is known is that he crossed the Danube at Rustchuck and reached Constantinople at least by 17 September when, according to Knapp, he cashed a letter of credit there and was presented to the Sultan Abdul Medjid. The problem that Borrow was encountering on this first leg of his journey was that a person alienated from his own society, as Borrow was, cannot remedy the situation, if he wishes to, merely by going somewhere else. His being in Spain had had a point: his travelling to Constantinople did not. He did not have the 'adventures' he was supposed to need for his book, or if he did have adventures they were not ones that he could use because, almost by definition, they would have had nothing to do with his 'life'. That complex of feelings which simultaneously constituted both his sense of self and his sense of what he could allow himself to write – that is, what his imagination produced which he did not delete – was not further modified, in any important way, by the casual events of the road. He did incorporate a Hungarian episode into *The Romany Rye* but his trip added little or nothing to *Lavengro*. He said little about casual events when he wrote to Ford and Hasfeld *en route*, as far as one can gather, that is, from their replies. Ford heard from Borrow several times and, when he did, wrote to Mrs Borrow: 'I hope he will get through next winter without any bronchitis and go on with the biography', he said characteristically on 6 October.[32] Hasfeld heard from Borrow at least twice. 'It was a heavy task to read the letter from Bucharest', said Hasfeld; 'it appeared to be written with shoe blacking.'[33] Unfortunately Borrow's letters to his friends have not survived, so we lack the probably important and, by its omissions, revealing account Borrow chose to give of his own trip. He travelled home by way of Salonika, Prevesa, Albania, Corfu, Venice, Rome, Marseilles and Paris, reaching Le Havre (for some reason!) by 16 November. And so to Oulton by way of London.

Back home, Borrow returned to the writing of *Lavengro* only very slowly, not just because he was still having difficulties with it but also because the Borrows were restless, wishing to move house but not feeling certain about where they should go. Mary Borrow finally gained sole possession of the Oulton Estate in 1846, and it was natural for them to wonder whether they should move into the larger house. While this was going on, it was difficult for Borrow to work, although it was in September of that year that Borrow began to give John Murray new assurances about the book. 'My work will be ready next year at about Christmas', he wrote on 17 September.[34] From this point on, Murray appears to have had no doubts about Borrow's intentions, or, if he had doubts, decided it was wiser to conceal them. Another year passed. Then when Borrow in December 1847 said that he would travel up to London early in the new year to make arrangements for publication, he assumed that the book was finished, continued to have faith in his author, and began to think of how and when the book should be produced. Either in January or in the spring Borrow sent him volume 1, and during the summer Murray listed the book in the *Quarterly Review* under the heading 'Mr. Murray's List of New Books in Preparation', giving the title as:

LAVENGRO, AN AUTOBIOGRAPHY
By George Borrow, Author of *The Bible in Spain*, etc.

When the first volume went to press in October 1848, Murray repeated the advertisement and listed *Lavengro* as a 'forthcoming work'. At roughly the same time he wrote to Borrow, still not aware, so it seems, that an almost insoluble problem had already been created. 'My object in writing', he said, 'is to ask you now to send up to Woodfall the MS of Lavengro in order that we may *begin printing*.'[35] That Borrow had sent Murray something, probably just the first volume, is shown by the fact that when the titlepage was printed in February 1849, it had been changed to:

LIFE, A DRAMA by GEORGE BORROW ESQ.

Borrow, though, had not yet finished the book. After another year had elapsed, Murray wrote again.

I think you will be disposed to give me credit for not bothering you unnecessarily on the subject of your book. I know that you are fastidious and that you desire to produce a work of distinguished excellence. I see the results of this labour in the sheets as they come from the press, and I think that when it does appear it will make a sensation. At the same time, the long period which has elapsed since the work was first sent to the press – *now nearly eighteen months ago* – has given rise to great evils and inconvenience both to Woodfall and myself, but, what is of more importance, is now acting detrimentally to the reception of the book.[36]

Murray's letters, at least by his own high standards, became more curt. Borrow replied that he was not idle, that he would return the proof-sheets in 'a day or two' and that the book would be ready – finished – by February. Murray therefore advertised the book in *The Athenaeum*, retaining the title *Lavengro, An Autobiography*. Despite the problems Borrow was having with the book and despite the psychological conflicts that these problems represented, Borrow chose not to disabuse the publisher as to *Lavengro*'s actual character, but left him with the impression that he was to be presented with a fully fashioned, and complete, autobiography, where 'complete' to Murray and his advisers would have entailed the inclusion of accounts of Borrow's adventures overseas to rival or surpass *The Bible in Spain*. Borrow may originally have thought that he could satisfy his publisher's expectations. In the course of writing *Lavengro*, however, he discovered that he could not. 'Upon the strength of your assurance that your book would be finished in February', wrote Murray, 'I offered it to the booksellers at my sale last week, and I have disposed of more than one thousand copies. Now I entreat you not to slacken in your labours, or I shall be in a bad plight, and your book will most certainly suffer if its publication be further delayed.'[37] Should he send proof-sheets to Lockhart so that there could be an early review of *Lavengro* in the *Quarterly Review*? On her husband's behalf, Mary Borrow replied that he did not wish his book to be reviewed in the next *Quarterly*.

In this way, in 1849, Mary Borrow became more directly involved in the business negotiations. Meanwhile, Murray discussed Borrow's intransigence with Ford, who wrote Borrow yet another friendly letter, and with Woodfall, who wrote him an impatient one.

I confess I have been not a little disappointed at not hearing from you on business matters. I do not, God knows! wish you to overtask yourself; but after what you last said, I thought I might fully calculate on your taking up, without further delay, the fragmentary portions of your 1st and 2nd volumes, and let us get them out of hand; as I have told you the locking up the types for so long a time is a decided inconvenience to me.[38]

Woodfall had been up to see Borrow in late December: now Mary Borrow wrote back to say that Borrow was doing his best, that he had been ill with overwork, that he had 'many plunges in the briny ocean which seemed to do him good',[39] that he had written 130 pages since Woodfall's visit, and that the book would be finished 'before long'. So the correspondence continued, with many instances of defensive, even paranoid, petulance on Borrow's side, until at long last, Mrs Borrow herself took the remaining parts of the manuscript to London. It had taken Borrow six additional years to complete a book that had been at least half written in 1844.

What had Borrow been doing during these years? His first

biographer referred to 'certain very humiliating circumstances' that made it difficult for Borrow to settle down to write. Certainly life at Oulton was different after Borrow returned from Constantinople in 1844. Up to that date life in Oulton Cottage had been dominated by *The Bible in Spain* and the excitement associated with it. After the trip to Turkey, Borrow had to face the question of how he would normally live, a question to which neither he nor his wife had the answer. Knapp turned his account of the Borrows' first years in Oulton Cottage to make it seem as though specific events were the 'humiliating circumstances' that impeded progress with *Lavengro*, events that varied in importance from a tiff with the local vicar about their dogs always fighting to the trauma of having the estate cut in half by a new railway. As to the dogs, the episode amounted to nothing more than that kind of angry exchange which people indulge in when they have nothing better to do. The Rev. Denniss' dog was no more at fault than Mr Borrow's 'which latter is of a very quarrelsome and savage disposition...and which has once bitten Mr. Denniss himself, and often times attacked him and his family'. Borrow declined to say anything further 'with respect to Mr. Denniss' recriminations on the quarrelsome disposition of his harmless house-dog', for 'no-one knows better than Mr. Denniss the value of his own assertions' and, though they would have to meet each other in church, 'the prayers of the Church of England are wholesome from whatever mouth they proceed'.[40] Dog-lovers deficient in common charity and a sense of humour are not rare beasts and, in this specific case, Borrow evidently found it difficult to accept that he was not a law unto himself, that he had neighbours with whom he might be expected to get on and that, if he wanted to be understood himself, he had better make an effort to understand them. The episode would be too trivial to recall, resting as it does on an incomplete transcript of a draft that only Knapp had seen, except for the fact that Knapp connected it with a note Borrow wrote to Murray the following week to say that he had been 'dreadfully unwell' – '*a regular nervous attack*'. Knapp found this 'amusing to note'.[41] Evidently Knapp found epilepsy unsavoury. Better for Borrow to have the reputation of an old curmudgeon, a hypochrondriac, an egoist and a bad neighbour, than for him to be thought of as genuinely ill. In this way, the George Borrow who had real anxieties, real frustrations, real fears – and real fits – was hidden away under a mass of anecdote, the cumulative effect of which was to make him seem impossibly, unreasonably, cantankerous and embittered.

The railway was a different matter. In 1846 Mary Borrow regained possession of the Oulton Hall Estate, obviously an important event in their lives, not least because the cottage was much too small for them for as long as Henrietta, now in her late twenties, remained at home. Later moves show that they were acutely conscious not just of the lack of space, though obviously a man who had had acute bronchitis could not live his life in a summer-house by the side of a lake, but also of the lack of congenial company, particularly for Henrietta, who could only expect to marry if she had a chance to meet eligible men. This was an issue in the Borrow household from at least as early as 1843. They were on top of each other all the time, yet without the activities or diversions that might make the overcrowding tolerable. A move to the Hall seemed a possible answer. As chance would have it, though, a local business man, Mr (later Sir) Samuel Morton Peto chose this time to build a railway from Lowestoft to Reedham, the line to run along the north side of Oulton Broad, cutting the Borrows' estate in half and separating the cottage from the Hall and the Hall from the water, which could only be reached, afterwards, by means of a small foot-bridge. The necessary Railway Act was passed in 1845 and the railway opened in 1847. The invective in *The Romany Rye* against a Sir Morton Peto thinly disguised as Mr Flamson is a sufficient reminder of Borrow's feelings on this matter. He was incensed, yes, but also profoundly upset, exactly as people still are, usually with good reason, when some remote power determines that across their idyllic land will pass an unwanted runway or arterial road, unwanted, that is, by those who have chosen that very place as their retreat from such things. Borrow's friends tried to calm him down. He should insist upon high compensation. There would only be a few trains a day. Once the railway was built the land would restore itself. To no avail. Providence, as Borrow would have said in his Spanish days, had conspired against him, and with such effect.

Preoccupied as he was by the question of the Hall and the railway, by the problem of the as-yet-unmarried Henrietta, and by his own, sometimes peaceful, sometimes troubled, relationship with his wife, Borrow let these years run away from him, many lazy agreeable months being interrupted by occasional 'incidents', which, however, only seem important in retrospect because, while one knows about them, there is no record of those other days, the majority, spent with dogs and horses, with fishing-line or gun, or with new acquaintances and friends. It is true that Borrow became upset, jealous and embittered when his old friend, Sir John Bowring, now M.P. for Bolton, seemed to use Borrow's knowledge of languages to get himself the job of British Minister in Hong Kong, a job that Borrow himself thought he would have liked, though there was never any question of his being considered for it except in his own mind. It is true that he was similiarly upset when the British Museum did not require his help in acquiring Greek documents that eventually went to Russia. It is true, too, that his pride was hurt when for a second time, in 1847, his attempt to become a magistrate failed. On the other hand, he was at the same time making new friendships and cementing old ones. There were visits from admirers of *The Bible in Spain*, dinner parties where he was lionised. He continued to see Dawson Turner and indeed one of Borrow's letters to him provides a hint, perhaps, that the railway had not completely ruined his existence: would Turner order for him, he asked, one dozen of Marcobrunner 1811 and one dozen of Hockheim 1834?[42] He made new friends in Bury St Edmunds, Elizabeth and Susan Harvey, and through them Thomas Hake and his family. The unmarried Harvey sisters provided a home from home for Henrietta in St Mary's Square in Bury, and Elizabeth Harvey, at the time of Borrow's death living at 1 Southgate House, was the executrix of Borrow's will. Thomas Hake, who had practised as a doctor in Bury St Edmunds since 1839, also became a close friend of the Borrows, as did the other members of his family. His seventh child was named Henrietta. Knapp had in his possession sixty-four letters from Hake to Borrow and Borrow to Hake, which he said showed there were many visits, both ways, up to 1853.[43] More than thirty years later, Hake vividly remembered the beginning of his friendship with Borrow. Few people had ever made as deep an impression on him.

His tall, broad figure, his stately bearing, his fine brown eyes, so bright yet soft, his thick white hair, his oval, beardless face, his loud, rich voice and bold heroic air were such as to impress the most indifferent of lookers-on. Added to this there was something not easily forgotten in the manner in which he would unexpectedly come to our gates, singing some gypsy song, and as suddenly depart. His conversation, too, was unlike that of any other man; whether he told a long story, or only commented on some ordinary topic, he was always quaint, often humourous.

Hake remembered him as 'whimsical and eccentric' but always presenting 'a stern front to humbug and cant'. Hake and Borrow became the closest of friends. Many a bottle of wine of rare vintage they had together in Oulton, for 'no man was more hearty than he over a glass'.[44] And perhaps it was not a coincidence that when the Hakes went to the United States in 1853, the Borrows also moved, for the two families had become very close, so close in fact that Knapp suppressed the correspondence.

When Borrow wrote to Lord Clarendon in January 1847 to reopen the negotiations for the position of local magistrate, he was restless because he missed his roving life and upset because he was powerless to stop Sir Morton Peto. Yet the reply of Lord Stradbroke, Lord Lieutenant of Suffolk, to Lord Clarendon was unexceptionable. 'I have lately made enquiry as to the number and efficiency of the magistrates in the vicinity of Lowestoft', he said,

and find that the Petty Sessions are well attended. No complaint exists of inattention to their public duties. Whenever it may be necessary to add to their strength, I shall be desirous of canvassing the assistance of those gentlemen residing in the neighbourhood who, living on terms of intimacy with them, will be able to maintain that union of good feeling which, I am happy to say, exists in all our benches of Petty Sessions, and if Mr. Borrow should be recommended to me by them, I shall have much pleasure in placing his name on the list for the approval of the Lord Chancellor.[45]

Someone alert to detect instances of class conspiracy might well seize upon this letter as an example of an old-boy network designed to ensure that troublesome fellows about the County of Suffolk were put down, put away, or put out. Borrow was not such a person. Nor was he a fool, however. Lord Stradbroke's letter was an unambiguous but polite no. Borrow knew this. What then was the importance of the episode as Borrow's critics recollected it? Surely it was not that a man aged forty-four who was living comfortably on his wife's income, had a still growing royalty income of his own, and was supposedly busy with his next book, which was to make him even more famous than he was already, cared desperately to be denied a job that he well knew was a pawn of Tory self-interest and a somewhat whimsical system of patronage? It was his wife who cared about his having a 'situation', having something to do, something that would be an antidote to his moods, his fits of depression, and his real fits, and literally make life bearable for them all by getting him out of the house. Unfortunately, her correspondence with her solicitor, John Pilgrim, on this subject was also suppressed by Knapp.[46] Knapp had, though, quoted the letter in which Borrow replied to his wife's suggestion that while in London, in 1843, he should find himself a 'situation'. In this same letter, Borrow said: 'I did very wrong not to bring you when I came, for without you I cannot get on at all. Left to myself a gloom comes over me which I cannot describe...My place seems to be in our own dear cottage, where, with your help, I hope to prepare for a better world.'[47] It is possible, of course, that Borrow could indeed be so dependent upon his wife as to be perfectly sincere when he said 'the poor bird when in trouble has no-one to fly to but his mate', and at the same time understand that being with his wife was part of that trouble, since it put a check on his idiosyncrasies, fantasies, evasions and the creation or re-creation of his autobiography. He had earlier, two months earlier, told John Murray that he was very unwell and that religious matters 'pained' him. 'These are strange and depressing times; Popery is springing up in every direction, and I have other duties to attend to besides those of an author. *There is no peace in this world*. I hope now you understand me.'[48] It is fairly obvious that the duties to which Borrow had to attend were matrimonial. It is surely also obvious that when he says there is no peace in this world, he does not mean that he is upset about the behaviour of a neighbour's dog. He means that he has not resolved the problem of living in Oulton Cottage with his wife. These in turn had a direct bearing upon *Lavengro*, in as far as he found it difficult to formulate a coherent account of the totality of his life up to the time of his marriage. She was beginning to have a clearer understanding of the man she had married: what she understood, however, he was not necessarily willing to state. 'My brain has been horribly worn and torn with writing this book', he had told Murray,[49] meaning that the self-scrutiny as well as the fabrication of the book had been a lacerating experience.

The correspondence in the John Murray archive shows that Mary Borrow not only protected her husband by corresponding herself with the publisher as the book at length neared completion, even to the extent of taking the finished manuscript to London, but that she also accepted responsibility for the proofs as well as for other important matters, such as the portrait used as a frontispiece (for which she gave approval without consulting her husband), the introduction that Borrow wrote in January 1850 – she held back Murray's comment that it seemed to have been 'got up for the present time and what is called Papal aggression'[50] – and the advance against royalties; she asked for and got £100 on account. Thanks to her labours both with the manuscript and the proofs *Lavengro* was eventually published – on 7 February 1851. Hake was later to describe how *Lavengro* had been written on small scraps of paper that Borrow passed out of his summer-house each morning for his wife to copy: the proof-reading Borrow prudently left almost entirely to his 'family'.[51] All in all, Mary and Henrietta could scarcely have done more to help him short of writing the book. That, however, was only within the powers of *Lavengro*'s highly eccentric author.

In a scabrous article in *The Daily Chronicle*, on 30 April 1900, the Rev. Dr Augustus Jessopp reviewed Knapp's new edition of *The Romany Rye* and, as a self-styled 'ardent Borrovian', took the occasion to vilify Borrow's reputation by innuendo. Knapp was right, Jessopp thinks, in saying that Borrow lacked an imagination, that in *Lavengro* and its sequel he only recorded his own experiences and that he was incapable of doing anything else.

The fact is that Borrow, if he set himself to write any story for love or money, could only have drawn upon his memory, and only did so. He was as absolutely wanting in the power of inventing or creating a romantic drama in three volumes as any man of real genius could be. He had, so to speak, no imagination to draw upon. What he had heard or seen, that he remembered, and that he had the power of reproducing with a strange vividness, and in a style peculiarly his own, which in its simplicity, directness and abruptness of rhythm the most skilled journalist will find very hard indeed to imitate or even parody for many pages. But Borrow was not a man of original genius.

Later on in the article, is a list of things of which Borrow in Jessopp's opinion was ignorant. We are informed, interestingly, that 'it is very improbable that he ever went into an art gallery after he left Norwich'.[52] Like much else in Jessopp's patronising piece, this remark is untrue. Borrow's brother was a painter. Through John Borrow, George met Benjamin Haydon. Through Haydon, he may have met other artists. And he himself records a visit to a London exhibition in 1843,[53] when there was at least the National Gallery to visit, but, of course, some years after his brother had died. More important, his way of coping with experience was essentially visual. It has often been pointed out that Borrow composed episodes into scenes, that he customarily rendered the psychological into the visual and that the 'strange vividness' to which Jessopp referred resulted from a habit of letting or making the reader see for himself without the imposition of any statement about the significance of what was seen. In achieving this effect, Borrow was at least as close to the artists of the picturesque as to any contemporary writer, and he was close in a way that is autobiographically important.

That Borrow had not visited many galleries in London during his first few years there is not to be doubted: the first public gallery was the National Gallery, which opened in 1838, so it was impossible for him to become familiar with great works in the same way as a young visitor to the Tate or Le Jeu de Paume could nowadays. Indeed, while Borrow was making heavy weather of the writing of *Lavengro*, the future members of the Pre-Raphaelite Brotherhood were lamenting their ignorance of the great masters, which they could only see by travelling abroad. Even someone as passionately interested as a Millais, a Holman Hunt or a Rossetti had to bide his time – why else those expeditions to Paris, Dresden and Rome? No: it was certainly not in a public gallery that Borrow's eye would have been trained. It was much more likely to have been brought up on engravings, engravings used to illustrate books and to reproduce oil paintings and watercolours, engravings moreover that much more reflected eighteenth-century notions of the sublime and the picturesque than any modern, that is to say, mid nineteenth-century view of the contemporary world. Art was not, then, an engagement with the contemporary, but represented the arousal of feelings by the depiction of a natural scene, where the feelings were a muddle of the moral and the aesthetic, while the natural scene was not natural at all but heightened to give an unusual sense of romantic isolation, romantic sympathy, or remote thrill: the wave-tossed ship, the solitary shepherd, the crippled beggar, the alpine guide, the battle against odds, but most of all the uninhabited or scarcely inhabited landscape, somewhat manipulated, so that its 'romantic' features were accentuated and its real-life features toned down.

The type of art that Borrow might have seen in London, in the 1820s for example, was that of Turner, especially the prints of Turner's *Liber Studiorum* and *Picturesque Views in England and Wales*. The publication of the latter series was a large-scale entrepreneurial enterprise by Turner and Charles Heath working in collaboration, Turner producing a large number of watercolours of different English and Welsh scenes, while Heath raised the capital – the initial capital – and organised the production of the engravings, which were then distributed by Robert Jennings and Co.[54] The first three parts of this great work, each part consisting of four engravings, were put on sale in 1827, and it is possible that Turner's views of Salisbury, Old Sarum and Stonehenge, corresponding to Borrow's depiction of the same subjects, appeared in the very first batch. To accelerate sales of a rapidly growing series in which a large amount of money had been invested, three exhibitions were later staged in each of which the public could see both watercolours and engravings. The first exhibition was held in the Large Gallery of the Egyptian Hall in Piccadilly, in June 1829. A review in *The Athenaeum* shows that Turner's watercolour of Stonehenge was included in this: 'the subject all will own was an ungracious one', said the reviewer, 'but this very defect has served to display the talent of Mr. Turner'.[55] The second exhibition of Turner's work, which Borrow might have visited, was at the Freemason's Tavern in January 1831 where an 'artists' and amateurs' conversazione' was held. And the third exhibition, the largest of the three with its sixty-six watercolours and still in progress while Borrow was in London conferring with the Bible Society's officers on the eve of his departure for Russia, was held in the gallery of Moon, Boys and Graves in June and July 1833. While nothing of an absolutely conclusive kind can be said about Borrow's knowledge of particular artists, these Turner exhibitions were undoubtedly the sort of artistic event he might well have known about. They represent the continued interest in the aesthetics of the picturesque, as well as a fashionable taste for rural England as a place to be looked at. Within this convention, Borrow later wrote about England in both *Lavengro* and *The Romany Rye*. He did not write about England in the style of Defoe's *Travels through England and Wales* or of Cobbett's *Rural Rides*, though he knew both books well: he rather tended to translate experience into the picturesque set-piece – that is, into the pictorial mode that remained prevalent in London at the time his imagination was being formed. And, of course, it was not necessary for him to have seen the water-colours and engravings of Turner to be familiar with this mode: since the publication of Thompson's *The Seasons*, most nature poetry had reflected the eighteenth-century preference for the 'sublime' and the 'picturesque'.

When Borrow wrote *The Bible in Spain* he tended to resort to the picturesque set-piece, which, as noted, was not always integral to the narrative, though it often was. When Borrow wrote *Lavengro*, he was much more skilful in this regard, at least to the extent that narrative and description seem to belong together, as here in the account of his leaving London and coming at dawn to Stonehenge – entirely by accident, he would have us believe.

After standing still a minute or two, considering what I should do, I moved down what appeared to be the street of a small straggling town; presently I passed by a church, which rose indistinctly on my right hand; anon there was the rustling of foliage and the rushing of waters. I reached a bridge, beneath which a small stream was running in the direction of the south. I stopped and leaned over the parapet, for I have always loved to look upon streams, especially at the still hours. 'What stream is this, I wonder?' said I, as I looked down from the parapet into the water, which whirled and gurgled below.

Leaving the bridge, I ascended a gentle acclivity, and presently reached what appeared to be a tract of moory undulating ground. It was now tolerably light, but there was a mist or haze abroad which prevented my seeing objects with much precision. I felt chill in the damp air of the early morn, and walked rapidly forward. In about half an hour I arrived where the road divided into two, at an angle or tongue of dark green sward. 'To the right or the left?' said I, and forthwith took, without knowing why, the left-hand road, along which I proceeded about a hundred yards, when, in the midst of the tongue of sward formed by the two roads, collaterally with myself, I perceived what I at first conceived to be a small grove of blighted trunks of oaks, barked and gray. I stood still for a moment, and then, turning off the road, advanced slowly towards it over the sward; as I drew nearer, I perceived that the objects which had attracted my curiosity, and which formed a kind of circle, were not trees, but immense upright stones. A thrill pervaded my system; just before me were two, the mightiest of the whole, tall as the stems of proud oaks, supporting on their tops a huge transverse stone, and forming a wonderful doorway. I knew now where I was, and laying down my stick and bundle, and taking off my hat, I advanced slowly, and cast myself – it was folly, perhaps, but I could not help what I did – cast myself, with my face on the dewy earth, in the middle of the portal of giants, beneath the transverse stone.

The spirit of Stonehenge was strong upon me!

And after I had remained with my face on the ground for some time, I arose, placed my hat on my head, and, taking up my stick and bundle, wandered round the wondrous circle, examining each individual stone, from the greatest to the least; and then, entering by the great door, seated myself upon an immense broad stone, one side of which was supported by several small ones, and the other slanted upon the earth; and there, in deep meditation, I sat for an hour or two, till the sun shone in my face above the tall stones of the eastern side.[56]

This does not have the ominous quality of Turner's watercolour: there is no vicious streak of lightning or sheep and shepherd killed by it. Nonetheless, there is a similarity, for the passage invites an aesthetic response, not an intellectual one. The economy of style ensures, as usual, that the reader will feel the immediacy of the description, while he is encouraged to believe in the appropriateness of an hour or two's meditation, without ever getting to know what Lavengro was thinking about while he watched the sunrise. Of course, supposing Borrow to have in fact visited Stonehenge, as he makes Lavengro visit it, the reader may have to conclude, not that the picturesque mode was the means by which he concealed what he thought, but that he did not think about very much at all. Even so, he obviously prefers, as author, to picture himself in aesthetically interesting or amusing situations, rather than relate his own experiences to the development of his own mind. He is not writing a prose version of *The Prelude* and he makes this clear.

Evidently, Borrow had become a master at manipulating visual experience, as this next passage – his view of Salisbury Cathedral – shows.

Leaving the shepherd, I bent my way in the direction pointed out by him as that in which the most remarkable of the strange remains of which he had spoken lay. I proceeded rapidly, making my way over the downs covered with coarse grass and fern; with respect to the river of which he had spoken, I reflected that, either by wading or swimming, I could easily transfer myself and what I bore to the opposite side. On arriving at its banks, I found it a beautiful stream, but shallow, with here and there a deep place where the water ran dark and still.

Always fond of the pure lymph, I undressed, and plunged into one of these gulfs, from which I emerged, my whole frame in a glow, and tingling with delicious sensations. After conveying my clothes and scanty baggage to the farther side, I dressed, and then with hurried steps bent my course in the direction of some lofty ground; I at length found myself on a high-road, leading over wide and arid downs; following the road for some miles without seeing anything remarkable, I supposed at length that I had taken the wrong path, and wended on slowly and disconsolately for some time, till, having nearly sur-mounted a steep hill, I knew at once, from certain appearances, that I was near the object of my search. Turning to the right near the brow of the hill, I proceeded along a path which brought me to a causeway leading over a deep ravine, and connecting the hill with another which had once formed part of it, for the ravine was evidently the work of art. I passed over the causeway, and found myself in a kind of gateway which admitted me into a square space of many acres, surrounded on all sides by mounds or ramparts of earth. Though I had never been in such a place before, I knew that I stood within the precincts of what had been a Roman encampment, and one probably of the largest size, for many thousand warriors might have found room to perform their evolutions in that space, in which corn was now growing, the green ears waving in the morning wind.

After I had gazed about the space for a time, standing in the gateway formed by the mounds, I clambered up the mound to the left hand, and on the top of that mound I found myself at a great altitude; beneath, at the distance of a mile, was a fair old city, situated amongst verdant meadows, watered with streams, and from the heart of that old city, from amidst mighty trees, I beheld towering to the sky the finest spire in the world.

And after I had looked from the Roman rampart for a long time, I hurried away, and, retracing my steps along the causeway, regained the road, and, passing over the brow of the hill, descended to the city of the spire.[57]

There are many other examples in *Lavengro* of Borrow's delicate pictorial handling of the physical scene, of what we could call his composing habit, his habit of training the reader's eye to an arrange-ment or disposition of objects in nature which, while it conjures pleasing effects, also denies the reader knowledge of the artist's partici-pation in the scene he portrays, since it is not possible to interrogate the picturesque: you take it or leave it as it is, enjoy or do not enjoy its conventional formulations. This technique, as utilised in *Lavengro*, whether by design or not, has two consequences – two at least. The first is that the English landscape is represented as uncluttered, serene, free of tension between person and person, free of tension between person and environment, and still accessible, meaningfully, to the foot-traveller. If Borrow had been trying to show what Britain was like in the late 1840s, what it was like socially and politically, he would have been open to the charge of deliberate falsification, but in fact his is not at all a documentary method but one limited to the particularities of fictional biography, in which the ego appears in a dream landscape, as Borrow accurately perceived when he changed his title. The second consequence of this technique of the picturesque is even more important. The scene observed is essentially a scene 'over there'. It is distant. The observer is not involved in what he sees. Even when the protagonist of *Lavengro* – its 'I' – is physically present in the scene being described, the author's habit of mind is such that any episode, for example an episode that is represented as really having occurred, is reformulated, reshaped, or reconstructed into a scene observed with a calm and scrupulous detachment. This absolved Borrow from the need to tell the truth about himself. The picturesque mode is anti-confessional in its effect and, although *Lavengro* is enlivened by a whole series of encounters between Borrow and people met on the road, this being a great part of its appeal, that such encounters are so immediate, varied and colourful and reconstructed in such vigorous dialogue, a common feature is that they never last. There are no permanent relations between people in *Lavengro*, relations that grow, develop and mature; and there are no instances of a serious challenge, as it were, to the fictional authority of the narrator. He decides what will and will not be revealed, the action never being so dramatised that a character might round upon the narrator and challenge his view of things. His view goes unchallenged, so it constitutes the totality of what the reader is given, which indeed is a lot. The point is, then, that not only does Borrow keep out of *Lavengro* anything like an honest account of his own adolescence, his own sexual experiences, his own personal disasters, his relations with his mother, father and brother, and not just his relations with them but also his knowledge of them, but that he chooses a style for the book, or hits upon it somehow in the process of writing, which constitutes an all-pervasive controlling device that allows him to protect his instinct for privacy while at the same time seeming to be open, bland, honest and sincerely, utterly involved. It is a fair guess that his eye and his sensibility had been trained on books like William Gilpin's *Observations relative chiefly to Picturesque Beauty*, that the type of watercolour he had seen with his brother at the early exhibitions of the Norwich Society of Artists was more important than, say, Augustus Jessopp later realised, and that his ironical comments on some of his own set-pieces indicate that he fully appreciated the convenience, to him personally, of an inherited and widely understood picturesque mode. He was essentially an artist not a reporter, an artist of the visible not of the invisible.

Borrow's adoption of a technique by which he could protect his own privacy is, of course, biographically significant. If his relations with his mother, father and brother had been formative, he did not think so. He thought he could write paragraphs in honour of his mother, because how she had behaved in *her* part did not affect him.

He thought he could honour his father, because his father's life was not his life. He thought he could write warm brotherly sentences about his brother, because it would have been indecorous and pointless to do otherwise. While it is highly probable that he got to know more about his family while writing *Lavengro* than he had known before, he did not wish to write about it. He wished to conceal it. His father had been a successful recruiting officer in a period when the press-gang became notorious for its cruelty. His mother had lived a much freer life in and about barracks than he would ever say. His brother had had a bohemian, promiscuous and reckless life. He himself had left home, rebelled against his Norwich training and made his own way in the world, often in extremely difficult circumstances. For all practical purposes, he lived his life without the support of his family, even though he lovingly and dutifully cared for his mother in her later years, as he had acted firmly, at an earlier stage, to secure for her his brother's pension after his death in Mexico. He was not without feeling. He did not cut his ties in order to be independent. On the other hand, he did think he was independent. He thought that he himself, not his own early experiences, fashioned his later life, the life he would write about perhaps in *Lavengro*. This is not to say that his urbanity of manner, his sense of self-sufficiency and his cool indifference to most of the hazards of existence had been easily achieved. They had been achieved by means of a successful repression of his anxieties about himself: his lack of faith, his being physically different from other people,[58] and his epilepsy. *Lavengro* is the autobiographical statement of a man who has brought the difficult things of his life under control – but at a cost: in some ways a terrible cost. Would he have written differently about his own formative experiences had he lived in the age of Freud rather than in the age of Victoria? Perhaps. But for Borrow repression was a strategy for living that worked. It would not have helped him in the slightest to have revealed his deepest fears, his most nagging and persistent thoughts, his darkest sense of his own fatality. Yet while *Lavengro* is the work that achieves serenity by means of thorough-going repression, the Appendix to *The Romany Rye* is the work that reveals, albeit indirectly, the terrifying pressures that bore upon Borrow's imagination, the needs that were inhibited and the psychological damage years of making his own way, privately, secretly, had worked.

The considerable charm of *Lavengro* which later generations of readers saw and felt easily enough was, however, at the time of publication, obscured by the controversy about Borrow's intentions that immediately arose. As John Murray had predicted, the book was not well received: 3,000 copies were printed of which only 2,000 were sold in 1851. Three years later Murray still had 833 copies on hand. He sold 250 to Mudie, presumably at an extremely low price, but failed to dispose of the others until the book was remaindered in 1869. These figures reflected a general dismay, a sense of disappointment that the book was not in the same vein as *The Bible in Spain* and, also, an often not very well-defined idea that Borrow had been dishonest in not narrating the experiences he was known to have had. He was forty-eight, but his autobiography terminated abruptly, without explanation, at the age of twenty-two or three. Some early reviewers, notably in *Blackwoods* and *The Athenaeum*, complained that the gypsy theme had been overexploited; others that there had been an overemphasis on 'low' life; others again, that Borrow had been over-complacent in indulging his own ego, as though the most trivial incident, if it concerned him, might be a substitute for an orderly account of the principal events of his own life. Most of all, the first readers were bewildered by the apparent blend of fact and fiction. On this subject, Knapp later said that Borrow himself had caused the problem, because when the book was finished 'that which served as scaffolding was cast aside, and Dream and Drama became so vivid, that the original sought to deny the likeness, and through his own vacillation the public raised the cry of *fiction*'.[59] 'There is no mystery about them, if you have the key', said Knapp. 'And what is the key? – only Sympathy! Believe them and read and weep and feel.'[60] This is exactly what early reviewers were not inclined to do. 'Few books have excited warmer expectations than this long-talked-of autobiography', pronounced *The Athenaeum*; 'and great is the disappointment which it will leave in the minds of those who expected anything beyond a collection of bold picaresque sketches. It is not an autobiography, even with the licence of fiction.'[61] This opinion was widely endorsed. Even though the book, as published, was entitled:

LAVENGRO

THE SCHOLAR   THE GYPSY   THE PRIEST

and even though Borrow began the preface by saying: 'In the following pages I have endeavoured to describe a dream, partly of study, partly of adventure, in which will be found copious notices of books, and many descriptions of life and manners, some in a very unusual form', he was nonetheless widely criticised not just for duping his expectant readers, but for duping them in this particular way, that is by perversely refusing to draw the self-portrait that was consistent with their image of him.

Had John Murray also been deceived? Had he read the third

volume of *Lavengro* in proof with the same care as he had read the first? Presumably not. He could not afford to adopt a nonchalant attitude to the public reception of *Lavengro*, however, because he had discussed it widely in advance of publication, described it vividly and with enthusiasm when selling copies in advance and endorsed the abrupt, unexplained conclusion. The problem would be resolved, he thought, if Borrow wrote a fourth volume which included an account of his later years, that is, which included the material that John Murray had been led to suppose would be in volume III. This he quickly urged Borrow to do.[62] Borrow could conceivably have at this point withdrawn from the fray. He was angry, hurt, bemused. But for two reasons, at least, he let pass the opportunity of saying that, because *Lavengro* had been badly mauled by reviewers, he saw no point in continuing it.

The first reason had to do with the personal nature of the criticism. There have been attempts in recent years to show that the early response to *Lavengro* was not as negative as Knapp and his contemporaries claimed[63] and there may well be a measure of truth in this. That Borrow was incensed by people's comments on the book is not, though, to be doubted, since it will be seen that he devoted a fifth of *Lavengro*'s eventual sequel to a particularly virulent form of rebuttal. At the time of publication, *The Times* had openly questioned Borrow's faith, so, after discussion with John Murray, he wrote a brief letter stating that he was a confirmed member of the Church of England. The other matters on which he felt he had been attacked, even savaged, he dealt with, one by one, in the famous Appendix to *The Romany Rye* where his outspoken, outrageously indiscreet, highly sensational self-defence quite adequately identifies the criticism he had found most offensive and difficult to stomach. If it is true that an author should endure in silence hostile reviews of his book, however misinformed, obtuse, mischievous and personally insulting or impudent they might be, Borrow broke this golden rule in a distinctly idiosyncratic, wilful and terrible manner, by immediately plotting and eventually perpetrating revenge. In fact, the six years between the publication of *Lavengro* in 1851 and *The Romany Rye* in 1857 were soured by this vengeful attitude. Eventually, he would get his own back, he thought. Eventually, he would make his enemies suffer.

The second reason for Borrow's willingness to accede to John Murray's request that he should quickly finish the story begun in *Lavengro* was that he had already written most of the book that was to become *The Romany Rye*. This was not what John Murray wanted, but it was what George Borrow wanted. Knapp noticed that a strong clue to this is provided by the dated watermarks of the paper on which *The Romany Rye* was written. If the watermarks are to be trusted, the following sections of the incomplete manuscript of *The Romany Rye* can be identified and dated.

Vol. i, pp. 361–72 and vol. ii, pp. 1–53	1844
Vol. ii, pp. 81–121	1848
Vol. i, pp. 1–360	1851
Vol. ii, Appendix, pp. 245–375	1853
Vol. ii, pp. 124–244	1854

These watermark dates and page numbers relate to the fair copy made by Mrs Borrow. They are not conclusive. Nonetheless there must be a strong presumption that much of *The Romany Rye* was written before *Lavengro* was published, that Borrow gave *Lavengro* its present shape because he had much too much material about his early years but scarcely anything usable about his later years, and that, though he may have reorganised, reshaped even in part rewritten the massive manuscript that could not be crammed into *Lavengro*, the essential creative work was well in the past when he began to discuss with John Murray the desired fourth volume that would finish the story. This clue is supported by internal evidence. The references in *The Romany Rye* to the police, the 'roads of metal', the railways and the corn-laws make an early composition date likely.[64] There is also a curious reference to Joseph Sell that seems to hark back to a much earlier period in Borrow's life.

There is no need to recapitulate in detail the correspondence between John Murray and George Borrow during the years immediately following the publication of *Lavengro*.[65] Murray would write a polite inquiry about the progress of the book only to be put off with a vague reply from either George or Mary Borrow. In November 1852, for example, Borrow said that he was 'occasionally occupied upon it' and that he would 'Probably add some *notes*', which is the first hint that the Appendix was on the stocks. Almost a year later, Mary Borrow reported that Borrow hoped 'shortly' to complete the book, which he now wanted to call *The Romany Rye – A Sequel to Lavengro*. She must almost have finished making the fair copy before they moved to Yarmouth in 1853 and began the new life that is the subject of chapter 9 of the present book. Borrow must almost have finished rewriting the last part of volume ii of *The Romany Rye*, if he had not in fact finished it. Their decision to go to Yarmouth must have been related to their combined labours on the manuscript and fair copy, even if they did not quite finish and even though Borrow did not give the book to Murray until after the Borrows had had a holiday in Wales in 1854. Both *Lavengro* and *The Romany Rye* belong to the years of seclusion in Oulton, in other words, even though *The Romany Rye* was not published until 1857.[66]

Borrow and Murray were now locked in a battle of wills. Murray wanted a book that would 'dissolve the mystery' of *Lavengro*. Borrow knew that he had *not* written the book Murray wanted but that he had written a book which *was* a continuation of the earlier narrative. Murray sent the manuscript to a reader, summarised the reader's comments and sent them to Borrow. Not for the first time an author was, or affected to be, enraged by the comments of an uncreative on a creative person, that anonymous consultant who so constantly bedevils relations between the principals in the publishing business. So thought Borrow, who had had his fill of criticism. A wild letter was concocted, written partly by Mary Borrow to George's dictation, partly by Borrow himself. 'You talk about *conditions* of publishing', he said in the first part. 'Mr. Borrow had not the slightest wish to publish the book. The MS was left with you because you wished to see it, and when left, you were particularly requested not to let it pass out of your hands.' This, of course, means that he did wish to have it published, that he resented comments and that he was determined to have his own way. Anyone with any experience of that type of critic, reader, reviewer or publisher's consultant who irritatingly discusses not the book that has in fact been written but the book he imagines he himself might have written had he been a writer of books, rather than a critic of other people's, will perhaps sympathise a little with Borrow at this point, wrong-headed though the author was undoubtedly being. He would not accept the criticism because 'the book is one of the most learned works ever written...It is treated just as if all the philological and historical facts were mere inventions, and the book a common novel.' If Borrow had suffered agonies during the period of self-scrutiny in Oulton, they were now thrust into the background for the sake of a struggle that Borrow could more readily handle. He would not give way!

Indeed, he took the occasion to give John Murray a piece of his mind on the subject of *Lavengro*, because Murray should have protected it, he claimed, from the 'infamous and undeserved' treatment it received.

It was attacked in every form that envy and malice could suggest, on account of Mr. Borrow's acquirements and the success of *The Bible in Spain*, and it was deserted by those whose duty it was, in some degree, to have protected it. No attempt was made to refute the vile calumny that it was a book got up against the Popish agitation of '51. It was written years previous to that period –

a fact of which none is better aware than the Publisher. Is that calumny to be still permitted to go unanswered?

That this descent to a level of carping and vindicative personal complaint would result in at least a temporary estrangement between author and publisher is in retrospect easy to see. No one likes an accusation of bad faith, whether it is recognised as valid or not. John Murray was in a difficult position but not so difficult as to make him enjoy this type of personal criticism.

Borrow at this point stopped dictating and finished the letter himself.

If these suggestions are attended to, well and good; if not, Mr. Borrow can bide his time. He is independent of the public and of everybody. Say no more on that Russian subject. Mr. Borrow has had quite enough of the press. If he wrote a book on Russia, it would be said to be like *The Bible in Spain*, or it would be said to be *un*like *The Bible in Spain*, and would be blamed in either case. He has written a book in connection with England such as no other body could have written, and he now rests from his labours. He has found England an ungrateful country. It owes much to him, and he owes nothing to it. If he had been a low ignorant imposter, like a person he could name, he would have been employed and honoured.[67]

George and Mary Borrow knew that the book George had written was the only one he would write. No amount of pressure could now alter this. Nor did there seem room for negotiation on the length of *The Romany Rye*. With different people, in different circumstances, there might have been talk of paring the manuscript to one volume and of omitting the inflammatory Appendix altogether. But Murray had a set idea of how large a volume should be, while Borrow had no intention of paring the book down. More time, therefore, passed. Mary Borrow asked for the manuscript back but did not receive it. Murray behaved as though he would publish the book but did not. Eventually, after further rancorous exchanges, the two men reached a point of no return. Murray said that it was impossible for him to publish the book at all, unless certain changes were made, and that there was one change which was an absolute condition of publication.[68] Borrow's response to this was sufficiently remarkable to merit quotation in full.

And now I must tell you that you are exceedingly injudicious. You call a chapter heavy, and I, not wishing to appear unaccommodating, remove or alter two or three passages for which I do not particularly care, whereupon you make most unnecessary comments, obtruding your private judgement upon matters with which you have no business and of which it is impossible that you should have a competent knowledge. If you disliked the passages, you might have said so; but you had no right to say anything more.

I believe that you not only meant no harm, but that your intentions were good. Unfortunately, however, people with the best intentions occasionally do a great deal of harm. In your language you are frequently in the highest degree injudicious; for example, in your last letter you talk of *obliging me by publishing my work*. Now is that not speaking very injudiciously? Surely you forget that I could return a most cutting answer were I disposed to do so.[69]

Evidently John Murray concluded that it was better to publish the book himself, with the minimal corrections that he personally required, than to have some other publisher put out an unrevised version in which he, too, might become a target for abuse. He must obviously have had a powerful private reason for condoning the Appendix, for under normal circumstances no publisher in his right mind would have had anything to do with it. Published it was, at any rate. *The Romany Rye* appeared on 18 May 1857 in an edition of 1,000 copies, of which 952 had been sold by June. The ledgers show that Borrow's half-share of the profits of this first edition amounted to £149 4s. 6d. and also that not Ford but a Mr Milton had been paid 8 guineas for reading the manuscript. As the dust of controversy settled, Borrow wrote to John Murray from Wales:

I was very anxious to bring it out, and I bless God that I had the courage and perseverance to do so. It is of course unpalatable to many; for it seems to foster delusion, to cry 'Peace, where there is no peace', and denounces boldly the evils which are hurrying the country to destruction, and which have kindled God's anger against it, namely, the pride, insolence, cruelty, covetousness, and hypocrisy of its people, and above all that rage for gentility which must be indulged in at the expense of every good and honourable feeling.[70]

Borrow, having got his way, was unrepentant. He noted that the publication of *The Romany Rye* coincided with the Indian Mutiny: was he not right, then, to think that the English had a lot to answer for? 'Instead of being ashamed', he wrote in his preface, 'has he not rather cause to be proud of a book which has had the honour of being rancorously abused and execrated *by every unmanly scoundrel, every sycophantic lacquey, and political and religious renegade in Britain?*' John Murray had persuaded Borrow to change the italicised words to 'by the very people of whom the country has least reason to be proud' but, if the phrasing suffered, the point remained the same – that point being, not just that Borrow was exultant, relieved and thankful to have a long ordeal behind him, but that, psychologically, the lonely human being who had laboured over so many manuscript pages, and for so long, found a pathetic, frightening type of comfort in castigating people who would not love him, think about him, honour him as he wished.

When Borrow said that he had 'written a book in connection with England such as no other body could have written', he meant what he said; the remark was a considered judgement or a reflection on the creative experience he had just been through. Not only had he not produced the narrative of adventures that had been called for; he did not produce that type of narrative at all. *The Romany Rye*, though it has the form of a journey, is no more about an actual journey than was *Lavengro*. It is more of a portrait of England presented through the consciousness of a traveller who gives a highly selective account of incidents on the road, an account so rigorously controlled that it never becomes nakedly autobiographical, crudely anecdotal or naively pictorial. The control is asserted through the character of the protagonist, the 'I' who tantalisingly is never utterly Borrow, never utterly a figment of his imagination: a character whose blandness, self-respect, coolness, resourcefulness and even temper together constitute the lens through which the reader is allowed to see events. Twice in *The Romany Rye* Borrow recalls the creative effort that had gone into the writing of the *Life of Joseph Sell*. 'When I reflected on the grisly sufferings which I had undergone whilst engaged in writing the *Life of Sell*, I shrank from the idea of a similar attempt; moreover, I doubted whether I possessed the power to write a similar work.' This power he had said earlier in the paragraph was the 'desperate effort' by which he had collected together the whole strength of his 'imagination'.[71] This applies equally to the effort of writing *The Romany Rye* itself: he had not sat calmly at a desk writing his memoirs; he had, rather, created a book from his intense feelings about his own youth and about the English countryside. But such is the marvel of his style that no trace of labour or effort remains on the page. Instead there is a deceptively limpid surface, a charm, a picturesque stability, the depths being charted much more by implication than by direct statement.

Borrow's bohemian character, 'Lavengro', is now, in *The Romany Rye*, first tinker, then hay and straw clerk in an inn, then horse-dealer – albeit one who qualifies for this quintessential gypsy occupation by buying and selling just one horse. He is still on the road; he crosses and re-crosses parts of southern England, ending up at the Horncastle horse-fair; and on the way meets a miscellany of deftly drawn, colourful people: Peter Williams, the preacher; Petulengro, Pakomovna, Ursula and other gypsies; Isopel Berners; Jack Dale; Murtagh; the tall Hungarian; the eccentric landowner, and a largish number of grooms, jockeys, landlords and pub *habitués*, in other words a pretty fair cross-section of rural society at that time. In drawing that picture of England which no one else could have drawn, Borrow is essentially oblique. In order to say something about contemporary poetry, he invents a character he finds snoring in a field, whose friends have treated him for insomnia by lending him a certain book, the poems of Wordsworth; Byron, for Borrow, is the true poet, but his 'rival will always stand a good chance of being worshipped by those whose ruined nerves are insensible to the narcotic powers of opinion and morphine'.[72] In order to say something about religion, he introduces a rather silly, covert Catholic nobleman, with whom he discusses the worship of images and the oriental origin of Christianity. He rinses out his shirt in a pond full of newts so that he can go to church with Mr and Mrs Petulengro, has more long talks with the Methodist preacher, talks with Murtagh about Murtagh's Catholic education overseas, and expatiates in passing on contemporary themes: the railways; the corn-laws and, of course, newspaper editors. 'Listen for an hour or two to the discourse of a set they call newspaper editors, and if you don't go out and eat grass, as a dog does when he's sick', says Mrs Petulengro, 'I'm no female woman.'[73] There is a deep but sure historical perspective to Borrow's vision of England. Krishna is immediately relevant when he thinks about Catholicism. In gypsy words and songs he hears the echoes of medieval history and the strength of oral traditions. And when Murtagh retells the story of Finn MacCoul Borrow recognises from his knowledge of Danish literature the earlier story of Sigrid Fafnirsbane. Mid nineteenth-century England is still inhabited by the representatives of the ancient Vikings and the gypsies make manifest important links with eastern cultures. These were the connections Borrow had in mind when he called *The Romany Rye* one of the most 'learned books ever written'.

Quite obviously, any reader might dispute Borrow's ideas, argue that there is no connection between Buddhism and Catholicism, that worshipping images is not basic to humanity at a certain stage, that the Scandinavian element in British life had long ago been replaced by, not absorbed within, the Norman, that Radical politics were not exotic but homebred and essential to England's health, and that cultural similarities between an Irish and a Danish folk tale have little bearing upon a people in the grip of capital and industry. This is true. Borrow is not writing a tract, even though he calls his book 'learned'. He is giving a picturesque view of those aspects of England he knows and loves, an England that still after all exists a hundred years after his death, though now much changed by events that he could only dimly have anticipated. His method remains urbane, descriptive, specific. Everything is brought onto the page with an economy that bespeaks direct observation, as here in his description of Mr and Mrs Petulengro, when they take tea with 'Lavengro' and Isopel Berners by their campsite.

Mr. Petulengro was dressed in Roman fashion, with a somewhat smartly cut sporting-coat, the buttons of which were half-crowns, and a waistcoat scarlet and black, the buttons of which were spaded half-guineas; his breeches were of a stuff half-velveteen, half-corduroy, the cords exceedingly broad. He had leggings of buff cloth, furred at the bottom, and upon his feet were highlows. Under his left arm was a long black whale-bone riding-whip, with a red lash, and an immense silver knob. Upon his head was a hat with a high peak, somewhat of the kind which the Spaniards call *calanes*, so much in favour with the bravos of Seville and Madrid. Now, when I have added that Mr. Petulengro had on a very fine white holland shirt, I think I have described his array. Mrs. Petulengro – I beg pardon for not having spoken of her first – was also arrayed very much in the Roman fashion. Her hair, which was exceedingly black and lustrous, fell in braids on either side of her head. In her ears were rings, with long drops of gold. Round her neck was a string of what seemed very much like very large pearls, somewhat tarnished, however, and apparently of considerable antiquity.[74]

The *naïveté*, the studied *naïveté*, or unaffectedness of this sort of passage is disarming: since the narrator seems only to tell the reader what he has experienced at first hand, and since whatever significance the creative strategy might have is extremely oblique, there is very little, really, to argue about. *The Romany Rye* is simply one man's view of things. Naturally a different person might have a different view.

The person who, in *The Romany Rye*, is represented as having this particular sympathetic yet careful view of England, is himself described as being so bland, so civilised, so agreeably ironic in attitude, and so calmly in control of himself, that for a reader to whip up an imaginary argument with him, as though there were dangerous points of doctrine, politics or morality to dispute, would be completely inappropriate, for the protagonist does not in the least show himself as dogmatic, closed-minded or truculent, but on the contrary leaves the reader plenty of space in which to reflect calmly on the scenes to which he is introduced. Here, for example, is 'Lavengro' remembering his cross-country expedition to the Horncastle horse-fair in Lincolnshire.

On the whole, I journeyed along very pleasantly, certainly quite as pleasantly as I do at present, now that I am become a gentleman and weigh sixteen stone, though some people would say that my present manner of travelling is much the most preferable, riding as I now do, instead of leading my horse; receiving the homage of ostlers instead of their familiar nods; sitting down to dinner in the parlour of the best inn I can find, instead of passing the brightest part of the day in the kitchen of a village ale-house; carrying on my argument after dinner on the subject of the corn-laws, with the best commercial gentlemen on the road, instead of being glad, whilst sipping a pint of beer, to get into conversation with blind trampers, or maimed Abraham sailors, regaling themselves on half-pints at the said village hostelries. Many people will doubtless say that things have altered wonderfully with me for the better, and they would say right, provided I possessed now what I then carried about with me in my journeys – the spirit of youth. Youth is the only season for enjoyment, and the first twenty-five years of one's life are worth all the rest of the longest life of man, even though those five-and-twenty be spent in penury and contempt, and the rest in the possession of wealth, honours, respectability, ay, and many of them in strength and health, such as will enable one to ride forty miles before dinner, and over one's pint of port – for the best gentleman in the land should not drink a bottle – carry on one's argument, with gravity and decorum, with any commercial gentleman who, responsive to one's challenge, takes the part of humanity and common sense against 'protection' and the lord of the land.[75]

Maybe, stylistically, Borrow owes a lot to Defoe, to Lamb and Hazlitt, to those legal writers whose words he transcribed for Phillips: he shares wtih them a worldly discursiveness which, though discursive, never diverges far from a precisely observed and intimately known 'real world', a place that actually exists, the reader is persuaded to believe, however improbable the events related. *The Romany Rye* is in fact superbly written and one can only lament its separation, or possible separation, from *Lavengro*. The two books are all of a piece, create the same atmosphere, have the same tone, give the same pleasure. Though *The Romany Rye* in a sense ends abruptly, too abruptly, with a one-and-a-half-page chapter that raises a hint of a trip to India, obviously something has been completed – a gypsy or bohemian ramble about England during the pre-industrial but post-war era. Certainly the reader has not been encouraged to believe that he is to begin a complete life, for amongst other things he knows well enough the whole action of *The Romany Rye* is just an interlude in the protagonist's story. So if a reader does not enjoy *The Romany Rye* it will not be because he was induced to expect a fully fledged autobiography.

Of course *The Romany Rye* did not actually end with the termination of Borrow's account of Lavengro's travels in 1824–6 because, instead of continuing the story, he used the rest of the final volume for what he at first called 'the notes' and later 'the appendix'. This amounted to about seventy pages, constituted an extremely hostile response to the critics' hostile remarks about *Lavengro*, and was widely criticised both because of the angry way in which he lambasted his opponents and because of the thinly veiled personal attacks on people who had offended him; Robert Curzon for denying him the chance to go to Greece on behalf of the British Museum, John Bowring for using Borrow's information to get a job in the Far East which Borrow himself wanted, Samuel Peto for being a *nouveau riche* railway magnate who had the gall to build a railway track across Borrow's land, John Murray for not defending him against the claim that *Lavengro* had been an opportunist publication and Lockhart for allowing or encouraging his literary rivals to review his books in a negative spirit.

These personal attacks are certainly not the best part of the Appendix. To the extent that the individuals under fire can be identified, the paragraphs devoted to them seem tasteless and beside the point. They show, too, that Borrow had been deeply wounded by a public indifference to him, that he very much had wanted a public role, and that, irrationally, ungraciously, ungenerously he lapsed into invective against those who, at least in a couple of cases, were doing what he would have done himself. As for the critics who had taken the pleasure out of Borrow's experience of publishing *Lavengro*, Borrow failed completely to see their complaints in any kind of perspective, and in particular failed to come to terms with the fact that they had expected an autobiography and legitimately, because of Murray's repeated statements about the book, felt duped. He therefore attacked them in the Appendix, as though they had had no right to be so idiotic as to have attacked him. The Appendix thus became a virulent, powerfully written, strongly or even savagely felt counter-blast and *credo*, and as such, because later readers cared not too much about John Bowring and Samuel Peto, remains one of the best things Borrow ever wrote, so much so that it seems best to quote a few longish passages so that the actual quality of the writing can be noticed and enjoyed. There is no translation or transformation, here, into the picturesque, no evasiveness, no troublesome distancing. Instead, Borrow writes directly about the criticisms that had upset him most: that *Lavengro* had been irreligious; that he had harped on the anti-Popery theme in order to get another job with the Bible Society; that the book was un-English; that he had been preoccupied with low life; that he had revealed an excessive love of beer and pugilism; and that his political views were suspect.[76] Borrow so strongly felt the need to answer these criticisms, real and imagined, that he produced a minor classic, a statement of faith, in a sense, of a man who loved England but who did not love the evangelical, moralistic and philistine attitudes of part of its middle class. He is so clear about all this that he must be allowed to speak for himself.

Here, first, is his statement, from the beginning of the Appendix, of what *he* thought *Lavengro* had been about.

Lavengro is the history up to a certain period of one of rather a peculiar mind and system of nerves, with an exterior shy and cold, under which lurk much curiosity, especially with regard to what is wild and extraordinary, a considerable quantity of energy and industry, and an unconquerable love of independence. It narrates his earliest dreams and feelings, dwells with minuteness on the ways, words and characters of his father, mother and brother, lingers on the occasional resting-places of his wandering half-military childhood, describes the gradual hardening of his bodily frame by robust exercises, his successive struggles, after his family and himself have settled down in a small local capital, to obtain knowledge of every kind, but more particluarly philological lore; his visits to the tent of the Romany chal, and the parlour of the Anglo-German philosopher; the effect produced upon his character by his flinging himself into contact with people all widely differing from each other, but all extraordinary; his reluctance to settle down to the ordinary pursuits of life; his struggles after moral truth; his glimpses of God and the obscuration of the Divine Being, to his mind's eye; and his being cast upon the world of London by the death of his father, at the age of nineteen. In the world within a world, the world of London, it shows him playing his part for some time as he best can, in the capacity of a writer for reviews and magazines, and describes what he saw and underwent whilst labouring in that capacity; it represents him, however, as never forgetting that he is the son of a brave but poor gentleman, and that if he is a hack author, he is likewise a scholar. It shows him doing no dishonourable jobs, and proves that if he occasionally associates with low characters, he does so chiefly to gratify the curiosity of a scholar. In his conversations with the apple-woman of London Bridge, the scholar is ever apparent, so again in his acquaintance with the man of the table; for the book is no raker up of the uncleanness of London, and if it gives what at first sight appears refuse, it invariably shows that a pearl of some kind, generally a philological one, is contained amongst it; it shows its hero always accompanied by his love of independence, scorning in the greatest poverty to receive favours from anybody, and describes him finally rescuing himself from peculiarly miserable circumstances by writing a book, an original book, within a week, even as Johnson is said to have written his *Rasselas*, and Beckford his *Vathek*, and tells how, leaving London, he betakes himself to the roads and fields.

In the country it shows him leading a life of roving adventure, becoming tinker, gypsy, postillion, ostler; associating with various kinds of people, chiefly of the lower classes, whose ways and habits are described; but, though leading this erratic life, we gather from the book that his habits are neither vulgar nor vicious, that he still follows to a certain extent his favourite pursuits, hunting after strange characters, or analysing strange words and names. At the conclusion of the fifth volume, which terminates the first part of the history, it hints that he is about to quit his native land on a grand philological expedition.[77]

This, surely, is to describe *Lavengro* for what it is, albeit in a somewhat disingenuous way. With the claim that the book was irreligious, he made short shrift. Had he not introduced a number of genuinely religious characters, like Peter Williams and the rich man who touches objects? And as for the charge of self-interest, was it not obvious that his association with the Bible Society was long in the past? And on the question of his being un-English, had he not dissociated himself from those who learnt foreign languages and affected foreign airs? But was it not possible, at the same time, to adopt a balanced, non-parochial, loving attitude to languages and foreign cultures; could one not value English literature *and* German literature: is it not possible to love one's own place *and* try to understand other people's places? Maybe Borrow alienated the contemporary reader by accusing him of talking non-sense, a word put to frequent use throughout the Appendix, but later readers did not feel that such remarks applied to them and so could more readily relish the directness and vigour of Borrow's style.

There are many species of nonsense to which the nation is much addicted, and of which the perusal of *Lavengro* ought to give them a wholesome shame. First of all, with respect to the foreign nonsense so prevalent now in England. The hero is a scholar; but, though possessed of a great many tongues, he affects to be neither Frenchman, nor German, nor this or that foreigner; he is one who loves his country, and the language and literature of his country, and speaks up for each and all when there is occasion to do so. Now what is the case with nine out of ten amongst those of the English who study foriegn languages? No sooner have they picked up a smattering of this or that speech than they begin to abuse their own country, and everything connected with it, more especially its language. This is particularly the case with those who call themselves German students. It is said, and the writer believes with truth, that when a woman falls in love with a particularly ugly fellow, she squeezes him with ten times more zest than she would a handsome one, if captivated by him. So it is with these German students; no sooner have they taken German in hand than there is nothing like German. Oh, the dear, delightful German! How proud I am that it is now my own, and that its divine literature is within my reach! And all this whilst mumbling the most uncouth speech, and crunching the most crabbed literature in Europe. The writer is not an exclusive admirer of everything English; he does not advise his country people never to go abroad, never to study foreign languages, and he does not wish to persuade them that there is nothing beautiful or valuable in foreign literature; he only wishes that they would not make themselves fools with respect to foreign people, foreign languages or reading; that if they chance to have been in Spain, and have picked up a little Spanish, they would not affect the airs of Spaniards; that if males they would not make Tom-fools of themselves by sticking cigars into their mouths, dressing themselves in *zamarras*, and saying, *carajo*! and if females that they would not make zanies of themselves by sticking cigars into their mouths, flinging mantillas over their heads, and by saying *carai*, and perhaps *carajo* too; or if they have been in France or Italy, and have picked up a little French or Italian, they would not affect to be French or Italians; and particularly, after having been a month or two in Germany, or picked up a little German in England, they would not make themselves foolish about everything German, as the Anglo-German in the book does – a real character, the founder of the Anglo-German school in England, and the cleverest Englishman who ever talked or wrote encomiastic nonsense about Germany and the Germans. Of all infatuations connected with what is foreign, the infatuation about everything that is German, to a certain extent prevalent in England, is assuredly the most ridiculous. One can find something like a palliation for people making them-selves somewhat foolish about particular languages, literatures and people. The Spanish certainly is a noble language, and there is something wild and captivating in the Spanish character, and its literature contains the grand book of the world. French is a manly language. The French are the great martial people in the world; and French literature is admirable in many respects. Italian is a sweet language, and of beautiful simplicity – its literature perhaps the first in the world. The Italians! – wonderful men have sprung up in Italy. Italy is not merely famous for painters, poets, musicians, singers and linguists – the greatest linguist the world ever saw, the late Cardinal Mezzofanti, was an Italian; but it is celebrated for men – men emphatically speaking: Columbus was an Italian, Alexander Farnese was an Italian, so was the mightiest of the mighty, Napoleon Bonaparte; but the German language, German literature, and the Germans! The writer has already stated his opinion with respect to German; he does not speak from ignorance or prejudice; he has heard German spoken, and many other languages. German literature! He does not speak from ignorance, he has read that and many a literature, and he repeats – however, he acknowledges that there is one fine poem in the German language, that poem is the *Oberon*; a poem, by-the-bye, ignored by the Germans – a speaking fact – and of course, by the Anglo-Germanists. The Germans! he has been amongst them, and amongst many other nations, and confesses that his opinion of the Germans, as men, is a very low one. Germany, it is true, has produced one very great man, the monk who fought the Pope, and nearly knocked him down; but this man his country-men – a telling fact – affect to despise, and, of course, the Anglo-Germanists: the father of Anglo-Germanism was very fond of inveighing against Luther.[78]

What Borrow says in the Appendix applies as much to late twentieth- as to late nineteenth-century England. Essentially, he distinguishes between true and false values, between common-sense and superficially acquired opinions, between fair dealing and hypocrisy, between a genuine concern for other people and a cynical adoption of the ways of the world, between a genuinely democratic sense of other people's existence and a social sense tuned to class perception, class power and class obtuseness. As Lavengro had walked across the land, he had met the people who lived on and by it, had talked with them, had sometimes lived with them, and so knew them. He also had extensive experience of the affectation and attitudinising of the urban philistine. Or he thought he had. At the heart, therefore, of his distinction between true and false values is the perhaps romantic notion that what a man is is more important than what he makes himself appear to be. Making yourself appear to be what you are not Borrow labels 'gentility', and in his eyes there is no worse offence: it is gentility that falsifies relationships between people, creates social differences where no differences need in fact exist, and induces an infatuation with the wealth necessary to purchase that facade of fine living that so effectively conceals or obliterates the fine feelings that would be a better basis for community and shared enterprise. He had been accused of not being a gentleman, of consorting with low characters, of living with a woman out of wedlock, and of being preoccupied with gypsies and other people whom the middle-class reviewer regard as parasitic. Here is his reply.

But what constitutes a gentleman? It is easy to say at once what constitutes a gentleman, and there are no distinctions in what is gentlemanly, as there are in what is genteel. The characteristics of a gentleman are high feeling – a determination never to take a cowardly advantage of another – a liberal education – absence of narrow views – generosity and courage, propriety of behaviour. Now a person may be genteel according to one or other of the three standards described above, and not possess one of the characteristics of a gentleman. Is the emperor a gentleman, with spatters of blood on his clothes, scourged from the backs of noble Hungarian women? Are the aristocracy gentlefolks, who admire him? Is Mr. Flamson a gentleman, although he has a million pounds? No! cowardly miscreants, admirers of cowardly miscreants, and people who make a million pounds by means compared with which those employed to make fortunes by the getters up of the South Sea Bubble might be called honest dealing, are decidedly not gentlefolks. Now as it is clearly demonstrable that a person may be perfectly genteel according to some standard or other, and yet be no gentleman, so it is demonstrable that a person may have no pretensions to gentility, and yet be a gentleman. For example, there is Lavengro! Would the admirers of the emperor, or the admirers of those who admire the emperor, or the admirers of Mr. Flamson, call him genteel? and gentility with them is everything! Assuredly they would not; and assuredly they would consider him respectively as a being to be shunned, despised, or hooted. Genteel! Why at one time he is a hack author – writes reviewals for eighteen-pence a page, edits a Newgate chronicle. At another he wanders the country with a face grimy from occasionally mending kettles; and there is no evidence that his clothes are not seedy and torn, and his shoes down at the heel; but by what process of reasoning will they prove that he is no gentleman? Is he not learned? Has he not generosity and courage? Whilst a hack author, does he pawn the books entrusted to him to review? Does he break his word to his publisher? Does he write begging letters? Does he get clothes or lodgings without paying for them? Again, whilst a wanderer, does he insult helpless women on the road with loose proposals or ribald discourse? Does he take what is not his own from the hedges? Does he play on the fiddle, or make faces in public-houses, in order to obtain pence or beer? or does he call for liquor, swallow it, and then say to a widowed landlady, 'Mistress, I have no brass?' In a word, what vice and crime does he perpetrate – what low acts does he commit? Therefore, with his endowments, who will venture to say that he is no gentleman? – unless it be an admirer of Mr. Flamson – a clown – who will, perhaps, shout: 'I say he is no gentleman; for who can be a gentleman who keeps no gig?'

The indifference exhibited by Lavengro for what is merely genteel, compared with his solicitude never to infringe the strict laws of honour, should read a salutary lesson. The generality of his countrymen are far more careful not to transgress the customs of what they call gentility, than to violate the laws of honour or morality. They will shrink from carrying their own carpet-bag, and from speaking to a person in seedy raiment, whilst to matters of much higher importance they are shamelessly indifferent. Not so Lavengro; he will do anything that he deems convenient, or which strikes his fancy, provided it does not outrage decency, or is unallied to profligacy; is not ashamed to speak to a beggar in rags, and will associate with anybody, provided he can gratify a laudable curiosity. He has no abstract love for what is low, or what the world calls low. He sees that many things which the world looks down upon are valuable, so he prizes much which the world contemns; he sees that many things which the world admires are contemptible, so he despises much which the world does not;

but when the world prizes what is really excellent, he does not contemn it, because the world regards it.[79]

Interestingly, Borrow also sees the application of this to the question of minority cultures. Middle-class 'gentility nonsense' is responsible, he says, for breaking up the 'venerable communities' of Jews, gypsies, and Quakers, by making them forsake their own customs in order to get on in life, by making them abandon their own literatures, by making them marry out of their own community, and by making them 'crazy after gentility diversions...and connections'. These were the minority groups about whom Borrow happened to know. That in this section of the Appendix he was not merely being argumentative is shown by the fact that he took trouble to visit those parts of Britain not dominated by the 'polite', the 'modish' and the 'genteel': Wales, Ireland, Cornwall, the Isle of Man, Scotland, Orkney, so presumably he would nowadays not only have tolerated with equanimity West Indian, Sikh, Pakistani, Chinese and other foreign sub-cultures in Britain, but have immersed himself in the business of trying to understand their ways and their words exactly in the same manner as he had done throughout his life with gypsies, whom he saw as more representative of world history than were, for example, the respectable citizens of the city of Norwich. People should not pretend to be what they are not, thought Borrow, which is the point of the story he has Jasper Petulengo tell about a gypsy who tried to make a living by disguising himself as a Chinese salesman. Cultural and racial differences should therefore be accepted and the social contributions of varied ethnic groups should be valued. At least the gypsy and the Jew had a culture, he thought, whereas the railway navvies whom Samuel Peto brought onto his land had not.

Although the Appendix is the clearest statement of what Borrow believed in, is indeed a minor masterpiece, some passages are difficult to interpret, even for a person who sees no point in reviving the acrimonious disputes between the eccentric author and his real and imagined enemies. At the very centre of the difficulty is the chapter on 'pseudo-critics', where Borrow breaks the rule that it is better to endure mean-spirited reviews in silence rather than enter into an unseemly controversy about a book that the intelligent reader will in any case judge on its own merits. Borrow thought that *Lavengro*'s fortunes had been affected adversely by critics who had attacked it with 'virulence and malice'. He therefore decided to give them a drubbing, ill-advisedly questioning their motives as well as their opinions. Why did they question his sincerity, he protested, why did they doubt the truth of what he wrote, when they are usually 'so enraptured with any fiction that is adapted to the purposes of humbug'? Would he not have heard less about its not being true, had it been written 'in order to further any of the thousand and one cants, and species of nonsense prevalent in England?'[80] 'Critics', he exclaimed, naively, 'when they review books, ought to have a competent knowledge of the subjects which those books discuss.' There would be more writers and fewer critics if this were the case. Borrow was so incensed by all this that he foolishly allowed himself to overlook, first, that any reader could see for himself that there were gaps in the narrative of *Lavengro*, secondly, that while writing *Lavengro* he had discovered there were things about himself he did not wish to disclose, and, thirdly, that his own behaviour in the past had been sufficiently idiosyncratic and, by ordinary standards, immoral for it to have been more prudent for him to have kept quiet about other people's failings.

The resentment, bitterness and animosity that inform parts of the Appendix reveal not just that a bohemian author would never accommodate the opinions of the literary establishment, whether legitimate or not, but also that as a person he had, at least temporarily, lapsed into an indulgent type of self-pity that absolved him from any need to achieve self-knowledge, or if not self-knowledge then just plain knowledge of the extremely limited significance of the human ego, even if wounded to the quick. In his summer-house, Borrow kept by him a manuscript verse fragment that read:

> To trust a man I never feel inclined,
> Unless I know his very inmost mind;
> Better an open foe your flesh should rend,
> Than you should deem a secret foe your friend.

A terrifying idea, if taken seriously. There was probably not a person in the world whose 'very inmost mind' Borrow knew, so to this extent he was, at the age of fifty, friendless. Shortly after the publication of *The Romany Rye*, Borrow wrote to Whitwell Elwin about the suicide of Benjamin Haydon, the painter. 'Poor Haydon', wrote Borrow, 'he thought to wound the world by cutting his own throat, the last of his many mistakes; the way to wound the world, if it is unkind to you, is to live on and snap your fingers at it.'[81] In this mood Borrow had certainly not become more sensitive to other people during his years at Oulton. He had alienated John Murray and he had sacrificed his friendship with Ford, by failing to write a suitable review for Ford's *Handbook*, a review that Ford thought Borrow owed him in exchange for Ford's earlier help with *The Bible in Spain*.[82] Irrationally, he thought there was virtue in savage attacks on the very public he expected to buy his books. Irrationally, he would snap his fingers at the world, yet he felt piqued for lack of preferment. They were the fools, not him. 'A fellow who unites in himself a bankrupt trader, the broken author, or rather book-maker, or the laughed-down single speech spouter in the House of Commons, may look forward, always supposing that at one time he has been a foaming radical, to the government of an important colony',[83] whereas that paragon of virtue, George Borrow, could not.

Borrow tried to deflect the criticism of *Lavengro* by arguing that it was not intended as autobiography, did not purvey that type of truth, was more concerned with philology than self-revelation, and was a creative work or, as he put it, the 'work of an independent mind'.

The writer begs leave to observe, that it would be well for people who profess to have a regard for truth, not to exhibit in every assertion which they make a most profligate disregard of it...In the preface *Lavengro* is stated to be a dream; and the writer takes this opportunity of stating that he never said it was an autobiography; never authorized any person to say that it was one; and that he had in innumerable instances declared in public and private, both before and after the work was published, that it was not what is generally termed an autobiography; but a set of people who pretend to write criticisms on books, hating the author for various reasons – amongst others, because, having the proper pride of a gentleman and a scholar, he did not, in the year '43, choose to permit himself to be exhibited and made a zany of in London, and especially because he will neither associate with, nor curry favour with, them who are neither gentlemen nor scholars – attack his book with abuse and calumny. He is, perhaps, condescending too much when he takes any notice of such people; as however, the English public is wonderfully led by cries and shouts, and generally ready to take part against any person who is either unwilling or unable to defend himself, he deems it advisable not to be altogether quiet with those who assail him. The best way to deal with vipers is to tear out their teeth; and the best way to deal with pseudo-critics is to deprive them of their poison-bag, which is easily done by exposing their ignorance.[84]

Though Borrow, when he wrote the Appendix, produced a fine piece of invective, a sustained and powerful addition to an already remarkable book, he failed to silence his critics and the merits of *The Romany Rye* were not recognised until years later, when people had forgotten all about George Borrow's disagreements with his publisher and his public. Once the controversy had been forgotten, or dampened down at least, it was seen that Borrow had not written a startlingly original philological book, for by the time people were reading *The Romany Rye* again the study of language had been placed upon a more exact professional level, but that he had written an original book, nonetheless, one that expressed the character of the author, as well as the quality of the type of life he preferred, with that vigour and clarity which assured him a place as one of the masters of English prose.

As to his character, he had successfully adopted that useful and well-established Victorian strategy of distinguishing sharply between the private and the public, so successfully, indeed, that some readers who wanted to know about his adventures did not believe he had ever in fact known anyone like Isopel Berners, who so dominates the end of *Lavengro* and the beginning of *The Romany Rye*. In the notice of a recent book called *The Forms of Autobiography* by William Spengemann, the construction of identity is treated as a twentieth-century phenomenon. 'This discovery', we are told on the dust-jacket, 'marks the dawning of the modern idea that autobiography is both impossible, since self does not exist apart from the act of writing about it, and unavoidable, since writing, like every other human action, invents a self which it also reflects.'[85] If the idea that self does not exist except in the act of writing about it has distinctly the smell of a university literature department, the formulation as a whole would seem to apply to Borrow, in that he found it impossible to write an autobiography that was a report on a person who already existed, but possible, though difficult, to write an autobiography in which a person was imagined as existing who was acceptable to the sensibility of the author. In *Lavengro* and *The Romany Rye* he became the person who he wanted to be, refused to present himself as the person others had seen that he was, and by creating a character called Lavengro, a scholar gypsy, freed himself imaginatively from the constraint of being no more than the sum of his own actions. The two books are a celebration of this remarkable feat. They are also a celebration of an almost mystical union between a human being and the land on which he lived, a union not contaminated by the belittling ideas of the mid nineteenth-century middle-class moralist. England was imagined and enjoyed by Borrow with a historical depth not reflected in the Great Exhibition of 1851 or the suppression of the Indian Mutiny in 1857, and in a way that was largely unaffected by the industrial revolution, of which for all practical purposes he remained ignorant. In the years that followed the publication of *The Romany Rye* this assertion of Borrow's that a bohemian existence was possible had a great appeal, because it was an imaginative escape route from Victorian prudery, jingoism, class consciousness and parochialism. The man of the road was a patriot, but one who had freed himself from those aspects of Empire that were a blight upon English life. So people as different as Matthew Arnold and Augustus John hailed Borrow, in his pages, as a colleague – a pal – until the modern bureaucrat took the pleasure out of eccentricity.

The years of discontent

It was convenient to look at *The Romany Rye* in the last chapter, simply because that book was a continuation of *Lavengro* and because Borrow had been preoccupied for so many years with the question of how to finish *Lavengro*. We must now go back to 1853, when there occurred a major change in the Borrows' family life. This was the decision to move into lodgings in Great Yarmouth, probably not for one reason but for many. George was bored with Oulton, particularly with the confined life of Oulton Cottage: whenever he was away from East Anglia for any length of time and his wife urged him to return, he would reply petulantly that there was nothing to return for. The Hall had after all been rented to a farmer, so the Borrows never lived in it, though Borrow sometimes gave it as his address. Most of the estate was rented out, too. The time he spent with his horses did not obscure the fact that there was little else to do. Henrietta, now thirty-six, was hardly having a full and rewarding life, despite her occasional expeditions to Bury St Edmunds. Mary Borrow's health had meanwhile begun to deteriorate, to the extent that their friend and counsellor, Dr Hake, urgently recommended a change of air. Her marriage of convenience had had, and indeed continued to have, its strains and stresses: she had never, in any real sense, shared her husband's life, and when, after the reception of *Lavengro* he retired into his shell, never genuinely to re-emerge, her lot became correspondingly difficult. It can be guessed that with their friends the Hakes, they talked a lot about the state of England, the problem of what to do with one's middle years and Borrow's pet subject of conversation, the tragic inability of the country to find employment for men of talent such as himself, unless, that is, they happened to be well connected or members of the aristocracy. In 1853, Dr Hake resolved this problem in a drastic fashion by taking his whole family to America, where they remained for seven years. At the same time, the Borrows moved to Great Yarmouth, where they remained, off and on, for the same seven-year period. If a major disruption concerning the two families precipitated the double move, it was quite adequately concealed from the world at large. At any rate Borrow and his family, without completely abandoning Oulton Cottage, spent the greater part of their time in various lodgings in Great Yarmouth, some of which Knapp was able to identify from papers in his possession. The first of these were at John Sharman's at 169 King Street.

Someone who knew Borrow well in his later years said that he was incapable of laughter. The person who knew him best, loved him most and studied his face most closely, was Henrietta and she knew well enough that behind the reserve was a personality capable of pleasure and fun. But Elizabeth Harvey, who also had seen the twinkle in his eye when he was enjoying himself, said that she 'never saw him even smiling'.[1] He lived his life very much on the defensive, was paranoid, secretive, uncommunicative and distrustful. Once he wrote to his wife from Tunbridge Wells a letter that characterises this nervousness about himself and about other people. 'Please to carry upstairs and lock in the drawer the little sack of letters in the parlour; lock it up with the bank book and put this along with it – also be sure to keep the window of my room fastened and the door locked, and keep the key in your pocket.'[2] Theodore Watts-Dunton, who got to know Borrow well later on in his life, recollected that there was always in Borrow's bearing towards other people what he called 'a kind of shy, defiant egoism'. Many people over the years had noted the apparent incongruity between Borrow's magnificent, athletic physique and his small, restless eyes, which they found in some way unsettling. Watts-Dunton put it in this way:

What Carlyle called the 'armed neutrality' of social intercourse oppressed him. He felt himself to be in the enemy's camp. In his eyes there was always a kind of watchfulness, as if he were taking stock of his interlocutor and weighing him against himself. He seemed to be observing what effect his words were having, and this approach repelled people at first.[3]

Nor was this a matter of the eyes only, for in casual conversation he tended to be belligerently, tediously dogmatic, as though challenging his companion, whoever it might be, to search for the real Borrow behind the usually exaggerated statement of mere opinion. If this was the dogmatism of the socially gauche or socially inept, it obviously had a deep-seated cause.

Few people, after 1853, had any reason to search out the cause, whether deep-seated or not. Borrow in his later years acquired the reputation of a curmudgeon, someone who made little attempt to get on with others and indeed took a kind of pride in offending them. He dismissed over the dinner table a 'very distinguished scholar' who

wanted to talk with him, with the one sentence: 'Sir, you're a fool.'[4]
He dismissed a man from the Russian embassy who came round for
a copy of *Targum* for the Czar. If the Czar wanted a copy, he should
come for it himself. Thackeray, at another dinner party, asked
Borrow – one egoist to another – whether he had been reading his
'Snob Papers' in *Punch*. 'In *Punch*? It is a periodical I never look at.'[5]
Hake recollected that on a similar occasion when a lady who sat by
him at dinner said: 'Oh, Mr. Borrow, I have been reading your books',
Borrow replied 'Pray, what books, Madam? Do you mean my account-
books?'[6] These brusque dismissals, which seem gratuitously careless of
others' feelings, and offensive, reflected both Borrow's continued resistance to the genteel and a pathological inability to accept for a
moment the role that others on good evidence assumed was his.
To others his peculiar hypocrisy was to insist upon a sincerity that was
inconsistent with the books that had by this time been so widely read.
He did not wish to be the person they saw he was. Because he very
well understood this, he became in society more and more petulant
and disagreeable.

John Murray told two stories in his *Good Words* which were
repeated by Jenkins as hitting off Borrow exactly.

Borrow was at a dinner-party in company with Whewell – both of them powerful men, and both of them, if report be true, having more than a superficial
knowledge of the art of self-defence. A controversy began, and waxed so warm
that Mrs. Whewell, believing a personal encounter to be imminent, fainted, and
had to be carried out of the room. Once when Borrow was dining with my
father, he disappeared into a small back room after dinner and could not be
found. At last he was discovered by a lady member of the family, stretched on a
sofa and groaning. On being spoken to and asked to join the other guests, he
suddenly said: 'Go away! Go away! I am not fit company for respectable people.'
There was no apparent cause for this strange conduct, unless it were due to one
of those unaccountable fits to which men of genius (and this description will be
allowed by many) are often subject.[7]

This was not an isolated instance. When he went once to see Anna
Gurney, her questions about Arabic so embarrassed him that he ran
out of the room without explanation.[8] At dinner parties, he would
frequently leave the table and be found in another part of the house
playing with the children. In particular he detested being interrogated
about his knowledge of languages, would reply ungraciously to polite
questions about linguistic matters, over which it would be claimed he
had boasted of his complete mastery, and reacted especially badly to
remarks that exposed his academic ignorance of languages that he
actually spoke. Frances Cobbe thought that this happened too frequently for him to be trusted, with the result that, in a much-quoted

phrase from her autobiography, she dismissed him out of hand as a hypocrite.

These anecdotes are collected here because they represent the mosaic of opinion created after Borrow's death by people who resented his intolerant attitude to what they took to be the normal pattern of existence, its normal civilities, communications and manners. They recollected what they knew, what they had experienced, but they did not know very much. The public often prefers a writer to bare his breast, so that, if eccentric, he must obligingly engage general sympathy for his eccentricity by providing in interestingly confessional acts salacious stories that there is never any need to emulate. Borrow declined to participate in his own story having once tried and failed. Ungraciously he refused the public access to his own history, his own activities and his own anxieties, so much so that when he met another human being, except when travelling incognito, he often had very little to talk about. His last years were therefore extremely lonely. He had to make do with the actuality of a self that, strong and constant though it was, did not grow and prosper under the influence of new ideas, new activities, or new friends.

Until he was about seventy, he remained fit and well, exceptionally so, seeming to attach importance to solitary athletic feats by which he proved to himself that he was still the rugged, tough individual he had always been. In Great Yarmouth, he swam almost every day in the sea, whatever the weather or the time of year. Indeed, shortly after his arrival there, or while he was searching out lodgings for his move, he was involved in a sea rescue that was widely reported. 'Intrepidity' was the newspaper headline, over the following account:

Yarmouth jetty presented an extraordinary and thrilling spectacle on Thursday, the 8th inst., about one o'clock. The sea raged frantically, and a ship's boat, endeavouring to land for water, was upset, and the men were engulfed in a wave some thirty feet high, and struggling with it in vain. The moment was an awful one, when George Borrow, the well-known author of *Lavengro* and *The Bible in Spain*, dashed into the surf and saved one life, and through his instrumentality the others were saved. We ourselves have known this brave and gifted man for years, and, daring as was this deed, we have known him more than once to risk his life for others. We are happy to add that he has sustained no material injury.[9]

Water was a natural element for him. 'Swimming is a noble exercise', he said in *The Bible in Spain*, 'but it certainly does not tend to mortify either the flesh or the spirit.'[10] At this period, that is in the early fifties, he recorded in a notebook, daily, the length of time he could stay under water after his first dive and the point on the other side of a river he could reach before surfacing.[11] The water temperature was

apparently unimportant to him. John Murray later recorded a story
told by his partner, Mr Cooke, who came to know the author quite
well.

Borrow, having stripped, took a header into the water and disappeared. More
than a minute had elapsed, and as there were no signs of his whereabouts,
Mr. Cooke was becoming alarmed, lest he had struck his head, or been entangled
in the weeds, when Borrow suddenly re-appeared a considerable distance off,
under the opposite bank of the stream, and called out 'What do you think of
that?'[12]

When Elizabeth Harvey repeated the same story in *The Eastern Daily
Press* she reported that Borrow had also said: 'There, if that had been
written in one of my books, they would have said it was a lie, wouldn't
they?'[13]

One of Borrow's neighbours remembered, after his death, how he
used to wander about the countryside by himself, his 'great delight'
being 'to plunge into the darkening mere at eventide, his great head
and heavy shoulders ruddy in the rays of the sun. Here he hissed and
roared and spluttered, sometimes frightening the eel-catcher sailing
home in the half-light, and remembering suddenly school legends of
river-sprites and monsters of the deep.'[14]

If all these stories are to be believed, and there are too many for us
to disregard them, Borrow rarely lost a chance to show off. When
Borrow was drifting, becalmed, with his solicitors, George Jay and
John Pilgrim, in Jay's 'old yacht', the *Widgeon*, Borrow made the
22-foot dive to the bottom and brought up a handful of mud to prove
that he had been there. The same informant recalled that he and his
mother had once met Borrow on Lowestoft beach, just after he had
swum out to the Ness Buoy, a difficult feat because of the currents.
This at the age of sixty-nine.[15] All in all, it seems fairly obvious that
Borrow not only continued to get a keen pleasure from swimming,
whatever the conditions might be, but also that satisfaction in his own
feats of strength and endurance compensated for other types of dissatisfaction, a supreme adequacy in one department of life compen-
sating, in the lonely individual, for inadequacies in other departments.

His pedestrian activities, though, were even more remarkable.
Between 1853, when he moved to Great Yarmouth, and 1860, when
he left to settle in London for a while, he walked many hundreds of
miles through Norfolk, Cornwall (from Liskeard to Land's End and
back), Wales (in three separate tours), the Isle of Man, Scotland and
Ireland, and maybe a few other places as well in expeditions of which
records have not survived. Certainly, he sometimes travelled by train

or coach. He sometimes began a trip in a coastal packet. Nonetheless, his journeys were often arduous and long: 600 miles on foot in Scotland, 400 miles in Wales. It must have been heartbreaking for this man when his vigour began to desert him and he had to sit at home, which, however, did not happen during his Great Yarmouth years.

During those years, Borrow participated in the vigorous nineteenth-century exploration of Great Britain by the British, as it was only natural (given his earlier experiences) that he should. Not surprisingly these travels took him more to far-flung Celtic places than anywhere else, the Viking predilections of his youth being powerfully sustained in old age. Though it might be intriguing to see him as a pacesetter for thousands and thousands of twentieth-century long-distance walkers, fell runners, climbers, youth-club adventurers and simple tourists, and though there is something bracing in his frank sympathy and interest in Celtic culture, feelings that he shared, of course, with other nineteenth-century writers who like him realised that the Scots, the Irish and the Welsh were not in the thrall of English class attitudes, might be in fact more honest, unaffected and genuine, not a lot is to be gained by following in Borrow's footsteps, though many of his admirers have done so in Wales and Spain – not, that is, if the nature of his achievement is seen as being mostly literary. The true enthusiast will of course wish to identify every place Borrow visited, ascertain the routes he followed, reconstruct his travels in a chronological order that makes sense and, where possible, get to know more about the people whom Borrow met or said he met. A detail-by-detail reconstruction of this type is a genuine and needful homage to a great man.

Only remotely, however, is it homage to a great writer, despite the fact that, as this large awe-inspiring figure with wide-brimmed hat, leather satchel, cape, green umbrella and notebook explored the re-moter regions of the British Isles, he was as surely feeling his way towards his next major work as he had been in Spain when he made notes for a book years before that book had clearly shaped itself in his mind. The snag about following in his footsteps is that the reality of a place seen as it is today, whether in Cornwall, Scotland, the Isle of Man, Ireland or Wales, has little to do with what those same places were like in the 1850s or with Borrow's personal, idiosyncratic, essentially literary transformations of experience, even when that experience as reported has a partly documentary character, and even though it seems to have been the case that Borrow never wrote about places he had not visited, people he had not met, or events that had not occurred. If biography is about the imagination, as this one aspires to be, that is, about how the mind works, how the whole being of a person functions and how experience in a particular set of cases is apprehended, not much is to be learnt from solitary, long-distance walking expeditions, beyond the obvious, which is that Borrow enjoyed, perhaps needed, the sustained physical exercise and the sense of physical well-being that went with it, perferred his own company and that of people met by chance to the company of people he knew, and for whatever reason accepted the traveller's view of things from the outside, whether to avoid a more profound or intimate type of knowledge or because profundity and intimacy had become unattainable.

Intimacy with other people, the one thing that might have affected the quality of his life, seems to have been unattainable during his Great Yarmouth years, when he was finishing *The Romany Rye* and turning his mind again to the publication of his translations. Deep friendship proved elusive as far as one can tell. Edward FitzGerald was a person with whom he corresponded and whom he saw from time to time, but there was a faltering in the relationship, despite the common interest in oriental literature, and FitzGerald brought it to a close, saying in 1875 that he assumed Borrow had 'slunk away from human company' as much as he had.[16] Hasfeld, whose letters hint of a steady warmth of regard over the years, visited Borrow from time to time, kept in touch and seems not to have wavered despite Borrow's crotchety, sometimes bitter, behaviour.[17] Borrow also continued to see Lucy Brightwell during this period, though there is not much to suggest that their friendship went deep.[18] Love, as well as friendship, proved elusive in fact and Borrow experienced the full loneliness of the person determined to be self-sufficient.

This was the emotional context, then, in which he began to explore once again his own country, something that began when distant relatives, who had seen in a newspaper the account of his rescuing someone from drowning, invited him to visit that part of Cornwall where his father had been born. That was for about two months between December 1853 and February 1854. He travelled down to Plymouth, walked from Plymouth to Liskeard, was entertained by descendants of his father's family, went to dinners, told stories and saw the sights, then walked to Land's End by himself and back again by the north coast at least as far as Tintagel, on his way chatting with strangers, playing amateur philologist with anyone who could speak Cornish, deciphering inscriptions, and unsystematically but with a genuine interest inquiring about folk history, folk tales and folk superstitions, always alert, as was Thomas Hardy later, to the residual surface signs of England's distant past, especially to anything that, because prior to the Norman Conquest, was uncontaminated by gentility nonsense.

This was to be one of the patterns of life during the whole of the fifties, indeed until his second visit to Scotland in 1866. He had already explored Norfolk on horseback, visiting – as tourist – places like Houghton Hall where the chapel was 'magnificent' and Cocksford Abbey where the large hall was 'wonderful'.[19] Not satisfied with this, he made his first extensive tour of Wales between 27 July and 16 November 1854, at first staying with Mary and Henrietta in Llangollen, then walking by himself to Anglesey on a little trip that took almost 11 days, doing the 33-mile stretch from Cerrig-y-Drudion to Bangor, incidentally, in one day, and finally on 26 October walking south, again by himself, through Bala, Machynlleth, Lampeter, Swansea, Neath, Merthyr Tydfil, Caerphilly, Newport and Chepstow, but often deviating by means of cross-country paths and mountain tracks, for example to see places associated with Glendower and Huw Morus.[20] It is this itinerary that was to form the basis of the journey described in *Wild Wales*. In September 1855, the three of them took their holiday on the Isle of Man and Borrow walked the length and breadth of the island, sustained by his usual interests and as usual making frequent entries in a pocket notebook.[21] In 1857, to Wales again, with parts of *Wild Wales* already written and the decision to go ahead with the book firmly in the past.[22] In 1858, after the death of his mother at the age of eighty-seven, on 16 August, to Scotland, an amazing journey through the Highlands and to Orkney, again with a notebook always at hand.[23] In 1859, to Ireland, this time with Mary and Henrietta, who stayed in Dublin at 75 St Stephen's Green South while Borrow walked west by himself.[24] He liked meeting interesting characters, though he resented invasions of his privacy and would turn his back on anyone who recognised him as the famous writer. Typical egoist that he was, he felt justified in observing others in ways he resented if applied to himself. He liked looking at anything connected with Celtic literature, of which his knowledge had been extensive since his early years, whether it was a bridge, a chair, a ruin, a monument or even someone with an ancient name. He liked amusing himself by testing his knowledge of the language on the locals, though they did not always understand him, or he them. And though he sometimes searched out a companion for his walks, even a guide when the terrain was difficult, he most of all liked being by himself, his view of the world being essentially that of a solitary and romantic, not a social or political, consciousness. As one looks back more than a hundred years to that decade during which Borrow walked such long distances through Britain, one can surely note a crucial difference between what happened to him on the road before he was thirty and what happened to him on the road after he was fifty, for whereas in the former case there were certainly events he declined to talk about, which in order to understand him we would like to know more about, in the latter case there were not. This is not to say that he revealed all, but only that when one uses his notebooks and his wife's account books[25] to reconstruct his journeys in detail not much of biographical significance is revealed beyond a small family's attempt to relieve the monotony of daily life in Oulton.

Almost inevitably, given his early acquisition of the Welsh language, his sustained interest in Welsh poetry, and his strong sympathy for the Celt, Wales emerged as *the* subject of his attention during these years, emerged in this case being the right word, not only because he from time to time thought he would write books about other regions of Britain, but also because he had simultaneously engaged in a new spell of work on his translations during the early 1850s. As to the first, an advertisement in *The Romany Rye* listed as forthcoming a two-volume work entitled *Penquite and Pentyre: or, The Head of the Forest and the Headland. A book on Cornwall*[26] and *Bayr Jairgey and Glion Doo...Wanderings in Quest of Manx Literature*,[27] neither of which ever materialised, or at least were ever published as books. Among the several other works listed in the same advertisement were *Songs of Europe or Metrical Translations from All the European Languages*,[28] *Kæmpe Viser; Songs about Gods and Heroes*,[29] *Celtic Bards, Chiefs and Kings*[30] and *Northern Skalds, Kings and Earls*,[31] all of which were given as 'ready for the press'. From a mass of manuscript material,[32] we know that Borrow spent many hours transcribing, correcting and editing his early translations, which were still close to his heart. While others were preoccupied with parliamentary reform, the status of women, the Irish question, India and the growth of empire, industry and the problems of industrialisation, Borrow chose to remain in the Celtic twilight of what to the contemporary English man was an irrelevant literature. In the event, none of the works mentioned above was published during his lifetime, though much of the material has been published posthumously by Borrovian enthusiasts. Nor, with two exceptions, were the other works listed: *The Turkish Jester*,[33] *Russian Popular Tales*,[34] and *The Death of Balder*,[35] the two exceptions being his Welsh books.

Borrow obviously anticipated by many years the interest in things Scandinavian that, partly as a result of Edmund Gosse's essays and translations, as well as of the first productions of Ibsen in the late eighties, became fashionable towards the end of the century. Equally, he thought the poems he translated had a vigour, mythic veracity and cosmopolitan appeal signally lacking in the insular, introverted, self-indulgent poetry being written by people like Arnold and Clough, which poetry, however, he seems not to have read. His interest was genuine, his enthusiasm unlimited, his determination almost lifelong. But he was not himself a poet, was not a good verse translator and indeed displayed a marked insensitivity to the English verse line and its traditional subtlety of sound: he would have had to have been a better poet himself, or at least a better writer of verse, to have interested the English reading public in what was to it, at that time, a very remote and unimportant culture. So Borrow was enlightened in his enthusiasm for other literatures, but as a translator doomed to failure.

Wales was a different matter. There was a growing English interest in things Welsh, an interest encapsulated later on in George Meredith's title *Celt and Saxon*, as much the result, maybe, of the growth of industry in the south, which Borrow, though, avoided, as of the discovery of the picturesque north, with 'scenes' that could be enjoyed in a simple Wordsworthian, egotistical manner.

Borrow began to write *Wild Wales* during the winter of 1854–5, continued to work at it throughout the following winter, the family having moved by this time to new lodgings at 37 Camperdown Place, and had something like a first draft in hand by the time *The Romany Rye* was published in May 1857, or at least by the time he went on his second expedition in Wales that August. On the way back from Wales, he gave Murray the manuscript of *The Sleeping Bard*, a complete verse translation of the late seventeenth-century work of Ellis Wynn, no doubt urging that it made sense for Murray to publish both it and *Wild Wales*, perhaps on the principle that if Murray were interested in the latter he would feel duty bound to publish the former. *The Sleeping Bard* had been on the shelf since 1830, when according to Borrow's account of the matter he almost but not quite found someone to print it. In the Preface he says that

the following translation of *The Sleeping Bard* has long existed in manuscript. It was made by the writer of these lines in 1830, at the request of a little Welsh bookseller of his acquaintance, who resided in the rather unfashionable neighbourhood of Smithfield, and who entertained an opinion that a version of the work of Ellis Wynn would enjoy a great sale, both in England and in Wales. On the eve of committing it to the press, however, the Cambro-Briton felt his small heart give way within him. 'Were I to print it,' said he, 'I should be ruined. The terrible descriptions of vice and torment would frighten the genteel part of the English public out of their wits, and I should to a certainty be prosecuted by Sir James Scarlett. I am much obliged to you for the trouble you have given yourself on my account; but *Myn Diaul*! I had no idea, till I read him in English, that Ellis Wynn had been such a terrible fellow!'[36]

Even in the late fifties, however, Murray was not interested. He had enough of a problem with *The Romany Rye*, was still smarting from the *Lavengro* affair and, of course, could not anticipate *Wild Wales*, so Borrow was obliged to return to Great Yarmouth, where he perhaps continued to work on *The Sleeping Bard* while he settled to the main work of completing *Wild Wales*. This took time. In 1859 the Borrows moved once again to new lodgings at 24 Trafalgar Place, a house kept by an Elizabeth King. Not until 1860, when the Hakes returned from America and set up house at Coombe End, Roehampton, and the Borrows moved first to lodgings at 21 Montague Street, Portman Square, in London, and then in September to a house at 22 Hereford Square, did he really succeed in coming to terms with his Welsh material.

Once in London, Borrow made a strong attempt to re-establish himself as the literary figure he had been in the mid-forties by publishing *The Sleeping Bard*, the essay called 'The Welsh and their Literature' and finally *Wild Wales*, about each of which a little must now be said. John Murray declined to publish *The Sleeping Bard* but allowed his name to be used on the limited edition of 250 copies that were printed in Yarmouth, probably at Borrow's expense. The author, or rather translator, then attempted to draw attention to the book by means of an anonymous review entitled 'The Welsh and their Literature' which he in fact wrote himself and published in *The Quarterly Review*.[37] Knapp quoted part of a letter, dated 1 February 1861, from Mary Borrow to one Thomas Lloyd of Newtown, Montgomery, in which she said: 'The work is now out of print, and it is probable that a new edition will be shortly published.'[38] As for the review, Knapp said that it was 'well written, and had the decisive result of selling off the whole edition in a month'.[39] However, in a letter dated 20 December 1909, William Webber, the Ipswich bookseller, told Frank Farrell: 'I have seen somewhere a statement of his in his usual tall way with reference to this work that the entire impression was sold within the year whereas I found the whole of it at Oulton and sold it nearly intact to a particular London bookseller.'[40] In other words, Borrow at the age of fifty-eight continued to desire recognition as a translator, continued to think of himself as scholar and philologist and, whether in ignorance of the changing world of letters or not, continued to believe that it was only right he should have his own way. He joins the ranks of those whose enthusiasms do not coincide with their talents, the circumstances of the publication of *The Sleeping Bard* showing in addition, not just that Borrow lacked self-knowledge in areas of life of crucial importance to himself, but also that both he and his wife were still prepared to manipulate the truth, preferring the false image to the more modest but secure public role of being known for what they were. This is not to say that it is entirely blameworthy to puff one's own publications.

As for *Wild Wales*, Borrow and John Murray eventually came to a compromise agreement, though the precise grounds on which the accommodation was based are not clear. Perhaps the cancelled chapter in the Norfolk Record Office in which Borrow defended Henry VIII and attacked his contemporaries, especially Wolsey and the Pope, was one of the sections Murray asked him or required him to omit. *Wild Wales* was published in December 1862 in an edition of 1,000 copies, which the ledgers show sold almost immediately, Borrow receiving just over £265 as his half of the profits. Many early critics disliked the book, because its dry tone, though less obviously ironic than in many parts of *The Bible in Spain*, made them worry once again about the veracity of the narrative. Borrow had not simply reported events as they occurred, and this worried them. But Cecil Price in the standard modern edition of *Wild Wales*, very justly says that

no modern reader cares whether these allegations are true or not. Borrow set out to communicate his enjoyment of a walk through Wales and to interpret the literature, history and people of the country to their neighbours over the border. In those aims he was completely successful. The charm of *Wild Wales*, as of all Borrow's work, depends not at all on factual or chronological accuracy, but on the way in which he discloses his own personality while also conveying the true spirit of Wales and its people.[41]

It is only natural that Borrow should have restructured his material, as indeed it has been interestingly demonstrated that he did,[42] and this, by and by, is why *Wild Wales* is so readable as compared with the unworked, unfinished notebooks of his other tours, which only the occasional phrase or detail bring to life. As Cecil Price says: 'All Borrow's art, his insight, keenness of observation and feeling for human destiny, were used to give his readers an affectionate interpretation of the Welsh and their history. His own character and interests gave shape, as well as humour and directness, to a wholly delightful book.'[43]

Borrow's art was, as ever, spare, visual, anecdotal, unpretentious, robust. His dialogues are as racy as in his earlier work. And his eye for detail is as sure. Take, for example, the way he talks about the replacement of gypsies, whom Borrow expected to find in Wales, by migrant Irish forced to leave Ireland by the economic conditions there. Characteristically he puts this into a conversation between himself and his guide, then lets the guide say:

I had been across the Berwyn to carry home a piece of weaving work to a person who employs me. It was night as I returned, and when I was half-way down the hill, at a place which is called Allt Paddy, because the Gwyddelod are in the habit of taking up their quarters there, I came upon a gang of them, who had come there and camped and lighted their fire, whilst I was on the other side of the hill. There were nearly twenty of them, men and women, and amongst the rest was a man standing naked in a tub of water with two women stroking him down with clouts. He was a large fierce-looking fellow, and his body, on which the flame of the fire glittered, was nearly covered with red hair. I never saw such a sight.[44]

Or take his again entirely characteristic arrival at the inn at Llyn Ceiriog, where 'a good fire was burning in the grate' of the large kitchen, where there was a long table in front of the fire, and a high settle on either side. While Borrow was drinking his pint of ale, two men came in out of the rain.

One who appeared to be the principal was a stout bluff-looking person between fifty and sixty dressed in a grey stuff coat and with a slouched hat on his head. This man bustled much about, and in a broad Yorkshire dialect ordered a fire to be lighted in another room, and a chamber to be prepared for him and his companion; the landlady, who appeared to know him, and to treat him with a kind of deference, asked if she should prepare two beds; whereupon he answered 'No! As we came together, and shall start together, so we shall sleep together; it will not be for the first time.'[45]

Borrow invariably lets the detail work for itself; he invariably cuts an episode short so that it is inconsequential in the mosaic of the book as a whole, and he invariably, though often with delicacy and tact, makes his own participation in the narrative its dominant feature. Sometimes the egoism and self-regard that spoilt the book for early readers are indeed overemphasised, but the book as a whole is more of a poem celebrating the affinity of a man and a place. Though it has a mellow character compared to the vigorous, enigmatic books that preceded it, *Wild Wales* has nonetheless stood the test of time, as many travellers through Wales still testify.

It was made clear at the outset that the present book is essentially an account of Borrow's writing life, a life which, in a very important sense, came to an end when he published *Wild Wales* at the age of fifty-nine. This is not a quibble. *Wild Wales* was Borrow's last creative work, a sort of miracle, really, when one looks back at the magical metamorphosis from crude notebook to urbane personal narrative; for if the book was nostalgic in its recollection of the picturesque, as it avowedly was from the first page and throughout, it was nonetheless an unqualified success within this genre. He did not cease at that point, in 1862, to be a person with literary interests, of course, even though his creative vigour deserted him. On the contrary, he saw the second edition of *Wild Wales* through the press in 1865, prepared a second edition of his 'Gypsy Luke' and published *Romano Lavo-Lil* in 1874, so that even in the seventh decade of his life he was far from idle. Nor did he cease to be out and about, for these were the days of his excursions to Roehampton and down into Surrey and Hampshire, while over and above his daily outdoor activities he managed two more walking-tours, the first to Scotland in 1866,[46] and the second to Wales and the New Forest in 1867.[47] Judging by the number of drawing-room stories told against him, he also seems, though this was against his nature, to have attempted a more sociable type of existence during his fourteen years in the house in Hereford Square. Why take up residence in London if not to meet people? But at his fairly advanced age Borrow's new life was vulnerable to change and inevitably changes occurred, changes that deeply affected him, slowed him down and robbed him of that outward domestic structuring of existence that held in check his lifelong disposition to depression. In 1865, Henrietta, then aged forty-five, married Dr William MacOubrey, took up residence in Charlotte Street, Fitzroy Square and subsequently moved to Belfast. Mary and George Borrow went to Belfast for a brief visit the following year, but a bond had been broken. Then in 1869, on 24 January, Mary Borrow died: though Borrow lived for another twelve years and indeed at some point made a proposal of marriage to his old friend Cecilia Lucy Brightwell, perhaps when he returned to Oulton in 1874 and realised that he needed companionship, it was too late for him to begin a new life, too late, probably, for him to desire to do so.

There are those who, firmly believing, apparently, that a man should cut his coat according to his cloth, criticised Borrow in his later years for being cantankerous and anti-social, but more particularly for having delusions of grandeur, for not being satisfied with the companionship of ordinary people and for too readily revealing, they thought, a belief in his own superiority, particularly as a traveller and as a linguist. These critics were for the most part not people who had enjoyed his friendship: they were the posthumous critics who thought that a writer should conveniently and politely forget his earlier literary success for the sake of getting on with people who showed they had more interest in anecdotes than in books. Borrow certainly provided a basis for such criticism, particularly when he published *Romano Lavo-*

Lil, because his publishing it late in life was taken to mean that he still thought of himself as an authority on gypsy language, perhaps the ultimate authority. By 1870, however, many other people knew as much about the gypsies and their language as he did. Some knew more. One of these was an American called Charles Leland, who through John Murray asked permission to dedicate to Borrow his forthcoming book called *The English Gypsies and their Language*. When Murray told Leland that Borrow was rambling about the country, Leland wrote Borrow a letter, which Borrow answered calmly and courteously.[48] Then less calmly he blew the dust off his own gypsy wordbook, which had existed in manuscript for many years, corrected it rapidly and took it to John Murray. In the event, Leland published first and his book was well received: Borrow's came out in March 1874 in an edition of 1,000 copies[49] and was immediately seen to be out of date. The ledgers reveal that 500 copies remained unsold in 1880. This much-talked-about episode certainly affected Borrow's reputation adversely during his last years, because it tended to make a new generation think of him not as the lively, eccentric person who had written *The Bible in Spain* but as the humourless egoist who could not understand that times had changed. Of course in this George Borrow was by no means unique. Not much occurs in life to make a person suppose that other human beings will judge him by his best actions or his best thoughts.

Borrow did not do so himself. Though he was certainly an egoist who thought that his own achievements were remarkable, that he himself was remarkable, he also knew perfectly well that his life lacked completeness, indeed was full of sorrow and frustration. He went to the grave with the major problems of his life unresolved. Looking back a hundred years, we see them not only as unresolved but also unresolvable. Take, for example, the immense contrast between his evident zest for existence and his apparent failure to achieve a relaxed, sustained type of friendship with anyone. The first is well characterised by his uninhibited enthusiasm for that breakfast he had in Bala in Wales. 'A noble breakfast it was; and indeed as I might have read of, but had never before seen. There was tea and coffee, a goodly white loaf and butter; there were a couple of eggs and two mutton chops. There was boiled and pickled salmon – there was fried trout – there were also potted trout and potted shrimps.'[50] How on earth would such a person have reacted, one thinks, to a diet of Pinter and Samuel Beckett, or even of Ibsen, Strindberg and O'Neill? The pleasure seems simple and uncomplicated. And Borrow went back for more, a little later on the same expedition. 'Having dressed myself', he said, 'I went to the coffee room and sat down to breakfast. What a breakfast! pot of hare; ditto of trout; pot of prepared shrimps; dish of plain shrimps; tin of sardines; beautiful beef-steak; eggs; muffin large loaf, and butter, not forgetting capital tea.'[51] Borrow's pages are full of exuberant descriptions such as this. Especially on the road, by himself, he seemed to have an unlimited capacity for enjoying in its own terms whatever happened to him.

Yet, as we have seen, he was also a complex person, someone who never overcame the psychological obstacles to intimacy with other people that he had first encountered during his youth. This shows up very clearly in his sense of his own marriage, which from the beginning lacked warmth. When he told his friend, Hasfeld, that he had married he evidently did so in such a toneless, general, unexcited way, that Hasfeld in his reply remonstrated and asked for the normal details. Who was this wife? What was she like? Borrow's reply, which was written in Spanish, rather sends a chill down the spine. 'She was a widow and has a daughter of twenty three who is a good girl, very meek, and with one of the best dispositions I have known in all my life. I live with them both in peace and tranquillity; they are determined to please me and for them my wish is law.'[52] That was in 1841. In the years that followed, Borrow came to depend upon Mary Clarke, in a way, a practical and material way, while she must have come to depend upon him. There is no evidence that she ever understood him, however, being prevented from doing so, not just by the man himself, but also by a deadly combination of lack of intelligence and a belief in Christianity. Even when she had lived with Borrow for twenty years she was still capable of telling John Murray that, although Borrow was sulking, he said his prayers each evening. There is no evidence, either, that they ever lived happily together, as opposed to 'in peace and tranquillity'. It is possible that the marriage remained unconsummated. Borrow took every opportunity that decency provided, and others that it did not, to be away from home, while as he told Hasfeld he worked off his boredom and sense of frustration in Oulton by cutting down dead trees with his great Norwegian axe, a symbolic activity if ever there was one. Stories were told after her death that Mary Borrow had died of nervous exhaustion, literally tired out by her husband's moods, by his quirky, often boorish, domestic behaviour and his tormented mental life that expressed itself in inconsistency and wrong-headedness. Someone of immense probity might say that she had got what she deserved, since she was undoubtedly more than fifty per cent responsible for the alliance in the first place. Such judgements, though, mean little. She was too simple a person, and

Borrow too complex, for them to have had much chance. She endured a lot. So, in quite a different sense, did he.

The existence of these unresolved and, at least for the time being, unresolvable elements means that a definitive life of Borrow will not be possible until more evidence has been gathered. The evidence that we have is too open to a variety of interpretations. Take, for example, Borrow's attitude to the Pope, something that has been underplayed in this account of his writing life. Throughout his whole career, Borrow was a strident anti-Catholic who wrote as though the Pope was a personal and very real enemy. Murray repeatedly had to ask him to tone down his passages against the Pope, which were vitriolic in the extreme. But why were they? Was it because he had had so many angry confrontations with Catholic priests in Spain? Was it because an angry or even hysterical anti-Catholic outburst would convince the listener of Borrow's own allegiance to the Church of England? Or had there been a more traumatic brush with Catholic authority at an earlier date in Italy? No answer to this can yet be given. Another example is his perplexing attitude to violence. He grew up during the war, obviously witnessed violence within his father's regiment, also witnessed violence on the streets of Norwich, and was part of a generation that accepted pugilism as a fact of life. After hobnobbing with Thurtell, in Norwich, he seemed in *Lavengro* to admire the prizefighter as something of a hero, though by the time *Lavengro* was published public attitudes had changed. *The Bible in Spain* reveals something of a fascination with the gory and the horrifying, though obviously Borrow concealed from his reader the full cruelty of war. Borrow often expresses the reserve, as well as the unbecoming sullenness of a man who has literally had to fight himself out of difficulty, or so it appears, yet even if this is true, one hesitates over the speculation and wants evidence of those early experiences that must have reinforced his basic attitudes. On a different level entirely, it must again be mentioned that not only were Borrow's personal papers scattered round the world after his death but also that many of them have yet to re-emerge. We are therefore many years away from a definitive view of the man, especially as much interesting work of a basic kind is in progress.

An instance of a notable recent success is the retrieval from the M.E. Saltykov-Shchedrin State Public Library in Leningrad of part of Borrow's correspondence with his Danish friend, Hasfeld. Obviously other significant collections of letters may turn up, such as that between Borrow and Hake, finds that might not only modify but radically alter our view of this amazing writer. How perplexing it is, though, when one tries to make sense of Borrow's life as a whole, of this man who so significantly lacked a moral centre, or rather located his being not at a centre at all, but in a preference for moral ambivalence which, if characteristically mid-Victorian, was also distinctly personal, for certainty eluded him, as it eludes many of us. Hasfeld told him at one point that he had had a good time in Stockholm and Borrow replies:

I really quite blushed when I read of your proceedings in Stockholm; what an extraordinary example you must have set to the youths entrusted (very improperly) to your care; and then you tell me you are unhappy, how should it be otherwise? Can winebibbers and haunters of brothels expect that peace of mind which only results from religion and orderly conduct? Take my advice: read the New Testament and ponder deeply on the important truths with which it abounds; devote yourself to study and give up that idle and desultory life which you have hitherto led.[53]

This is obviously an important statement. It shows Borrow taking a strong moral line, in which he seems to believe. At the same time, he had had, and was to have, experiences inconsistent with the position he adopted when writing to Hasfeld. He had lived with Isopel Berners: whether sexual or not that had obviously been a close relationship. He had lived with Mary Clarke out of wedlock. Even if he did not sleep with her in Seville, their being together at all was more profoundly unconventional than anything Hasfeld had ever done. He sustained a somewhat bizarre relationship with Henrietta,[54] who had a deep if mostly unexpressed affection for him, a strong clue to which is her having listed Borrow's works on her tombstone in Oulton churchyard as though to make absolutely clear that she wished to be remembered for her association with him. She was steadily affectionate, and the possibility remains that Borrow would have married her had her mother not been determined to marry him. Then again, on a less serious but nonetheless revealing level, he allowed himself to make statements calculated more to open the door to speculation than to assure the reader of a rigid morality, as for example when he says of the gypsy fortune-teller, shoplifter and procuress of Cordova, whose licentiousness he describes to make the point that gypsy women were invariably chaste, that 'she even made her propositions to myself, I will not say with what result'.[55] One does not need to maintain that Borrow had a sexual encounter with this Spanish gypsy similar to those Hasfeld had in the brothels of Stockholm to argue that Borrow liked inhabiting the world of the undefined or ill-defined and either made no effort to resolve the contradiction between the predilection for the specific and his evasion of the general truth, or, in making the effort, failed.

He himself knew that he was some sort of vagabond, was literally 'eccentric', away from the centre, so – to quote further from the Hasfeld correspondence – he recognised before not after his great books were published that the unique quality of his writing was a function of his own personality. Just as he had to tell Brandram that he was not writing a simple travel book about Spain, so he told Hasfeld, earlier, that he wanted to live in Moscow for two or three months 'to rub up my acquaintance with Russian life' but not for the sake of writing a travelogue. 'No no I write epic poems in prose the salt of which consists in a species of *Eulenspieglerey* which lurks at the bottom of my inkstand.'[56]

In the late 1870s Borrow lived for a while in Norwich, and it was from this period that many people remembered him, but eventually the MacOubreys moved to Oulton so that he, too, could live out his days in his old home. There he died on 26 July 1881, with, according to his death certificate, Henrietta in attendance, though the story was put about that he had been left by himself and died while the MacOubreys were in Lowestoft. In his will, which was dated 1 December 1880, he left everything to his old friend Elizabeth Harvey of 1 Southgate House, Bury St Edmunds, in trust for Henrietta, but Elizabeth Harvey, who was old, immediately 'renounced the Probate and Execution of the Will' so that Henrietta became sole executrix.[57] It is important to recall, perhaps, that there is no mention in this will of Borrow's literary effects, nor any statement about his unpublished work. He was childless. Henrietta MacOubrey, his executrix, was childless. The illegitimate children of his dead brother had disappeared. Bit by bit his papers were sold, as we have seen, to Webber, W. I. Knapp, T. J. Wise and Clement Shorter, who in turn re-sold them, mostly through the sale-room, to various libraries and private collections, thus making the opportunities for these posthumous publications that have been noted in this book. It cannot be that any interest, other than an academic interest, remains.[58] No mention was made in the will, either, of the Oulton or Mattishall Burgh estates, though the annual income from the former was noted on the probated copy.[59] Henrietta lived in Oulton Cottage for three years more, until her husband died in 1884, at which point the only real home that Borrow had had was sold off, as a 'Genuine Fishing box, with stable, carriage house, lawn, rookery, plantation, gardens and meadow', to a Mrs Caldecott for £6,375, of which Henrietta's share, once legal costs had been met and the mortgage paid of, was just over £1,000.[60] The Mattishall Burgh property was sold at the same time, effectively terminating the Norfolk residence of George Borrow's family. A few years later, his summer-house was pulled down, leaving as monuments only the cottage itself and the graves, in Oulton churchyard, of Ann

Borrow, Dr MacOubrey and Henrietta. Borrow himself was buried, near his wife, in Brompton Cemetery, where in 1981 an appropriate ceremony marked the centenary of his death.

Essentially Borrow had been an early-Victorian, sharing the perplexities of the pre-industrial period but not experiencing the satisfactions, such as they were, of industry and empire. By 1860 he was both out of touch and out of date, yet he lived for twenty more years, during which period he failed to adapt to circumstances, but retained the mental habits of a contemporary of J. S. Mill, Southey, Hazlitt and Byron.

'The idea to me is intolerable', he said, 'that when I am dead and gone my naked thoughts and unguarded expressions may be raked up and made to serve some dirty purpose or other. I have already had enough of notoriety.'[61] No dirty purpose has been intended here, but only a centenary celebration of the masterwork of an eccentric Victorian writer; yet, on second thoughts, who would not want to ponder the statements of someone prepared to say, as Borrow did: 'After all what a beautiful thing it is not to be but to have been a genius.'

Abbreviations used in the notes

Archive	The ledgers and daybooks of John Murray, Albemarle Street, London.
Beinecke	The Beinecke Manuscript Library and Rare Book Room, Yale University.
Berg	The Henry W. and Albert A. Berg Collection, the New York Public Library.
Bodleian	The Bodleian Library, Oxford.
Brotherton	The Brotherton Library, Leeds University.
Duke	The William R. Perkins Library, Duke University.
Darlow	*Letters of George Borrow to the British and Foreign Bible Society*, published by direction of the Committee, ed. T. H. Darlow (London: Hodder and Stoughton, 1911).
Fales	The Fales Library, New York University at Washington Square.
Fréchet	René Fréchet, *George Borrow (1803–1881) Vagabond – Polyglotte – Agent Biblique – Ecrivain* (Paris: Didier, 1956).
Harvard	The Houghton Library, Harvard University.
Hispanic Society	The Library of the Hispanic Society of America, New York.
Knapp	W. I. Knapp, *Life Writings and Correspondence of George Borrow* (2 vols., London: John Murray, 1899).
Jenkins	Herbert Jenkins, *The Life of George Borrow* (London: John Murray, 1914).
Leningrad	Collection P. N. Tikhanov, the M. E. Saltykov-Shchedrin State Public Library, Leningrad.
Norwich	The Norfolk Record Office.
Shorter	C. K. Shorter, *George Borrow and his Circle* (London: Hodder and Stoughton, 1913).
Texas	The Library of the Humanities Research Centre, University of Texas, Austin.
Trinity	The Wren Library, Trinity College, Cambridge.
Wise	T. J. Wise, *A Bibliography of the Writings in Prose and Verse of George Henry Borrow* (London: printed for private circulation only by Richard Clay & Sons, Ltd., 1914; reprinted for Dawsons of Pall Mall, London, 1966).
York	The Scott Library, York University, Toronto.

Notes

Chapter 1
The son of a recruiting sergeant

1 Autograph fragment (York).
2 Autograph fragment (York). Whether this is merely a translation, as used in *The Zincali*, or a verbal recollection triggered by something actually seen, is difficult to determine.
3 A. Egmont Hake, 'Recollections of George Borrow', *The Athenaeum*, 2807 (13 August 1881), 209.
4 ALS dated 15 December 1909 (Norwich).
5 ALS to Wentworth Webster dated 27 February 1894 (Bodleian).
6 ALS dated 26 March 1894 (Bodleian MS Eng. Misc. C. fols. 131–82). The quoted sentence follows Knapp's saying that Borrow became a changed man when Mrs Clarke went out to Seville.
7 As he said he might and as a pencilled note there indicates he did.
8 Knapp, *Life Writings and Correspondence of George Borrow*, vol. II, p. 97. Although there are many discrepancies between the autograph text of Borrow's letters, where these have survived, and the text as published by Borrow's early biographers, and although Knapp in particular tended to reproduce the text of Borrow's fair copy rather than that of the letter as sent, the printed text has in this book been preferred for reasons of convenience, except where the discrepancy is of substantive significance. The task of establishing the text of Borrow's letters has still to be tackled. Other early biographies were C. K. Shorter's *George Borrow and His Circle*, which utilised papers Shorter had obtained from Henrietta MacOubrey's executors, and Herbert Jenkins' *The Life of George Borrow*, the first book to take into account Borrow's letters to the Bible Society. An important, more recent, study is René Fréchet's *George Borrow (1803–1881) Vagabond Polyglotte–Agent Biblique–Ecrivain*.
9 Gordon Thomas Hake, *Memoirs of Eighty Years* (London: R. Bentley and Sons, 1892). When Hake refers to 'our portrait gallery', he means literally the National Portrait Gallery, where he went to remind himself of what Borrow looked like. What he describes, though, is the portrait of Borrow by Phillips, painted some years before Borrow and Hake met. Phillips had idealised his subject, as he was expected to.
10 'Literature', *The Athenaeum*, 3726 (25 March 1899), 361 (review of Knapp's *Life Writings and Correspondence of George Borrow*).
11 When Henrietta MacOubrey left the Oulton Estate, she kept his cloak and his axe as precious relics. ALS dated 19 February 1881 (York).

12 Theodore Watts-Dunton, 'Reminiscences of George Borrow', *The Athenaeum*, 2810 (3 September 1881), 307.

13 F. H. Groome, *The Bookman* (February 1893) (see Jenkins, p. 465).

14 *Lavengro* (3 vols., John Murray, 1851), vol. i, p. 13. All references to *Lavengro* will be to this, the first edition, unless otherwise stated.

15 *Ibid.* vol. iii, pp. 193–203.

16 In the fit described in *Lavengro* Borrow retained an awareness of what was happening to him, which is not consistent with *a grand mal* attack. On other occasions, though, he seems to have been completely incapacitated.

17 This story is apocryphal, however, being part of Knapp's whitewash strategy.

18 There exists no account of this period with the Guards.

19 Not East Dereham as claimed by Knapp. See A. M. Fraser, 'George Borrow's Birthplace and "Gypsy" Ancestry', *Journal of the Gypsy Lore Society*, 3rd series, 51 (1972), 60–81.

20 *Lavengro*, vol. i, p. 3.

21 *Ibid.* vol. i, pp. 3–4. Knapp pointed out that the decisive championship fight between Brain and Johnson was on 17 January 1791.

22 The entry for Ann in the East Dereham baptismal register for 1772 reads: 'Parfrement Ann 2ⁿᵈ daugʳ of Samuel and Mary Perfrement perhaps Palfriman i.e., a groom Jany 18 (birth) Jany 23 (baptism)'. The phrase 'perhaps Palfriman i.e., a groom' is a later addition.

23 Fraser, 'George Borrow's Birthplace and "Gypsy" Ancestry', pp. 60–81.

24 Knapp identified the farm from an enclosure-award map dated 1815 as 'Farm No. 200, belonging to Elizabeth Coe, formerly Cooper' (Knapp, vol. i, p. 20). A. M. Fraser in his article on Borrow's birthplace convincingly demolished Knapp's line of thought, showing, also, that while Samuel Perfrement rented the property (no. 191 on earlier award maps) from Mr Starling, when the property changed hands in 1804 the name Samuel Perfrement simultaneously disappeared not just from this but from all extant East Dereham records. The place and year of Samuel Perfrement's death remain unknown, but it seems reasonable to suppose either that he died in 1803 or that he moved away, perhaps to Scarning where his wife died in 1814.

25 The children of Samuel and Mary Perfrement were: Elizabeth, born 1 August 1767, baptised 2 August 1767; William, born 25 August 1769, baptised 17 September 1769; Ann, born 18 January 1772, baptised 23 January 1772; James, born 3 November 1773, baptised 10 November 1773; Samuel, born 16 December 1775, baptised 9 April 1776; Mary Sophia, baptised 4 June 1778; Philip, born 8 August 1779, baptised 20 October 1779; Sarah, born 1 March 1783, baptised 4 March 1783.

When the Borrows finally settled in Norwich in 1816, the state of Ann's family was as follows. Her parents were both dead; her brother, William, and her sister, Sarah, were also dead; Elizabeth had 'married into obscurity'; James had married in Dereham but had moved to King's Lynn where he brought up a large family; Samuel had married, had three children and had moved to Salthouse, where he was a farm-labourer; Mary had married John Burcham in Scarning. It seems impossible to determine whether Ann had kept in touch with any of her brothers and sisters during the previous twenty-four years. She might well have seen James' family in King's Lynn, but there is no firm evidence. Nor is there any evidence to suggest that George Borrow ever had any contact with his mother's family, though he must have known Thomas Borrow Burcham, son of Mary, who attended Norwich School from 1816 to 1825.

26 As advanced by Brian Vesey-Fitzgerald in *Gypsy Borrow* (London: D. Dobson, 1953). Frances Cobbe, in her catty way, said of Borrow that 'if he were not a gypsy by blood, he ought to have been one' (*Life of Frances Power Cobbe* (London: Richard Bentley, 1894), p. 117).

27 Knapp, vol. 1, p. 16.

28 Shorter, p. 8.

29 In his 'George Borrow's Birthplace and "Gypsy" Ancestry', A. M. Fraser notes the sources of information on the West Norfolk Militia on p. 69 and in the footnote to that page, i.e., WO 68/467; WO 13/1560–77; WO 17/953–4; WO 68/495. The West Norfolk Militia was in Portsea Barracks, Portsmouth, during the first half of 1801. In 1800, they had been in Braintree in April, at Chelmsford from May to July and at Portsmouth from August to December.

30 *Lavengro*, vol. 1, p. 8.

31 Everyone interested in Borrow must be indebted to the scrupulous inquiries of A. M. Fraser into Borrow's family background. See, again, Fraser's 'George Borrow's Birthplace and "Gypsy" Ancestry', referred to above.

32 There is no evidence of the Borrows ever having had a permanent home during the years of active service.

33 This was the full pay of the lieutenant (8*s*. a day) not of a captain (9*s*. 6*d*.).

34 *Lavengro*, vol. 1, pp. 46–8.

35 *Ibid*. vol. 1, p. 44.

36 *Ibid*. vol. 1, p. 31.

37 *Ibid*. vol. 1, p. 39.

38 *Ibid*. vol. 1, p. 40.

39 Unpublished autograph 'essay' in the Lilly Library at the University of Indiana, Bloomington.

40 This subject, 'George Borrow as a Linguist', is being examined with great thoroughness by Mrs A. M. Ridler in an almost complete CNAA doctoral dissertation.

41 *Lavengro*, vol. 1, p. 80.

42 *Ibid*. vol. 1, p. 81.

43 *Ibid*. vol. 1, pp. 169–70.

44 *Ibid*. vol. 1, pp. 170–2.

45 *Ibid*. vol. 1, p. 143. 'What a contemptible trade is the author's compared with that of a jockey', he said once, while breaking in a savage half-Arab. Knapp, vol. 11, p. 308.

46 *Ibid*. vol. 1, pp. 194–6. Note that in the deleted passage, included in the so-called definitive edition published by John Murray in 1899 as edited by Knapp, D'Eterville tells the story of how he carried loaded pistols when visiting pupils in the country (*Lavengro* (John Murray, 1899), pp. 558–9).

47 See Knapp, vol. 1, p. 60; Shorter, p. 75.

48 Shorter, p. 77.

49 Borrow seems to have worked mostly with Simpson, though it was Rackham who signed the contract with Borrow's father. See the 'Affidavit of due

execution of clerkship: Common Pleas, 2 April 1819' (Public Records Office, with a copy in the Norfolk Record Office).

50 *Norvicensian* (1888), 177. See Knapp, vol. 1, p. 68.

51 Grandson of Sir Roger Kerrison, Sheriff of Norwich in 1774, Mayor in 1778. His father, Thomas Allday Kerrison, who had been Mayor of Norwich in 1806, died in 1818. Despite his advice to Borrow, Roger became a solicitor and practised in Norwich. He had two brothers: Allday and Edmund. Allday went to Mexico, prior to which George, in 1824–5, had taught him Spanish.

52 *Lavengro*, vol. 1, p. 241.

53 *Ibid.* pp. 240–1.

54 *Harriet Martineau's Autobiography*, with memorials by Maria Weston Chapman (London: Smith, Elder and Co., 1877), pp. 300–1.

55 *Lavengro*, vol. 11, p. 359.

56 Recorded in 'A Schoolfellow of *Lavengro*', *The Britannia* (26 April 1851), (See Jenkins, p. 37.)

57 See J. W. Robberd's *A Memoir of the Life and Writings of Taylor of Norwich* (2 vols., London: John Murray, 1825), vol. 11, p. 495.

58 Autograph fragment (Norwich).

59 *Lavengro*, vol. 1, p. 275.

60 *Ibid.* vol. 1, pp. 24–6.

61 *Ibid.* vol. 1, p. 279.

62 *Ibid.* vol. 1, p. 288.

63 John Borrow's appointment as ensign had been dated 29 May 1815. See H. W. Saunders, 'A Contribution towards the Biography of George Borrow', *The History Teacher's Miscellany*, 2 (Norwich, November 1923), 6–9.

Chapter 2
Borrow in New Grub Street

1 ALS dated 20 January 1824, addressed to 18 Millman Street, Bedford Row. A note in a different hand on the outer fold of this letter gives the date as 18 January 1824. About two months later, Borrow wrote to Roger Kerrison again to say that he was on his way and was sending a chest of books in advance. ALS, 14 March 1824 (University of Rochester Library).

2 *Celebrated Trials and Remarkable Cases of Criminal Jurisprudence from the Earliest Records to the Year 1825* (6 vols., London: Knight and Lacey, 1825).

3 *Lavengro*, vol. 11, pp. 75–6.

4 Preface to *Celebrated Trials*, p. vii.

5 'Danish Poetry and Ballad Writing', *The Monthly Magazine*, 56 (1 November 1823), 306–9.

6 'Danish Traditions and Superstitions', *The Monthly Magazine*, 58 (1 August 1824), 19–22; 58 (1 January 1825), 498–500; 59 (1 February 1825), 25–6; 59 (1 March 1825), 103–4; 59 (1 May 1825), 308; 59 (1 June 1825), 411; 59 (1 July 1825), 507; 60 (1 November 1825), 296–7; 60 (1 December 1825), 424–5.

7 *Lavengro*, vol. 11, p. 73.

8 *Ibid.* pp. 74–5. It has to be noted that there is no sure way of identifying all Borrow's contributions to periodicals at this time. Knapp and Wise

provide only a starting-point, but since the contributions in question were anonymous, these may be false attributions on the one hand, while on the other a few authentic Borrow items may still have escaped notice.

9 Borrow had probably been reading Charles Bray's two-volume *The Philosophy of Necessity: or the Law of Consequences, as applicable to mental, moral and social science* (London: Longman, Orme, Brown, Green and Longmans) which, however, was only published in 1841. In other words it is a reminder of the important fact that *Lavengro* was 'recollected in tranquillity'.

10 *Lavengro*, vol. II, p. 77.

11 A passage deleted from an autograph draft to the preface to *Lavengro* (Hispanic Society).

12 *Lavengro*, vol. II, pp. 77–8 (likewise the continuation that follows).

13 *Faustus: His Life, Death and Descent into Hell. Translated from the German* (London: W. Simpkin and R. Marshall, 1825). A second edition was published in London by Kent in 1864.

14 See A. M. Fraser, 'Some Pitfalls in Collecting George Borrow', *Antiquarian Book Monthly Review*, 8, 10, issue 78 (October 1980), 473.

15 *Lavengro*, vol. II, pp. 249–50.

16 Knapp said that *Joseph Sell* was 'not a book at all' but at best a story contributed to a larger volume (Knapp, vol. I, p. 103). Knapp was mistaken, thought Herbert Jenkins, because no one would have paid Borrow £20 for a story written in just a single weekend. Fréchet said he agreed with Jenkins (Fréchet, p. 1901). As for Clement Shorter, 'there was, we may be perfectly sure, no Joseph Sell', he said (p. 102), meaning that there had never been in Borrow's life an actual person with that name. In *George Borrow and his Circle*, Shorter announced that 'Joseph Sell' was no more than the name used in *Lavengro* for Borrow's translation called *Faustus*, a theory that by itself is utterly implausible, as Shorter evidently understood, for an autograph note by Shorter in Walter Jerrold's copy of *Tales of The Wild and the Wonderful* in Texas shows that Shorter changed his mind when he read Jerrold's article, 'George Borrow's Joseph Sell' in the *Cornhill Magazine*, 123 (January 1923), 48–56.

17 BM 10826.aa.2, tentatively dated 1825. No other copies have been found.

18 *Lavengro*, vol. II, p. 251.

19 *The Romany Rye; A Sequel to 'Lavengro'* (2 vols., London: John Murray, 1857), p. 81. Although *The Romany Rye* was not published until 1857, this particular passage was written during the winter of 1843–4.

20 See A. M. Fraser, 'More About Mumper's Dingle', *The Blackcountryman*, 13, 1 (1980), 38–41. Very reasonably Fraser says: 'Borrovians have longed to know the exact locality of this dingle, where some of the most memorable scenes of *Lavengro* and *The Romany Rye* were enacted.' The article is an extremely thorough and helpful discussion of the various theories put forward on this subject. It is so good, in fact, that it throws into sharp contrast the difference between those who wish to document scrupulously every aspect of Borrow's life, down to the last detail, and those who believe that the Borrow world only really exists as part of the imaginative fabric of *Lavengro* and *The Romany Rye*.

21 See Ivor Evans, 'The Quest for Isopel Berners', *Journal of the Gypsy Lore Society*, 31, 1–2 (1952), 13–16. A. M. Fraser has challenged this on the

ground that Ivor Evans only took from the register the information about Elizabeth Jarvis that suited his case.

22 *Wild Wales* (3 vols., John Murray, 1862), vol. III, p. 348.

23 *The Romany Rye*, vol. I, p. 208.

24 A. M. Fraser, 'George Borrow and John Hasfeld', *Etudes anglaises*, 34, 3 (1981), 319.

25 Knapp, vol. II, pp. 265–6.

26 Wise, p. 24.

27 See A. M. Fraser, 'George Borrow and "The Painter of the Heroic" ', *Notes and Queries*, 216 (October 1971), 380–6.

28 The autograph of this letter is in the possession of A. M. Fraser.

29 For the information about Borrow's use of Norwich libraries I am indebted to Ann Ridler, who generously showed me her forthcoming article on this subject, to be published in *Library History*. In the case of 1827, entries made by Borrow in his mother's account book (entries dated 29 September, 7, 13 and 25 October, and 9 and 13 November) presumably show that he was in Norwich that autumn.

30 *The Zincali*, vol. I, p. 23.

31 *The Bible in Spain*, vol. III, p. 259.

32 *Ibid.* vol. I, pp. 95–6.

33 This is a notebook, bound in vellum, in the Berg Collection of the New York Public Library. Borrow used it in Spain before he knew he would write two books about his experiences there: thus some parts are used in *The Zincali* while others, the greater number, are used in *The Bible in Spain*.

34 I am indebted to A. M. Fraser whose very thorough inquiries resulted in his 'John Borrow's Disembodied Allowance', published in *Notes and Queries* (February 1969), 64–70. Much of the information about John Borrow in the next few pages derives directly, though in severely summarised form, from this excellent and indispensable article. Fraser shows, *inter alia*, that the first request to the Army Pay Office on behalf of John Borrow was dated June 1829, an important date because it shows that George Borrow was back in Norwich or London.

35 Here, for example, is one of the letters quoted by Knapp (vol. II, p. 277): 'Sir, – I take the liberty of troubling you with these lines for the purpose of enquiring whether there is any objection to the giving of the disembodied allowance of my brother, Lieut. John Borrow, of the West Norfolk Militia, who is at present abroad. I do this by the advice of the Army Pay Office, a Power of Attorney having been granted to me by Lieut. B. for the purpose of receiving the said allowance. I beg leave to add that my brother was present at the last training of his regiment that he went abroad with the permission of his commanding officer who has never recalled him; that he has sent home the necessary affidavits, and that there is no clause in the pay and clothing act which can authorize the stopping of his allowance – I have the honour to remain, Sir, Your most obedient humble servant.'

36 Shorter, p. 35. If there were a suspicion of irony here, it would provide further evidence of the whitewash activities of the early biographers.

37 Knapp, vol. I, p. 206. Knapp had in his possession the letters of John Borrow to his mother and brother, copies of which were later deposited in the Library of the Hispanic Society of America in New York. A. M. Fraser has

pointed out, as have others, that both Knapp and Shorter worked from drafts. Knapp's selective quotations were obviously designed to give the impression that John and George enjoyed a friendly, even an intimate, relationship, that John, in writing about the possibility of joining him in Mexico, was genuinely solicitous, and that nothing was omitted that was of great biographical significance. Shorter claimed he was quoting verbatim letters from George Borrow dated 8 September 1831; 17 September 1831; 24 November 1831; 13 December 1831; and 24 May 1833 (Shorter, pp. 28–33).

38 *The Romany Rye*, vol. II, pp. 359–60.

39 It was published in 1889 by Jarrold and Sons as *The Death of Balder from the Danish of Johannes Ewald (1773) translated by George Borrow Author of 'Bible in Spain,' 'Lavengro,' 'Wild Wales' etc.* Although 1889 is the date on the titlepage, it seems fairly certain that the book was actually published in 1892, the year in which the British Library, Cambridge University Library and the Bodleian received their deposit copies. The paper has an 1891 watermark. At the same time, corrected proof-sheets have survived dated 1886. Knapp had encouraged Webber's interest in the papers he had purchased from Oulton, thus creating a very choice situation for the bibliographer to disentangle.

40 Shorter, p. 143.

41 *Ibid.* p. 144.

42 *Ibid.* p. 147.

43 *Ibid.* p. 147.

44 *Ibid.* p. 148.

45 *The Foreign Quarterly Review*, 6, 11 (June 1830), 48–87.

46 Shorter, p. 151.

47 This quotation is from an unpublished four-page draft at Texas. It is difficult to know whether Knapp silently excised it from his version (see Knapp, p. 144) or whether it is an entirely different version, as on the surface it appears to be.

48 Shorter, p. 151.

49 ALS, GB to Bowring, 12 January 1831 (in the collection of Mrs Ann Ridler).

50 Knapp, vol. I, pp. 145–6.

Chapter 3
Russia: 1832–1835

1 William Canton, *History of the British and Foreign Bible Society* (5 vols., London: John Murray, 1904–10), vol. II, p. 271.

2 *Ibid.* vol. II, p. 271.

3 *Ibid.* vol. II, p. 264.

4 Darlow, *Letters of George Borrow to the British and Foreign Bible Society*, p. 4.

5 *Ibid.* p. 1.

6 *Ibid.* p. 3. See also Knapp, vol. I, p. 152; vol. II, p. 211.

7 Knapp, vol. II, pp. 267–8.

8 Darlow, p. 7.

9 *Ibid.* p. 9.

10 *Ibid.* p. 10. There is no evidence to support Knapp's contention (Knapp, vol. I, p. 143) that, while studying Manchu, Borrow also translated St Luke's gospel into Nahuatl, a Mexican dialect.

11 *Ibid.* p. 12.

12 *Ibid.* pp. 14–15.

13 *Ibid.* p. 13.

14 *Ibid.* p. 16.

15 *Ibid.* pp. 16–17.

16 *Ibid.* p. 17.

17 *Ibid.* pp. 18–19.

18 *Ibid.* pp. 19–20.

19 See Darlow, p. 52. Bible Society records show that Borrow also visited Bremen. See Knapp, vol. I, p. 151.

20 Edward Jerrman, *Pictures from St. Petersburg*, translated from the German by Frederick Hardman (London: Longman, Brown, Green and Longman, 1852), pp. 13–14. (There is a high likelihood that Jerrman is a pseudonym.)

21 A. B. Glanville, *St. Petersburg. A Journal of Travels to and from that Capital*, 2nd ed. 'carefully revised and with considerable additions' (2 vols., London: Henry Colburn, 1829).

22 Elizabeth Rigby (Lady Eastlake), *Letters from the Shores of the Baltic*, 2nd ed. (2 vols., John Murray, 1842), pp. 75–6.

23 Darlow, pp. 24–5.

24 Glanville, *St. Petersburg*, vol. I, p. 414.

25 *Ibid.* p. 416.

26 Darlow, p. 25.

27 Letter dated 1/13 May 1834 printed in Knapp, vol. I, p. 29.

28 The Norwich Edition of the Works of George Borrow (London: Constable, 1923), vol. XVI, p. 400.

29 *The Zincali* (2 vols., John Murray, 1841), vol. I, pp. 83–4.

30 Darlow, pp. 24–5.

31 *Wild Wales*, vol. III, p. 368.

32 Jerrman, *Pictures from St. Petersburg*, p. 15.

33 Darlow, p. 27. Shorter says that Borrow worked at the transcription eight hours a day from August to 18 October (Shorter, p. 171).

34 *Ibid.* p. 28.

35 *Ibid.* p. 32.

36 *Ibid.* p. 38.

37 *Ibid.* p. 31.

38 Captain John Dundas Cochrane, R.N., *Narrative of a Pedestrian Journey Through Russia and Siberian Tartary, from the Frontiers of China to the Frozen Sea and Kamtchatka*, 2nd ed., printed for Charles Knight (London, 1825), p. 112 .

39 Darlow, pp. 36–7.

40 *Ibid.* pp. 37–8.

41 *Ibid.* p. 35.

42 *Ibid.* p. 45.

43 *Ibid.* p. 35.

44 *Ibid.* p. 43.

45 *Ibid.* p. 47.

46 *Ibid.* p. 50.

47 *Ibid.* pp. 51–2.
48 *Ibid.* p. 54.
49 All the quotations in this paragraph are from Borrow's letter to Jowett dated 8 October 1834 (Darlow, pp. 55–62).
50 *Ibid.* p. 63.
51 *Ibid.* p. 66. All the quotations in this paragraph and the next are from Borrow's letter to Jowett dated 13 October 1834. Note his saying that he learned Turkish 'from friendship with Mohammitans' (Darlow, pp. 63–7).
52 Norwich MS 11319/8; Shorter, pp. 175–6.
53 *The Turkish Jester; or, The Pleasantries of Cogia Nasr Eddin Effendi*, translated from the Turkish by George Borrow (Ipswich: W. Webber, 1884). This translation was found amongst Borrow's papers at Oulton some time after his death. That he probably made this translation in Russia is indirectly corroborated by the fact that the BL catalogue seems not to reveal a possible text.
54 Fales ALS dated 10 May 1835 but for some reason given, often, as 1833. See also Jenkins, p. 111.
55 Knapp, vol. 1. For Borrow's friendship with Hasfeld see Knapp, vol. 1, pp. 173ff, and A. M. Fraser 'George Borrow and John Hasfeld', *Etudes anglaises*, 34, 3 (1981), 311–21.
56 Fraser, *ibid.* p. 313.
57 Darlow, pp. 87–96. See also the version published in *The Athenaeum*, 460 (20 August 1836), 387–8. Passages omitted from the printed text are given by Knapp (Knapp, vol. 1, pp. 192–3).
58 Rigby, *Letters from the Shores of the Baltic*, p. 233.
59 *Ibid.* p. 233.
60 Glanville, *St. Petersburg*, vol. 1, pp. 243–4.
61 A. G. Cross, 'George Borrow and Russia', *MLR*, 64 (April 1969), 2, 363–71. Cross' references are to: 'Pis'mo Pushkin k Dzhondzhu Borro', *Vestnik Leningradskago universiteta*, 6 (1949), 133–9; M. P. Alekseyev, 'Pushkin na Zapade', *Vremennik Pushkinskoy komissii*, 3 (Moscow–Leningrad, 1937), 124; and *Literaturnoye nasledstvo*, in which Alekseyev said the surviving Hasfeld–Borrow correspondence was to be published. This is the correspondence, referred to above, that A. M. Fraser has written about and partly reproduced.
62 *Targum*, p. iv.
63 Cross, 'George Borrow and Russia'.
64 Knapp, vol. 1, p. 225.
65 'The Story of Tim', *Once a Week*, 7 (4 October 1862), 403–6; 'The Story of Yvashka with the Bear's Ear', *Once a Week*, 6 (17 May 1862), 572–4; 'Emelian the Fool', *Once a Week*, 6 (8 March 1862), 289–94.
66 'The Story of Yvashka with the Bear's Ear', p. 572.
67 Darlow, p. 84.
68 *Ibid.* p. 83.
69 Jenkins, p. 146.

Chapter 4

The first visit to Spain: November 1835–September 1836

1 *The Bible in Spain*, 1st ed. (3 vols., John Murray, 1843). All the quotations in the first few paragraphs of chapter 4 of this book are from

chapter 30 of *The Bible in Spain*. All subsequent quotations are from the first edition.

2 In the defamatory attacks towards the end of the century, some critics of Borrow claimed that he was beardless and had never had to shave, implying that he was impotent; equally that he had white hair from birth. He himself stated in *The Bible in Spain* that he shaved, while people who met him in Spain reported that the hair depicted as dark in the portrait by his brother, was only then turning white. (see also p. 267, note 58).

3 *The Bible in Spain*, vol. ii, p. 221.

4 This is the last of the quotations from chapter 30 of *The Bible in Spain*.

5 J. Stoughton, *Religion in England from 1800 to 1850: a history* (London, Hodder and Stoughton, 1884), vol. ii, p. 377.

6 Darlow, p. 98. Borrow had also discussed the possibility of translations from the Armenian that might interest the Bible Society. That this remained in mind the later references in *Lavengro* and *The Romany Rye* demonstrate.

7 Darlow, p. 99.

8 A useful and relevant summary of the political situation may be found in U. R. Burke's two-volume edition of *The Bible in Spain*, published by John Murray in 1898.

9 Chile by 1818, Paraguay by 1814, La Plata by 1816, Mexico by 1821, and Peru and Bolivia by 1824.

10 Darlow, p. 100.

11 Borrow's reputation between his death in 1881 and the First World War was much affected by dinner-table gossip. Caroline Fox was one of the people who implied that Borrow had simply ignored his instructions while in Spain, damning him posthumously by innuendo. Whether she would have liked it more had he been a devout cleric or zealous missionary is open to doubt. That Borrow had Brandram's authority to travel in Spain is clear: that the two had discussed which part of Spain was to be Borrow's territory is also clear from the fact that he stayed in the west.

12 Knapp, vol. i, pp. 232–3.

13 There are autograph manuscripts of parts of *The Bible in Spain* in the Berg Collection of the New York Public Library, the Library of the Hispanic Society of America, the Brotherton Library, Rutgers University Library and the York Gate Library in Adelaide. Of these, the two important ones are the notebook Borrow used in Spain, in the Berg, and that part of the manuscript which concerned the expedition to Tangiers, in the Hispanic Society. The copy that Borrow gave to Murray for publication consisted of (*a*) passages copied from the Berg notebook; (*b*) edited copies of his letters to the Bible Society; (*c*) the journal of an Excursion to Tangiers (which he later gave to Dawson Turner); (*d*) connecting passages, which are more substantial than were for many years supposed. There has not yet been a detailed textual study of *The Bible in Spain*.

14 Darlow, p. viii. I have checked the text of Darlow against the originals in the library of Bible House. While there are inevitably a few dubious transcriptions, there is no doubt that Darlow did his level best to edit scrupulously and to present as fairly as possible the relationship of the incoming letters to the business of the Society, as recorded in committee and council minutes. Some of the letters that were once in the possession of the Society have disappeared. Equally, not all of Brandram's communications to

Borrow have found their way, as copies, into the files of outgoing correspondence.

15 Correspondence in Bible House shows that, understandably, both Darlow and Jenkins took steps to protect their interests and to maximise the impact of the newly discovered letters. Hodder and Stoughton, who published the letters, wanted to be sure that Jenkins would not steal their thunder; John Murray, who published Jenkins, wanted some assurance that the interest of a new biography would not be reduced by the prior publication of the letters. This correspondence has a bearing on Jenkins' attitude to the new material he had at hand, because it shows that as first user he did not feel free, or did not wish, to analyse or interpret either Borrow's letters or Borrow's relationship with the Society. This is not to say that he would have grasped the opportunity had it been there: presumably he genuinely believed Borrow to be a sincere missionary, as he frequently asserted. With this same correspondence are amusingly high-handed letters from Clement Shorter (see p. 271, n. 58).

16 It has already been mentioned that he did this deliberately. If he had at hand the papers he claimed he had, he obviously knew more about Borrow's comings and goings than he chose to reveal.

17 *The Bible in Spain*, vol. 1, p. 57.

18 *Ibid.* vol. 1, pp. 10–12.

19 Darlow, p. 106.

20 *Ibid.* p. 115.

21 See, for example, Jenkins, pp. 161, 171, 193, 219. Jenkins said Borrow had never 'been equalled as a missionary' (p. 210); that 'there was something magnificent in his Christianity' (p. 278); and that 'Borrow was instinctively a missionary, even a great missionary' (p. 303).

22 *The Bible in Spain*, vol. 1, p. 25.

23 *Ibid.* vol. 1, pp. 34–5.

24 *Ibid.* vol. 1, p. 115.

25 *Ibid.* vol. 1, pp. 40–1.

26 *Ibid.* vol. 1, pp. 42–3.

27 *Ibid.* vol. 1, p. 51.

28 *Ibid.* vol. 1, p. 62.

29 *Ibid.* vol. 1, pp. 95–6.

30 *Ibid.* vol. 1, p. 99.

31 The first four editions of *The Bible in Spain* in 1843 are textually different from each other only in the preface. For the first single-volume edition Borrow made a number of changes to the text itself to accommodate criticism. These revisions were not extensive.

32 *The Bible in Spain*, vol. 1, pp. 96–7.

33 *Ibid.* vol. 1, pp. 105–6.

34 *Ibid.* vol. 1, p. 110.

35 *Ibid.* vol. 1, p. 124.

36 *Ibid.* vol. 1, p. 125.

37 *Ibid.* vol. 1, p. 129.

38 Darlow, p. 143.

39 These lodgings had apparently been used on an earlier occasion by Lt Graydon, the other agent of the British and Foreign Bible Society in Spain.

40 *The Bible in Spain*, vol. 1, p. 238.

41 *Ibid.* vol. 1, p. 242.

42 Benedict Mol is the name Borrow gave to someone whom he said he met frequently in various parts of Spain. Biographers and critics who claimed Borrow told the truth and nothing but the truth in *The Bible in Spain* baulked at the peculiar figure of Benedict Mol, who thus became the test case in the controversy. Since it is not assumed in the present book that Borrow told the literal truth, Benedict Mol can step back into the ranks of the many bizarre and colourful characters whom Borrow created or recreated while writing *The Bible in Spain*.

43 *The Bible in Spain*, vol. 1, pp. 251–3.

44 George William Villiers, later Fourth Earl of Clarendon, 1800–70, British Ambassador in Spain for all but the last year of Borrow's stay there. The Clarendon papers, including correspondence relating to Villiers' dealings with Borrow, are in the Bodleian.

45 Borrow's reduction of the complex issue of why Spaniards remained adamant in their attitude to the Bible to the mere reiteration by a secretary of a remote reference to the Council of Trent, which he does not explain, is characteristic of his procedure throughout. New readers of Borrow who are uncertain whether to believe him or not will at least wish to notice, perhaps, that he habitually understates, often when on one level it seems most likely that he is exaggerating.

46 Knapp, vol. 1, pp. 254–5.

47 Jenkins, p. 179; see also Darlow, pp. 162–3.

48 Darlow, p. 164.

49 *Ibid.* p. 171.

Chapter 5
The second visit to Spain: November 1836–September 1838

1 *The Bible in Spain*, vol. 1, pp. 309–10.

2 *Ibid.* vol. 1, p. 310.

3 *Ibid.* vol. 1, p. 312.

4 *Ibid.* vol. 1, p. 316.

5 *Ibid.* vol. 1, p. 315.

6 *Ibid.* vol. 1, p. 323.

7 Darlow, p. 190.

8 *The Bible in Spain*, vol. 1, p. 344.

9 Darlow, p. 191.

10 *Ibid.* p. 196.

11 See Knapp, vol. 1, pp. 266–7, for the detailed itinerary.

12 Darlow, p. 194.

13 *Ibid.* pp. 196–200.

14 *Ibid.* pp. 205–6.

15 *Ibid.* p. 208.

16 *Ibid.* p. 209.

17 *Ibid.* p. 198.

18 *Ibid.* p. 203.

19 *Ibid.* p. 204.

20 *Ibid.* p. 212.

21 *Ibid.* p. 213.
22 *Ibid.* p. 222.
23 *Ibid.* vol. I, p. 247.
24 *Ibid.* vol. I, p. 249.
25 *Ibid.* pp. 271–2.
26 *Ibid.* p. 278.
27 *Ibid.* p. 278.
28 *Ibid.* p. 278.
29 *Ibid.* p. 280.
30 A fair copy, untranslated, is in the Bodleian.
31 Bodleian, GB to Sir George Villiers, 23 February 1838 (75, Clar. dep. C. 469). This is the complete text of the letter.
32 Darlow, p. 282.
33 *Ibid.* p. 298.
34 Bible Society minute no. 36, 2 April 1838: 'Resolved that Mr. Borrow be informed that it is the wish of the Committee that he remain at present at Madrid and that he be desired to get the Spanish Bible received from Barcelona bound, in order to be ready for distribution as opportunity may offer.'
35 *The Bible in Spain*, vol. III, p. 12.
36 *Ibid.* vol. III, p. 14.
37 Jenkins, pp. 231–2.
38 *The Bible in Spain*, vol. III, p. 16.
39 *Ibid.* vol. III, p. 15.
40 Jenkins, pp. 240–1.
41 See Darlow, pp. 310–11.
42 Darlow, p. 343.
43 *Ibid.* p. 304. Note that Hasfeld read about Borrow's arrest in *Preussische Staats-Zeitung*, which suggests that the episode was widely reported.
44 Darlow, p. 305.
45 *Ibid.* p. 313.
46 See *ibid.* pp. 331–2, for the relevant minutes: 'resolved that, as there are many points on which it is highly desirable to confer with Mr. Borrow respecting his future proceedings, it is recommended to the General Committee to authorize him to visit this country, provided that he thinks he may, without injury to the cause, leave Spain for a reason'. (Actually, Darlow transcribed this as 'leave Spain this season', a minor example of the unimportant ways in which he sometimes deviated from the autograph.)
47 This is one of the documents in the Bodleian cited above.
48 Jenkins, p. 271.
49 *Ibid.* p. 272.
50 *The Bible in Spain*, vol. III, p. 140.

Chapter 6
Seville and Tangiers: December 1838–April 1840

1 24 October 1838 to Jowett (Bible Society Archives).
2 Knapp, vol. II, p. 286.
3 *Ibid.* vol. I, p. 151.
4 *Ibid.* vol. I, p. 186.

5 *Ibid.* vol. I, p. 184.
6 *Ibid.* vol. I, p. 295.
7 Shorter, pp. 219–20.
8 Knapp, vol. I, p. 300.
9 Darlow (Brandram to Borrow).
10 A. M. Fraser, 'George Borrow and John Hasfeld', *Etudes anglaises*, 34, 3 (1981), pp. 314–15.
11 Knapp, vol. I, p. 305.
12 *The Bible in Spain*, vol. III, p. 148.
13 *Ibid.* vol. III, p. 147.
14 *Ibid.* vol. III, p. 150.
15 *Ibid.* vol. III, p. 168.
16 ALS, 10 January 1839 (Berg).
17 Knapp, vol. II, pp. 290–1.
18 *Ibid.* vol. I, p. 317.
19 *The Bible in Spain*, vol. III, p. 169.
20 *Ibid.* vol. III, p. 169.
21 *Ibid.* vol. III, pp. 178–9.
22 *Ibid.* vol. III, p. 180.
23 *Ibid.* vol. III, p. 186.
24 *Ibid.* vol. III, p. 187.
25 Knapp, vol. I, pp. 313–14.
26 He says, for example: 'I had flattered myself, previous to my departure for Madrid, that I should have experienced but little difficulty in the circulation of the Gospel in Andalusia' (*The Bible in Spain*, vol. III, p. 198).
27 Knapp, vol. I, p. 285.
28 *The Bible in Spain*, vol. III, pp. 193–4.
29 *Ibid.* vol. III, p. 207.
30 *Ibid.* vol. III, pp. 208–9.
31 Knapp, vol. I, p. 318.
32 *Ibid.* vol. I, pp. 324–5.
33 *Ibid.* vol. I, pp. 325–7.
34 *Ibid.* vol. II, p. 310.
35 *The Zincali*, vol. I, p. 114.
36 Knapp, vol. I, p. 138.
37 *The Zincali*, vol. I, p. 266.
38 *The Bible in Spain*, vol. III, pp. 228–9.
39 *Ibid.* vol. III, p. 236.
40 *Ibid.* vol. III, p. 242.
41 *Ibid.* vol. III, p. 253.
42 *Ibid.* vol. III, p. 257.
43 *Ibid.* vol. III, p. 264.
44 *Ibid.* vol. III, p. 314.
45 *Ibid.* vol. III, pp. 273–4.
46 Knapp, vol. I, p. 331.
47 *Ibid.* vol. I, p. 332.
48 *Ibid.* vol. I, p. 334.
49 *Ibid.* vol. I, p. 336.

Chapter 7

The books about Spain

1 Archive.
2 Knapp, vol. II, p. 284.
3 Borrow to John Murray (Archive).
4 Archive.
5 *The Zincali*, vol. I, p. 6.
6 *Ibid.* vol. I, p. 12.
7 *Ibid.* vol. I, p. 18.
8 *Ibid.* vol. I, p. 29.
9 *Ibid.* vol. I, pp. 23–5.
10 *Ibid.* vol. I, p. 14.
11 *Ibid.* vol. I, p. 117.
12 *Ibid.* vol. I, p. 239.
13 *Ibid.* vol. I, p. 46.
14 *Ibid.* vol. I, p. 47.
15 *Ibid.* vol. I, p. 351.
16 Knapp, vol. I, pp. 382–3.
17 *Ibid.* vol. II, p. 300.
18 *Ibid.* vol. II, pp. 4 and 302.
19 *Ibid.* vol. II, p. 4.
20 GB to Andrew Brandram: 27 May 1841 (Bible Society Archive).
21 GB to Andrew Brandram: 27 June 1841 (Bible Society Archive).
22 GB to JM: 23 August 1841 (Archive). See also Knapp, vol. II, p. 304.
23 Eighty-two pages representing, with revision, vol. III, pp. 223–304. When Dawson Turner asked Borrow for some of the manuscript, he said he only had the one section. 'The rest is written higgledy-piggledy in account books etc., containing much extraneous material connected with the Bible Society and my own private affairs' (Knapp, vol. I, p. 393).
24 GB to JM: 13 January 1842 (Archive). See also Knapp, vol. II, p. 307.
25 GB to JM: 22 January 1842 (Archive). See also Knapp, vol. II, p. 308.
26 GB to JM: 22 February 1842 (Archive).
27 GB to JM: 4 March 1842 (Archive).
28 Knapp, vol. I, pp. 383–5.
29 GB to JM: 10 May 1842.
30 GB to Dawson Turner: 3 June 1842 (Trinity).
31 Knapp, vol. II, p. 310.
32 *Ibid.* vol. II, pp. 310–12.
33 GB to Dawson Turner: 5 December 1842 (Trinity).
34 'I returned yesterday the last proof', GB to JM: 25 November 1842 (Archive). Ford was also being sent proofs. See Knapp, vol. II, p. 313.
35 Knapp, vol. II, pp. 314–15.
36 *Ibid.* vol. I, p. 396.
37 GB to JM: 31 December 1842 (Archive).
38 GB to J. Sparham (Harvard).
39 Wise, p. 71.
40 The publication details are dealt with in greater detail in the forthcoming *George Borrow: A Bibliographical Study* being prepared by A. M. Fraser and Michael Collie.

41 GB to JM: 24 June 1843 (Archive).
42 JM to GB: 21 September 1843 (Archive).
43 GB to JM: 18 September 1843 (Archive).
44 GB to JM: 17 September 1843 (Archive).
45 JM to GB: 24 November 1843 (Archive).
46 GB to JM: 24 November 1843 (Archive).
47 GB to JM: 6 November 1843 (Archive).
48 GB to JM: 15 November 1843 (Archive).
49 15 October 1843 (Archive).
50 Knapp to JM: 5 January 1899.
51 Putnam to JM: 19 December 1898.
52 *The Zincali* was issued in the Home and Colonial Library in 1846, but did not do as well: 7,500 copies of each part were issued in 1847 but on 30 June 1852, John Murray still had 3,175 copies from 15,000 left.

Chapter 8
Lavengro: the 'book which is no humbug'

1 Borrow to Lord Clarendon. Undated draft (Texas).
2 Knapp, vol. II, p. 42. The full text of Clarendon's letter as quoted by Knapp reads as follows:

> Grosvenor Crescent, June 10th, 1841.
> My Dear Sir, — It would afford me pleasure to promote any wish of yours, but I know by experience that it is quite hopeless to ask a Consulship from Lord Palmerston. That portion of his patronage is more coveted than any other, and you will easily believe that he is overwhelmed with applications, and that he cannot serve a twentieth part of those who have claims upon him. I have myself on two occasions, but in vain, applied to him in behalf of friends who were desirous of Consulships.
> I am well aware of your great philological proficiency, and I wish it were employed in the public service; but I hardly see how the Government could facilitate your travelling in various parts of the world, nor in what capacity you could carry such a project into effect. If you have any definite views upon the subject that you can communicate to me, I will gladly take them into consideration, and if they appear practicable I will bring them before Lord Palmerston. — I am, dear Sir, yours faithfully —
> CLARENDON.

3 Ward, Lock and Co., 1893; Macmillan, 1896; Newnes, 1897; Walter Scott, 1848; Gresham Publishing, 1900; John Lane, 1900; Methuen and Co., 1901; Blackie and Son, 1904; Grant Richards, 1904; Routledge, 1906; Dent, 1906; Nelson, 1909; Cassell, 1909; Collins, 1910; Oxford, 1904; Milford, 1914.
4 'Mr. Borrow', *The Athenaeum*, 2806 (6 August 1881), 177.
5 *Views and Reviews: Essays in Appreciation* (London: David Nutt, 1890), pp. 133–8.
6 *Outlook*, 1 (April 1899).
7 *The Quarterly Review*, 189 (1899), 472–91.
8 Introduction to Methuen's two volume edition (1901).
9 *English Literature: an Illustrated Record* (4 vols., London: William Heinemann, 1903–4), vol. IV, pp. 270–1.
10 (Dent, 1906), p. xxv.

11 *A Survey of English Literature: 1830–1880* (2 vols. London: Edward Arnold, 1920), vol. I, pp. 319–29.

12 Borrow to John Murray, 1 December 1842 (Archive). Knapp's date for this letter appears to be incorrect.

13 2 October 1843 (Archive) and Knapp, vol. II, p. 10.

14 Knapp, vol. II, p. 8.

15 *Ibid.* vol. II, p. 8. Borrow to Hasfeld, 21 January 1843.

16 *Ibid.* vol. II, p. 8.

17 *Ibid.* vol. II, pp. 8–9.

18 Borrow to John Murray, 4 April 1843 (Archive). See also Knapp, vol. II, p. 9.

19 Knapp, vol. II, pp. 10–11.

20 *Ibid.* vol. II, p. 9.

21 *Ibid.* vol. II, p. 9. Letter dated 3 October 1843.

22 Unpublished letter dated 18 January 1844 (Trinity).

23 Jenkins, p. 387.

24 Knapp, vol. II, p. 12.

25 Mary Borrow to Dawson Turner, 8 May 1844. A. M. Fraser's edition of letters relating to Borrow's expedition to Constantinople includes a useful and interesting introduction. See A. M. Fraser, *A Journey to Eastern Europe in 1844 (Thirteen Letters)* by George Borrow (Edinburgh: The Tragara Press, 1981).

26 Borrow to Mary Borrow, 16 May 1844 (Texas).

27 *The Zincali*, vol. I, pp. 11–12.

28 *Ibid.* vol. I, p. 13.

29 E. O. Winstedt, 'Borrow's Hungarian-Romani Vocabulary', *The Journal of the Gypsy Lore Society*, 29 (1950), 46–54, 104–15; 30 (1951), 50–61.

30 *The Romany Rye*, vol. II, p. 318.

31 Borrow to Mary Borrow, 5 August 1844 (Texas).

32 Knapp, vol. II, p. 324.

33 Hasfeld to Borrow, 23 November/5 December 1844 (Norfolk).

34 Borrow to John Murray, 17 September 1846 (Archive).

35 Knapp, vol. II, p. 15.

36 *Ibid.* vol. II, p. 17. Letter dated 27 November 1849.

37 *Ibid.* vol. II, p. 18.

38 *Ibid.* vol. II, p. 19.

39 *Ibid.* vol. II, p. 19.

40 *Ibid.* vol. II, pp. 40–1.

41 *Ibid.* vol. II, p. 41.

42 Borrow to Dawson Turner, 9 October 1848 (Trinity).

43 Knapp, vol. II, pp. 61–2.

44 'Recollections of George Borrow', *The Athenaeum*, 2807, (13 August 1881), 209.

45 Knapp, vol. II, p. 57.

46 See Knapp, vol. II, p. 57, for a list of the relevant letters.

47 *Ibid.* vol. II, pp. 39–40.

48 *Ibid.* vol. II, p. 39.

49 Borrow to John Murray, 23 June 1848 (Archive).

50 See John Murray to Borrow: 'It looks too much as though got up for the present time and what is called Papal aggression'; and Woodfall to Borrow:

'It might be fancied that the book was written to suit the crisis' (Knapp, vol. II, p. 23).

51 The incomplete set of proofs in the Berg Collection were, however, marked by Borrow.

52 'Lights on Borrow', *The Daily Chronicle* (30 April 1900), 3.

53 Unpublished letter. Borrow to Dawson Turner, 6 March 1843 (Trinity).

54 Eric Shanes, *Turner's Picturesque Views in England and Wales* (Chatto and Windus, 1979).

55 'Turner's Drawings', *The Athenaeum*, 85 (10 June 1829), 363.

56 *Lavengro*, pp. 278–80.

57 *Ibid.* pp. 331–2.

58 There is, however no firm evidence to support Augustus Jessopp's contention that Borrow was impotent, although the following passage was damaging to Borrow's reputation during the early years of this century:

> There is a mystery about his life, as I have said. That life was not a happy life, not a gay life.
>
> Of anything like animal passion there is not a trace in all his many volumes. Not a hint that he ever kissed a woman or ever took a little child upon his knee. He was beardless; his voice was not the voice of a man. His outbursts of wrath never translated themselves into uncontrollable acts of violence; they showed themselves in all the rancorous hatred that could be put into words – a fire smouldered in that sad heart of his. Those big bones and huge muscles and strong brain were never to be reproduced in an offspring to be proud of. How if he were the Narses of Literature – one who could be only what he was, though we are always inclined to lament that he was not something more? ('Lights on Borrow', p. 3).

Borrow was not beardless: he would from time to time get Henrietta to bring him a new razor from London. And though his marriage was not a happy one, it is impossible to know whether it was consummated or not. If not, the fault would just as likely have been Mary's as his.

59 Knapp, vol. II, p. 166.

60 *Ibid.* vol. II, p. 164.

61 *Ibid.* vol. I, pp. 29–30.

62 Jenkins, p. 399.

63 See Jenkins, pp. 390ff.

64 *The Romany Rye*, vol. I, p. 75 (police and railways); pp. 314–15 (railways); pp. 295, 348 and 356–7 (corn-laws). With equal certainty, some passages can be seen as late additions: for example, the story of the salmon and the blistered thumb at *The Romany Rye*, vol. II, pp. 199–205 (See Knapp vol. II, p. 86).

65 Summarised by Knapp, vol. II, pp. 166–72.

66 The autograph fair copy of *Lavengro*, in three volumes, is in the Library of the Hispanic Society. There are now 14 chapters (238 pages) and a few fragments of an early version that is roughly identical, but does not coincide precisely, with the first-edition text in the Berg Collection. There are other autograph fragments in the Brotherton Library, at Texas, at Duke, and in the Norfolk Record Office.

67 Knapp, vol. II, pp. 167–8.

68 John Murray to Borrow, 23 December 1854 (Archive). This letter contained the list of passages John Murray thought should be omitted. Presumably many of these passages coincide with the widely scattered autograph fragments in research libraries and private collections.

69 Knapp, vol. II, p. 169.

70 *Ibid.* vol. II, p. 171.

71 *The Romany Rye*, vol. I, pp. 164–5.

72 *Ibid.* vol. I, p. 272.

73 *Ibid.* vol. I, p. 66.

74 *Ibid.* vol. I, pp. 64–5.

75 *Ibid.* vol. I, pp. 355–7.

76 See Knapp, vol. II, pp. 24–5, and Shorter, pp. 281–2. For other reviews see Knapp.

77 *The Romany Rye*, vol. II, pp. 245–7.

78 *Ibid.* vol. II, pp. 271–4.

79 *Ibid.* vol. II, pp. 281–4.

80 *Ibid.* vol. II, pp. 335–6.

81 George Borrow to Whitwell Elwin, 25 October 1853 (Texas).

82 Ford had asked Borrow to write such a review, saying that he would make a 'crack reviewer' if he would just write a long spontaneous letter. He tried to arrange this in 1843 with Lockhart and Murray, 'behind the scenes' as he put it. When the time came, however, Borrow wrote a thirty-seven-page article on Spain, with scarcely a mention of Ford and his *Handbook*. Lockhart refused to publish it as a review without changes; Borrow refused to make such changes; Ford wrote to Borrow to smooth the matter over; the friendship gradually petered out. (See Knapp, vol. II, pp. 45–52). Ford had always treated Borrow in a friendly way, so in a sense he deserved friendship in return. On the other hand, he persisted in treating Borrow as a 'natural', a sort of unsophisticated rustic. 'Avoid all attempts to write *fine*', he kept saying: 'just dart down the first genuine up-pouring idea and thought in the plainest language' (Texas). Possibly Borrow had grown rather tired of these remarks and all that they implied. Possibly, therefore, he did not regret the break.

83 *The Romany Rye*, vol. II, pp. 264–5.

84 *Ibid.* vol. II, pp. 336–7.

85 William Spengemann, *The Forms of Autobiography* (Yale University Press, 1980).

Chapter 9
The years of discontent

1 *The Eastern Daily Press* (1 October 1892).

2 Shorter, p. 319.

3 'Literature', *The Athenaeum*, 3726 (25 March 1899), 361.

4 Jenkins, p. 447.

5 *Ibid.* p. 382.

6 A. Egmont Hake, 'Recollections of George Borrow', *The Athenaeum*, 2807 (13 August 1881), 209–10.

7 John Murray, *Good Words*. (Quoted by Jenkins, pp. 385–6.)

8 Shorter, p. 316.

9 Jenkins, p. 404. A quotation from a note in *The Bury Post* (17 September 1852), probably written by Hake.

10 *The Bible in Spain*, p. 668.

11 Unpublished notebook (Texas).

12 Jenkins, p. 404, who is quoting from John Murray's *Good Words*.

13 *The Eastern Daily Press* (1 October 1892), also quoted at Jenkins, p. 404.

14 'Vestiges of Borrow: Some Personal Reminiscences', *The Globe* (21 July 1896). (Jenkins, p. 423.)

15 Shorter, p. 420.

16 Jenkins, p. 467. In his letter from Woodbridge, FitzGerald said: 'I remember first seeing you at Oulton; then at Donne's in London; then at my own happy home in Regent's Park; then *ditto* at Gorleston – after which, I have seen nobody, except the nephews and nieces left me by my good sister Kerrich. So shall things rest?' This had been a friendship of mutual respect and shared interest, though FitzGerald bridled at the attempt to bring the two 'old men' together.

17 A. M. Fraser has pointed out that the correspondence between Hasfeld and Borrow contains 'no dramatic revelations'. See his 'George Borrow and John Hasfeld', *Etudes anglaises*, 34, 3 (1981), 311–21. Borrow saw Hasfeld briefly in Oulton in 1852, Great Yarmouth in 1857 and London in 1862.

18 See A. M. Fraser, 'George Borrow and Lucy Brightwell', *Notes and Queries*, 220, (March 1975), 109–11. Though the evidence is not conclusive, Fraser suggests that if Borrow proposed to his old friend it would have been after his wife's death, not before his own marriage. Lucy Brightwell was the daughter of Thomas Brightwell, a solicitor and former mayor of Norwich. Borrow had known the family throughout his adult life, as Lucy Brightwell's diary, now in the Norfolk Record Office, makes clear.

19 The unpublished notebook that contains entries from both the Norfolk and Manx tours is in Texas.

20 See A. M. Fraser, 'The Diaries of George Borrow's Walking Tours', *Journal of the Gypsy Lore Society* (3), 49 (1970), 25–34; and 'George Borrow's Walking Tours: the Welsh Diary, 2–6 September 1854', *Journal of the Gypsy Lore Society* (3), 49 (1970), 97–110.

21 See A. M. Fraser, 'George Borrow's Wanderings in Quest of Manx Literature', *Proceedings of the Isle of Man Natural History and Antiquarian Society*, 8, 3 (1980), 296–314.

22 A. M. Fraser is the authority on Borrow in Wales, and anyone interested in the details of Borrow's itineraries should start with his articles rather than with the now out-of-date early twentieth-century biographies. It is worth noting that Borrow never explains why he chose, finally, to write about Wales rather than about the other parts of the British Isles he had visited.

23 See F. James Johnson, 'Mystery Tour of George Borrow', *Country Quest*, 9, 2 (October 1968), 16–18; F. G. Blair, 'George Borrow in Orkney and Shetland', *Journal of the Gypsy Lore Society*, 41 (January–April 1962), 62–5; 'George Borrow's Walking Tours: the Scottish Diary, 4–7 August 1866', *Journal of the Gypsy Lore Society* (3), 50 (1971), 20–4.

24 Borrow's expedition to Connemara and the Giant's Causeway was escapist rather than literary as far as one can tell.

25 In the Norfolk Record Office the account books are full of interesting details. They show, for example, that the Borrows spent £120 on their Welsh trip

in 1854 and £200 when they went to Ireland in 1859. Of special interest are the disbursements to Borrow from his wife. Whatever their relationship, she held the purse strings.

26 See A. L. Salmon, 'George Borrow in Cornwall', *Literary Rambles in the West of England* (London: Chatto and Windus, 1906), pp. 30–50.

27 See Fraser, 'George Borrow's Wanderings in Quest of Manx Literature'.

28 Reconstituted by R. B. Johnson from texts supplied by Herbert Wright and published by Alston Rivers in 1927 as *Ballads of All Nations*.

29 Various fragments have survived from this period including an autograph draft of part of an introduction, which reads:

> Above the writer has endeavoured to give a clear yet concise account of the Kæmpe Viser, a collection of ancient Danish Ballads, the substance of a greater part of which is common to the entire north – the best of them he now offers in English tongue to an English public, a public which is bound to receive them (Texas).

The manuscript of the introduction and notes for the proposed *Songs of Scandinavia* is now in the Library of Rutgers University, the poems themselves being widely scattered.

30 Reconstituted from Borrow's manuscripts by H. G. Wright and published in 1928 as *Celtic Bards, Chiefs and Kings* (London: Chatto and Windus). See also Ernest Rhys, *Welsh Poems and Ballads* (London: Jarrold and Sons, 1915).

31 Unpublished and difficult to identify.

32 Wise referred correctly to two sets of autograph manuscripts of verse, the first having been in existence prior to 1830 and the second dating from after 1850. These are now widely distributed.

33 Published in 1884 by W. Webber of Ipswich as *The Turkish Jester; or, The Pleasantries of Cogia Nasr Eddin Effendi*; 150 copies were printed, some of which were taken over by Jarrolds of Norwich when Webber joined Jarrold's staff.

34 This volume would have included three stories published in *Once a Week*: 'Emelian the Fool', 6 (8 March 1862), 289–94; 'The Story of Yvashka with the Bear's Ear', 6 (17 May 1862), 572–4; and 'The Story of Tim', 7 (4 October 1862), 403–6. All three stories were reprinted as 'Avon Booklets' in 1904 and by Wise in 1913.

35 *The Death of Balder from the Danish of Johannes Ewald* (London: Jarrold and Sons, 1889). This is undoubtedly the work of Borrow, not a forgery associated with Wise as was once argued. The edition was a long time in the making; see p. 256, n. 39 for the details.

36 Preface to *The Sleeping Bard*.

37 *The Quarterly Review* (January 1861), 38–63.

38 Knapp, vol. II, p. 197.

39 *Ibid.* vol. II, p. 196.

40 Unpublished letter (Norfolk).

41 *Wild Wales* (Collins, 1955), pp. 14–15.

42 See A. M. Fraser, 'George Borrow's *Wild Wales*: Fact and Fabrication', *Transactions of the Honourable Society of Cymmrodorion* (1980), 163–73.

43 See Cecil Price's introduction to the Collins edition of *Wild Wales*.

44 *Wild Wales* (Collins), pp. 78–9.

45 *Ibid.* p. 91.

46 See the Norwich Edition of the Works of George Borrow.

47 See A. M. Fraser, 'George Borrow's Third Tour in Wales (1867)', *Transactions of the Honourable Society of Cymmrodorion* (1978), 262-4.

48 ALS Borrow to Charles Leland, 2 November 1871 (Texas): 'I have received your letter, and am gratified by the desire you express to make my acquaintance.'

49 *Romano Lavo-Lil; Word-book of the Romany; Or, English Gypsy Language* (London: John Murray, 1874). There are corrected proof-sheets in the Beinecke Library and at Norwich.

50 *Wild Wales*, p. 264.

51 *Ibid.* p. 356.

52 Borrow to Hasfeld, 30 August 1841 (Leningrad) quoted in Fraser, 'George Borrow and John Hasfeld', p. 316. It can be assumed that Borrow wrote in Spanish because his letters were read by his wife.

53 Borrow to Hasfeld, 15 February 1837 (Leningrad, as quoted by Fraser).

54 Bizarre because characteristically ambivalent. They walk arm in arm to the summit of Snowdon together singing. She called him, in letters, 'dear friend'. She commemorated him on her gravestone. But unfortunately there are no third-party reports to give us an inkling of the extent of intimacy, which the Victorian would have known very well how to conceal.

55 *The Zincali*, vol. I, p. 347.

56 Borrow to Hasfeld, 24 March 1843 (Leningrad).

57 Borrow's will was signed by his solicitor, R. H. Reeves of Lowestoft, and Reeves' clerk, Henry Spear. The gross amount left was £519 13s. 4d.; the net amount £363 5s. 8d.

58 Clement Shorter claimed an interest in all of Borrow's unpublished papers when he purchased some of them from Henrietta MacOubrey's executor. In his book he said that Borrow's letters 'were kindly placed at my disposal by Mr. Wilfred J. Bowring, Sir John Bowring's grandson. The rights which I hold through the executors of George Borrow's stepdaughter, Mrs. MacOubrey, over the Borrow correspondence enable me to publish in their completeness letters which three biographers, all of whom have handled the correspondence, have published mainly in fragments' (Shorter, p. 142). Though he knew better, he was confusing the ownership of the letters that he had in his possession with the larger, or at least different, question of copyright. When Darlow was editing Borrow's letters to the British and Foreign Bible Society (see p. 260, n. 15), Shorter tried to impede their publication by claiming that he had purchased the copyright of Borrow's letters from Russia. He threatened legal action but was deterred by a counter-threat of expulsion from a London club! The correspondence relating to this matter is in the Library at Bible House. Shorter had a financial interest only in the papers he had purchased, but these papers he later sold.

Henrietta MacOubrey continued to receive royalties on *Romano Lavo-Lil* and the Murray collected edition, until John Murray indicated that all of Borrow's works were out of copyright: the documents relating to this, including the final statement of account, are in the Scott Library at York University.

59 Henrietta's copy of Borrow's will is in the Scott Library at York University. With the will are statements of account with her lawyer for Mattishall

Burgh and Oulton Hall, as well as the Settled Land Act account with the trustees.

60 The estate was sold in twelve lots at the Suffolk Hotel in Lowestoft on 10 September. The Hall, the Cottage and most of the land composed Lots 1, 2, 3 and 4. The malthouse, eight cottages, and associated fields and woods were sold separately.

61 Borrow to Hasfeld, 23 June 1843 (Leningrad).

Index

Index